THE INSTITUTIONAL STRUCTURE OF ANTITRUST ENFORCEMENT

THE INSTITUTIONAL STRUCTURE OF ANTITRUST ENFORCEMENT

DANIEL A. CRANE

OXFORD
UNIVERSITY PRESS

OXFORD
UNIVERSITY PRESS

Oxford University Press, Inc., publishes works that further Oxford University's objective of excellence in research, scholarship, and education.

Oxford New York
Auckland Cape Town Dar es Salaam Hong Kong Karachi Kuala Lumpur Madrid Melbourne Mexico City Nairobi New Delhi Shanghai Taipei Toronto

With offices in
Argentina Austria Brazil Chile Czech Republic France Greece Guatemala Hungary Italy Japan Poland Portugal Singapore South Korea Switzerland Thailand Turkey Ukraine Vietnam

Published by Oxford University Press, Inc.
198 Madison Avenue, New York, New York 10016

Library of Congress Cataloging-in-Publication Data

Crane, Daniel A.
The institutional structure of antitrust enforcement / Daniel A. Crane.
p. cm.
Includes bibliographical references and index.
ISBN 978-0-19-537265-6 (hardback : alk. paper)
1. Antitrust law—United States. I. Title.
KF1652.C73 2011
343.73'0721—dc22

2010043763

Note to Readers
This publication is designed to provide accurate and authoritative information in regard to the subject matter covered. It is based upon sources believed to be accurate and reliable and is intended to be current as of the time it was written. It is sold with the understanding that the publisher is not engaged in rendering legal, accounting, or other professional services. If legal advice or other expert assistance is required, the services of a competent professional person should be sought. Also, to confirm that the information has not been affected or changed by recent developments, traditional legal research techniques should be used, including checking primary sources where appropriate.

(Based on the Declaration of Principles jointly adopted by a Committee of the American Bar Association and a Committee of Publishers and Associations.)

To Saara, Elie, and Pascal

CONTENTS

ACKNOWLEDGMENTS

This book is the product of numerous discussions, conversations, and exchanges with many people. None of them bears any culpability for the book's content, but all deserve thanks for enriching the project. Alas, it will be impossible to recall or mention every worthy person.

Portions of some of the chapters were previously published as articles. The following legal journals graciously assented to the edited republication of the relevant portions: the Vanderbilt Law Review, the California Law Review, the Texas Law Review, and the Chicago Journal of International Law. Many individuals contributed to improving those articles, and are thanked in the articles themselves. Drafts of the articles or other portions of this book received considerable aid from presentations at workshops at the University of Virginia, NYU, the Benjamin N. Cardozo School of Law (Yeshiva University), Stanford University, Loyola University Chicago, William & Mary, Vanderbilt, the University of Michigan, the University of Chicago, the European University Institute, and the University of Toronto.

A number of individuals read and commented on portions of the book. I am particularly indebted to Bruce Hoffman, Graciela Miralles, Danny Sokol, Spencer Waller, and Tom Krattenmaker for editorial suggestions. Tom Krattenmaker and Bill Kovacic deserve special recognition for pushing me to focus on issues of institutional structure and helping to frame many of the ideas expressed in the book. Eleanor Fox and Harry First provided encouragement and suggestions during the book's early development. Christopher Lentowski, Joe Coburn, and Larisa Vaysman provided invaluable research assistance.

Finally, I am very grateful to the five institutions under whose auspices this book was written: the Benjamin N. Cardozo School of Law (Yeshiva University), which generously supported my research as a junior faculty member; the University of Michigan, my current home institution; and three universities where I was visitor when substantial portions of this book were written: NYU, the University of Chicago, and the Universidade Católica Portuguesa.

INTRODUCTION

Antitrust enjoys a strong tradition of relatively short monographs that cover the entire field from a theoretical, historical, and normative perspective. Among them are Richard Posner's path-breaking 1976 *Antitrust Law* (substantially updated in 2001); Robert Bork's 1978 Chicago School Bible, *The Antitrust Paradox*; Keith Hylton's 2003 economically oriented *Antitrust Law: Economic Theory and Common Law Evolution*; and Herbert Hovenkamp's 2005 *The Antitrust Enterprise*. Each of these books focuses primarily on substantive antitrust norms (i.e., merger or predatory pricing law) and the appropriate level of regulatory intervention in particular industrial segments (i.e., the new economy or regulated industries). To date, no one has tried to present a comprehensive account of the institutions that implement antitrust law. This book makes such an attempt.

As the focus on substantive antitrust norms in the major antitrust monographs makes clear, the legal academy has primarily valued analysis of substantive rules. And yet changes in substantive rules often have relatively little effect on observed behaviors. If legal norms and legal institutions are the inputs that interact to create outcomes—behaviors in real markets—and changes in legal norms fail to change behaviors, institutions must be doing a good bit of the work. For example, it is conventional wisdom that in light of pro-defendant liability norms created by the U.S. Supreme Court in the 1980s and 1990s, plaintiffs have no chance of winning predatory pricing cases.[1] And yet plaintiffs have filed scores of predatory pricing cases since those pro-defendant decisions, and defendants have paid out hundreds of millions of dollars in settlements and modified their pricing behavior in the face of predatory pricing litigation.[2] If the liability rules are stacked in favor of the defendants, the institutional structures—particularly the availability of jury trials (see Chapter 6)—may be stacked in favor of the plaintiffs. The substance of predatory pricing liability rules is, at most, half of the story about the effect of the predatory pricing law on business behavior.

Institutions, then, are a critical and underappreciated driver of an antitrust policy that interacts in many subtle ways with substantive antitrust rules and decisions. In order to set the stage, let us introduce each of our starring characters.

1. *See* Daniel A. Crane, *The Paradox of Predatory Pricing*, 91 Cornell L. Rev. 1, 4–5 (2005).

2. *Id.*

I. INSTITUTIONS

In economic theory, the category "institution" is so capacious as to include virtually everything that a law student would study in an antitrust course. For example, the introduction to the *Handbook of New Institutional Economics* defines institutions as "the written and unwritten rules, norms and constraints that humans devise to reduce uncertainty and control their environment" and explains that these include "(i) written rules and agreements that govern contractual relations and corporate governance, (ii) constitutions, laws and rules that govern politics, government, finance, and society more broadly, and (iii) unwritten codes of conduct, norms of behavior, and beliefs."[3] Following such a broad definition would require a treatment of antitrust institutions to cover the entire spectrum of substantive legal norms, procedural rules, and informal mechanisms that comprise the antitrust enterprise.

A narrower understanding of antitrust institutions would focus solely on formally established governmental bodies such as the Federal Trade Commission, Justice Department's Antitrust Division, state attorney general's offices, and the federal courts. Limiting the study of antitrust institutions so narrowly would unduly constrict coverage and miss many of the most important determinants of the antitrust system's direction. Many of antitrust's critical drivers are not institutions in a formal sense but nonetheless vie with, or supplement, the formal institutions. Examples include the private enforcement system, criminal leniency rules, the shadow of the civil jury (as we will see, the jury's shadow does much more work than the jury itself does), and the Hart-Scott-Rodino premerger notification requirement.

My goal in this book is to fall somewhere between the broad economic definition and the narrower legal one. It is to study antitrust's institutional structure broadly—to understand the system's transsubstantive determinants, their interactions, and outputs—without dipping more than necessary into the substance of antitrust rules. Of course, the legal realist movement taught us that the distinction between substance and procedure is illusory,[4] and I shall not pretend that one can intelligently speak about antitrust's institutional structure without also implicating its substantive goals, ideological commitments, rules, and attitudes toward the competitive process. Yet my overall project is, as much as possible, to isolate antitrust's institutional structure from the complex of substantive norms that make up the ordinary course of study in antitrust law.

Just as important as institutions are *anti-institutions*—political or legal forces that arise to counter the directional pull of institutions. Examples of

---

3. Claude Ménard & Mary M. Shirley, *Introduction*, in HANDBOOK OF NEW INSTITUTIONAL ECONOMICS 1 (Claude Ménard & Mary M. Shirley eds., 2005).

4. For an early version of this insight, *see* CHARLES F. CHAMBERLAYNE, EVIDENCE § 191 (1911) ("The distinction between substantive and procedural law is artificial and illusory").

anti-institutions include jury-avoidance procedural rules, draconian standing rules that stymie private litigation, federalism constraints on state antitrust enforcement, and canons of appellate judicial review that diminish the influence of the FTC. While the story of antitrust's institutions is well known to most practitioners in the field, the story of its anti-institutions and their consequences for substantive norms have been comparatively underappreciated. Hence, this book often has as much to say about the anti-institutions as it does about the institutions themselves.

II. STRUCTURE

In institutionalist literature, "design" and "structure" are often used interchangeably, but there is an important difference between the two concepts. "Institutional design" suggests the conscious construction of an apparatus or edifice. For example, the Sixty-third Congress of 1914 designed the FTC to have certain features—i.e., five commissioners of diverse political parties and with seven-year terms and the power to make adjudicatory decisions subject to judicial review by federal appellate courts. These features and others reflect the institutional design of the FTC. However, the deliberate design features of the FTC tell us relatively little about the FTC's real structure as an institution. As we will see, the way that the FTC functions in the antitrust arena is a product of its history and development, its interaction with other legal and economic institutions, and its molding by external political, social, and economic forces.

To fully understand the effect of the FTC (and all of the other antitrust institutions to which this book is devoted) on competition policy, one must study the edifice not merely as an architect pouring over blueprints but as an engineer evaluating the building's soundness and effectiveness 100 years later. Architectural design is only one element of structural integrity, and legislative design is only one element of institutional integrity. This book is dedicated to the structure of antitrust institutions as they have stood—and adapted—over the years and as they stand today.

III. ANTITRUST

Since I have defined the scope of this book to exclude direct examination of the substance of antitrust law—or what legal academics would refer to as antitrust liability rules—a brief word should be said about the background norms that the following discussion will assume. At a very high level of generality, antitrust could be defined as the rules governing the competitive process that market-oriented legal regimes adopt to control market power. This definition may be overbroad, since many legal and regulatory mechanisms—for example, telecommunications regulation and rules for bidding on government contracts—govern competition other than those traditionally in the antitrust fold. As Herbert Hovenkamp has noted, antitrust is really a "residual regulator" that comes into play when other legal and regulatory mechanisms are not in play.[5]

Perhaps the best way to understand the antitrust enterprise is to consider the three common "evils" that most antitrust regimes are designed to police. First, there are agreements in restraint of trade that are prohibited in the United States by Section 1 of the Sherman Act, which prohibits "[e]very contract, combination in the form of trust or otherwise, or conspiracy, in restraint of trade or commerce."[6] Article 101 of the Treaty on the Functioning of the European Union (TFEU) contains a similar prohibition on concerted anticompetitive restraints. A classic example of an unlawful restraint of trade is a price-fixing cartel, which is per se illegal and would be criminally prosecuted in the United States and in many other antitrust jurisdictions. But there are other less obviously anticompetitive agreements in restraint that are judged not under a rule of per se illegality but rather under a "rule of reason."

A second category of unlawful activity consists of exclusionary acts that lead to monopoly power. The most salient statute in the United States is Section 2 of the Sherman Act, which prohibits monopolizing, attempting to monopolize, or combining or conspiring to monopolize.[7] Other statutes that contain more specific provisions against various forms of exclusionary conduct include the Clayton Act and the Robinson Patman Act, which prohibit various forms of tying, exclusive dealing, and price discrimination. Article 102 of the TFEU's prohibition on "abuse of a dominant position" captures a similar range of unilateral exclusionary conduct.

A third broad category consists of mergers or asset acquisitions that result in market dominance. Such mergers are prohibited in the United States by Section 7 of the Clayton Act and in the EU by the Merger Regulation.

These three broad categories of antitrust concern often overlap. At their core, all three of the paradigmatic evils involve conduct that facilitates the acquisition or enhancement of market power and does so without a sufficient efficiency justification. Today, in the United States at least, antitrust law is generally understood as a mechanism for promoting industrial competition for the benefit of consumers. The Supreme Court has described the Sherman Act (the first and most general of the antitrust statutes) as a "consumer welfare prescription."[8] The Court has also made clear that antitrust law is not concerned with protecting individual businesses against immoral or unethical business conduct, noting

5. Herbert Hovenkamp, The Antitrust Enterprise: Principle and Execution 13 (2005).

6. 15 U.S.C. § 1.

7. 15 U.S.C. § 2.

8. *Reiter v. Sonotone Corp.*, 442 U.S. 330, 343 (1979).

that "[e]ven an act of pure malice by one business competitor against another does not, without more, state a claim under the federal antitrust laws."[9] Unless a plaintiff can describe the defendant's conduct as harming the process of economic rivalry in a way that harms consumers, she probably does not have an antitrust claim.

As we shall see at various junctures, economic efficiency and consumer welfare (which are not always the same thing) are merely one possible set of goals for antitrust. Other possible goals (among many) include dispersing economic power, achieving a common market, protecting powerless commercial actors from powerful ones, creating opportunity for all people to enter the business of their choosing, and maintaining ultimate state control over the economic system. A critical theme, mostly developed in the third part of this book, is how a jurisdiction's goals for the antitrust enterprise can shape the design and development of its antitrust institutions.

IV. ENFORCEMENT

"Enforcement" is the bête noire of my title because it implies that antitrust is a system of legal sanctions that must be wielded against recalcitrant subjects. This is the way that the antitrust statutes and cases read. But there are alternative approaches to achieving antitrust's regulatory goals, many of which I will argue are preferable to the "enforcement" model. For example, Chapter 5 considers the informal administrative-regulatory model that characterizes much merger review today. Chapter 9 argues in favor of private administrative solutions to certain problems of market power. These are examples of institutional arrangements to police market power that do not follow a prohibition or deterrence-oriented enforcement model.

It is often assumed that regulation and antitrust are the two possible models for controlling market power in capitalist societies. Regulation controls outcomes and antitrust controls processes. In Chapter 5, I describe a middle ground that I refer to as administration. Administration avoids both the ex ante command-and-control model of regulation and the ex post deterrence or punishment model of traditional antitrust. It is antitrust "enforcement" in a very different sense.

V. ORGANIZATION

This book unfolds in three sections. Section I focuses on the origins and development of U.S. antitrust institutions. It begins by telling a "deep" story

9. *Brooke Group Ltd. v. Brown & Williamson Tobacco Corp.*, 509 U.S. 209, 225 (1993).

about long-standing competition between adjudicatory and corporate regulatory models of antitrust from the framing of the U.S. Constitution to the creation of the FTC during the Progressive Era. It then addresses the curious case of dual federal enforcement, the growth and backlash to private enforcement, and the technocratic shift that occurred beginning in the middle of the twentieth century.

Section II shifts from history and description to a critical assessment and improvement agenda for modern antitrust institutions. In Chapter 5, it outlines a typology of approaches to antitrust enforcement—regulation, adjudication, and administration—and promotes the virtues of administration. Later chapters focus on specific institutions or enforcement structures including juries, the federal agencies, federalism, and private enforcement.

Part III briefly introduces comparative and international perspectives. The obvious counterpoint to the U.S. story is the European Union model, and Chapter 10 is devoted to describing and comparing institutional mechanisms in the United States and Europe. Chapter 11 surveys developing antitrust institutions around the world and provides some typologies that may be useful to condensing this vast subject matter. The book closes with the controversial topic of global antitrust institutions—a perhaps Utopian topic but one that also may represent the wave of the future.

PART I

ORIGINS AND DEVELOPMENT OF U.S. ANTITRUST INSTITUTIONS

1. ANTIFEDERALISM AND CORPORATE REGULATION

Foreign observers of the American system of antitrust enforcement are often puzzled by the system's heavily adjudicatory bent. A large part of U.S. antitrust enforcement happens in courtrooms before generalist judges and juries who make binary decisions about whether the defendant's conduct conformed to some abstract norm of industrial competition. It is mostly backward looking and deterrence oriented rather than forward looking or structurally oriented. Despite complaints that private antitrust enforcers are not often motivated by the public interest, private enforcement outstrips public enforcement by a ten-to-one ratio. For a system that is supposed to be about economic efficiency rather than morality, fairness, or populist sentiment, the U.S. enforcement system seems inefficient.

U.S. scholars often try to explain the institutional features of U.S. antitrust enforcement by examining the legislative history of the Sherman Act and the Clayton Act—the 1890 and 1914 statutes that created most of our existing antitrust institutions. This approach usually leads to frustration for several reasons. For one, the Sherman Act's legislative history is notoriously tortured and unhelpful.[1] On institutional structure matters, the Clayton Act's legislative history is far richer, but it presents only one slice of a long-standing historical dialectic between competing ideas about federal management of commercial enterprises. Understanding U.S. antitrust institutions requires examining a much broader set of ideological, constitutional, and political tensions about the role of the federal government in superintending the structure and behavior of large corporations.

In particular, it is necessary to understand the relationship between antitrust law and corporate law and assumptions about the wisdom and constitutionality of giving Congress the power to grant charters of incorporation. These conversations began much earlier than antitrust's formative period but underlay discussion about the institutional structure of antitrust law during its formative moments. The story of U.S. antitrust institutions is in many ways a story about constitutional and political impulses that resulted in the divorce of corporate law

1. *See* E. Thomas Sullivan, The Political Economy of the Sherman Act: The First One Hundred Years 20–160 (1991); I Phillip E. Areeda & Herbert Hovenkamp, Antitrust Law 59 (2d ed. 2000) ("Taking the legislative history of the antitrust laws as a whole, we would give it relatively little weight on the fundamental question whether economic efficiency, injury to competitors, or some alternative 'populist' goal should guide antitrust policy."); Robert H. Lande, *Wealth Transfers as the Original and Primary Concern of Antitrust: The Efficiency Interpretation Challenged*, 34 Hastings L.J. 67, 68 (1982); Robert H. Bork, *Legislative Intent and the Policy of the Sherman Act*, 9 J.L. & Econ. 7 (1966).

and antitrust law. Because of this divorce, antitrust law was unmoored from corporate regulation and left to develop on its own as a freestanding prohibition on certain types of "bad acts." Many of the distinctively American antitrust enforcement mechanisms—binary adjudication, treble damages, juries, private litigation, and so forth—are products of this constitutionally animated divorce of corporate regulation and antitrust law. This chapter traces the development of the ideological impulses that contributed to U.S. antitrust's institutional status quo.

I. THE ANTIMONOPOLY TRADITION AT THE FOUNDING

At the time of the Constitution's framing, the former colonies inherited from British common law a suspicion of corporate charters based on the view that such special privileges generally led to monopoly.[2] Further, since many of the foreign trading companies that colonized the reaches of the British Empire were explicitly granted monopoly rights in their charters—exclusive trading privileges in specified regions—the American colonists tended to associate the corporation with explicit monopoly.[3] Abhorrence of monopoly was early to become an American tradition, and it was associated almost entirely with the business corporation. Hence, most preconstitutional corporations were noncommercial—charitable, educational, or religious institutions like Dartmouth College, whose 1754 charter from George III and the governor of New Hampshire gave rise to the famous *Dartmouth College* case that established corporate charters as inviolable contracts.[4] Before the adoption of the Constitution, the colonies chartered only twenty-one business corporations, which consisted of thirteen canal, navigation, or bridge companies; six banks or trading companies; and only one manufacturing company.[5] The dominant business model remained the sole proprietorship or general partnership.[6]

---

2. William Letwin, Law and Economic Policy in America: The Evolution of the Sherman Antitrust Act 62–63 (1965); James Willard Hurst, The Legitimacy of the Business Corporation in the Law of the United States: 1780–1970 (1970).

3. Letwin, *supra* note 2, at 63.

4. *Trustees of Dartmouth College v. Woodward*, 17 U.S. (4 Wheat.) 518 (1819).

5. Simeon E. Baldwin, Introduction to Two Centuries Growth of American Law 275, 296 (1901).

6. *See* Lawrence Friedman, A History of American Law 190 (2d ed. 1985). Although the Continental Congress had chartered The Bank of North America without any express delegation of power to do so in the Article of Confederation, the bank raised little criticism because it was perceived as critical to the war. Janet A. Reisman, *Money, Credit and Federalist Political Economy*, *in* Beyond Confederation: Origins of the Constitution and American National Identity 128, 138–49 (Richard Beeman et al. eds., 1987). Indeed, seven states enacted legislation granting the bank monopoly status and assuring that no competitive state bank would be chartered for the duration of the war. Davis, II Essays in

The Federalist framers of the new Constitution were dissatisfied with the pace of growth in the agrarian localized economy under the Articles of Confederation. They aimed for a far more interventionist federal government. The Federalists' economic architect-in-chief, Alexander Hamilton, envisioned a mercantilist federal government stimulating growth through subsidies, tariffs, and grants of monopoly privileges to specially chartered business corporations. Hamilton's vision was bound to collide with the Jeffersonian vision of an agrarian nation of yeoman farmers, and the power to incorporate was to become one of the defining friction points in the confrontation between the mercantilist Federalists and the classicist Antifederalists.

The earliest skirmish between the opposing views—between what I will anachronistically call antitrust federalism and antitrust antifederalism—occurred almost by accident during the Philadelphia Constitutional Convention during the summer of 1787. On August 18, James Madison moved a reference to the Committee of Detail of a series of additional enumerated powers. Among these were the precursors to the copyright and patent clauses and a power "[t]o grant charters of incorporation in cases where the Public good may require them, and the authority of a single State may be incompetent."[7] Madison may have meant to propose a fairly limited federal incorporation power and certainly reinterpreted his views as classicist, Republican, and anti-mercantilist in his later Jeffersonian incarnation.[8] The "Public good" caveat could have limited the federal incorporation power to common carriers or other firms "affected with the public interest" and performing public or quasi-governmental functions.[9] Madison probably did not imagine that Congress would charter manufacturing or commercial corporations, which were still rare.[10]

THE EARLIER HISTORY OF AMERICAN CORPORATIONS 38 (1917). After 1784, the bank's charter was repealed and replaced with a Pennsylvania-specific bank. *Id.* at 41–43.

7. James Madison, Notes on the Constitutional Convention (Aug. 18, 1787) (proposal of James Madison), *in* 2 THE RECORDS OF THE FEDERAL CONVENTION OF 1787, at 324, 325 (Max Farrand ed., 1966) [hereinafter Farrand's Records].

8. Later in life, Madison wrote that "Monopolies though in certain cases useful ought to be granted with caution, and guarded with strictness against abuse. The Constitution of the U.S. has limited them to two cases, the authors of Books, and of useful inventions, in both which they are considered as a compensation for a benefit actually gained to the community as a purchase of property which the owner otherwise might withhold from public use." JAMES MADISON, WRITINGS 756 (Jack N. Rakove ed., 1999).

9. On the "affected with the public interest" idea that the colonies inherited from British common law, *see* MARTIN LOUGHLIN, THE IDEA OF PUBLIC LAW 6, 77–80 (2003). In *Munn v. Illinois*, the Supreme Court justified rate regulation of an unincorporated grain elevator firm on the grounds that it was affected with the public interest, and traced this distinction to common law. 94 U.S. 113, 125–26 (1876).

10. In response to Madison's proposal, Charles Pinkney offered a list of ten additional proposed powers, which included a broader power "To grant charters of incorporation." Farrand's Records, *supra* note 7, at 325.

Madison's proposal went nowhere until, during a meeting of the full Convention a month later, Benjamin Franklin moved to add "a power to provide for cutting for canals where deemed necessary" following the clause that became Article I, Section 8, Clause 7 (establishment of post offices and post roads).[11] In the debate that ensued, Roger Sherman expressed concern that the federal government would bear all of the cost of the canals and that local interests would receive all of the benefits.[12] Madison responded by reintroducing his incorporation proposal, this time as an "enlargement" on Franklin's canals motion. Instead of bearing the costs of cutting canals directly, the federal government could incorporate private firms to undertake this and other interstate commercial ventures at their own risk and expense. Thus, Madison proposed to add a power "to grant charters of incorporation where the interest of the U.S. might require & the legislative provisions of individual States may be incompetent."[13] Whether intentionally or not, Madison had removed the language that could have limited federal corporations to common carriers and other enterprises "affected with the public interest" from his original proposal.

Madison's proposal engendered two very different kinds of reactions in the Convention. James Wilson—a strong Federalist—supported the proposal on the ground that granting Congress such an incorporation power was necessary "to prevent a State from obstructing the general welfare."[14] Wilson apparently had in mind the use of federal incorporations to preempt provincial state legislation and other local impediments to free trade. On the other hand, Rufus King expressed concern that the Antifederalists would seize on the clause as permitting the incorporation of a national bank and mercantile monopolies.[15] In a lapse into inadvisable candor, Wilson responded that the power to incorporate "mercantile monopolies" was already included in the commerce clause power.[16] Wilson's admission drew a rise out of Antifederalist George Mason, who "was afraid of monopolies of every sort, which he did not think were by any means already implied by the Constitution as supposed by Mr. Wilson."[17] Having reached an impasse on the general incorporation power, the Convention returned to Franklin's original proposal for a canals power.[18]

11. Farrand's Records, *supra* note 7, at 615.
12. *Id.*
13. *Id.*
14. *Id.*
15. *See id.* at 616.
16. See *id.*
17. *Id.*
18. *Id.*

Scholars sometimes interpret the defeat of Madison's proposal as an Antifederalist victory against mercantilist monopolies.[19] Opposing the incorporation of the First Bank of the United States a few years later, Madison interpreted the defeat of his proposal as entailing the absence of federal power to incorporate.[20] But the Antifederalists eventually lost that fight in *McCulloch v. Maryland*. Even at the moment that Madison's proposal was abandoned, the reason for its failure was inconclusive. Was it because federal incorporations could become monopolistic and therefore should be rejected or because Congress had an incorporation power anyway, and spelling this out explicitly would merely raise red flags for Antifederalists?

The Antifederalists chose to believe the latter. George Mason refused to sign the proposed Constitution because "[u]nder their own construction of the general clause at the End of the enumerated Powers, the Congress may grant Monopolies in Trade & Commerce."[21] Elbridge Gerry withheld his signature for the same reason.[22] A slew of Antifederalist writers attacked the proposed Constitution as setting up a congressional power to grant mercantile monopolies.[23] The ratifying conventions of Massachusetts, New Hampshire, and North Carolina requested, in their proposed bill of rights, an amendment providing

---

19. *E.g.*, Dotan Oliar, *Making Sense of the Intellectual Property Clause: Promotion of Progress as a Limitation on Congress's Intellectual Property Power*, 94 Geo. L.J. 1771, 1800–1801 (2006) ("An anti-monopolistic sentiment was present during the Convention's debates, which seems to be the reason why the Framers rejected other proposals by Madison and Pinckney for a federal incorporation power."); *see also* Steven A. Bank, *Entity Theory as Myth in the Origins of the Corporate Income Tax*, 43 Wm. & Mary L. Rev. 447, 470 n. 112 (2001); Thomas B. McAfee, *The Federal System as Bill of Rights: Original Understandings, Modern Misreadings*, 43 Vill. L. Rev. 17, 117–18 (1998); Daniel A. Farber & Suzanna Sherry, A History of the American Constitution 141 (1990).

20. *The Bank Bill* (Feb. 2, 1791), *in* 13 The Papers of James Madison 377–78 (Robert A. Rutland, et al. eds., 1975); David P. Currie, The Constitution in Congress, at 78–80 (1997).

21. 8 The Documentary History of the Ratification of the Constitution 45 (Merrill Jensen ed., 1976) [hereinafter Documentary History].

22. 4 Documentary History, *supra* note 21, at 14.

23. *See Son of Liberty*, 13 Documentary History, *supra* note 21, at 482 ("Monopolies in trade [will be] granted to the favorites of government, by which the spirit of adventure will be destroyed, and the citizens subjected to the extortion of those companies who will have an exclusive right"); *Agrippa*, 4 Documentary History, *supra note* 21, at 428 ("The unlimited right to regulate trade, includes the right of granting exclusive charters. . . . We hardly find a country in Europe which has not felt the ill effects of such a power."); *Centinel*, 1 The Debate on the Constitution: Federalist and Antifederalist Speeches, Articles, and Letters During the Struggle Over Ratification 89 (Bernard Bailyn ed., 1993) (complaining that proposed Constitution failed to specify that "monopolies in trade or arts other than to authors of books or inventors of useful arts, for a reasonable time, ought not to be suffered").

"that congress erect no company of merchants, with exclusive advantages of commerce," and New York proposed a similar provision.[24] After the ratification, Thomas Jefferson, in private correspondence to Madison, expressed the need for an antimonopoly provision in the Bill of Rights.[25]

In sum, Madison's proposal was a catalyst for the antitrust antifederalist impulse. The Antifederalists had seen the possibility of federal charters with exclusive privileges when Madison, perhaps unintentionally, had blundered into it. They were even more troubled by Wilson's admission that the Federalists would pursue a mercantilist incorporationist agenda with or without an express incorporation power. The ambiguous skirmish over Madison's proposal in Philadelphia set the stage for a much more heated battle over Hamilton's national bank.

II. JACKSONIANISM AND THE SECOND BANK OF THE UNITED STATES

The Antifederalist prediction that powerful federal corporations would arise despite the rejection of Madison's federal incorporation proposal proved correct. In 1791, at Hamilton's instance, Congress chartered the Bank of the United States with a capitalization of $10 million, five times the total capitalization of the three existing state banks.[26] Hamilton designed the bank as a private commercial corporation "under a *private* not *public* direction—under the guidance of *individual interest,* not of *public policy.*"[27] Just as alarming to the Antifederalists (turned Republicans, shortly to become Democrats) was Hamilton's argument that the Constitution implied a virtually unlimited right to incorporate national corporations: "A power to regulate trade, is a power to make all needful rules and regulations concerning trade. Why may it not, then, include that of erecting a trading company?"[28]

The charter of the first Bank of the United States expired after twenty years.[29] By 1811, the Federalist era had long ended and neo-Antifederalism was politically ascendant. Madison, however, had shifted from pro-incorporationist framer

---

24. 2 The Documentary History of the Constitution of the United States of America 1786–1870, at 95, 142, 274 (1894).

25. Letter from Jefferson to Madison (Aug. 28, 1789), *in* 15 The Papers of Thomas Jefferson 367–68 (1958) (proposing a provision that "Monopolies may be allowed to persons for their own productions in literature and their own inventions in the arts for a term not exceeding _ years but for no longer term and for no other purpose").

26. *See* John Steel Gordon, Hamilton's Blessing: The Extraordinary Life and Times of Our National Debt 34 (1997).

27. *Id.*

28. Horace L. Wilgus, *Need of National Incorporation Law,* 2 Mich. L. Rev. 358, 380 (1904).

29. Gordon, *supra* n. 26, at 46.

to anti-incorporationist Representative to pro-incorporationist president.[30] He instructed Albert Gallatin, his treasury secretary, to seek renewal of the charter.[31] The bill failed in the Senate when Vice President George Clinton bucked Madison's will and cast the tie-breaking vote against it.[32] But, saddled with a fiscal crisis resulting from the War of 1812, Congress finally gave Madison the Second Bank of the United States in 1816.[33]

The second bank's charter gave rise to a decisive battle over the constitutionality of federal incorporations and the scope of Congress's enumerated powers more generally. In *McCulloch v. Maryland*, the Hamiltonian-Federalist vision prevailed as a matter of constitutional law. The Supreme Court held that incorporating a bank was within Congress's "necessary and proper" powers.[34] Since *McCulloch*, it has become clear that "Congress. . . may create corporations as appropriate means of executing the powers of government, as, for instance, a bank for the purpose of carrying on the fiscal operations of the United States, or a railroad corporation for the purpose of promoting commerce among the states."[35] Congress could charter corporations as "necessary and proper" to the exercise of its enumerated powers, to which the Supreme Court eventually gave a broad construction. The Court thus effectively granted Congress the broad power to incorporate business firms despite the defeat of Madison's proposal for an enumerated power to that effect.

But if *McCulloch* served the Hamilton-Federalist vision a constitutional law victory, it also handed it a long-term political defeat. Citing the powers of the "monster" bank to "make money plenty or scarce at its pleasure, at any time and in any quarter of the Union," Andrew Jackson vetoed the renewal charter of the Second Bank of the United States in 1836.[36] The bank embodied old Antifederalist fears of a monopolistic, mercantilist, nationally dominant corporation. Antifederalism had lost on the constitutional law question but nonetheless defeated the Bank and established an important political precedent against federal incorporations. A new national bank—the federal reserve—would not be created until 1913 during the Progressive Era, by which time its symbolic importance as the embodiment of the federal incorporation power had long

30. *Id.* at 46–47.

31. *Id. at* 47.

32. *Id.*

33. *Id.* at 53.

34. Currie, *supra* note 20, at 160–68.

35. *Luxton v. North River Bridge Co.*, 153 U.S. 525, 529 (1894) (*citing McCulloch v. Maryland*, 4 Wheat. 316, 411 (1819).

36. Tony A. Freyer, Producers Versus Capitalists: Constitutional Conflict in Antebellum America 33, 44, 83–84 (1994).

since passed.[37] By 1913, general incorporation had become, perhaps irretrievably, a state law prerogative.

However, the triumph of Jacksonianism did not result in fewer incorporations. Indeed, Jackson supported state general incorporation statutes on the ground that they were a necessary antidote to the corrupting influence of the special charter system that favored established and politically powerful commercial incumbents at the expense of newcomers.[38] The policy of Jacksonianism became to "reduce the privilege of incorporation, not by taking it from the few, but by opening it to the many."[39]

Jackson's administration marked an ideological shift from the mercantilism of the Federalist era to the classicism that would prevail until the turn of the century. One of the important attributes of the emerging classicism was an emphasis on equality of access to incorporation privileges granted by the state. In the antebellum and Reconstruction eras, the general corporate charter would become the dominant means of doing business on a medium or large scale.

The expansion of the corporate charter and the eventual liberalization of its terms facilitated increasingly large aggregations of capital which, in turn, contributed to the rise of the "trusts" problem in the late nineteenth century.

III. CORPORATISM AND THE SHERMAN ACT

Jacksonianism gave a boost to general incorporation statutes, but it took some time for the states to liberalize corporate law to the point that large, and potentially monopolistic, aggregations of capital were frequent. At the time of the Civil War, most business corporations still were limited by their corporate charter to a single line of business.[40] Following the Civil War, however, states began to liberalize their incorporation statutes, with an eye toward attracting firms to incorporate in their state. Thus began the "race to the bottom" in state corporation law. States competing to become incorporation havens eventually permitted corporations to own stock of other companies, granted favorable tax treatment

---

37. On the establishment of the federal reserve system, *see* RICHARD T. MCCULLEY, BANKS AND POLITICS DURING THE PROGRESSIVE ERA: THE ORIGINS OF THE FEDERAL RESERVE SYSTEM 1897–1913 (1992).

38. HERBERT HOVENKAMP, ENTERPRISE AND AMERICAN LAW 1836–1937 37 (1991) [hereinafter HOVENKAMP, ENTERPRISE AND AMERICAN LAW]. Hovenkamp notes that "Jackson's outspoken opposition to reincorporation of the Second National Bank was based on his hatred of hard money and the National Bank's dominance over state banks, not on any general hostility toward the corporation as a method of doing business." *Id.*

39. LETWIN, *supra* note 2, at 65; *see also* J. CADMAN, THE CORPORATION IN NEW JERSEY, BUSINESS AND POLITICS, 1791–1875, at 188 (1949).

40. Melvin I. Urofsky, *Proposed Federal Incorporation in the Progressive Era*, 26 AM. J.L. HIST. 160, 161 (1982).

for out-of-state earnings, allowed corporate charters "for any lawful business purpose whatsoever," dispensed with requirements that directors be state residents and that corporate meetings be held within the state, allowed unlimited capitalization, eliminated shareholder liability for corporate debts, and stopped requiring public disclosure of annual reports.[41]

The incentives on state legislatures to liberalize their own corporate statutes were extraordinarily powerful. New Jersey became known as the "traitor state" for its Holding Company Act of 1891, which facilitated the Standard Oil and Northern Securities trusts, among others.[42] But even rival state legislatures found it hard to fault New Jersey when they considered the extent to which the state benefited from its new incorporation regime. From 1896 to 1901, corporate filing fees and franchise taxes swelled from $800,000 to $2,189,000, accounting for 60 percent of the state's revenues.[43] By 1901, 95 percent of the nation's large corporations were incorporated in New Jersey.[44] By 1902, New Jersey had earned so much from corporate filing fees and franchise taxes that it had paid off the state debt and abolished property taxes. By 1905, it had a surplus of nearly $3 million in the treasury, mostly attributable to its corporate liberalization initiative.[45] It was little wonder that, despite grumbling about the "traitor state," most other states soon followed suit.[46]

Even as state incorporation law began to move along an inexorable path toward liberalization, an array of voices across the political spectrum began to complain about these laws' capital-concentrating effects. General incorporation laws made it easier for the capitalist class to concentrate the management of large enterprises in a few hands, whether by acquiring assets under common ownership or placing the shares of the corporations into "trusts" administered by common management. As early as 1874, the conservative judge and future Interstate Commerce Commission member Thomas Cooley warned that "the most enormous and threatening powers in our country have been created; some of the great and wealthy corporations [have] greater influence in the country at large and upon the legislation of the country than the States to which they owe

41. Ernst Von Halle, Trusts, Or, Industrial Combinations and Coalitions in the United States 94–96 (1900).

42. Phillip I. Blumberg, *The Transformation of Modern Corporation Law: The Law of Corporate Groups*, 37 Conn. L. Rev. 605, 607 (2005); Marc Winerman, *The Origins of the FTC: Concentration, Cooperation, Control, and Competition*, 71 Antitrust L.J. 1, 6 (2003).

43. Urofsky, *supra* note 40, at 164.

44. *Id.*

45. *Id.*

46. The trend toward corporate liberalization began well before the passage of the Sherman Act and accelerated in the wake of the Sherman Act, facilitating the great merger wave that occurred between 1895 and 1904. Naomi R. Lamoreaux, The Great Merger Movement in American Business 1895–1904 (1985).

their corporate existence."[47] Such warnings became ever more dire as the race to the bottom and the formation of the great industrial trusts of the Gilded Age accelerated. In 1895, the German economist Ernst Von Halle noted the irony of the simultaneous liberalization of corporate law and adoption of antitrust law:

> We now have the strange spectacle of the enactment of the most severe laws against trusts and combinations on the one hand, and on the other of a transformation of the corporation law which facilitated the remodeling of the trusts, and their continued transaction of business in the state.[48]

In 1900, the treatise-writer Christopher Tiedeman would blame the entire trust problem on state corporate law and propose a return to incorporation by special legislation only.[49]

The absence of a federal incorporation statute and, hence, the absence of many federal corporations, made early antitrust control an exclusively state matter. During the Reconstruction era, state attorneys general began to use state corporation law as a form of crude antitrust law to resist the capital-intensifying trends accompanying postbellum economic expansion.[50] State enforcers employed the *quo warranto* writ to challenge as *ultra vires* the corporate charter various activities, such as doing business outside the state, conducting business outside the scope of the charter, and owning the shares of other corporations.[51] But although the attorneys general met with success in some individual cases,[52] *quo warranto* enforcement of state corporate law proved to be an abysmal failure in the long run, for at least two reasons. First, clever corporate lawyers frustrated state regulators by inventing sophisticated common-law trusts that replicated the structure of multistate, conglomerate or vertically-integrated corporations through contract rather than direct corporate structuring.[53] Second, the competitive interstate pressures previously discussed created incentives for state legislatures to "cheat" on their neighbors and liberalize the very corporate rules that their attorneys general sought to rely on to control the power of large corporations.

---

47. Thomas Cooley, A Treatise on the Constitutional Limitations which Rest Upon the Legislative Power of the United States of the American Union 279 n.2 (3d ed. 1874).

48. Von Halle, *supra* note 41, at 92–97.

49. 1 Christopher G. Tiedeman, A Treatise on State and Federal Control of Persons and Property in the United States 609–10 (1900).

50. *See* Rudolph J.R. Peritz, Competition Policy in America: 1888–1992: History, Rhetoric, Law 10 (1996); Jonathan W. Singer, Broken Trusts: The Texas Attorney General Versus the Oil Industry 1889–1909 (2002).

51. Hovenkamp, Enterprise and American Law, *supra* note 38, at 63.

52. *E.g., State ex rel. Att'y Gen'l v. Standard Oil Co.*, 49 Ohio St. 137, 30 N.E. 279 (1892).

53. Hovenkamp, Enterprise and American Law, *supra* note 38, at 249.

It was thus not surprising that toward the end of the nineteenth century, calls for a federal response to the "trust" problem intensified.[54] The states had shown themselves incapable of dealing with the problem as a matter of corporate law, and therefore a federal solution was needed. But what federal solution? As Herbert Hovenkamp has argued, Congress had a choice of two models.[55] First, it could follow a structural model similar to the state *quo warranto* approach but without the inconvenience of interstate competition driving legal standards down to the lowest common denominator. At the time of the Sherman Act's adoption in 1890, there had already been calls for a federal incorporation statute,[56] and those calls intensified significantly during the two decades following the Act's passage.[57] Congress might well have chosen to require all corporations operating in interstate commerce to be federally chartered and subject to direct regulation by competition law bureaucrats in Washington. As discussed in the next section, such proposals came close to passing during the Progressive Era.

The second approach—the one actually adopted in the 1890 Sherman Act—was to divorce antitrust law from corporate law and model it instead on the common law's prohibition on restraints of trade. Congress, in fact, went far beyond the common law by making restraints of trade not merely void or unenforceable, as they were at common law, but a species of wrong against others and against the state—a tort and a crime. The Sherman Act contains two prohibitory sections—Section 1, which prohibits "every contract, combination in the form of trust or otherwise, or conspiracy, in restraint of trade";[58] and Section 2, which prohibits monopolizing, attempting to monopolize, or conspiring to monopolize.[59] The statute applies to all "persons" rather than simply to corporations; far from being targeted at corporate regulation, the statute goes out of its way to make clear that corporations and associations are covered as well.[60]

The Sherman Act's legislative history is notoriously tortured and unilluminating, and what motivated individual congressmen to support the crime-tort model instead of the corporate regulatory model is debatable. A corporate regulatory model was never formally proposed during the legislative maneuvering that brought about the 1890 statute.[61] Hovenkamp, however, argues that Congress

54. Theodore H. Davis, *Corporate Privileges for the Public Benefit: The Progressive Federal Incorporation Movement and the Modern Regulatory State*, 77 VA. L. REV. 603, 619–21 (1991).

55. *Id.* at 244–49.

56. Urofsky, *supra* note 40, at 164–65.

57. MARTIN J. SKLAR, THE CORPORATE RECONSTRUCTION OF AMERICAN CAPITALISM, 1890–1916: THE MARKET, THE LAW, AND POLITICS 203–28 (1988).

58. 15 U.S.C. § 1.

59. 15 U.S.C. § 2.

60. 15 U.S.C. § 7.

61. The leading study of the Sherman Act's legislative history is HANS B. THORELLI, THE FEDERAL ANTITRUST POLICY: ORIGINATION OF AN AMERICAN TRADITION 164–225 (1955).

chose its model wisely because the corporate regulatory model was subject to significant weaknesses. In particular, Hovenkamp notes that the corporate law rules limiting corporate activities to state boundaries, prohibiting ownership of shares of other corporations, and prohibiting mergers by stock transfer trust indiscriminately prohibited many efficient practices and were not tailored to the problem of anticompetitive trusts.[62]

To be sure, many of the corporate regulatory rules used by state attorneys general in the formative era of antitrust were not designed to advance competition values and were ill-suited for promoting market efficiency. That does not mean, however, that divorcing antitrust from corporate law in favor of a crime-tort model was a preferable solution. Replacing the corporate regulatory model with the crime-tort model created a number of systemic problems for antitrust enforcement that have persisted and in many cases become aggravated over time. As the Progressive Era began, some of these disadvantages of the crime-tort model became apparent, and Progressives returned to the possibility of a federal incorporation statute and direct federal superintendence of corporations.

IV. ANTICORPORATISM IN THE PROGRESSIVE ERA

Progressive Era lawyers, economists, and politicians were dissatisfied with the federal judiciary's interpretation of the Sherman Act.[63] During its first decade, the act was rarely used and, when it was, its ax most often fell on labor rather than capital. Many Progressives felt that Congress had chosen a weak conceptual model for antitrust in patterning it on the common law's restraint of trade jurisprudence instead of adopting a direct corporate control model. A more robust and interventionist model was needed.

Around the turn of the century, the possibility of a federal incorporation statute became a popular topic among academics and prominent members of the bar.[64] The voices in favor of such legislation included James Dill, the author of New Jersey's much-maligned Holding Company Act, who denied that he had unleashed a trust-building race to the bottom. Dill nonetheless argued that

---

62. Hovenkamp, Enterprise and American Law, *supra* note 38, at 247–48.

63. Friedman, *supra* n. 6 at 1391–96.

64. *See* Wilgus, supra note 28; E. W. Huffcut, *Constitutional Aspects of the Federal Control of Corporations*, 34 Am. L. Rev. 186 (1900); James B. Dill, *National Incorporation Laws for Trusts*, 11 Yale L.J. 273 (1902); John Bell Sanborn, *Federal Control of Corporations*, 37 Am. L. Rev. 703 (1903); Walter S. Logan, *National Incorporation and Control of Corporations*, 37 Am. L. Rev. 237 (1903); John E. Parsons, *Federal Regulation of Corporations: A Dangerous Departure*, 17 Green Bag 135 (1905); Thomas Thacher, *Federal Control of Corporations*, 14 Yale L.J. 301 (1905); E. Prentice, The Federal Power Over Carriers and Corporations 155 (1907); Charles W. Bunn, *Federal Incorporation of Railway Companies*, 30 Harv. L. Rev. 589 (1917).

"[t]he country demands uniform corporate legislation, formulated upon the good of the country as a whole, and not sectional legislation, state by state."[65] Dill and other proponents of federal incorporation argued that the trust problem was created by the diversity of state incorporation law and the absence of a national regulatory force that could supervise the activities of the gigantic interstate trusts and prevent them from exercising monopolistic power.[66]

Opponents of federal incorporation, led by Yale Law Professor Thomas Thacher, invoked old Antifederalist themes.[67] Thacher worried that ceding incorporation power to the government would be to "bid farewell to the fundamental theory of the Federal Constitution and to call the wisdom of the [founding] Fathers folly when applied to the conditions of to-day."[68] Responding to Attorney General Philander Knox's argument that an incorporation power was necessary to prevent fraud, Thacher noted that corporate fraud such as overcapitalization "affects only those who become participants in corporate enterprises," not the general public.[69] Since Thacher did not believe that the federal incorporation and corporate disclosure model would make the trusts more competitive, he worried that proponents of the plan had an ulterior motive. Contextualizing for an early twentieth-century audience, Thacher warned that the incorporation proposal was "a long step toward Federal socialism."[70] Thacher and others feared, perhaps with some good reason, that Roosevelt's ultimate goal was to use federal incorporation to wrest federal control over the national economy. The economy would be "socialized" not in the conventional sense that the state would own and operate the means of production but rather in the looser sense that federal regulators—in tandem with corporate managers—would oversee the management of vast corporate enterprises.

Outside of academic circles, calls for a federal incorporation statute grew louder as disappointment with early returns under the Sherman Act increased. An 1899 Chicago Conference on Trusts, sponsored by the Chicago Civic Federation, led a number of prominent public figures to call for direct federal control of the trusts.[71] William Jennings Bryan, the 1896 Democratic presidential candidate, led the charge, advocating mandatory federal incorporation for corporations doing business outside their home state and accompanying stringent requirements regarding capitalization and business policies.[72] Soon, federal incorporation became a widely favored strategy in the political mainstream.

---

65. Dill, *supra* note 64, at 274.

66. *Id.*

67. *See* Thacher, *supra* note 64; *see also* Parsons, *supra* note 64; Prentice, *supra* note 64.

68. Thacher, *supra* note 64, at 305.

69. *Id.* at 307.

70. *Id.* at 311.

71. Sklar, *supra* n. 57 at 207.

72. *Id.*

Despite personal misgivings about the value of antitrust law and conservative opposition from within his own party, Teddy Roosevelt made corporate control legislation the keynote of his first annual message to Congress. Even before assuming the presidency upon McKinley's assassination, Roosevelt had come to believe that "[m]ore and more it is evident that the State, and if necessary the nation, has got to possess the right of supervision and control as regards the great corporations which are its creatures."[73] In his 1901 message, he identified the trusts problem as one of corporate law:

> It is not limitation upon property rights or freedom of contract to require that when men receive from government the privilege of doing business under corporate form. . . they shall do so upon absolutely truthful representations. . . Great corporations exist only because they are safeguarded by our institutions; and it is therefore our right and duty to see that they work in harmony with these institutions.[74]

This "creatures of the state may be regulated by the state" justification for antitrust regulation advanced by Roosevelt found a home in antitrust jurisprudence. When the Supreme Court upheld Roosevelt's antitrust suit against J.P. Morgan's railroad merger, Justice Brewer noted in his concurrence that a "corporation. . . is not endowed with the inalienable rights of a natural person. It is an artificial person, created and existing only for the convenient transaction of business."[75] Even the *Northern Securities* dissenters agreed with that proposition.[76] The freedom of contract arguments that prevailed the following year in *Lochner*[77] found no traction as applied to efforts to curtail the harms created by large aggregations of capital occasioned by the liberalization of corporate law.[78]

But if the corporate control model of antitrust found a place in constitutional rhetoric, it found little success in antitrust reform, despite broad political support. Even prior to Roosevelt's charge to Congress, Congressmen began to introduce proposals for a federal incorporation statute that would have placed corporate control at the center of federal antitrust policy.[79] Beginning in 1900, congressmen introduced a series of bills that would have required firms operating in interstate commerce to be federally licensed and comply with certain requirements.

---

73. EDMUND MORRIS, THEODORE REX 30 (2001).

74. *Id.* at 73.

75. *N. Sec. Co. v. United States*, 193 U.S. 197, 362 (1904) (Brewer, J., concurring).

76. *See id.* at 398 (White, J., dissenting) (conceding that "the corporation is created by the state, and holds rights subject to the conditions attached to the grant, or to such regulations as they creator, the state, may lawfully impose upon its creature, the corporation").

77. *Lochner v. New York*, 198 U.S. 45 (1905).

78. *See generally* Daniel A. Crane, *Lochnerian Antitrust*, 1 N.Y.U. J.L. & LIBERTY 496 (2005).

79. *See* Herbert Hovenkamp, *Antitrust Policy, Federalism, and the Theory of the Firm: A Historical Perspective*, 59 ANTITRUST L.J. 75, 77 (1990).

Roosevelt threw his considerable weight behind such corporate control legislation. For example, in his December 3, 1907, Annual Message to Congress, he advocated the adoption of a general incorporation statute under which a federal board or commission would decide whether an applicant for a federal charter was already in violation of federal law, and if the charter was issued, assume jurisdiction over the corporation to enforce federal law.[80] The proposed legislation would have also added further content to the antitrust laws (somewhat along the lines eventually adopted in the Clayton Act) by prohibiting pricing at a loss to drive out competitors, entering into exclusive dealing or tying contracts, and defrauding investors and gauging consumers.[81] But by 1907, six such bills had died in committee.[82]

Roosevelt did achieve a modest step toward direct federal superintendence of large corporations operating in interstate commerce in a 1903 act of Congress that created a Bureau of Corporations as an agency of the newly formed Department of Commerce.[83] The new bureau was charged with investigating and reporting on interstate corporations. Between 1906 and 1913, the bureau investigated and issued reports on the petroleum, tobacco, steel, and farm implement industries.[84] However, the bureau lacked enforcement or regulatory authority and insisted that its only authority was investigatory, with an eye toward proposing new legislation.[85]

In the meantime, Roosevelt continued to press for antitrust legislation giving the federal government direct supervisory authority over interstate corporations. Even after his administration scored a major victory in *Northern Securities*, Roosevelt fumed that antitrust litigation was too slow and cumbersome a means of regulatory control, and that "[n]o judicial tribunal has the knowledge or the experience to determine in the first place whether a given combination is advisable or necessary in the interest of the public."[86] True to the spirit of the Progressive Era, Roosevelt argued that the crime-tort model of the Sherman Act, committed as it was to the care of the federal courts, needed to be replaced with a regulatory model where complex decisions about the propriety of "trusts" could be made by specialized bureaucrats. Between 1906 and 1908, Roosevelt's annual message repeatedly urged Congress to "grant [] supervisory power to the government over these big concerns engaged in interstate business."[87]

---

80. Sklar, *supra* n. 57 at 216–17.

81. *Id.*

82. Gabriel. Kolko, The Triumph of Conservatism 133 (1963).

83. Act of Feb. 14, 1903, 32 Stat. 827.

84. *See FTC v. Gratz*, 253 U.S. 421, 433 (1920).

85. Report of the Commissioner of Corporations, 1904 (58th Cong. 3rd Sess. H.R. Doc. 165) 34.

86. Roosevelt, Special Message to Congress, the Senate, and House of Representatives 71937 (Apr. 27, 1908) in Joint Committee on Printing, 16 A Compilation of the Messages and Papers of the Presidents (1897).

87. Letwin, *supra* note 2, at 246.

Roosevelt came closest to getting a corporate control bill when, on March 23, 1908, Congressman William Hepburn of the Committee on Interstate Commerce introduced what became known as the Hepburn Bill.[88] The bill provided that corporations could, at their option, register with the commissioner of corporations.[89] To register, the corporation would have to make full disclosure of its finances and business methods. Registered companies could file any potentially anticompetitive agreements with the commissioner.[90] Within thirty days, the commissioner could declare the contract an unreasonable restraint of trade and void, but if he did not do so, the contract would become immune from attack by the government.[91] The bill also cut back on private rights of action by de-trebling damages as to any registered contract and prohibiting any private or public suits as to contracts predating 1908.[92] In effect, the Hepburn Bill would have replaced much of the Sherman Act's model of antitrust with a corporate regulatory model, albeit a voluntary one.[93]

At first, the Hepburn Bill enjoyed strong support from a wide array of constituencies, including Roosevelt, business, labor, and Progressive reformers. But as the bill languished in committee, big business began to push for revisions that would have reduced the power of the commissioner of corporations, Roosevelt and labor reformers worried that the bill was becoming diluted, and eventually both labor and business began to grumble against the bill.[94] When Roosevelt left office in 1909, the bill was dead.

Roosevelt's successor, William Howard Taft, continued to promote the need for a federal incorporation bill. His proposal, however, would have made federal incorporation and regulatory superintendence mandatory for businesses operating in interstate commerce.[95] But Taft's proposal was forgotten in the furor surrounding the Supreme Court's *Standard Oil* decision in 1911.[96] Although the Court ordered Rockefeller's trust disbanded, Justice White's opinion squarely affirmed that the Sherman Act prohibited not all restraints of trade but only unreasonable ones.[97] Many Progressives thought *Standard Oil* gutted the Sherman

---

88. 60th Con. I Sess., H.R. 19745.

89. SKLAR, *supra* n. 57 at 232.

90. *Id.*

91. *Id.*

92. *See* LETWIN, *supra* note 2, at 248–49.

93. On the history of the Hepburn bill, *see* Sklar, *supra* n. 57 at 228–85.

94. *Id.* at 249–50.

95. *See* LETWIN, *supra* note 2, at 252.

96. *Standard Oil Co. v. United States*, 221 U.S. 1 (1911). The public reaction to the *Standard Oil* decision was intense. It has been compared to *Dred Scott, Brown v. Board of Education* and *Roe v. Wade*. *See* NATHAN GASKILL, THE REGULATION OF COMPETITION 15 (1936); PERITZ, *supra* note 51, at 61.

97. On the *Standard Oil* decision, *see* James May, *The Story of Standard Oil Co. v. United States*, in ANTITRUST STORIES (Eleanor Fox & Daniel A. Crane, eds. 2007).

Act and opened the door to large combinations of capital.[98] For example, the 1912 Democractic Party platform lamented that the opinion had deprived the Sherman Act "of much of its efficacy." The party proposed legislation to "restore to the statute the strength of which it has been deprived by such interpretation."[99]

In the 1912 election, Woodrow Wilson defeated the reinvented Roosevelt and his plan for direct federal regulation of corporations, paving the way for the major antitrust legislation of 1914.[100] Louis Brandeis, who served as Wilson's chief antitrust braintrust, argued that Roosevelt proposed to "'regulate monopoly' whereas Wilson" proposed to "regulate competition."[101] In Wilson's view, the Rooseveltian model of direct federal creation and regulation of corporations was a recipe for government-created monopoly. Unlike Brandeis, however, Wilson did not share the Progressive Era infatuation with government by experts. Reacting to a proposed antitrust commission in 1912, he caustically remarked: "I don't want a smug lot of experts to sit down behind closed doors in Washington and play providence to me."[102] Further, Wilson distinguished between proper prohibitory regulation—for example, a law against anticompetitive behavior by trusts and improper "direct administrative regulation"—for example, structuring corporations to facilitate competition, which, like Thacher, he equated with socialism.[103] Thus, when Senator Cummins issued a report proposing various powers for the soon-to-be created Federal Trade Commission, Wilson objected to only one of them: the power directly to structure interstate corporations through regulation.[104] Although Cummins argued that such prophylactic "quasi-judicial" power would allow the Commission to make competition policy "vastly more effectually" than could the courts, Wilson saw this as nothing other than Roosevelt's model of an unholy partnership between the government and the trusts. Wilson declared that although "the opinion of the country" supported a commission, "it would not wish to see it empowered to make terms with monopoly or in any sort to assume control of business, as if the government made itself responsible."[105] The Commission's powers would have to be prohibitory, not structural.

98. *See* Robert L. Rabin, *Federal Regulation in Historical Perspective*, 38 STAN. L. REV. 1189, 1219 (1986); Rudolph J. Peritz, *A Counter–History of Antitrust Law*, 1990 DUKE L.J. 263, 278 (1990).

99. KIRK H. PORTER & DONALD BRUCE JOHNSON, NATIONAL PARTY PLATFORMS 1840–1960 169 (2d ed. 1961).

100. On shifts in Roosevelt's thinking on antitrust matters during the Taft administration and 1912 election cycle, *see* SKLAR, *supra* n. 57 at 359–64.

101. LETWIN, *supra* note 2, at 269.

102. A campaign address in Sioux City, Iowa, Sept. 17, 1912, *in* 25 PAPERS OF WOODROW WILSON 148, 154 (Arthur S. Link, ed.) (1978).

103. Winerman, *supra* n. 42, at 42. On Wilson's aversion to ceding antitrust power to economic experts, *see id.* at 45–47.

104. *See* LETWIN, *supra* note 2, at 272.

105. *Id.* at 273.

The year 1914 saw the adoption of two significant pieces of antitrust legislation: the Clayton Act, which strengthened and expanded the substantive reach of the Sherman Act; and the Federal Trade Commission (FTC) Act, which replaced the Bureau of Corporations with an independent and powerful antitrust enforcement agency.[106] But despite the FTC's independence, it lacked the corporate regulatory powers that many Progressives had envisioned for the new antitrust commission. Its received powers to enforce a new competitive norm created by statute,[107] not to regulate corporations, and its decisions were ultimately reviewable by Article III courts.[108] The FTC reflected Wilson's vision of "regulating business methods through a mix of commission and judicial enforcement of a common law-based antitrust law, with ultimate judicial supremacy in the process as a whole."[109]

This same year, 1914, was also the year in which antitrust Antifederalism become ever more firmly entrenched. Just as the Antifederalists had before him, Wilson feared that direct federal regulatory power over corporations would lead to industrial monopolies as the corporations captured their regulators and turned regulation to their advantage.[110] Safer, then, to retain antitrust policy as a prohibition on bad conduct delegated to generalist courts.[111]

V. SECURITIES AND CORPORATIONS IN THE NEW DEAL

Wilson's rejection of a federal incorporation statute and the passage of the Clayton and FTC Acts ended any serious possibility of a federal incorporation statute in the Progressive Era, and probably for a very long time thereafter. Antitrust law had been set on the modified common law path chosen by the framers of the Sherman Act, as reinforced by the 1914 statutes. Nonetheless, the possibility of federal incorporation resurfaced during the New Deal in connection with post-Depression calls for securities regulation.

---

106. 15 U.S.C. 15 §§ 12–27 (2000); U.S.C. §§ 41–58 (2000).

107. 15 U.S.C. §45(a) ("Unfair methods of competition in or affecting commerce, and unfair or deceptive acts or practices in or affecting commerce, are hereby declared unlawful.").

108. 15 U.S.C. § 45(c) (allowing for judicial review of FTC decisions in any circuit court of appeals where the method of competition or act in question was used).

109. Sklar, *supra* n. 57, at 381.

110. Wilson's concerns were not frivolous. Although much of the external momentum for direct federal control of corporations came from populist voices, much of the proposed legislation was shaped by corporate interests, as was the Sherman Act itself. For instance, the House of Morgan apparently drafted the Hepburn Bill. *See* Kolko, *supra* note 82, at 134.

111. On the causes of the failure of federal incorporation proposals during the Progressive Era, *see* Davis, *supra* n. 6 at 625–29.

The connection between securities regulation and antitrust dates back to the nineteenth century. In 1898, Congress created an Industrial Commission to investigate combinations in restraint of trade.[112] When the Commission published its report in 1902, its recommendations made the trust problem sound primarily like one of investor deception rather than harm to consumers. The Commission stated that its primary objective was "to prevent the organizers of corporations or industrial combinations from deceiving investors and the public, either through suppression of material facts or by making misleading statements."[113] It recommended that "the larger corporations—the so-called trusts—should be required to publish annually a properly audited report, showing in reasonable detail their assets and liabilities, with profit and loss; such a report and audit under oath to be subject to government regulation."[114]

The Commission apparently failed to understand that the trust "restraint of trade" problem was a very different one than fraud on investors.[115] As a class, investors are benefited by anticompetitive restraints of trade, which tend to create monopoly rents and thereby inflate the value of their shares.[116] On the other hand, consumers as a class tend to be harmed by anticompetitive conduct. Shareholders, as a class, may be benefited by disclosure of corporate finances, but consumers are little helped against monopolistic practice by such disclosure, except to the extent that it helps regulators identify and countermand unlawful conduct.

Nonetheless, the idea of a financial disclosure model gained some traction during the founding era of antitrust when the Bureau of Corporations requested the power "to directly inspect corporate accounts to protect the public interest."[117] The Bureau's proposal, however, was linked to more specifically antitrust-oriented proposals to require federal incorporation and licensing of the trusts, and shared the fate of those proposals during the Progressive Era.

---

112. Gary John Previts & Barbara Bubis Merino, A History of Accountancy in the United States: The Cultural Significance of Accounting 184 (1998).

113. *Id.* at 185.

114. *Id.*

115. Defenders of the corporate disclosure model of trust control typically argued that public disclosure of the inner workings of the trusts was necessary for the public to understand how to deal with the trusts. *See, e.g.*, Dill, *supra* note 64, at 290 ("Publicity will give a clear insight into the operation and workings of a trust and when this is fully known the public will know how to deal with the proposition as a whole.").

116. Of course, some shareholders will lose from anticompetitive restraints if their corporation is anticompetitively excluded from a market. On balance, however, the returns to shareholders from anticompetitive conduct tend to be positive, except to the extent that costly efforts to obtain monopoly profits eat into the monopoly rents or management internally consumes the monopoly rents through lack of industry or innovation.

117. First Annual Report, Bureau of Corporations (1904).

The Great Depression reinvigorated the idea of federal incorporation and licensing of large corporations. Already during the brief era of the National Industrial Recovery Act, a group within the Department of Justice began to investigate the potential of a federal incorporation statute to solve a variety of social ills attendant to large aggregations of capital, including anticompetitive conduct, fraud on shareholders, and labor and employment abuses.[118] The passage of the securities acts of 1933 and 1934, which created a regime of registration and disclosure for nationally traded securities and created a new agency to oversee corporate financial disclosure obligations,[119] encouraged various New Deal factions to believe that a more comprehensive federal incorporation scheme was possible. A significant piece of the Progressive agenda for direct federal regulation of corporations, dating back to the Industrial Commission's 1902 report, had been realized. Just as Congress had found state blue sky laws inadequate to protect investors,[120] so too Congress might now find state incorporation law combined with the crime-tort-modeled Sherman Act insufficient to protect consumers and small businessmen from the overwhelming power of large corporations.

With the demise of the National Industrial Recovery Act's associationalist regime in 1935,[121] a Brandeisian wing took control of the Antitrust Division of the Justice Department and gained strength within the Roosevelt administration.[122] The new antitrustrusters were troubled by the laxity of state incorporation laws, and believed that "this 'competition in laxity' had produced giant 'tramp' corporations, great sprawling empires with more power than the states that created them."[123] Eventually, they found a sympathetic ear in Congress. In 1937, Senators William Borah and Joseph C. O'Mahoney introduced a joint bill that required corporations engaged in interstate commerce to be licensed with the FTC, and imposed a variety of restrictions on licensed corporations, including child labor and anti-gender-discrimination provisions, prohibitions on anti-union activities, a requirement that they maintain their principal place of business in the state where they were organized, and a requirement that they observe

---

118. *See* Ellis W. Hawley, The New Deal and the Problem of Monopoly: A Study in Economic Ambivalence 371 (1966).

119. Securities Exchange Act of 1934 §4(a), 48 Stat. at 885 (codified as amended at 15 U.S.C. §78d(a) (2000).

120. State blue sky laws were generally adopted between 1911 and 1933 and prohibited the sale of worthless investment vehicles—or "blue sky." Jonathan R. Macey & Geoffrey P. Miller, *Origin of the Blue Sky* Laws, 70 Tex. L. Rev. 347, 348–49 (1991).

121. *See Panama Refining Co. v. Amazon Petroleum Corp.*, 293 U.S. 388 (1935); *A.L.A. Schechter v. United States*, 295 U.S. 495 (1935).

122. *See generally* Daniel A. Crane, *The Story of United States v. Socony-Vacuum: Hot Oil and Antitrust in the Two New Deals*, in Antitrust Stories (Eleanor Fox & Daniel A. Crane eds. 2007).

123. Hawley, *supra* note 118, at 371.

all antitrust law, eliminate all non-voting stock, and refrain from practices that were designed to inflate their capital structure or deceive their shareholders.[124]

Despite some initial momentum, the Borah-Mahoney Bill never had profound support in Congress.[125] Several factors contributed to its failure. First, the passage of the Securities Acts of 1933 and 1934 created a form of direct federal superintendence of large interstate corporations, and any significant appetite for further intrusions on traditional state prerogatives may have been lacking. Second, the Robinson Patman Act of 1936[126] responded to the New Deal's political need for some form of new antitrust legislation to show that it was responding to competitive abuses. Third, Robert Jackson and Thurman Arnold's reinvigoration of antitrust enforcement as successive heads of the Justice Department's antitrust division showed that the current laws could work to curb competitive abuses.[127] Arnold's influential book *The Bottlenecks of Business* argued that the existing antitrust laws could be effectively used to promote competition, thus undermining any claim that a more radical displacement of traditional state prerogatives with respect to corporations was needed.[128] Finally, Franklin Roosevelt did not have as great an appetite for antitrust enforcement as Jackson or Arnold, particularly when the war began and various dominant national industries became critical to the war effort.

Once again, a version of the Madisonian proposal had reared its head only to be defeated. The state incorporation system survived untouched by Congress, except to the extent that investor protection became a regulatory function of the newly minted Securities and Exchange Commission.[129] The corporate regulatory model had found a home in federal law, but only to the extent of investor protection.[130] Antitrust law remained a statutory crime and tort, equally applicable to the large corporation and the small sole proprietorship.

---

124. *Id.* at 371–72.

125. *See id.* at 427 n.5.

126. 15 U.S.C. § 13 (2000).

127. *See generally* H. Hewitt Pate, *Robert H. Jackson at the Antitrust Division*, 68 Alb. L. Rev. 787 (2005); Spencer Weber Waller, Thurman Arnold: A Biography 78–110 (2005).

128. Hawley, *supra* note 118, at 426 n.5.

129. The commission was established by the Securities Exchange Act of 1934, 15 U.S.C. §§78a–78mm (2000).

130. *See* Steven A. Bank, *Tax, Corporate Governance, and Norms*, 61 Wash. & Lee L. Rev. 1159, 1162 n.5 (2004) ("In large part, the securities laws enacted in 1933 and 1934 served as a de facto federal corporations law."); Robert B. Thompson & Hillary A. Sale, *Securities Fraud as Corporate Governance: Reflections upon Federalism*, 56 Vand. L. Rev. 859, 869 (2003) ("The government response to the excesses of the 1920s and to the pain of the Great Depression again led to calls for federal corporations law, but the New Deal Congress that passed securities legislation in 1933 and 1934 chose less intrusive means.").

VI. STRUCTURALISM AND ANTITRUST INERTIA

The Borah-Mahoney Bill was the last serious congressional attempt at a federal incorporation proposal designed to remedy the antitrust problem. Since then, the voices advocating federal regulation as a competition law measure have been relegated to the margins of American political discourse.[131] In the 1970s, a vigorous discussion emerged about the possibility of federal incorporation, or at least minimum federal standards for state incorporation law, but it focused almost entirely on problems of shareholder protection and corporate governance.[132] In 1976, the Senate Committee on Commerce held six days of hearings on "why we should continue the present arrangements of state chartering of corporations or arguments for alternatives," but antitrust concerns were not the focus.[133]

In one way, it is surprising that direct federal superintendence of corporations as an antitrust solution did not emerge as a conversation topic during the structuralist heydays of the 1960s and 1970s. Following Joe Bain's seminal work,[134] a structuralist school (often called the Harvard School, although the modern Harvard School discussed in later chapters is considerably different) asserted that a market's structure almost invariably dictated the competitive conduct of its participants, whose conduct invariably determined the performance of the market.[135] Structuralism's important implication for antitrust law was to diminish the

---

131. *See, e.g.*, RALPH NADER, TAMING THE GIANT CORPORATIONS (1976); Ralph Nader, *The Case for Federal Chartering*, *in* CORPORATE POWER IN AMERICA (Ralph Nader & Mark J. Green eds., 1973). Nader proposed a federal incorporation law with related antimonopoly provisions, applicable to all industrial, retail, and transportation companies that sold over $250 million in goods or services in the United States or employed more than 10,000 employees. *See also* Donald E. Schwartz, *Federal Chartering of Corporations: An Introduction*, 61 GEO. L.J. 71 (1972); Seymour J. Rubin, *Corporations and Society: The Remedy of Federal and International Incorporation*, 23 AM. U. L. REV. 263 (1973).

132. *See, e.g.*, William L. Cary, *Federalism and Corporate law: Reflections Upon Delaware*, 83 YALE L. J. 663 (1974); Donald E. Schwartz, *A Case for Federal Chartering of Corporations*, 31 BUS. L.J. 1125 (1976); Daniel Fischel, *The "Race to the Bottom" Revisited: Reflections on Recent Developments in Delaware's Corporation Law*, 76 NW. U. L. REV. 913, 920 (1982); Angela Karmel, *Is it Time for a Federal Corporation Law?*, 57 BROOK. L. REV. 55 (1991); *see generally* 1 LOUIS LOSS & JOEL SELIGMAN, SECURITIES REGULATION 155–57 (3d ed. 1998).

133. Corporate Rights and Responsibilities, Serial No. 94-95, Hearings Before the Senate Committee on Commerce, United States Senate, 94th Cong., 2d Sess. (1976) (statement of Sen. Durkin). *See* JOEL SELIGMAN, THE TRANSFORMATION OF WALL STREET 205–10 (3rd ed. 2003).

134. JOE BAIN, INDUSTRIAL ORGANIZATION (2d ed. 1968).

135. *See* Robert J. Larner & James W. Meehan, Jr., *The Structural School, Its Critics, and its Progeny: An Assessment*, *in* ECONOMICS AND ANTITRUST POLICY 179, 180–91 (Robert J. Larner & James W. Meehan, Jr. eds., 1989); Leonard W. Weiss, *The Structure-Conduct-Performance Paradigm and Antitrust*, 127 U. PA. L. REV. 1104, 1104–23 (1979).

importance of anticompetitive conduct in antitrust analysis, since anticompetitive results were assumed to follow invariably from concentrated markets.[136] Although the ascendant Chicago School attacked structuralism's assumptions in the 1970s,[137] structuralism received a boost as late as 1979. That year, the National Commission for the Review of Antitrust Laws and Procedures unsuccessfully advocated amending Section 2 of the Sherman Act to permit the government to seek equitable structural relief to dissolve persistent monopoly power, even absent any showing of wrongdoing by the monopolist.[138]

Structuralism would seemingly have provided a natural segue back into discussions about a federal incorporation power or a federal regulatory role in superintending large, interstate corporations. When the framers of the Sherman Act chose the crime-tort model, they elevated the importance of conduct in antitrust analysis and rejected the alternative regulatory possibility that would have focused instead on corporate structure. But if direct federal regulation of interstate corporations would have been a logical complement to structuralism, its absence from the range of proposals suggested by structuralists can be explained by the dominance of the antitrust Antifederalist impulse in American political discourse. Antifederalist opposition to a federal regulatory role in structuring and supervising corporations had weathered so many challenges over the preceding two centuries that its continued dominance as an American political idea seemed inevitable.

In a twist of historical fate, by the time that structuralism arose as a political possibility, the logic behind the antitrust Antifederalist impulse had dissipated. From 1787 through the early twentieth century, it was generally assumed that federal incorporation and federal corporate regulation were mutually necessary: federal regulation of corporations could only be justified as to federal incorporations and federal incorporation would require federal regulation to prevent monopolistic aggregations of capital. By the second half of the twentieth century, alternate models of federal corporate regulation were available—particularly the securities acts of the 1930s—but there was insufficient political interest in the institutional structure of antitrust to force a major reexamination of foundational principles. For better or worse, antifederalism won its battles during early framing moments in the institutional development of U.S. antitrust and has maintained its sway since then through inertia.

This whirlwind tour of two centuries years of American political, legal, and economic history sets the stage for an examination of U.S. antitrust institutions as they have evolved since their inception. Although the corporate regulatory

136. For example, structuralists generally assumed that concentrated markets result in higher prices, even in the absence of seller collusion. *See* Weiss, *supra* n. 135 at 106–15.

137. On the debate over structuralism, *see* Larner & Meehan, *supra* note 135.

138. *See Report to the President and the Attorney General of the National Commission for the Review of Antitrust Laws and Procedures* 151–63 (Jan. 22, 1970).

route turned out to be the road not followed, we will encounter examples of that model cropping up over time. Still, the crime-tort model and its implicit delegation of authority to generalist judges, juries, and private litigants remains the dominant model. As we shall see, its imprint on the institutional structure of U.S. antitrust is deep.

2. THE CURIOUS CASE OF DUAL FEDERAL ENFORCEMENT

The dialectic between two competing conceptualizations of antitrust—one based on federal regulation of large corporations and the other based on enforcement of a generalized competition norm—led to the creation of two federal antitrust agencies or departments: the Federal Trade Commission (FTC) and the Justice Department's Antitrust Division. The Antitrust Division corresponds entirely to the crime-tort conceptualization. It enforces the antitrust laws, both criminally and civilly, always in front of generalist judges, and sometimes in front of juries. The FTC, by contrast, represents a hybrid of the two visions. As we saw in the previous chapter, the impetus for its creation was Progressive and technocratic, but it was ultimately not given a strong norm-creation function. It thus assumed the character of an expert law enforcement agency, different in structure and political accountability but not that different in function from the Antitrust Division.

It is not unusual for different law enforcement or regulatory agencies to have overlapping jurisdiction and for interagency turf wars to erupt.[1] Thus, there is nothing particularly notable about the mere fact that the FTC and Department of Justice Antitrust Division have overlapping jurisdiction to enforce the antitrust laws and sometimes get into scraps over turf. Nor are the FTC and Antitrust Division purely duplicative agencies. For one, the FTC has an entire consumer protection side that is separate from, and about 25 percent larger than,[2] the FTC's competition policy function. On the other hand, the Antitrust Division presides over all criminal enforcement of the Sherman Act;[3] the FTC has no criminal jurisdiction.

And, yet, despite the fact the fact that the two agencies are not purely redundant and that overlapping agency jurisdiction is not uncommon, there is something curious about dual-agency structure of federal antitrust enforcement. Unlike most instances of overlapping enforcement, the FTC and Antitrust Division do not overlap because they are regulatory neighbors with fuzzy borders (as is true, say, of the Department of Agriculture and the Environmental

1. For convenience, I will use the word "agency" to describe both the FTC and Antitrust Division, recognizing that "agency" is sometimes given more specific definitions that would preclude one or the other from being an "agency."

2. *See* Federal Trade Commission, Performance and Accountability Report, Fiscal Year 2008, http://www.ftc.gov/opp/gpra/2008parreport.pdf (reporting competition policy expenses of $105 million and consumer protection expenses of $141 million).

3. Many cartel prosecutions are handed by regional U.S. attorney's offices with relatively little input from the Antitrust Division.

Protection Agency) or because they are asked to regulate the same activities but for different purposes (as is true, say, of the Food and Drug Administration and the Patent and Trademark Office). With a few important qualifications, the FTC and Antitrust Division overlap because Congress has assigned them the identical mission and for the identical purpose.

Does this make any sense? Would a sensible designer of legal and regulatory institutions commit functionally identical jurisdiction to two separate agencies in the same government? Does this not inevitably lead to waste, bickering, strategic gamesmanship, regulatory uncertainty, and excessive regulation?

As we will see, the answers to these questions are complex. The design of the antitrust agencies was not the product of a unified draftsman—not even a politically fragmented committee like the Philadelphia Constitutional Convention that produced the Federal Constitution in 1787. The structure is inelegant, redundant, and often problematic. And, yet, efforts to alter the essential structure have repeatedly failed, largely for want of a strong enough sense that the system has failed.

I. A BRIEF HISTORY OF THE AGENCIES

By most scores, the Antitrust Division is a more significant player than the FTC's competition wing. Its budget is about 50 percent larger,[4] it employs a staff that is over 40 percent larger,[5] it undertakes as many or more merger reviews,[6] and it handles all criminal enforcement. Nonetheless, there has been much more systematic study of the FTC as an institution than there has been of the Antitrust Division. At least ten books and countless articles have been written about the

4. For 2008, the FTC's competition budget was $104 million. Federal Trade Commission, Fiscal Year 2009, Congressional Budget Justification Summary at 39, http://www.ftc.gov/ftc/oed/fmo/budgetsummary09.pdf. For the same year, the Antitrust Division's budget was $148 million. Appropriation Figures for the Antitrust Division Fiscal Years 1903–2009, http://www.usdoj.gov/atr/public/10804a.htm.

5. For 2008, the FTC had 503 full-time equivalents (FTEs) employed in the "maintaining competition" program. *See* Federal Trade Commission, Fiscal Year 2009, Congressional Budget Justification Summary at 39, http://www.ftc.gov/ftc/oed/fmo/budgetsummary09.pdf. For the same year, the Antitrust Division had had 851 FTEs. U.S. Dept. of Justice FY 2008 Budget and Performance Summary, http://www.usdoj.gov/jmd/2008summary/pdf/078_atr.pdf.

6. In 2007, the Antitrust Division received 2201 Hart-Scott-Rodino filings and issued 32 second requests. Antitrust Division, Workload Statistics 1998–2007, http://www.usdoj.gov/atr/public/workstats.htm. For the same period, the FTC received 2108 Hart-Scott filings and issued 31 second requests. The FTC in 2008; A Force for Consumers and Competition, http://www.ftc.gov/os/2008/03/ChairmansReport2008.pdf.

FTC and very few about the Antitrust Division.[7] What accounts for the fact that the "larger" antitrust institution in the federal government has received comparatively less attention than the smaller one?

Part of the answer is that the FTC as a whole—including its consumer protection function—has historically had a significantly larger budget than the Antitrust Division and has taken on consumer protection projects with a much more visible public profile than the arcane complexities of antitrust law.[8] But there is a more fundamental reason for the FTC's prominence in academic case studies: The FTC is an institutional curiosity in the American political system. It is a hybrid of legislative, executive, and judicial functions, independent from the three mainstream branches of government, insulated from direct political control, and statutorily multipartisan. The Antitrust Division, by contrast, is simply a subset of the executive's law enforcement department—an ordinary and unexceptional feature of the American political landscape.

Because of the FTC's political exoticism, there is a dearth of "deep" comparisons of the two agencies. The FTC is usually studied in isolation and the Antitrust Division ignored. Yet, in seeking to understand the story of U.S. antitrust institutions, it is important to examine the FTC and Antitrust Division side by side as the two agencies navigated the vicissitudes of twentieth-century history.

---

7. Books on the FTC include ROBERT V. LABAREE, THE FEDERAL TRADE COMMISSION: A GUIDE TO SOURCES (2000); PUBLIC CHOICE AND REGULATION: A VIEW FROM INSIDE THE FEDERAL TRADE COMMISSION (Robert J. Mackay, James C. Miller III and Bruce Yandle eds., 1987); Bernice Rothman Hasin, CONSUMERS, COMMISSIONS, AND CONGRESS: LAW, THEORY, AND THE FEDERAL TRADE COMMISSION, 1968–1985 (1987); ROBERT A. KATZMAN, REGULATORY BUREAUCRACY: THE FEDERAL TRADE COMMISSION AND ANTITRUST POLICY (1980); PRISCILLA LA BARBERA, CONSUMERS AND THE FEDERAL TRADE COMMISSION: AN EMPIRICAL INVESTIGATION (1977); EDWARD F. COX, ROBERT C. FELLMETH & JOHN E. SCHULZ, THE NADER REPORT ON THE FEDERAL TRADE COMMISSION (1969); THOMAS C. BLAISDELL, JR., THE FEDERAL TRADE COMMISSION: AN EXPERIMENT IN THE CONTROL OF BUSINESS (1932); GERARD C. HENDERSON, THE FEDERAL TRADE COMMISSION: A STUDY IN ADMINISTRATIVE LAW AND PROCEDURE (1924); WILLIAM STULL HOLT, THE FEDERAL TRADE COMMISSION: ITS HISTORY, ACTIVITIES, AND ORGANIZATION (1922); JOHN MAYNARD HARLAN & LEWIS W. MCCANDLESS, THE FEDERAL TRADE COMMISSION: ITS NATURE AND POWERS (1916). A comprehensive but somewhat dated compendium of sources on the FTC appears in the bibliography of MACKAY et al., *supra*.

8. *See* Richard S. Higgins, William F. Shughart II & Robert D. Tollison, *Dual Enforcement of Antitrust Laws, in* MacKay et al., eds., *supra* n. 7 at 172 Table 7.2 (detailing annual budgetary appropriations for FTC and Antitrust Division for 1915 through 1981). The formal separation between the FTC's antitrust and consumer protection functions is of relatively recent vintage. It was not until the Wheeler-Lea Amendment to the FTC Act in 1938 that the FTC received an explicit statutory consumer protection goal. Federal Trade Commission Act, ch. 49, 52 stat. 111 (1938). The consumer protection and antitrust functions were not formally separated into their current departments (Bureau of Consumer Protection and Bureau of Competition) until 1960.

By some measures, antitrust enforcement in the Justice Department enjoyed a twenty-four year head start on the FTC. The Sherman Act committed antitrust enforcement to the U.S. Attorneys in 1890, and the FTC did not come into existence until 1914. But although federal prosecutors and civil lawyers had been working on antitrust matters since the last decade of the nineteenth century, Congress did not establish a separate Assistant Attorney General for an antitrust post or fund a separate antitrust budget until 1903.[9] The initial appropriation of $500,000 was required to last until 1908, when federal antitrust enforcement received additional annual funding of $250,000. The Antitrust Division was not formed as a separate unit until 1933. The FTC came on the scene in 1915 and obtained a budget that more than doubled the Justice Department's antitrust appropriation within two years. Thus, the FTC has, by many measures, a longer institutional history than does the Antitrust Division.

The budgetary story, told in figure 2.1 below,[10] provides a quick snapshot of the agencies' funding—which one might consider a rough proxy for their political support in Congress. Let us use trends in budgetary appropriations to frame a rough historical narrative. The early years of the dual-agency model—from roughly 1915 until the early New Deal—coincided with the Progressive Era and its prevailing belief in expert agencies. Hence, during this period, the FTC was comparatively well fed and the Justice Department's antitrust program starved. The Justice Department was victimized first by enthusiasm for the technocratic potential of its rival agency, then by Republican administrations during the 1920s that had little use for executive enforcement of the antitrust laws, and then by an early New Deal culture in which competition was normatively displaced by an associationalist model that suspended antitrust law in favor of industry codes.[11]

After 1935, however, there was an abrupt shift in ideological influence within the FDR administration and a reinvigoration of the Antitrust Division under political luminaries Robert Jackson and Thurman Arnold.[12] Shortly thereafter, during the 1940s and early'50s, there was a political reaction to the agency-control model that so strongly characterized early New Deal thinking. A modernized

9. The figures in this paragraph are drawn from Appropriation Figures for the Antitrust Division Fiscal Years 1903–2009, http://www.usdoj.gov/atr/public/10804a.htm.

10. The figures in the table are drawn from Appropriation Figures for the Antitrust Division Fiscal Years 1903–2009, http://www.usdoj.gov/atr/public/10804a.htm. The FTC's budgetary summary is drawn from Higgins et al., *supra* n. 8 and http://www.ftc.gov/ftc/oed/fmo/appropriationhistory.shtm. Annual budgets are converted into real 2007 dollars using the Consumer Price Index as the inflationary control. The FTC budget includes both antitrust and consumer protection functions.

11. *See generally* Ellis W. Hawley, The New Deal and the Problem of Monopoly: A Study in Economic Ambivalence (1966).

12. *See* Daniel A. Crane, *The Story of United States v. Socony-Vacuum: Hot Oil and Antitrust in the Two New Deals*, in Antitrust Stories 91–119 (Eleanor M. Fox & Daniel A. Crane eds., 2007).

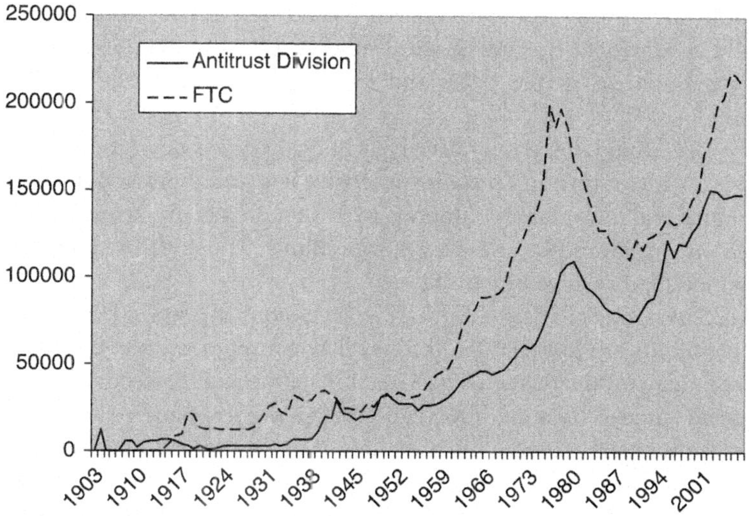

FIGURE 2.1 FTC AND ANTITRUST DIVISION BUDGETS (REAL 2007 DOLLARS IN THOUSANDS)

and reinvigorated Antitrust Division received considerable increases in funding while the FTC's budget remained flat. The agencies' funding equalized and remained on par for a decade.

In the 1960s, as the FTC began to diversify its policy objectives and explicitly shift its emphasis from competition policy to consumer protection, the FTC again pulled away from a budgetary perspective. For example, the FTC's prestige increased with the promulgation of the 1964 "Cigarette Rule," which required cigarette companies to advertise the unsafeness of their product.[13]

The FTC, however, quickly lost its comparative luster. In 1969, a scathing report by Ralph Nader,[14] followed up by an only somewhat less scathing report by the American Bar Association (commissioned by President Richard Nixon) indicted the FTC for ineffectiveness.[15] In the late 1970s, the Commission suffered further discredit as the ordinarily friendly *Washington Post* labeled the agency the "national nanny"—a cruel label that stuck—over a series of proposed consumer protection rules, culminating in its proposed "kid vid" rules relating to advertising to children.[16] The FTC's comparative luster was therefore already waning when the Reagan Revolution in 1980 caused both agencies' budgets to

13. Unfair or Deceptive Advertising and Labeling of Cigarettes in Relation to the Health Hazards of Smoking, 29 Fed. Reg. 8324 (1964).

14. EDWARD F. COX, ROBERT C. FELLMETH & JOHN E. SCHULZ, THE NADER REPORT ON THE FEDERAL TRADE COMMISSION (1969).

15. *See generally* Edward F. Cox, *Reinvigorating the FTC: The Nader Report and the Rise of Consumer Advocacy*, 72 ANTITRUST L.J. 899 (2005).

16. Editorial, *The FTC as National Nanny*, WASH. POST, March 1, 1978, at A22.

decline significantly in both real and nominal dollars. Thereafter, the agencies' budgets would largely move in parallel, with equivalent Reagan-era punishment for the perceived excesses of the 1970s and reinvigoration during the Clinton administration.

Finally, the FTC would move away decisively in the first decade of the twenty-first century as its increasing and resource-intensive consumer protection functions in the digital and information economy—Do Not Call registry, spam e-mail, identity theft, etc.—required ever larger appropriations. The antitrust budgets, however, retained their relative proportions.

With the recent financial crisis—the "Great Recession" of 2008–2009—there is again the possibility of a political shift in the relative importance and positions of the FTC and Justice Department. The Consumer Financial Protection Act of 2010[17] has created a new consumer financial protection agency and reduced the FTC's consumer financial protection jurisdiction. While the effects of this bill on the FTC's overall prestige and position—including its antitrust position—remain to be seen, this is a good time to reconsider the justifications for an independent Federal Trade Commission in relation to other organs of government.

II. HUMPHREY'S EXECUTOR AND THE NOBLE NARRATIVE

There are many ways to evaluate the institutional positions of the FTC and Justice Department. Much of the comparative institutionalist literature tries to model optimal institutional outcomes, given resource limitations and other constraints. With the U.S. antitrust agencies, however, we are not dealing with idealized statutory models but rather with institutions that have grown, shrunk, adapted, morphed, and developed personalities over their hundred-year histories. Rather than asking how institutions with a particular design are likely to behave, we can ask how these particular institutions have actually behaved.

In keeping with the prevailing academic infatuation with the FTC, we will frame our comparison of the two agencies with reference to FTC's supposed institutional advantages. Specifically, we will evaluate the two agencies through the rose-colored glasses worn by the Supreme Court in expounding upon the Commission's technocratic virtues. Having identified the FTC's supposed virtues, we can then ask whether the Commission actually enjoys its supposed advantages. But, first, the noble narrative about the FTC, as told in the Supreme Court's landmark constitutional decision in *Humphrey's Executor.*[18]

In 1925, Calvin Coolidge appointed William E. Humphrey as a commissioner of the FTC. In 1931, Herbert Hoover appointed him to a second, seven-year term

---

17. Pub.L. 111-203, H.R. 4173.

18. *Humphrey's Ex'r v. U.S.*, 295 U.S. 602 (1935).

on the Commission. From the outset, Humphrey proved a most controversial commissioner. He made vociferously clear his opposition to almost any coercive action by the Commission to reign in business and lambasted the Commission's interventionist agenda. Humphrey decried the FTC's "old policy of litigation" that had ostensibly made the Commission "an instrument of oppression and disturbance and injury instead of a help to business."[19] He vowed not to approve any Commission action that did not have as its goal to "help business help itself."[20] Humphrey pushed a policy of behind-the-scenes negotiation with industry to resolve matters quietly and without the imposition of legally enforceable sanctions. He went so far as to threaten criminal prosecution against other commissioners who publicly dissented, contrary to new FTC rules.[21] When the Commission voted to investigate ties between DuPont, U.S. Steel, and General Motors, Humphrey, displaying his usual tact, called his fellow commissioners men "drunk with their own greatness."[22]

Needless to say, Humphrey made some enemies. Congressmen who favored an interventionist FTC introduced legislation to abolish the agency altogether.[23] The newly inaugurated Franklin Delano Roosevelt, however, had a better idea. On July 25, 1933, a few months into his first term, Roosevelt wrote Humphrey, politely requesting his resignation.[24] Humphrey demurred, and Roosevelt wrote again—more forcefully—on August 31, 1933. This time, the president explained that while he had no problem with Humphrey personally, "[y]ou will, I know, realize that I do not feel that your mind and my mind go along together on either the policies or the administering of the Federal Trade Commission, and, frankly, I think it is best for the people of this country that I should have a full confidence."[25] Humphrey again demurred. On October 8, 1933, FDR again wrote Humphrey, this time simply firing him.[26]

Humphrey died just five months later, on February 14, 1934,[27] but his passing did not moot the controversy concerning the legality of the president's removal of an FTC commissioner for political reasons. The executor of Humphrey's estate, Samuel F. Rathun, brought suit on Humphrey's behalf for the five months

---

19. William E. Kovacic, *The Federal Trade Commission and Congressional Oversight of Antitrust Enforcement: A Historical Perspective*, *in* Mackay, Miller, Yandle, *supra* n. 7 at 105 n. 93, *citing* E. Pendleton Herring, Public Administration and the Public Interest 125 (1936).

20. *Id.*

21. Marc Winerman, *The FTC at Ninety: History Through Headlines*, 72 Antitrust L.J. 871, 878–79 (2005).

22. *Id.* at 879.

23. Kovacic, *supra* n. 19 at 78.

24. *Humphrey's Ex'r,* 295 U.S. at 618.

25. *Id.* at 619.

26. *Id.*

27. *Id.* at 618.

of salary that Humphrey allegedly should have earned between his unlawful removal and his death. And that suit—over a picayune sum[28] but an expansive principle—gave rise to the Supreme Court's *Humphrey's Executor* decision.

Humphrey won a final battle from the grave when the Supreme Court ruled in his favor, thus establishing the principle that the president may not remove FTC commissioners for political reasons but only for good cause (defined in the statute as "inefficiency, neglect of duty, or malfeasance in office").[29] That holding alone is a significant fact in understanding federal agency dualism—the FTC is as independent from the president as is the Supreme Court (the president appoints both bodies' members but loses control thereafter). But the reasons given by the Court for protecting the FTC's independence from the president are much more far-reaching in their implications. In explaining why FDR could not remove Humphrey just because the president disagreed with Humphrey's policies, the Court articulated what I will call a "noble narrative" about the role of the FTC in the determination of U.S. competition policy.

The essence of the noble narrative is a Progressive Era view of the agency as a staunchly independent, objective, and technocratic body detached from the hurly-burly of politics and formulating industrial policy in the clear light of the public interest. Thus, the FTC is "a body which shall be independent of executive authority, except in its selection, and free to exercise its judgment without leave or hindrance of any other official or any department of the government."[30] And why should we believe that the FTC will be so objective and detached? "The commission is to be nonpartisan; and it must, from the very nature of its duties, act with entire impartiality."[31] And why will political considerations not creep into a body that is not *nonpartisan*—the commissioners have usually been a mix of Republicans and Democrats—but only *multipartisan*? "It is charged with the enforcement of no policy except the policy of the law."[32] But, surely law itself is not politically neutral. Even in 1935, that was becoming apparent. Yes, indeed, but the sort of "law" practiced by the Commission was not ordinary law enforcement. "Its duties are neither political nor executive, but predominantly quasi judicial and quasi legislative."[33] And why should we think that the Commission will be better at this sort of "law" than Congress and the courts? "Like the Interstate Commerce Commission, its members are called upon to exercise the trained judgment of a body of experts 'appointed by law and informed by experience.'"[34]

---

28. Rathbun sought to recover $3043.06 plus interest. Brief for Samuel F. Rathbun, Executor, 1935 WL 32964 (March 19, 1935).

29. 295 U.S. at 619.

30. *Id.* at 625–26.

31. *Id.* at 624.

32. *Id.*

33. *Id.*

34. *Id.* (citation omitted).

There we have the outline of the noble narrative, frequently repeated in justifying the existence of an independent FTC. One could quibble with many of its assumptions—that experts are better than generalists at making regulatory policy, that detached technocracy is normatively preferable to democratically responsive governmental agents, that a "neutral" construction of law is ever possible. Nonetheless, our goal here is not to evaluate the noble narrative categorically. Rather, it is to understand whether the noble narrative has a sufficient basis in reality to justify the existence of two federal antitrust agencies. As we shall see, on that score, the empirical case is rather weak.

III. EVALUATING THE NOBLE NARRATIVE

The noble narrative can be distilled into three primary virtues: independence, expertise, and a hybrid agency model that creates decisional advantages. As it turns out, the FTC has exhibited these three virtues only weakly over the course of its history.

A. Political Independence

The leading edge of the noble narrative is the FTC's political independence. Unlike the Antitrust Division, which is directly accountable to the president, the FTC is supposed to exercise independent technical judgment in the interests of the American people. Does it actually do that?

To answer that question, we should put aside a normative evaluation of the FTC's decisions and simply try to understand whether the FTC is independent from the one political organ that exerts the greatest influence over it—Congress. The president lacks the power to remove commissioners, but Congress does not lack the power to remove their funding (or, conversely, to give them more). A series of empirical studies collected in 1987 tried to gauge the extent of this purse-string influence.[35] Tellingly, the studies uniformly showed that congressional influence had a significant explanatory effect on FTC outcomes. For example, a study by Roger Faith, Donald Leavens, and Robert Tollison found that case dismissals at the FTC were nonrandomly concentrated on defendants headquartered in the home districts of congressmen on committees and subcommittees with budgetary and oversight jurisdiction over the FTC.[36] Bill Kovacic, who later went on to become the FTC's chair, found that the FTC has consistently chosen policy programs that follow the expressed will of the FTC's oversight committees in Congress.[37]

---

35. The studies are collected in Mackay, Miller & Yandle, *supra* n. 7.

36. Roger L. Faith, Donald R. Leavens & Robert D. Tollison, *Antitrust Pork Barrel, in* Mackay, Miller & Yandle, *supra* n. 7 at 15–29.

37. Kovacic, *supra* n. 19 at 63.

To say that the FTC responds to the will of Congress—or, more particularly, the will of the congressmen with the greatest control over the FTC's purse strings—is not necessarily to criticize the FTC for being a "political" institution. In a democracy, having a politically accountable agency may be desirable. But what these studies do accomplish is to lessen the argument for dual federal enforcement because the "nonpolitical" FTC will balance out the "political" Antitrust Division. There is a "checks-and-balances" argument to be made, but it is for a "political" agency controlled by Congress to be checking another "political" agency controlled by the president.

A related argument for multiple enforcement agencies is that the existence of multiple and independent law enforcement agencies will tend to ensure that antitrust enforcement continues in periods during which one branch abdicates its enforcement responsibilities. This is particularly thought to be the case of the "politically independent" FTC, which should check the occasional delinquency of the Antitrust Division.

Experience, however, shows that the agencies largely "hunt in pairs." That is to say, both agencies tend to bring more cases during periods of pro-enforcement sentiment and fewer cases during periods of anti-enforcement sentiment. Figure 2.2 below shows the trend lines in FTC and Antitrust Division enforcement actions.[38] From the inception of FTC enforcement in 1915 to roughly 1940, there is a fair amount of volatility in the trend lines. With the institutionalization of the antitrust division and the radical shift in New Deal thinking in the mid-1930s, civil enforcement at both agencies settles into a largely symmetrical pattern. Total Antitrust Division complaints continue to move independently from FTC complaints—largely because of the volatility in the amount of criminal enforcement. However, simply comparing the activities on which the agencies coincide—merger and other civil enforcement—there is a high degree of correspondence. The trend lines briefly cross in the late 1980s, but there is no overall pattern of one agency taking up the other agency's slack.

The raw numerical story is, of course, incomplete. It could be that even focusing just on civil enforcement, agencies chose a different mix of cases. To be sure, there have been times when one or the other agency chose to pursue a particular

38. The Antitrust Division data were drawn from a dataset provided by the Antitrust Division records department. The FTC data were drawn from two sources. For 1915–1969, they were drawn from Richard A. Posner, *A Statistical Study of Antitrust Enforcement, in* The Causes and Consequences of Antitrust: A Public Choice Perspective 77 (Fred S. McChesney & William F. Shughart II, eds. 1995). For 1970–1999, the data were drawn from FTC Annual Reports. For 1970–1999, the "complaints" that were counted were administrative complaints and actions for a preliminary injunction. Consent decrees and other enforcement actions were not counted. Due to changes in reporting formats, it was not possible to obtain data for 1999 forward. However, in order to complete the 1995–1999 period, 1999 was assumed to have the same number of complaints as the average of the previous four years.

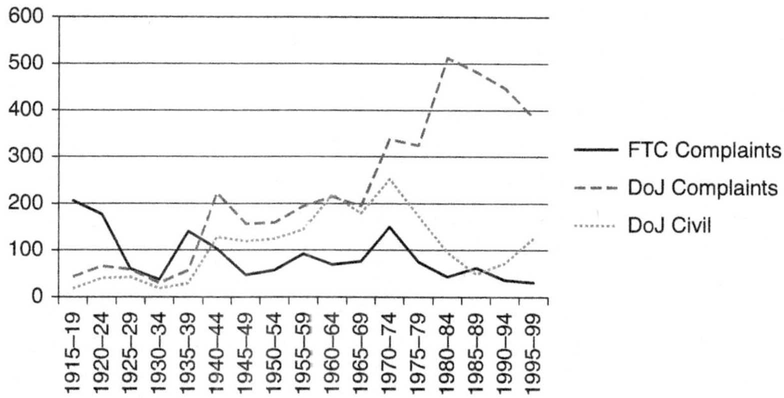

FIGURE 2.2 FTC AND DOJ ENFORCEMENT ACTIONS

kind of case that the other agency was not bringing.[39] However, there is little evidence of *counter-cyclical* tendencies—of one agency abandoning a particular kind of theory and the other agency picking it up in order to keep the ball rolling.

If anything, the two-agency model represents a law enforcement diversification strategy—put multiple enforcers in different institutional contexts, and it is more likely that they will identify more things that are anticompetitive than if they are all lumped in a single agency. That is a very different story than the counter-cyclical smoothing story and has its own set of problems. In particular, it is not clear whether what we want in antitrust enforcement is a wide but shallow reach over lots of different competition problems or the narrow but deep enforcement in the most obviously problematic areas. If we assume that the total amount of resources allocated to federal antitrust enforcement remains relatively constant whether there are two agencies or one, it could be the case that diversifying federal enforcement leads us to spend too few dollars on clearly problematic practices (like hard-core cartels) and too many dollars on marginally anticompetitive practices (like strikes by disaffected government-employed trial lawyers).[40]

Further, even assuming that there is some benefit to diversification, it is not clear that we need two agencies to achieve it. Given that the availability of the private antitrust remedy (discussed in Chapter 3) and state Attorney General

39. For example, during the 1970s and early 1980s, the Justice Department not only ignored the Robinson-Patman Act but went so far as to argue for its repeal at the same time that the FTC was bringing a significant number of Robinson-Patman cases. *See generally* Hugh C. Hansen, *Robinson-Patman Law: Review and Analysis*, 51 FORDHAM L. REV. 1113 (1983).

40. *See Superior Court Trial Lawyers Ass'n v. FTC*, 493 U.S. 411 (1990).

enforcement (discussed in Chapter 8), we may already have achieved (or exceeded) the optimal level of diversification.

B. Expertise

One of the Progressive Era's durable ideological commitments was expertise in regulatory decision making. As we saw in Chapter 1 and will examine in greater detail in Chapter 5, the FTC's technocratic potential was tempered by Woodrow Wilson's concern over experts convening behind closed doors to decide matters of industrial policy. Nonetheless, the technical expertise of the FTC in antitrust matters remains a strong part of the "noble narrative."

In later chapters, I will argue for expertise in antitrust decision making and, comparatively, against the role of the generalist judge or lay juryman. So let us assume, for the sake of the argument, that expertise in decision makers should count as a virtue. What are the implications for dual enforcement?

The answer is that there is no particular reason to think that today, the FTC has any greater antitrust expertise than does the Antitrust Division. To be sure, there was a time when the FTC had a comparative advantage over the FTC in economic sophistication. When the FTC came into being in 1914, it inherited the Economic Department (later transformed into the Economic Division and then the Bureau of Economics) of its predecessor—the Bureau of Corporations.[41] The Antitrust Division did not hire its first economist or create an economics unit until 1936.[42] Until the early 1970s, economists played a relatively small role in the division—mostly in data gathering and statistical litigation support.[43] The FTC's economics unit, by contrast, enjoyed earlier influence within the agency.[44] Today, however, there is little distinction between the agencies on this score. At the Antitrust Division, a deputy assistant attorney general for economics—usually a prominent academic economist—heads a staff of approximately 60 Ph.D.-level economists.[45] At the FTC, the Bureau of Economics features about 70 Ph.D.-level economists (although they spend about a quarter of their time on consumer protection issues).[46] The bureau director is also usually a prominent academic economist, and it is typical to have an economist among the commissioners. Historically, the commissioners have not been leading experts in their fields when appointed and have not stayed at the Commission long enough to acquire

---

41. Lawrence J. White, *Economics, Economists, and Antitrust: A Tale of Growing Influence*, NYU Law and Economics Research Paper No. 08–07, *available at* http://papers.ssrn.com/sol3/papers.cfm?abstract_id=1091531.

42. R. Hewitt Pate, *Robert H. Jackson at the Antitrust Division*, 68 Alb. L. Rev. 787, 791 n. 12 (2005).

43. White, *supra* n. 41 at 11.

44. *Id.*

45. *Id.* at 13.

46. *Id.*

expertise.[47] In terms of economic brainpower and prestige of leadership, there is no substantial difference between the agencies.

What if the relevant expertise is not in economics but in legal strategy? Again, there is no reason to believe that the FTC has a comparative advantage over the Antitrust Division. Both employ skilled lawyers to litigate their cases, or if they lack a lawyer with the right skill set, they can farm out work to private lawyers as the Justice Department did when it retained the prominent litigator David Boies to try the Microsoft case.

The one kind of expertise that the agencies do not mutually share is expertise in particular industries. The agencies have historically divided up the cases they bring based on their prior work with particular industries.[48] Thus, for example, the FTC has much experience with pharmaceuticals and health care, and the Antitrust Division has considerable experience with airlines and computer software. Thus, disbanding one or the other of the agencies could entail a loss in expertise (unless the personnel and institutional memory of the two agencies could be preserved through a seamless merger) but for historical rather than structural reasons. Expertise may be a compelling reason to retain the dualistic status quo, but it is not a compelling reason to choose a dual-agency model in the first place. There is nothing to prevent a single agency—whether as a branch of the executive or as an independent agency—from becoming optimally expert.

C. Agency Model

The final prong of the noble narrative concerns the advantages of the agency model. Critical to the *Humphrey's Executor* decision was the Supreme Court's belief that the FTC differed from ordinary law enforcement—a clearly executive function—insofar as it wielded both judicial and legislative functions in addition to its law enforcement functions. The hybrid agency model can be used to explain not only why the FTC should be independent but why we should have an FTC at all. In particular, if we think that the antitrust statutes are highly indeterminate—going little beyond such generalities as "restraints of trade," "monopolization," "lessening competition," and "unfair methods of competition"—then there is quite a bit of policy making to be done before the statutes can be applied to particular circumstances. Perhaps this "legislative" function should be done by administrators who have tools at their disposal to gather facts and, unlike judges, are not limited to the records presented to them by litigants. Similarly, given the highly specialized and technical work required of making and enforcing competition policy, perhaps it makes sense to have the primary adjudicatory function wielded by administrative law judges who frequently see competition issues and are somewhat specialized in the field.

47. *See* Richard A. Posner, *The Federal Trade Commission: A Retrospective*, 72 ANTITRUST L. J. 761, 768 (2005).

48. *See* Daniel A. Crane, *Technocracy and Antitrust*, 86 TEX. L. REV. 1159, 1199 (2008).

Turning first to the FTC's legislative function, it seems that the sort of "legislation" the Supreme Court had in mind in *Humphrey's Executor* was the promulgation of regulations. During the 1970s, administrative law maven Kenneth Culp Davis argued that the FTC's primary institutional advantage was its power to promulgate rules.[49] Whether for good or ill, however, the FTC has never been an antitrust rule maker. Certainly, the FTC has promulgated influential rules on the consumer protection side—the Cigarette Rule and the Do Not Call Registry come notably to mind—but it has published almost no antitrust rules.[50] Indeed, the opinion of the antitrust establishment seems to incline against any such role for the agency. A 1989 ABA report on the FTC concluded that "we are not optimistic about the chances that the FTC could codify antitrust-oriented prohibitions on specific types of business conduct."[51]

In Chapter 7, we shall consider the possibility that the FTC should have a greater norm-creation role, perhaps through the promulgation of rules. For now, however, it is sufficient to observe that the FTC has not performed a legislative function in antitrust cases at all. Indeed, even if we conceive of the legislative function as broader than the formulation of administrative regulations, the FTC is accorded no deference on its interpretations of the law. Early during the history of the FTC, the Supreme Court rejected the view that the Commission should have any special position when it came to the meaning of the FTC Act.[52] In later cases, the Supreme Court took back this restrictive view of agency interpretation,[53] but the official position remains that the FTC gets very little deference on questions of law.[54] Thus, on the antitrust side, the FTC does not have a real legislative function but is essentially an enforcer of norms created by the courts.[55] In that, it is not any different from the Antitrust Division.

There is one potentially significant structural difference between the FTC and Antitrust Division, related to the judicial function identified in *Humphrey's Executor*. The Antitrust Division can only sue in court, but the FTC staff can also bring administrative proceedings before administrative law judges, with an appeal to the Commission. Two significant points should be kept in mind.

---

49. KENNETH CULP DAVIS, DISCRETIONARY JUSTICE: A PRELIMINARY INQUIRY 70–74 (1969).

50. A 1989 ABA report found only one instance of the FTC promulgating an antitrust rule. *Report of the American Bar Association Section of Antitrust Law Special Committee to Study the Role of the Federal Trade Commission*, 58 ANTITRUST L. J. 43, 91 n.103 (1989).

51. *Id.*

52. *FTC v. Gratz*, 253 U.S. 421, 427 (1920) ("The words 'unfair competition' are not defined by the statute and their exact meaning is in dispute. It is for the courts, not the commission, ultimately to determine as a matter of law what they include.").

53. *See FTC v. Brown Shoe Corp.*, 384 U.S. 316, 320–21 (1966).

54. *See FTC v. Indiana Federation of Dentists*, 476 U.S. 447, 454–55 (1986).

55. *See* Posner, *Retrospective, supra* n. 47 at 768 (observing that the FTC has become "a conventional law enforcement agency").

First, the FTC brings as many or more injunctive actions in district court as it does administrative actions. During the 1990s, for example, the FTC brought slightly more injunctive actions in district court than it did administrative actions.[56] Thus, while the FTC enjoys the flexibility of choice, it often chooses the conventional law enforcer route—in which capacity it is essentially identical to the Antitrust Division.

Second, even as to cases that the FTC brings administratively, the ultimate decision is usually in the Court of Appeals or Supreme Court, which accord the FTC deference only on findings of fact. As noted in Chapter 1, this is owing to Woodrow Wilson's unwillingness to allow experts to "sit behind closed doors and play Providence" without judicial review. The FTC's enforcement staff enjoy tremendous success in adjudication at the Commission level. One recent study found that between 1983 and 2008 the staff won all 16 cases adjudicated by the Commission.[57] However, the federal courts of appeal tend to treat appeals from FTC decisions as fresh opportunities for making regulatory policy, which accords the Commission's adjudicatory function relatively little importance.

Ironically, given the Supreme Court's assumptions in *Humphrey's Executor*, the one place where the FTC may actually have a significant statutory advantage over the Justice Department is not as a legislator or adjudicator but as a prosecutor. Under Section 13(b) of the FTC Act (or Section 53(b) of Title 15, as it is often called), the FTC sometimes receives greater deference than the Justice Department when seeking to block a merger in district court in order thereafter to initiate administrative proceedings. Some courts have interpreted Section 13(b) as relieving the FTC of having to show the traditional requirement of a substantial likelihood of success on merits and creating a presumption that the Commission will be accorded a preliminary injunction so long as it raises "serious, substantial, difficult, and doubtful" issues about the merger.[58] Although there is some doubt as to the correctness of this interpretation of the FTC Act, for now the Commission is sometimes able to score preliminary injunction wins—which, in the merger context are usually case dispositive—with the help of this unique statutory advantage. Whether or not such an advantage is justified, it cannot be justified on *Humphrey's Executor* grounds as a product of the

---

56. According to a tally from the FTC's annual reports, during the 1990–1998 period, the FTC brought thirty-one administrative complaints and thirty-three district court actions. (The 1999 annual report does not report the data in a way that allows the comparison.)

57. A. Douglas Melamed, *The Wisdom of Using the "Unfair Methods of Competition" Prong of Section 5*, COMPETITION POLICY INTERNATIONAL (Nov. 2008). The study Melamed cites found that the respondents won 4 of the 16 cases before the Administrative Law Judge, but then lost those cases before the Commission.

58. *FTC v. Whole Foods, Inc.*, 548 F.3d 1028, 1035 (D.C. Cir. 2008) (citation omitted).

Commission's hybrid status as a legislative and adjudicatory body. Section 13(b) is a *prosecutorial* advantage.

IV. THE PATHOLOGIES OF DUALISM

The noble narrative has failed to live up to its bidding. Worse, having two agencies has created a number of pathological interactions in antitrust enforcement.

A. Clearance Confusion

Since much of the FTC and Justice Department's jurisdiction is duplicative, both agencies could theoretically investigate or sue over the same activity. This is particularly a problem in merger cases, where the Hart-Scott-Rodino Act (discussed in greater detail in Chapter 5) requires merging firms to give premerger notification to both agencies 30 days before closing the merger. At times, much of the thirty-day process—during which the agencies should hopefully be trying to understand whether they should investigate (and hence, delay) the merger and the parties should be cooperating with the agencies quickly to address any concerns—is eaten up in a clearance process, during which time no one inside or outside the agency knows which agency will ultimately assume jurisdiction.[59] Improved clearance processes can ameliorate but never entirely eliminate this cost of committing overlapping enforcement authority to multiple agencies.

B. Cost Duplication

In one sense, having two antitrust enforcement agencies does not result in much cost duplication, since once the agencies have resolved any initial clearance confusion, they generally do not work on the same matters.[60] Duplication, however, can occur in another sense: the failure to achieve economies of scale. It is in the latter sense that the dual-agency structure is suboptimal.

Consider the dual-agency problem from the perspective of a business activity that the agencies pervasively regulate: mergers. Mergers are justified from a business perspective when two firms could, by combining, consolidate operations under highly skilled (and hence scarce) management, integrate complementary functions, more efficiently deploy firm resources by assigning employees to more specialized tasks, and eliminate duplicative cost centers. Many of these good reasons that firms have for merging would apply to a consolidation of the agencies.

For example, the FTC has experience with computer hardware markets (handles Intel) and the Antitrust Division has experience with software markets

59. *See* Antitrust Modernization Commission Report and Recommendations at 132–37 (April 2007).

60. *See* id. at 129.

(handles Microsoft).[61] Of course, computer software and hardware are complementary products, and many antitrust cases turn on the relationship between the two. Combining knowledge centers about both products within a single firm is the very sort of efficiency that the agencies consider virtuous when undertaking merger review.[62] A unified antitrust agency could take advantage of economies of scale and scope to a greater degree than is possible in the fractured dual-agency system.

C. Inconsistent Treatment

The Antitrust Division and FTC have essentially a market-division approach to jurisdiction, with each agency laying claim to the industries with which they have the greater experience. As we have seen, there is little to distinguish the two agencies in terms of their real capabilities. But to the extent that agencies have significantly different statutory positions on particular functions, this means that firms in different industries are treated differently based on the happenstance of which agency considers itself their industrial patron.

For example, we noted above that some courts accord the FTC special presumptions when it seeks a preliminary injunction under Section 13(b). This means that a controversial hardware merger might be tougher to pull off than a controversial software merger (such as the Oracle-PeopleSoft merger that the Justice Department was unable to block).[63] In Chapter 7, we shall see that the substantive reach of Section 5 of the FTC Act may sometimes extend beyond the substantive reach of the Sherman Act. If so, then monopolistic practices by Intel (hardware) might be judged more harshly than monopolistic practices by Microsoft (software). Or, a firm like Apple that makes both hardware and software might face different liability rules depending on which side of its business was at issue.

There is no logical justification for such an arbitrary disparity in governing legal rules on a sectoral basis. If the FTC should enjoy distinctive powers because of its position as an administrative agency, then these powers should apply with equal weight and vigor across all industries. If the FTC should not enjoy distinctive powers because of its position as an administrative agency, then it is hard to see why we should have an FTC.

---

61. *See* Memorandum of Agreement Between the Federal Trade Commission and the Antitrust Division of the United States Department of Justice Concerning Clearance Procedures for Investigations (2002), *available at* http://www.ftc.gov/opa/2002/04/clearanceoverview.shtm.

62. *See* U.S. Dep't of Justice and FTC Joint Horizontal Merger Guidelines § 4 (1992).

63. *U.S. v. Oracle Corp.*, 331 F. Supp. 2d 1098 (N.D. Cal. 2004).

D. Squabbling

From time to time, the FTC and Antitrust Division fall into squabbling. For example, a recent bout of apparent bad blood began with the FTC's enforcement action against Schering-Plough over several of Schering's patent litigation settlements involving "reverse payments" (payments from the branded drug maker to the generic drug maker not to enter the market).[64] The FTC suffered a stinging defeat in the United States Court of Appeals for the Eleventh Circuit and sought a writ of certiorari in the Supreme Court.[65] The Solicitor General and the Antitrust Division then filed their own brief (at the invitation of the Supreme Court), recommending that the Court deny certiorari,[66] which the Court did.[67] The FTC was highly displeased—and not merely with the courts. A sister agency had not even accorded them the courtesy of agreeing that the Supreme Court should hear the case.

But soon it would be payback time. In 2007, in a private lawsuit, the United States Court of Appeals for the Ninth Circuit ruled that an Internet service provider (ISP) could maintain a "price-squeeze" claim against the local telephone company for charging the ISP too high a price at wholesale in relation to the telephone company's retail prices for DSL service.[68] Displeased with this result, the Solicitor General and the Antitrust Division filed an amicus curiae brief supporting the phone company's certiorari petition in the Supreme Court.[69] The FTC then issued a lengthy press release explaining that it strongly disagreed with the Justice Department and refused to join the brief.[70]

The bickering was about to get worse. For several years, the agencies had been collaborating on a report on unilateral exclusionary conduct. They held numerous joint hearings, organized and staffed by members of both agencies. Since unilateral exclusionary conduct was a hot issue in the antitrust community, the joint report was much anticipated. But when the report was released in September 2008, it was unilateral in two senses: it discussed unilateral conduct, and the FTC refused to join.[71] Instead, the FTC issued a harshly worded dissent, complaining

---

64. *Schering-Plough Corp. v. FTC*, 402 F.3d 1056 (11th Cir. 2005).

65. *FTC v. Schering-Plough Corp.*, Petition for a Writ of Certiorari, 2005 WL 2105243 (Aug. 29, 2005).

66. *FTC v. Schering-Plough Corp.*, Brief for the United States as Amicus Curiae, 2006 WL 1358441 (May 17, 2006).

67. *FTC v. Schering-Plough Corp.*, Order denying certiorari, 548 U.S. 919 (2006).

68. *linkLine Communications, Inc. v. SBC California, Inc.*, 503 F.3d 876 (9th Cir. 2007).

69. *Pacific Bell Telephone Co. v. linkLine Communications, Inc.*, Brief for the United States as Amicus Curiae, 2008 WL 2155265 (May 22, 2008).

70. *Statement of the Federal Trade Commission*, Petition for a Writ of Certiorari *Pacific Tel. Co. d/b/a AT&T California v. linkLine Comms., Inc.* (No. 07-512), http://www.ftc.gov/os/2008/05/P072104stmt.pdf (May 23, 2008).

71. U.S. Dep't of Justice, *Competition and Monopoly: Single-Firm Conduct Under Section 2 of the Sherman Act* (2008), http://www.usdoj.gov/atr/public/reports/236681.htm.

that the report "would be a blueprint for radically weakened enforcement of Section 2 of the Sherman Act," asserting that "the testimony gathered during the hearings was not representative of the views of all Section 2 stakeholders,"[72] and threatening that the FTC "stands ready to fill any Sherman Act enforcement void that might be created if the Department actually implements the policy decisions expressed in its Report."[73] The unilateral conduct report turned into an embarrassment to federal antitrust enforcement. One surmises that it was the culmination of a slow-developing schism that began with the *Schering* affair (although differing ideology surely played a part as well).

Should it bother us that the two federal agencies in charge of antitrust enforcement publicly disagree? Perhaps such public dialogue is simply part of the optimal give and take that democracy requires. After all, we do not think it at all odd—indeed we think it healthy—when FTC commissioners publicly disagree with each other and when judges dissent from their colleagues' opinions. We also usually do not have any conceptual problem when two regulatory agencies—say the Labor Department and the Office of the U.S. Trade Representative—disagree on some policy matter. Further, even within the discipline of antitrust, we usually find it beneficial that private enforcement puts a check on public enforcement (more on this in Chapter 9) and that state enforcement puts a check on federal enforcement (more on this in Chapter 8). So why should it bother anyone that the two federal antitrust agencies fall into public disputation?

The answer is that not all dissent is created equal. From a systemic perspective, there can be suboptimal levels of dissent and suboptimal distribution of dissent among the various decision-making or policy-influencing institutions. One way to look at the problem is through the lens of informational modularity. For ultimate policy makers (the Supreme Court or Congress) to make informed decisions about complex issues like antitrust policy, they can acquire information in bits in pieces or in packets. It is hard to determine the optimal level of modularity in the abstract, but it clearly would not work, for example, to have each commissioner of the FTC and each senior official in the FTC submitting a separate brief urging his own point of view. Congress and the courts would prefer to interact with fewer modules of information.

Although each module requires reliable processes for producing information—including internal dissent and discussion—the ultimate module becomes a unified encapsulation of the internal work product and does not reveal all of its internal processes. Even the presence of majority and dissenting opinions only slightly frays the borders of the module. The fact that the majority opinion is the decision

72. It is particularly difficult to understand this procedural complaint, since the FTC was just as involved as the Antitrust Division in organizing the hearings.

73. FTC Commissioners React to Department of Justice Report, *Competition and Monopoly: Single-Firm Conduct Under Section 2 of the Sherman Act* (Sept. 8, 2008), http://www2.ftc.gov/opa/2008/09/section2.shtm.

of the Commission counts in ways that a mere tally of views does not: in the same way that an election counts in a way that an opinion poll does not. The winner can act on behalf of the entire electorate whether he won by 50 or 90 percent.

Having two competing modules of agency antitrust information (for example, in legal briefs or policy reports) diminishes the influence of agency antitrust information as a class. Agency antitrust information already has to compete with other modules of information—i.e., other agencies, private litigants, state attorneys general, bodies of scholarship. When the two agencies disagree, their cumulative influence falls more than their cumulative influence rises when they agree. It is easy to dismiss entirely the competing positions advanced by two agencies on the theory that "if the antitrust agencies can't agree among themselves, why should we listen to them at all." During periods of dissent, the dual-agency model thus tends to diminish the influence of the agencies over antitrust decision making. The unilateral conduct fiasco likely means that the courts will severely discount what either agency has to say on monopolization and fall back on other sources of information.

Of course, this is only a problem if we think that on average, the information provided by the agencies is valuable compared to information provided by other sources. In later chapters, we will develop such an argument around the technocratic potential of antitrust experts. For now, it is enough to observe that squabbling between the agencies is not merely "healthy dissent." Instead, it reduces their overall influence by diminishing the value of the information modules they produce.

V. THE PERSISTENCE OF DUALISM

The dual-agency system is inelegant on paper and imperfect in practice. It has little to commend to other jurisdictions. Why, then, does it persist? The answer seems to be that the system is not broken *enough* to warrant fixing.

Consider the most recent occasion on which a high-profile body gave serious consideration to consolidating antitrust enforcement. In 2007, the bipartisan, congressionally appointed Antitrust Modernization Commission released an evaluative report on the entire gambit of modern antitrust law. Among other things, the twelve members of the Commission considered whether dual federal enforcement should continue. Three of the twelve—including two former heads of the Antitrust Division—voted to recommend abolishing the FTC's antitrust enforcement authority and vesting responsibility for all antitrust enforcement with the Justice Department.[74] But the majority recommended retailing the

74. Antitrust Modernization Commission, Report and Recommendations II.A at 129 (footnote).

dual-enforcement structure. With the benefit of nearly one hundred years of dual-agency history, the commissioners sounded none of the "noble narrative" themes described above. They admitted that the two agencies did not provide counter-cyclical checks on each other—no, the two agencies "typically have worked together to develop similar, if not identical, approaches to substantive antitrust policy."[75] The commissioners made clear the real justification for continuing with dual enforcement: "Although concentrating enforcement authority in a single agency generally would be a superior institutional structure, the significant costs and disruption of moving to a single-agency system at this point in time would likely exceed the benefits."[76] The commissioners noted further practical difficulties with such a switch: "there is no consensus as to which agency would preferably retain antitrust enforcement authority," and any such move "would likely be politically very difficult."[77]

In contemplating the Commission's reasoning, which echoes similar observations made by others over the years, consider some remarks by James Bryce, the late nineteenth-century British commentator on the American political system.[78] Bryce identified many theoretical flaws in the design of the American system but noted that the American republic had survived the centripetal forces of federalism and "the furnace of civil war" with its institutions intact.[79] Thus, although "[o]bjections may taken to particular features [of the American system and that] most American thinkers are agreed, to practical improvements which would preserve the excellence and remove some of the inconvenience," the American people "submit, not merely patiently but hopefully, to the defects of their government."[80] Why not experiment with institutional modifications to change the universally agreed-upon defects? The answer, wrote Bryce, lay in the success of the existing institutions in producing felicitous results. "The vessel may not be any better built, or found, or rigged than are those which carry the fortunes of the great nations of Europe. She is certainly not better navigated. But for the present at least—it may not always be so—she sails upon a summer sea."[81] As the eminent American legal scholar and Judge Thomas Cooley put it

---

75. *Id.* at 129.

76. *Id.* at 129–30.

77. *Id.* at 130.

78. Bryce's magisterial work is The American Commonwealth, first published in 1896.

79. James Bryce, The American Commonwealth 222 (MacMillan 1904). Among other things, Bryce believed that the American legislative process was ill-conceived. He noted that legislation was accomplished largely by unspecialized committees, meeting only briefly each year, where individual committee members largely hold a veto over the progress of legislation.

80. *Id.* at 222–23.

81. *Id.* at 222.

two decades earlier, "the advantages of government are not to be found in its forms exclusively: they must be perceived also in its results."[82]

What conclusions, then, may we draw from the history of two-headed enforcement in the United States? One conclusion is that, on balance, there is no good reason to commend the inelegant dual-agency model to the rest of the world. The other is that there is wisdom in conservative impulse not to alter existing structures that seem to be working passably well, even if their theoretical basis is shaky. If there is one abiding principle of American pragmatism, it's "if it ain't broke, don't fix it." Dual enforcement may not be broken enough to fix.

Whether this sentiment is pragmatic common sense or just timidity and inertia, there is likely to come a time when political forces transpire to bring the American dual-agency structure into the public spotlight. If ever there arises the political will for serious institutional reform in antitrust, there will not be a shortage of options, including ones that preserve an antitrust role for both agencies. For example, one could imagine handing over all of the civil antitrust portfolio to the FTC and allowing the Justice Department to continue its criminal anti-cartel program. Or the FTC could handle all merger cases—thus exploiting its Section 13(b) advantage—and the Justice Department could handle everything else. The political will to make such changes is remote, but the advantage to making them is not.

---

82. Thomas M. Cooley, *Limits to State Control of Private Business*, 1878 PRINCETON REV. 233, 240.

3. PRIVATE ENFORCEMENT
Growth, Backlash, and Spillovers

One consequence of the decision to divorce antitrust from corporate regulation and conceptualize it as a freestanding tort (as described in Chapter 1) was the creation of a private right of action for damages. If the antitrust laws created a generalized norm of competitive conduct, it followed that anyone injured by a violation of the norm should be entitled to redress. The 1890 Sherman Act thus provided a right of action for any person "injured in his business or property" by virtue of an antitrust violation to sue for "three fold the damages by him sustained, and the costs of suit, including a reasonable attorney's fee."[1]

The allowance for private enforcement and treble damages was not entirely an American innovation. Conceptually, it derived from the 1623 English statute of monopolies, passed by Parliament during the reign of James I in the wake of Sir Edward Coke's landmark decision in *Darcy v. Allein* (usually called "the case of monopolies").[2] There was, however, a very significant difference between the private right of action created under the statute of monopolies and that created under the Sherman Act. The Statute of Monopolies right of action only applied to damages sustained by virtue of actions taken under color of monopolies illegitimately granted by the government.[3] Although the common law expressed a more general pro-competition policy, it was only a defense to the enforcement of anticompetitive contractual terms or other legal entitlements, not a source of independent liability.[4] In the great English common law cases like

1. 51 Cong. Ch. 647, July 2, 1890, 26 Stat. 209, § 7 (1890). The private right of action provision was slightly modified in 1914 in Section 4 of the Clayton Act. 63 Cong. Ch. 323, 38 Stat. 730, § 4 (1914).

2. Statute of Monopolies, 21 Jam. I, c. 3 (1623) (Eng.). In *Darcy v. Allein*, 11 Co. Rep. 84b, 77 Eng. Rep. 1260 (K.B. 1602), the King's Bench held unlawful a playing card monopoly granted by Queen Elizabeth.

3. Section 4 of the statute provided, in relevant part: "And if any person. . . shall be hindered, grieved, disturbed, or disquieted, or his or their goods or chattels any way seized, attached, distrained, taken, carried away, or detained by occasion or pretext of any monopoly, or of any such commission, grant, license, power, liberty, faculty, letters patents, proclamation, inhibition, restraint, warrant of assistance, or any other matter or thing tended as aforesaid, and will sue to be relieved in or for any premises, that then and in every such case the same person and persons shall have and may have his remedy for the same at common law. . . and every such person. . . shall recover three times so much as the damages which he or they sustained. . . and double costs."

4. *See, e.g.*, Herbert Hovenkamp, Enterprise and American Law, 1836–1937 274 (1991) ("Although completely voluntary agreements to eliminate competition, such as

Mitchell v. Reynolds[5] and *The Case of Monopolies*,[6] what we would think of today as the antitrust claim was raised as a defense to the enforcement of other legal rights, such as covenants not to compete. Thus, for example, in the *Mogul Steamship* case,[7] the House of Lords held that a shipping association's agreement to engage in a number of exclusionary acts against a rival shipping company was possibly unlawful in the sense that courts would not enforce the agreement, but that the agreement itself was not "contrary to law." The excluded competitor, a stranger to the association's agreement, had no legal recourse.

By the time of the Sherman Act, however, the concept of monopoly had shifted from its earlier meaning of an exclusive governmental grant to a more general meaning of any strongly held market position, whether derivative of a governmental grant or purely private industrial power.[8] Further, the Sherman Act did not limit the private right of action for damages to unlawful monopolies but also included agreements in restraint of trade. The Sherman Act's private right of actions therefore set the United States on a course for a much more expansive role for private damages litigation than that known at common law. Over time,

---

price-fixing, were not generally enforceable in court, neither were they indictable offenses or even challengeable by third parties in civil actions."). William Letwin's survey of English common law and statutory law on various competitive offenses suggests a few ways in which the common law may have gone beyond merely voiding anticompetitive agreements. *See* WILLIAM LETWIN, LAW AND ECONOMIC POLICY IN AMERICA: THE EVOLUTION OF THE SHERMAN ANTITRUST ACT 18–52 (1965). The crimes of forestalling, engrossing, and regrating were relatively narrow offenses somewhat akin to price-gouging that had been effectively abandoned by the time of William Blackstone and Adam Smith in the late eighteenth century and were finally abolished by an act of Parliament in 1844. *Id.* at 38.

5. 1 *Peere Wms.* 181 (1711).

6. *Darcy v. Allein*, 11 Co. Rep. 84, Moore 671 (K.B. 1599), Noy 173.

7. *Mogul Steamship Co. v. McGregor*, [1892] App. Cas. 25.

8. At common law, a "monopoly" was understood as an exclusive governmentally granted privilege. Twenty years after the enactment of the Statute of Monopolies, Sir Edward Coke defined a monopoly as "[A]n institution, or allowance by the king by his grant, commission, or otherwise to any person or persons, bodies politique, or corporate, of or for the sole buying, selling, making, working, or using of any thing, whereby any person or persons, bodies politique, or corporate, are sought to be restrained of any freedome, or liberty that they had before, or hindred in their lawfull trade." EDWARD COKE, THE THIRD PART OF THE INSTITUTES OF THE LAWS OF ENGLAND 181 (London, W. Clarke and Sons, 1644). *See generally* Herbert Hovenkamp, *The Monopolization Offense*, 61 OHIO ST. L. J. 1035, 1035 (2000) ("The history of the term 'monopoly' prior to 1890, when the Sherman Act was passed, indicates that most people understood 'monopoly' to mean a grant of exclusive privileges from the government. . .. But the legislative history of the Sherman Act shows virtually no concern at all for monopolies created by government grant. Rather, Congess was concerned with large firms who acquired their dominant positions without the explicit aid of government intervention.").

the private right of action would displace public enforcement as the principal driver of federal antitrust policy.

I. PRIVATE ENFORCEMENT IN THE EARLY YEARS—A SLOW BEGINNING

The framers of the Sherman Act seem to have imagined that private enforcement would be essentially a supplement to public enforcement, exercised primarily in the event that public enforcers were delinquent. For example, Representative Webb opined that "[i]f the Attorney General should be negligent, the individual himself has a wide-open door to go into court and sue."[9] The framers seem to have imagined that the persons with standing to prosecute private claims under the newly minted Sherman Act would be consumers[10] and competitors.[11] The framers also seem to have contemplated that some sort of claim aggregation device might be necessary to make the private remedy effective in the event of widely distributed harms,[12] although it is doubtful that they would have anticipated the rise of the class-action mechanism in its full modern uses.

In the earlier years, the framers' vision of private antitrust as a modest supplement to public enforcement proved to be the norm. Private antitrust litigation was rare. During the Sherman Act's first decade, there were only six reported private antitrust cases.[13] There were eight more cases between 1899 and 1904 and about four additional cases per year until World War II.[14] Although the Sherman Act was raised as a defense to the enforcement of contracts in restraint

---

9. 3 Legislative History of the Federal Antitrust Laws and Related Statutes 2771–72 (E. Kintner ed., 1978) [hereinafter Legislative History].

10. "Who is this party injured, when. . . there has been an advance in the price by the combination?. . . The consumer is the party 'damnified or injured.'" DDD' 21 Cong. Rec. 1767 (1890), *reprinted in* 1 Legislative History, *supra* note 9, at 99 (statement of Sen. George).

11. 21 Cong. Rec. 3147 (1890) (statement of Sen. George) ("By the use of this organized force of wealth and money the small men engaged in competition. . . are crushed out, and that is the great evil at which all this legislation ought to be directed."), *reprinted in* 1 Legislative History, *supra* note 9, at 284; *see also* 51 Cong. Rec. 9090 (1914) (statement of Rep. Mitchell) ("[T]hose who had been crushed and driven out of business were left without a remedy. . . ."), *reprinted in* 2 Legislative History, *supra* note 9, at 1229.

12. 21 Cong. Rec. 3148 (1890) (remarks of Sen. George, arguing for aggregation of small claims), *reprinted in* 1 Legislative History, *supra* note 9, at 285; *see also* 21 Cong. Rec. 1768 (1890) (remarks of Sen. George) ("It is manifest that in nearly every instance the damage by the advanced price of each article affected by these combinations would be—though in the aggregate large, indeed—so small as not to justify the expense and trouble of a suit in a distant court."), *reprinted in* 1 Legislative History, *supra* note 9, at 100.

13. Douglas H. Ginsburg & Leah Brannon, *Determinants of Private Antitrust Enforcement in the United States*, Competition Policy Int'l, Autumn 2005 at 31.

14. *Id.* at 31–32.

of trade in some earlier cases,[15] the first treble-damages case by a private litigant did not reach the Supreme Court until twelve years after the Sherman Act's promulgation.[16] The Court first affirmed a treble-damages award in 1904.[17] During the first half of the twentieth century, private litigation continued to have only modest influence in the development of Sherman Act norms. When antitrust law appeared in private litigation, it often was as defense to patent infringement or breach-of-contract claims.[18] Up to three-quarters of all private antitrust lawsuits for damages were follow-ons to government lawsuits,[19] meaning that the private lawsuit did relatively little work in establishing new antitrust norms.

Figure 3.1 below shows the level of private antitrust filings (grouped into five-year clusters—which accentuate the movements) in the federal courts from the passage of the Sherman Act in 1890 to the present.[20] We will return to different movements in the curve at various junctures, but for now we should simply note that from the passage of the Sherman Act until the end of World War II, private antitrust enforcement was relatively insignificant. Most of the big cases—the ones that could make important precedent or reshape industries—were brought by the Antitrust Division or the Federal Trade Commission.

In light of the explosion of private cases that followed the war, one may wonder why private litigation took so long to take off. After all, many of the features that foreign commentators often associate with the American model of

---

15. *E.g., Dickerman v. Northern Trust Co.*, 176 U.S. 181, 195 (1900).

16. *Connolly v. Union Sewer Pipe Co.*, 184 U.S. 540 (1902). Indeed, *Connolly* arguably was not even a treble-damages claim, since the buyer merely sought a treble-damages set-off for the price-fixed goods against the amount of money he owed the seller.

17. *W.W. Montague & Co. v. Lowry*, 193 U.S. 38 (1904).

18. *E.g., E. Bement & Sons v. Nat'l Harrow Co.*, 186 U.S. 70 (1902) (finding that resale price maintenance provisions in patent license did not violate the Sherman Act).

19. *See* Comment, *Consent Decrees and Private Antitrust Actions: An Antitrust Dilemma*, 53 CAL. L. REV. 627, 628 n. 7 (1965) (estimating that 75 percent of private antitrust cases filed before 1960 were follow-ons to government cases); *see also* John D. Guilfoil, *Private Enforcement of U.S. Antitrust Law*, 10 ANTITRUST BULL. 747 (1965).

20. The data are compiled from two separate sources. For the years 1890–1969, the data come from Richard A. Posner, *A Statistical Study of Antitrust Enforcement*, *in* THE CAUSES AND CONSEQUENCES OF ANTITRUST: THE PUBLIC-CHOICE PERSPECTIVE 79 Table 5.3 (Fred S. McChesney & William F. Shughart II eds., 1995). Posner's data for the years before 1938 are estimated from the general ratio of reported decisions to all antitrust cases. For the period 1938 forward, Posner employs data made available by the administrative offices of the United States courts. They exclude 1940, for which Posner found no available data. Posner also excludes the electrical equipment cases from the early 1960s, which would add 2233 cases (most of them filed in 1962) but would provide a misleading picture since they all arose from a few indictments. *Id.* at 79. For the periods 1970–forward, I relied directly on data from the administrative offices. The period 2005–2009 includes an estimate for 2009, based on the average number of cases in the four preceding years.

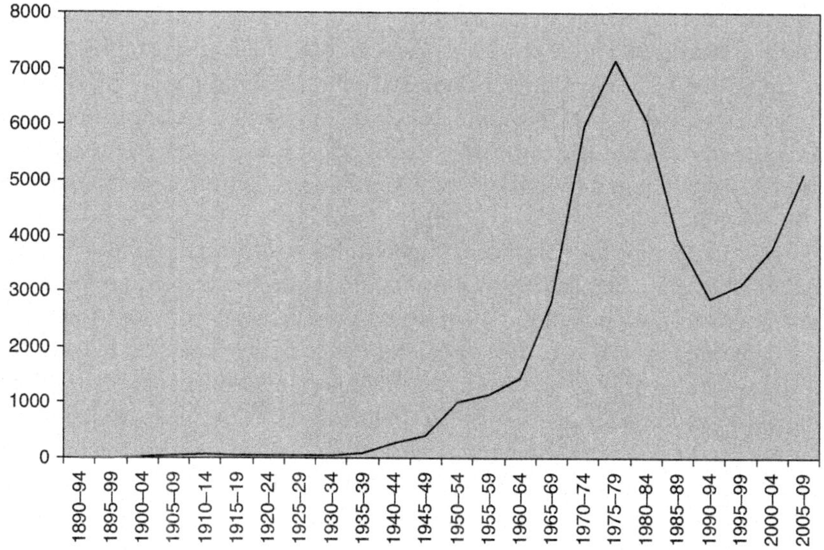

FIGURE 3.1 PRIVATE ANTITRUST FILLINGS BY FIVE-YEAR PERIOD

"out of control" private antitrust enforcement—the treble-damages bounty, one-way attorney-fee shifting in favor of the plaintiff, liberal discovery rights, and some possibility of class action treatment—were all in place in the first half of the twentieth century (although, in the case of discovery and class actions, they were significantly liberalized in the second half of the century). Nonetheless, private litigation remained a very modest supplement to public enforcement for the better part of fifty years.

While it is difficult to fully explain why the counterfactual did not occur, one can at least draw the following inference for countries that are considering moving toward a private litigation system and are worried about the volume of private litigation in the United States: The availability of private rights of action and even of features like treble damages, discovery, class actions, and attorney's-fee shifting that make the deployment of the right attractive, do not inexorably lead to an explosion of private litigation or a displacement of public litigation. The forces that cause such booms are far more complex than just the theoretical availability of plaintiff-friendly litigation rules.

II. THE BOOM

Beginning in the post-war era, private antitrust enforcement boomed dramatically. The number of new filings more than doubled from the period 1945–1949 to the period 1950–1954. Private litigation surpassed government litigation (in pure numerical terms) in the 1940s. From the 1940s to about 1965, the ratio between private and public litigation was about 6–1.[21] Thereafter, private litigation continued to grow at an astronomical rate, reaching a peak of 1611 new private cases filed in 1977, with a 20–1 ratio in favor of private litigation.[22] Subsequently, the number of private cases declined for reasons we will explore in the next section, and the ratio between public and private cases stabilized in the 10–1 range.

What accounts for the private enforcement boom during the 1950s, '60s, and '70s? One possibility is that the post-war boom in antitrust was merely part of a larger boom in civil litigation. Whether or not such a "boom" or "explosion" really happened is subject to disagreement; critics of the explosion theory argue that the real rates of litigation were not that much higher than at earlier times, and that litigation run amok is simply a rhetorical device employed to justify pro-business legal reforms.[23] The post-war era undoubtedly saw significant growth in some areas of civil litigation in federal court, but at least, in part, because new liability regimes, like the civil rights statutes of the 1960s, came into effect in that era. Litigation growth because of the creation of new rights of action would not seem to have a direct effect on the incidence of antitrust litigation.

Although a more general increase in overall litigation levels may very well have affected antitrust, private antitrust litigation experienced enough idiosyncratic developments that overall litigation patterns do not provide a complete explanation. Figure 3.2 below presents the number of new private filings on an annual basis for antitrust and four of its closest analogues: securities, trademark, patent, and copyright, for 1961–2008.[24] There is little correlation in patterns of increases and decreases. Antitrust and securities both grew dramatically in the late 1960s and early '70s, but securities grew in the 1980s when antitrust plummeted. Antitrust then began to enjoy a revival during the 2000s, when securities lawsuits were headed sharply in the other direction (no doubt as a result of restrictive private securities litigation reforms in the late 1990s).[25] Copyright and trademark began their dizzying assents in the 1970s, just when antitrust was

---

21. Steven C. Salop & Lawrence J. White, *Economic Analysis of Private Antitrust Litigation*, 74 Geo. L. J. 1001, 1002–03 (1986).

22. *Id.* at 1003.

23. *See, e.g.*, A. Benjamin Spencer, *Understanding Pleading Doctrine*, 108 Mich. L. Rev. 1, 3 n.6 (2009) (collecting authorities disputing the fact of the litigation explosion).

24. All data are compiled from the administrative offices of the U.S. Courts. 1961 was chosen as the starting year because of data reporting changes in that year that allowed the previously unavailable break-out of private and government cases for some categories of cases.

25. Private Securities Litigation Reform Act of 1995, Pub. L. 104–67, tit. 1, §101(b), 109 Stat. 737, 743 (codified at 15 U.S.C. §78u-4 (2000); Securities Litigation Uniform Standards Act of 1998 (SLUSA), Publ. L. No. 105–353, 112 Stat. 3227 (codified as amended in scattered sections of 15 U.S.C.).

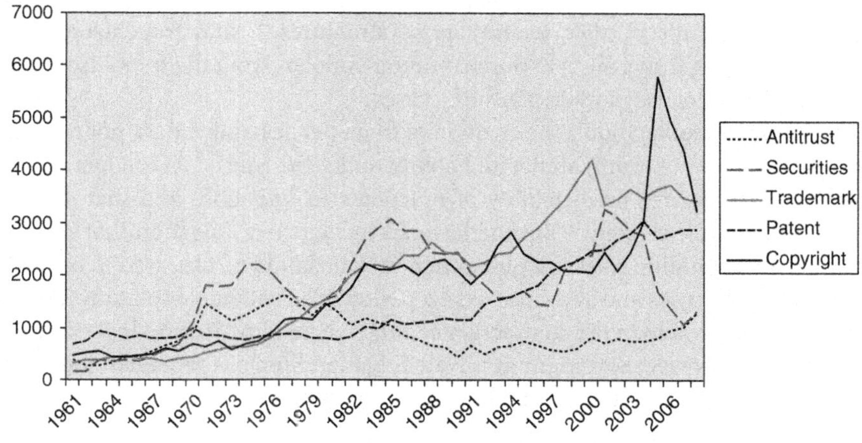

FIGURE 3.2 COMPARISON OF PRIVATE CASES FILED IN FEDERAL COURT 1961–2008

heading south. Patent and antitrust crossed paths in the mid-1980s; their trend lines moved in opposite directions for the better part of two decades.

If overall trends in litigation patterns do not furnish a satisfactory answer, the explanation must lie in changes in antitrust rules themselves. Scholars have furnished various explanations to this effect. Richard Posner has identified the significant factors as the Supreme Court's 1946 decision in *Bigeleow v. RKO Radio Pictures, Inc.*,[26] which greatly reduced a plaintiff's burden to prove damages in antitrust cases and a variety of procedural rulings that made antitrust cases easier to bring.[27] One significant ruling, which initially expanded liability but sowed the seeds for later contraction, was the Supreme Court's denial of a "passing on" defense,[28] thus allowing direct purchasers of price-fixed goods to sue for the full overcharge even if they passed along much or all of the overcharge downstream.

Judicial creation of more plaintiff-friendly liability norms also contributed to plaintiffs' willingness to sue. Doug Ginsburg and Leah Brannon have argued that judicial resolution of antitrust cases in the 1960s created a "'plaintiff's picnic,' with the courts construing the antitrust laws to protect firms from their competitors without regard to whether the defendant had caused any injury to the competitive process."[29] Ginsburg and Brannon find that the creation of rules

26. 327 U.S. 251 (1946).

27. Posner, *Statistical Study*, *supra* n. 20 at 80. Among the procedural cases Posner identifies is *Hanover Shoe, Inc. v. United Shoe Machinery Corp.*, 392 U.S. 481 (1968), which we consider further below.

28. *Hanover Shoe Inc. v. United Shoe Machinery Corp.*, 392 U.S. 481 (1968).

29. Ginsburg & Brannan, *supra* n. 13 at 37.

of per se illegality or near per se illegality for such species of conduct as vertical territorial restraints,[30] "deteriorating price structures,"[31] and franchise agreements requiring franchisees to purchase their supplies from the franchisor[32] led to an explosion of easy-to-win plaintiff's cases.[33]

Like earlier explanations, the creation of more per se liability does not provide a complete account. Compared with liability under the rule of reason, per se liability creates greater predictability of outcomes in litigation, and that should make litigation less likely.[34] But the lowered incidence of litigation that should come with bright-line rules is a phenomenon that should be observed in equilibrium, and the sixties and seventies were a period of considerable volatility in first the expansion and then the contraction of antitrust liability. So one final explanation for the post-war movement in private litigation filings is rapid development of liability norms, leading to waves of experimentation in liability theories and defenses.

III. BACKLASH

Figure 3.1 shows a steep decline in private antitrust litigation that began in the late 1970s and continued until the mid-1990s, when private litigation began to creep back up again. What caused this decline? The theory just articulated for the expansion of private enforcement in the fifties, sixties, and early seventies provides a possible explanation. Private litigation grew exponentially during a period of rapid change in liability norms, which created uncertainty about litigation outcomes. Once the norms crystallized and the outcomes became more predictable, parties had less to litigate over. But, as usual, the stories are far more complex. Most significantly, the just-offered story does not work so well because the liability norms that had shifted rapidly in a pro-plaintiff direction, primarily during the sixties and early seventies, made a dramatic turn in the pro-defendant direction, beginning in the late 1970s. The new liability norms were not only more pro-defendant but also more complex—the rules shifted from per se illegality to an open-ended rule of reason. The greater complexity of the rules should have invited *more* litigation, but their pro-defendant shift should have had the opposite effect. It is very difficult to determine in the abstract which influence likely had the greater effect. So we will once again need to interpret our graph in light of a variety of influences.

---

30. *United States v. Arnold, Schwinn & Co.*, 388 U.S. 365 (1963).

31. *Utah Pie Co. v. Cont'l Baking Co.*, 386 U.S. 685 (1967).

32. *Siegel v. Chicken Delight, Inc.*, 448 F.2d 43 (9th Cir. 1971).

33. Ginsburg & Brannon, *supra* n. 13 at 37–39.

34. *See generally* George L. Priest & Benjamin Klein, *The Selection of Disputes for Litigation*, 13 J. LEGAL STUD. 1 (1984).

One possibly contributing factor was the decline in public litigation. As previously noted, prior to the 1960s, a very large percentage of all private cases were follow-ons to government cases, so a decline in public litigation could also result in a decline in private litigation. Using data from the Georgetown study to be discussed momentarily, Tom Kauper and Edward Snyder found that roughly a quarter of the private cases studied from 1973 to 1983 were follow-ons to prior government cases.[35] Since public antitrust enforcement decreased somewhat during the 1980s and 1990s (more on this in Chapter 4), there could have been some effect on private litigation. But the effect would be far too small to explain the precipitous drop, both because the decline in government enforcement was modest, and the number of cases depending on prior government enforcement was small.[36] Further explanations are required.

To get at least a part of the answer, it's worth spending a moment on the only comprehensive study of private litigation in the United States conducted to date. The Georgetown Private Antitrust Litigation Project studied 2350 private antitrust cases filed in federal court in five judicial districts between 1973 and 1983.[37] The survey results provided some interesting insights into what kinds of cases were being filed and who was filing them. For one, complaints of vertical misconduct outnumbered horizontal complaints.[38] Second, most private cases were brought by businesses vertically related to the defendant, such as dealers, licensees, and franchisees or by competitors.[39] Competitors brought 35.5 percent of all cases, dealers 27.3 percent, and suppliers 5.6 percent and franchisees and licensees cumulatively around 3 percent.[40] Customers—the ostensible beneficiaries of antitrust law—played a comparatively minor role. Final or end customers brought 8.7 percent of cases, perhaps not surprisingly in light of the Supreme Court's limitation of indirect purchaser standing.[41] But customer companies filed only 12.5 percent,[42] hence all customer complaints accounted for only about a fifth of antitrust filings. Third, around 88 percent of the cases settled; only about 5 percent of cases went to trial.[43] Fourth, judges apparently used dismissal sparingly, dismissing fewer than 25 percent of all cases.[44] Fifth, the average

---

35. Thomas Kauper & Edward Snyder, *Private Antitrust Cases that Follow On Government Cases*, *in* PRIVATE ANTITRUST LITIGATION: NEW EVIDENCE, NEW LEARNING 358 (Lawrence J. White ed., 1988).

36. *See generally* Ginsburg & Brannon, *supra* n. 13 at 37 (finding the thesis that private litigation declined as a result of fewer government cases "plausible but incomplete").

37. Salop & White, *supra* n. 21 at 1001–02.

38. *Id.* at 2005.

39. *Id.*

40. *Id.* at 1008, Table 5.

41. *Illinois Brick Co. v. Illinois*, 431 U.S. 720 (1977).

42. Salop & White, *supra* n. 21 at 1008, Table 5.

43. *Id.* at 1011.

44. *Id.* at 1011.

settlement was either $547,000 or $1,244,000, depending on whether one chose to include a $50 million outlier settlement.[45] Either way, the numbers seemed significant. Finally, the combined cost (in 1984 dollars) of litigating the cases was estimated to be around $200,000–$250,000.[46]

One could draw many different lessons from the Georgetown study, but one set of conclusions could easily feed into the rising "Chicago School" critique that was beginning to prevail in the courts.[47] Private antitrust litigation was fueled primarily by disgruntled competitors, dealers, franchisees, and licensees whose interests were adverse to those of consumers. The bulk of private cases challenged vertical practices that the Chicago School considered likely to be benign, rather than horizontal practices that the Chicago School might have conceded could be more problematic. The cases were easy to bring, costly to defend, unlikely to be involuntarily dismissed by the courts, and hence likely to coerce the defendant to pay a substantial settlement to be rid of the case.

The Georgetown study generated a large amount of scholarship on private litigation, much of it critical. An important theme that emerged from the study was that much private antitrust litigation was motivated by businesses seeking a strategic advantage in the marketplace rather than by publicly minded private attorneys general. Kenneth Elzinga and William Wood's work with the Georgetown data led them to the conclusion that "only a minority of the cases in the data set, and presumably in private antitrust cases generally, have any connection with improving or maintaining efficiency."[48] Elzinga and Wood concluded that many private antitrust lawsuits were strategically motivated. Edward Synder and Tom Kauper similarly analyzed the Georgetown data and found evidence that the private antitrust remedy was often used to subvert, rather than promote, competition.[49]

Although an important source of information and fount of valuable scholarship on private antitrust litigation, the Georgetown study was not the triggering event in judicial retrenchment of private antitrust litigation. For example, the

45. *Id.* at 1012.

46. *Id.* at 1015–16.

47. The Chicago School is identified with scholars at the University of Chicago who began to make a systematic critique of interventionist antitrust law during the 1950s and 60s. The Chicago School was ultimately successful in contributing to a dramatic transformation of antitrust law in the United States in the 1970s and 80s. *See* Daniel A. Crane, *Chicago, Post-Chicago, and Neo-Chicago,* 64 U. Chi. L. Rev. 1911 (2009), *reviewing* How the Chicago School Overshot the Mark (Oxford University Press, Robert Pitofsky, ed., 2008).

48. Kenneth G. Elzinga & William C. Wood, *The Costs of the Legal System in Private Antitrust Enforcement, in* Private Antitrust Litigation: New Evidence, New Learning 134 (Lawrence J. White ed., 1988).

49. Edward A. Snyder & Thomas E. Kauper, *Misuses of the Antitrust Laws: The Competitor Plaintiff,* 90 Mich. L. Rev. 551 (1991).

idea that plaintiffs strategically misused antitrust law to subvert wholesome competition had been proposed in a number of books and articles that preceded the Georgetown study.[50] Rather, the Georgetown study provided empirical evidence of intuitions or suspicions that lots of lawyers, economists, and judges had begun to hold about private antitrust enforcement since its boom in the post-war era. By the time the Georgetown study was released in the mid-1980s, the courts had already been cutting back on private antitrust cases for many of the reasons that Georgetown subsequently made explicit.

Many of the "backlash" cases that contributed to the fall in private antitrust litigation rates during the late 1970s and '80s involved questions unique to private litigation—particularly standing and the use of procedural mechanisms to screen out unmeritorious cases. In 1977, in the *Brunswick* case, the Supreme Court held that it was not enough for a plaintiff to prove an antitrust violation—it needed to prove injury of a kind with which the antitrust laws were concerned or "antitrust injury."[51] *Brunswick* was a merger case, but the Supreme Court subsequently extended its reasoning to private competitor cases challenging resale price maintenance schemes that were illegal per se under then-prevailing precedents.[52] In 1977, the same year it decided *Brunswick*, the Court also held that indirect purchasers—those that made their purchases from an intermediary like a wholesaler or retailer rather than directly from the defendant—had no standing to seek recovery for overcharges.[53] In a subsequent case, the Court created a similar standing roadblock for nonpurchaser plaintiffs who were not the direct victims of the antitrust violations but still felt its effects.[54] Then, in 1986, the Court significantly elevated the availability of summary judgment as a screen in antitrust cases. The Court held that trial judges should inquire into the economic plausibility of the plaintiff's assertions and only allow ones to proceed to trial cases that had both record support and sound economic theories behind them.[55] In 2007, the Court extended this reasoning to the motion to dismiss stage, ruling that antitrust plaintiffs cannot survive a motion to dismiss and obtain discovery unless they can plead facts plausibly entitling them to relief.[56] Although the long-term effects of *Twombly* are still uncertain, the decision seems to invite district

---

50. *See, e.g.*, Richard A. Posner, Antitrust Law: An Economic Perspective 228 (1976); Frank H. Easterbrook, *The Limits of Antitrust*, 63 Tex. L. Rev. 1, 37 (1984); William J. Baumol & Janusz A. Ordover, *Use of Antitrust to Subvert Competition*, 28 J.L. & Econ. 247, 256–59 (1985).

51. *Brunswick v. Pueblo Bowl-O-Mat, Inc.*, 429 U.S. 477 (1977).

52. *Atlantic Richfield v. USA Petroleum*, 495 U.S. 328 (1990).

53. *Illinois Brick Co. v. Illinois*, 431 U.S. 720 (1977).

54. *Associated General Contractors v. California State Council of Carpenters*, 459 U.S. 519 (1983).

55. *Matsushita Elec. Indus. Co. v. Zenith Radio Corp.*, 475 U.S. 574 (1986).

56. *Bell Atlantic Corp. v. Twombly*, 550 U.S. 544 (2007).

judges to play a much more aggressive role in dismissing cases before discovery even begins.

The cases discussed in the previous paragraphs reflect a backlash against private enforcement expressed as a curtailment of *private enforcement*. But, during the same time frame as the courts were cutting back private enforcement, they were also cutting back on the substantive norms of illegality in antitrust cases, most of which happened to be private cases. The courts sharply constricted liability norms for all intra-brand vertical restraints,[57] predatory pricing,[58] refusals to deal,[59] tying,[60] and boycotts.[61] One of the impulses that drove this retrenchment in liability norms was the triumph of the Chicago School, to be discussed momentarily, in persuading judges that many practices once thought to be anticompetitive were perfectly benign. But an equally important impulse was a deep suspicion that the institutional apparatuses of private litigation—particularly competitor plaintiffs, easy class certification, treble damages, attorney-fee shifting, and generalist judges and juries—created the potential for tremendous abuses.

In the last few years, scholars have begun to explain the antitrust revolution of the late 1970s, 1980s, and 1990s as the product of two very different schools of thought: Harvard and Chicago.[62] The Chicago School, often associated with such names as Richard Posner, Frank Easterbrook, Robert Bork, and Anthony Scalia is associated with a generally conservative view of judicial intervention into markets and government regulation.[63] In the Chicago School perspective, antitrust interventions as to many previously suspected commercial practices such as intra-brand vertical restraints, predatory pricing, tying, exclusive dealing, and most vertical and even horizontal mergers are unnecessary because the practices are competitively benign, and the market works better than legal interventions at curing any imperfections. The Harvard School, associated with Philip Areeda, Donald Turner, Herbert Hovenkamp, and Stephen Breyer is associated with a concern that generalist judges and juries are unable to navigate the shoals of complex antirust cases very well and that other features of the civil litigation system, such as treble damages and class actions, may distort the process of private antitrust adjudication. Each of these schools deeply mistrusts the other,

57. *Leegin Creative Leather Prods., Inc. v. PSKS, Inc.*, 551 U.S. 877 (2007).

58. *Brooke Group Ltd. v. Brown & Williamson Tobacco Corp.*, 509 U.S. 209 (1993).

59. *Verizon Comms., Inc. v. Law Offices of Curtis V. Trinko*, LLP, 540 U.S. 398 (2004).

60. *Jefferson Parish Hosp. No. 2 v. Hyde*, 466 U.S. 2 (1984).

61. *NYNEX Corp. v. Discon, Inc.*, 525 U.S. 128 (1998).

62. *See*, e.g., Daniel A. Crane, *linkLine's Institutional Suspicions*, 2009 CATO S. CT. REV. 111; Crane, *Chicago, Post-Chicago*, *supra* n. 47; William E. Kovacic, *The Intellectual DNA of Modern U.S. Competition Law for Dominant Firm Conduct: The Chicago/Harvard Double Helix*, 2007 COLUM BUS L REV 1; Einer Elhauge, *Harvard, Not Chicago: Which Antitrust School Drives Recent U.S. Supreme Court Decisions*, 3 COMP POLICY INT'L 59 (2007).

63. In *Chicago, Post-Chicago*, *supra* n. 47, I qualify this perspective on Chicago in a number of ways.

but they have tended to converge on outcomes in the last three decades. Thus, for example, from 1994 when Breyer joined the Supreme Court to 2010, the Court decided fifteen antitrust cases. In those cases, there were 117 votes for the majority position and only 14 votes in dissent.

The upshot has been that during the period of private antitrust litigation retrenchment, the onslaught of opinions that have contracted liability norms (as opposed to the procedural aspects such as standing and pleading, previously discussed) have reflected both substantive and institutionalist concerns. It is often difficult to ferret out how much of an opinion rests on substantive concerns that antitrust law simply should not penalize certain kinds of behavior versus institutionalist concerns that a particular plaintiff or procedural context is inappropriate for vindicating otherwise legitimate substantive norms. Supreme Court opinions speak for up to nine Justices and are the result of compromises among judges with different viewpoints and agendas. But there is no doubt that institutionalist concerns have played a major role in shaping contemporary Sherman Act norms.

Consider, for example, two opinions written by Stephen Breyer, the most influential Harvard School jurist, while he was an appellate court judge. *Barry Wright*[64] became highly influential in the development of restrictive liability norms in exclusive dealing and predatory pricing cases, and *Town of Concord*[65] was a significant influence in the Supreme Court's eventual rejection of price-squeeze liability.[66] In *Barry Wright*, Breyer justified a restrictive view of predatory pricing on an important difference between "technical economic discussion" and the practical competence of "an administrative system the effects of which depend upon the content of rules and precedents only as they are applied by judges and juries in courts and by lawyers advising their clients."[67] Breyer dismissed the possibility of whether a firm had engaged in short-run profit-maximizing pricing, observing that "[o]ne can foresee conflicting testimony by economic experts, with the eventual determination made, not by economists or accounts, but by a jury."[68] He also noted that "if private plaintiffs are allowed to attack 'above total costs disciplinary price,' we are unlikely to lack for plaintiffs willing to make the effort."[69] Breyer reprised these institutionalist themes in *Town of Concord*, explaining that "we shall take account of the institutional fact that antitrust rules are court-administered rules."[70] As in *Barry Wright*, these

64. *Barry Wright Corp. v. ITT Grinnell Corp.*, 724 F.2d 227 (1983).
65. *Town of Concord v. Boston Edison Co.*, 915 F.2d 17 (1st Cir. 1990).
66. *See Pacific Bell Tel. Co. v. linkLine Comms., Inc.*, 129 S. Ct. 1109, 1121–22 (2009).
67. 724 F.2d at 234.
68. *Id.* at 235.
69. *Id.*
70. 915 F.2d at 22.

institutionalist concerns, raised in the context of a private damages action, justified a constricted liability norm.

These institutionalist thematics played out heavily in private antitrust cases during the period of antitrust contraction beginning in the late 1970s. On the Supreme Court, Breyer has plainly called into question the competence of generalist judges and, in particular, juries in antitrust cases[71] and denounced the pull of treble damages.[72] More generally, the Court embraced many of the themes coming out of the Georgetown study as reasons to constrict liability norms in antitrust cases. In the leading predatory pricing case, for example, the Court explained that "[i]t would be ironic indeed if the standards for predatory pricing liability were so low that antitrust suits themselves became a tool for keeping prices high."[73] Without directly citing the "competitor plaintiff" literature discussed above, the Court clearly tipped its hand, revealing a suspicion that many antitrust cases were driven by competitors perversely eager to secure anticompetitive benefits from a statute designed to enhance competition.

Two of the themes emerging from the Supreme Court decisions were the dangers of "false positives" and the "practical ability of a judicial tribunal" to control anticompetitive conduct.[74] These themes were not necessarily unique to private litigation, but they were doubtlessly accentuated in the private litigation context. Frank Easterbrook's influential article, "The Limits of Antitrust," described a systemic bias toward false positives in private antitrust litigation as victims of Joseph Schumpeter's "gale of creative destruction"—competitors—rushed to court with complaints of their business injuries before economic theory had been able to explain why the defendant's conduct was socially beneficial.[75] Against this backdrop of continual pressure to appease aggrieved competitors and other business interests, generalist judges and, particularly, juries, had few resources at their disposal to create rules that advanced the welfare of consumers.

The retrenchment in antitrust liability norms that began in the late 1970s and has largely carried forward to this day was not solely the product of a backlash against private antitrust litigation, but that backlash was a major

---

71. *See, e.g., Credit Suisse Secs., (USA) LLC v. Billings*, 551 U.S. 264, 127 S. Ct. 2383, 2395 (2007) (observing the risks of inconsistency entailed in entrusting decisional authority to "different nonexpert judges and different nonexpert juries"); *Leegin Creative Leather Prods., Inc. v. PSKS, Inc.*, 551 U.S. 877, 127 S. Ct. 2705, 2730 (2007) (Breyer, J., dissenting) (arguing that "[o]ne cannot fairly expect judges and juries in [resale price maintenance] cases to apply complex economic criteria without making a considerable number of mistakes, which themselves may impose serious costs").

72. *NYNEX Corp. v. Discon, Inc.*, 525 U.S. 128, 137 (1998).

73. *Brooke Group, Inc. v. Brown & Williamson Tobacco Corp.*, 509 U.S. 209, 226–27 (1993).

74. *See, e.g., Verizon Comms. v. Trinko*, 540 U.S. 398, 414–18 (2004).

75. Frank H. Easterbrook, *The Limits of Antitrust*, 63 Tex. L. Rev. 1, 5–6 (1984).

contributing cause.[76] As we will see in the next section, the effects of that retrenchment did not remain confined to private cases.

IV. SPILLOVERS TO PUBLIC ENFORCEMENT

We have previously observed that changes in the incidence of government litigation have effects on private litigation. The converse is also true. Changes in the incidence of private litigation can have very significant effects on the incidence and strength of government litigation. The sharply pro-defendant turn in liability norms that began in the late 1970s has had profound effects on the government's enforcement powers.

Private antitrust lawsuits influence the government's enforcement powers primarily by providing occasions for the creation of constricted liability norms that the courts then tend to apply without modification to government enforcement actions, even though many of the concerns that led to the contraction of liability norms in the private cases do not apply to government actions. Given that there are ten or more private cases for every public case, liability norms are being created far more often in private cases than in government cases. As of this writing, it has been over a decade since a government antitrust case has reached the Supreme Court. The FTC last reached the court (in its antitrust capacity) in 1999,[77] and the Antitrust Division last reached the Court on an antitrust issue a quarter of a century ago.[78] To be sure, both agencies routinely submit amicus curiae briefs expressing their views on the merits or publish reports or guidelines on antitrust enforcement, but that makes them sideline participants in the development of liability rules, not the drivers and shapers of antitrust theory.[79]

As the courts began to react to perceived abuses in private litigation by sharply contracting liability norms, the spillover effects on public litigation were not unavoidable. The courts could have ruled that different liability norms applied in

---

76. The diminution in the number of private antitrust cases does not necessarily mean that total number of litigated disputes went down. In light of the backlash to private antitrust cases, some plaintiffs have shifted to other legal theories, such as state dealer protection statutes, franchise laws, or tort or contract theories.

77. *California Dental Ass'n v. FTC*, 526 U.S. 756 (1999).

78. *Southern Motor Carriers Rate Conf., Inc. v. U.S.*, 471 U.S. 48 (1985). The Justice Department had a Sherman Act case go to the Supreme Court on criminal procedure issues in 1987. *U.S. v. John Doe, Inc. I.*, 481 U.S. 102 (1987).

79. This is not to say that the agencies have no influence over the shaping of antitrust norms when they act outside the courtroom, for example by promulgating guidelines or position papers or issuing business review letters. *See* Spencer Weber Waller, *Prosecution by Regulation: The Changing Nature of Antitrust Enforcement*, 77 ORE. L. REV. 1383 (1998) (describing the non-litigation influence of the antitrust agencies in the formation of antitrust norms).

government actions. Indeed, some of the Harvard School judges that contributed to the contraction of antitrust liability norms in private cases have made exactly such an argument. In a recent private action in which the Supreme Court unanimously rejected "price-squeeze" liability, Justice Breyer's concurring opinion, joined by the Court's three more liberal Justices, argued that although the private claim was properly rejected, "[a] 'price-squeeze' claim finds its natural home in a Sherman Act § 2 claim where *the Government* as plaintiff seeks to show that a defendant's monopoly power rests, not upon 'skill, foresight and industry,' but upon exclusionary conduct."[80] Breyer does not explain why it should matter to the viability of a price-squeeze claim that the government, rather than a private party, is the plaintiff. But Breyer's clear aim was to rehabilitate the Justice Department's successful price-squeeze claim against *Alcoa* in the 1940s,[81] snubbed by the Chicago School majority as overridden by subsequent "developments in economic theory and antitrust jurisprudence."[82] The Harvard School Justices were implicitly arguing that their willingness to cut back on private antitrust cases did not extend to government enforcement actions in a different institutional context.

The difficulty for the Harvard School position, at least in Justice Department cases, is that the Justice Department and private plaintiffs enforce the same statute: the Sherman Act. If the courts enforce the open-textured Sherman Act not to prohibit prize squeezes in a private case, it is awkward to explain how the same statutory language does prohibit them in a government case. That makes the meaning of the statute turn on the identity of the plaintiff, which seems inconsistent with the rule of law.

In fact, the courts have not applied a different liability norm to Justice Department enforcement actions. Take, for example, predatory pricing law. During the 1980s and '90s, in a series of private cases, the federal courts sharply constricted the right of action for predatory pricing.[83] As we have seen, the courts justified restrictive predation liability rules by claiming that opportunistic private plaintiffs could chill rivals' aggressive pricing by bringing predatory pricing lawsuits for treble damages.[84] During the years that the courts were developing these restrictive liability norms, neither the FTC nor the Department of Justice brought any predatory pricing lawsuits. The liability rules were created with the institutional limitations of private litigation in mind. Then, in 1999, the Justice Department brought its first predatory pricing lawsuit in decades, against

---

80. 129 S. Ct. at 1124 (citing *United States v. Aluminum Co. of America*, 148 F.2d 416, 430 (2d Cir. 1945) (Alcoa)) (emphasis added).

81. *U.S. v. Aluminum Co. of America*, 148 F.2d 416 (2d Cir. 1945).

82. 129 S. Ct. at 1120.

83. *See generally* Daniel A. Crane, *The Paradox of Predatory Pricing*, 91 CORNELL L. REV. 1, 3 (2005).

84. *Id.*

American Airlines.[85] The government lost the case on summary judgment in the district court and then again in Tenth Circuit, largely because the courts applied off-the-rack predatory pricing liability rules designed to avoid abusive private litigation.[86] If the law of predatory pricing had developed with the institutional parameters of public enforcement in mind, it is doubtful that the resulting liability rules would have been so deferential to pricing decisions by dominant firms.[87]

The Justice Department may not be able to avoid these spillover effects of private litigation, but the FTC has one significant advantage here: It does *not* enforce the same statute as the Justice Department and private litigants. The FTC enforces Section 5 of the FTC Act, which prohibits "unfair methods of competition. . . and unfair or deceptive [trade] practices."[88] The Commission's powers under Section 5 are at least coextensive with the substantive reach of the Sherman Act—in other words, that anything that is illegal under the Sherman Act is also illegal under the FTC Act.[89] But the Supreme Court has also held that the FTC may go further than the Sherman Act and "stop in their incipiency acts and practices which, when full blown, would violate those Acts."[90] Thus, "the standard of unfairness under the FTC Act. . . encompass[es] not only practices that violate the Sherman Act and the other antitrust laws. . . but also practices that the Commission determines are against public policy for other reasons."[91]

This suggests that the private litigation should not have the same spillover effects on FTC cases as it has on Justice Department cases. But it has. Even though the FTC is theoretically unconstrained by the meaning of the Sherman Act, since at least the 1980s, the courts have tended to superimpose their prior interpretations of the Sherman Act onto the FTC Act. In three high-profile cases in the early 1980s—*Official Airlines*,[92] *Boise Cascade*,[93] and *Ethyl*,[94] the Commission experienced embarrassing setbacks as the courts of appeal rejected the Commission's efforts to extend Section 5 beyond the Sherman Act.

---

85. *U.S. v. AMR Corp.*, 335 F.3d 1109 (10th Cir. 2003).

86. For example, the Tenth Circuit relied on earlier precedent from predatory pricing cases that justified underinclusive liability norms because of the high costs of false positives. 335 F.3d at 1114. Such concerns are far greater in private actions for treble damages than in injunctive actions by the government seeking to interdict future misbehavior.

87. For a thoughtful postmortem on the case, *see* Gregory J. Werden, *The American Airlines Decision: Not With a Bang But a Whimper*, 18 Fall ANTITRUST 32 (2003).

88. 15 U.S.C. § 45.

89. *FTC v. Cement Inst.*, 333 U.S. 683, 694 (1948).

90. *FTC v. Brown Shoe Co.*, 348 U.S. 316, 322 (1966).

91. *FTC v. Indiana Federation of Dentists*, 476 U.S. 447, 454 (1986).

92. *Official Airlnes Guides, Inc. v FTC*, 630 F.2d 920 (2d Cir. 1980).

93. *Boise Cascade Corp. v. FTC*, 637 F.2d 573 (9th Cir. 1980).

94. *E.I. du Pont de Nemours & Co. v. FTC*, 729 F.2d 128 (2d Cir. 1984).

After experiencing these setbacks, the FTC fell into a pattern of asserting that it wanted to be treated no differently from any other litigant, whether the Justice Department or a private litigant. In its filings, the Commission would state, or implicitly assume, that the substantive standards for illegality under Section 5 of the FTC Act were "co-extensive with the Sherman Act."[95] Predictably, the courts then applied the Sherman Act norms wholesale to the Commission.

The upshot was that, like the Justice Department, the FTC assumed liability norms that had already been, and were continuing to be, constricted at least in part because of institutionalist concerns that should not have applied to public enforcers. It seems likely that some of the FTC's high-profile defeats in court in the last several decades have owed in large measure to the baggage of private litigation stowed in Sherman Act liability norms.

Take, for example, the Commission's disappointing loss in *Rambus*.[96] Rambus was a technology company that had patents on various computer memory functions. During the 1990s, Rambus participated in the Joint Electron Device Engineering Council (JEDEC), which was then in the process of formulating new computer memory standards.[97] At some point before the finalization of the new standards, Rambus withdrew from JEDEC. According to the FTC's subsequent administrative complaint, Rambus failed to disclose that it had various patents or patent applications on technologies that would be essential to practicing the new standard. After the standard's adoption, Rambus began to demand royalties from firms practicing the standard.

The FTC decided that Rambus violated Section 2 of the Sherman Act (as enforced through Section 5 of the FTC Act) by deceiving JEDEC about its patents and patent applications. The FTC explicitly stated that it was relying on general Sherman Act, Section 2 law in bringing its challenge to Rambus's comment.[98] The D.C. Circuit reversed the Commission's decision, finding that the Commission had not shown that any deception or fraud had impaired the competitive function of the market. In support of this holding, the court relied heavily on antitrust doctrines created in private cases, particularly the Supreme Court's decision in *NYNEX*.[99] In *NYNEX*, Justice Breyer's opinion rejecting fraud on rate regulators as a ground for antitrust liability worried that applying antitrust rules to "regulatory fraud. . . would transform cases involving business behavior that is improper for various reasons, say, cases involving nepotism or personal pique,

95. *See, e.g., In re Schering-Plough Corp.,* Opinion of the Commission at 83 n. 107, Docket No. 9297 (FTC, Dec. 18, 2003), *available at* http://www.ftc.gov/os/adjpro/d9297/index.shtm.

96. *Rambus, Inc. v. FTC*, 522 F.3d 456 (D.C. Cir. 2008).

97. *Id.* at 458–60.

98. 522 F.3d at 462.

99. *NYNEX Corp. v. Discon, Inc.*, 525 U.S. 128, 137 (1998).

into treble-damages antitrust cases."[100] Obviously, the concern over abusive treble-damages lawsuits by frustrated competitors had nothing to do with the FTC's case in *Rambus*, but since the FTC had hitched its wagon to the Sherman Act, it also had to take this act with all of its institutionalist baggage.

We should be careful not to overstate the claim that institutionalist concerns about private litigation are the reason for the relative frailty of public antitrust enforcement today. Certainly, there are many other explanations, including the Chicago School's substantive views that many previously condemned forms of business behavior are pro-competitive and therefore should be lawful, no matter who their challenger. Still, there is little doubt that the post-war explosion of private antitrust litigation in the United States and the backlash that it engendered has, to some degree, stymied the effectiveness of public enforcement.

The private litigation model—and its spillover effects on public enforcement—are hardly unique to antitrust enforcement. As a general matter, the United States tends to rely considerably more on private litigation than do economically comparable countries in Europe, which achieve many similar functions using bureaucratic or administrative models.[101] Private enforcement survived the backlash in the 1970s–1990s and appears to be once more in a growth trend. It is with us to stay. In future chapters, we shall consider potential reforms to separate public and private enforcement norms and other reforms that could make private enforcement more successful within its own sphere at achieving consumer welfare objectives.

---

100. 525 U.S. at 136–37.

101. *See generally* Robert A. Kagan, Adversarial Legalism: The American Way of Life (2001); Thomas F. Burke, Lawyers, Lawsuits, and Legal Rights: The Battle Over Litigation in American Society (2002).

4. SHIFTING TOWARD TECHNOCRACY

U.S. antitrust institutions were born during the Progressive Era, but they were not strongly imprinted with that era's idealistic markers. As we saw in Chapters 1 and 2, despite serious efforts to give the FTC a technocratic, regulatory bent, the Commission ultimately assumed a conventional law enforcement character. The legislative interventions of 1890 and 1914 cast antitrust as a crime and tort to be addressed by generalist prosecutors, judges, juries, private plaintiffs, and commissioners closely accountable to appellate judges. In its initial stages, then, antitrust's institutional design owed a great deal more to Populism than to Progressivism.

Over time, however, antitrust began to lose its hold on the popular imagination and, consequently, much of its early populist orientation. During antitrust's formative era, from the passage of the Sherman Act until the beginning of World War I, antitrust ideology played out dramatically on the public stage. Presidents trumpeted its virtues, public intellectuals debated its merits, and the political elite recognized its power in mobilizing support. But, little by little, antitrust began to go underground. It did not vanish in importance, but it largely vanished from the public eye.

This chapter describes antitrust's twentieth-century shift toward "technocracy." As we shall see, the shift was dramatic but only partial. Antitrust disappeared from the public imagination and lost the interest of the political elite. Its day-to-day implementation became the province of bureaucrats and private sector specialists, working largely behind closed doors and away from the newspapers and cameras. Yet, there were relatively few formal changes to antitrust's institutional infrastructure. Antitrust retained its populist institutions, even while shifting at an ideological level toward technocracy. This shift has important implications for the functioning of antitrust's institutions and the possible direction of future reforms.

I. AN OVERVIEW OF THE TECHNOCRATIC SHIFT

In its original sense, technocracy described a school of thought that grew out of Progressive ideology and held sway as a political movement from the beginning of the twentieth century until the later portion of the New Deal and the beginning of World War II.[1] The technocrats believed that "the newly emerging industrial

1. *See generally* William E. Akin, Technocracy and the American Dream: The Technocrat Movement, 1900–1941 1–26 (1977 (summarizing the rise and fall of the technocratic movement).

state and the corporate organization of production could be directed by man's rationality to bring about a social reformation where poverty, injustice, superstition, and class conflict would be abolished."[2] Achieving this rationalization of the economic order "required the separation of politics from administration."[3] Regulation of industry required the objective and detached rule of industrial and scientific experts and problem solvers.

The original technocrats were "progressive" or "leftist" in the sense that they viewed private ordering of markets as grossly inefficient, opposed the price-wage system that underlay the capitalist order, and favored strong centralization of regulatory power in the government.[4] Yet, as the American technocratic movement first splintered and then dissolved as an organized political movement (having exercised little direct effect on its most likely constituency—the New Deal administration of Franklin Roosevelt),[5] technocratic ideas were absorbed by the political mainstream. Over time, "technocracy" became associated not so much with *how much* governmental regulation there should be but *with whom* governmental powers should lie. In its contemporary sense, technocracy refers to the insulation of a governmental function from popular political pressures and its administration by experts rather than generalists. In this sense, technocracy does not have to imply a greater degree of governmental intervention in markets than there would be under technocracy's opposite: populism. It is possible that the technocrats who have been delegated a particular government function—environmental protection, compensating for personal injuries, determining product safety, policing securities markets, etc.—will decide that it is best to maintain a laissez faire approach. Thus, for example, calls for a technocratic approach to risk regulation have tended to have conservative political implications insofar they have suggested that the general public often overreacts to risks, thus prompting excessive levels of risk regulation.[6]

In the years following its formative era, antitrust underwent a technocratic shift in the more general sense of the word. The antitrust enterprise became more technocratic in the sense that antitrust decision making became increasingly insulated from popular political pressures and delegated to industrial policy specialists and problem solvers. Although the original technocrats favored displacing private market ordering with centralized governmental administration, the technocratic shift in antitrust has tended to correlate with a trend in just the opposite direction—toward greater faith in private market ordering and deregulation and

2. *Id.* at 1.

3. *Id.*

4. *Id.* at x.

5. *Id.*

6. Samuel R. Bagenstos, *The Americans With Disabilities Act as Risk Regulation*, 101 Colum. L. Rev. 1479, 1482 (2001).

a rejection of central planning as an administrative modality.[7] Antitrust's modern technocrats see their task largely as enforcing a set of legal-industrial norms predicated on a competitive-market capitalist system.

The technocratic shift began almost immediately after the passage of the FTC and Clayton Acts. Historian Martin Sklar finds that the passage of the 1914 statutes "took the trust question and the central bank question 'out of politics'—by beginning the settling down in law. . . of rudimentary adjustments to, and regulation of, the domestic and international requirements of corporate capitalism."[8] But while antitrust may have shifted from political frenzy to incremental administration after 1914, it remained far from dead as a political issue. In 1964, a time at which, from the contemporary perspective, antitrust appears to have been in political bloom, the historian Richard Hofstadter described a much more recent technocratic shift in antitrust enforcement. Hofstadter contended that the "antitrust movement is one of the faded passions of American reform,"[9] but that the passion faded only within the past twenty years. According to Hofstadter, the public had come to peace with large corporations as a result of the post-World War II economic boom, and big business was no longer routinely vilified in American political pageantry.[10] But though invisible to the public, antitrust remained a potent legal control on the behavior of dominant firms: "Antitrust has become almost exclusively the concern of small groups of legal and economic specialists, who carry on their work without widespread public interest or support."[11] Hofstadter found that antitrust had "cease[ed] to be largely an ideology and [had become] largely a technique" administered by "a small group of influential and deeply concerned specialists" in "differentiated, specialized, and bureaucratized" administrative institutions.[12]

Hofstadter traced the beginnings of the technocratic model to the reinvigoration of the Antitrust Division under Thurman Arnold in the late New Deal.[13] Ironically, before his appointment to the Antitrust Division, Arnold had belittled antitrust enforcement as political theater—as hyper-democratic absurdity.[14]

---

7. As explained below, the rejection of centralized economic administration has not entailed abandonment of antitrust enforcement.

8. Martin J. Sklar, The Corporate Reconstruction of American Capitalism, 1890–1916: The Market, the Law, and Politics 425 (1988).

9. Richard Hofstadter, *What Happened to the Antitrust Movement?*, *in* The Paranoid Style in American Politics and Other Essays 188 (1966).

10. *Id.* at 218–24.

11. *Id.* at 194.

12. *Id.* at 235.

13. Hofstadter, *supra* n. 9 at 230. Arnold took over the reigns of the Antitrust Division from Robert Jackson on March 7, 1938.

14. Thurman W. Arnold, The Folklore of Capitalism (1937). *See generally* Spencer Weber Waller, Thurman Arnold: A Biography 69 (2005) (noting that "Arnold [] ridiculed the antitrust laws as empty symbolic vehicles designed to assuage popular fears of

Nonetheless, it was Arnold who transformed the Antitrust Division into a professional, active, and, in Hofstadter's view, quietly technocratic and successful enterprise.[15]

Hofstadter made these observations over forty years ago, before the Hart-Scott-Rodino Antitrust Improvements Act turned merger control into an almost purely administrative process (an issue we will examine in Chapter 5),[16] before the neoclassical assumptions of the Chicago School revolutionized antitrust law and discredited many of the interventionist views that prevailed in the 1950s and'60s,[17] and before the Reagan Revolution completed the large corporation's transition from "trust" to "trusted." With hindsight, it is clear that Hofstadter made his observations while the technocratic model was ascendant but nascent.

Much has changed in the antitrust world since the 1960s, and not all of these changes point toward a continuing technocratic shift. Antitrust has become less politically visible than it was when Hofstadter wrote *What Happened to the Antitrust Movement?* but that does not necessarily mean that antitrust has become ever more the province of faceless technocrats. It could be that antitrust has disappeared politically because it is no longer valued or practiced. In order to conclude that antitrust has shifted toward technocracy, it is necessary to establish that antitrust has lost its political salience even while remaining active in society—questions to which we now turn.

II. THE DECLINING POLITICAL SALIENCE OF ANTITRUST

A. Presidential Speeches and Party Platforms

It is commonly held that antitrust has lost the political grandeur of its founding era.[18] Antitrust was highly visible and publicly debated from the passage of the

---

bigness and power without actually constraining the behavior of the modern business corporation.").

15. Hofstadter, supra n. 9 at 230–32. *See generally* Spencer Weber Waller, *The Antitrust Legacy of Thurman Arnold*, 78 St. John's L. Rev. 569 (2004). For a contrary view on the political nature of some of Arnold's enforcement actions, *see* Daniel A. Crane, *The Story of United States v. Socony-Vacuum: Antitrust and Hot Oil in the Two New Deals, in* Antitrust Stories (Eleanor M. Fox & Daniel A. Crane eds., 2007).

16. *See* Daniel A. Crane, *Antitrust Antifederalism*, 91 Cal. L. Rev. 1, 51–57 (2007) (describing effects of Hart-Scott-Rodino); E. Thomas Sullivan, *The Antitrust Division as Regulatory Agency: An Enforcement Policy in Transition*, 64 Wash. U. L. Q. 997, 1024–42 (1986) (describing shift toward regulatory model of merger review following adoption of Department of Justice merger guidelines in 1968 and Hart-Scott in 1976).

17. *See* Richard A. Posner, *The Chicago School of Antitrust Analysis*, 127 U. Pa. L. Rev. 925, 925–28 (1979) (describing pre-Chicago interventionist views).

18. Jonathan B. Baker, *Competition Policy as a Political Bargain*, 73 Antitrust L.J. 483 (2006).

Sherman Act in 1890 to the passage of the Federal Trade Commission and Clayton Acts in 1914.[19] But when, after that, did it lose its political luster? In order to address this issue concretely rather than impressionistically, I conducted a systematic search of references to antitrust in two bellwethers of political salience: presidential speeches and party platforms.[20] Presidents and parties generally speak about topics that they think resonate with the public, so the level of references to antitrust in presidential speeches and party platform provides a reasonably good proxy for antitrust's national political salience.

A search of the electronic database of presidential speeches maintained by the University of California at Santa Barbara reveals that antitrust has faded from presidential discourse in recent times, but that it maintained a substantial presence well after Hofstadter made his observations in 1964. The last president to invoke antitrust in an inaugural address was William Howard Taft, author of the landmark *Addyston Pipe*[21] decision, while a judge on the Sixth Circuit and of an influential book about antitrust.[22] Not surprisingly, Presidents Roosevelt, Taft, and Wilson made frequent references to antitrust during the period of controversy over the direction of antitrust law that was resolved in the Federal Trade Commission and Clayton Acts in 1914.[23] But antitrust continued to make regular appearances in State of Union addresses, appearing twenty times from the Wilson administration through the end of the Carter administration and appearing for the last time in 1979, when Jimmy Carter vowed to "fight inflation by

---

19. *See generally* SKLAR, *supra* n. 8 (providing history of relevant period).

20. Previous studies have concluded that Congress exercises comparatively little control over the antitrust agencies. *See* Evan J. Ringquist, Jeff Worsham & Marc Allen Eisner, *Salience, Complexity, and the Legislative Direction of Regulatory Bureaucracies*, 13 J. PUB. ADMIN. RES. & THEORY 141 (2003) (characterizing antitrust enforcement as a low salience and high complexity enterprise over which Congress exercises comparatively little oversight); M. Albert Vachris, *Federal Antitrust Enforcement: A Principal-Agent Perspective*, 88 PUB. Choice 223, 236 (1996) (finding that "while congressional oversight does play a role in the determination of bureaucratic behavior, the Congress does not, in effect, dominate the [antitrust] bureaucracy"). I chose to focus on presidential rhetoric and control and political party platforms because of their reflection of national political perspectives and their trendability.

21. *United States v. Addyston Pipe & Steel Co.*, 85 F. 271 (6th Cir. 1898) *aff'd*, 175 U.S. 211 (1899).

22. WILLIAM HOWARD TAFT, THE ANTI-TRUST ACT AND THE SUPREME COURT 47 (1914). Taft discussed antitrust in his March 4, 1909 Inaugural Address. *See* http://www.presidency.ucsb.edu/ws/index.php. Taft declared that he hoped "to be able to submit at the first regular session of the incoming Congress, in December next, definite suggestions in respect to the needed amendments to the antitrust and the interstate commerce law and the changes required in the executive departments concerned in their enforcement."

23. *See generally* SKLAR, *supra* n. 8.

improvements and better enforcement of our antitrust laws."[24] Following Carter, the word "antitrust" is relegated to more specialized speeches and announcements or off-the-cuff references or jokes.[25]Figure 4.1 shows the number of antitrust references in major political speeches, including all messages to Congress (including State of the Union addresses); speeches on proposed or signed legislation; convention acceptance speeches; and inaugural addresses, by presidential term.[26] The results show a period of intense antitrust references during the

---

24. The State of the Union Address Delivered Before a Joint Session of the Congress (Jan. 23, 1979), http://www.presidency.ucsb.edu/ws/index.php. President Carter said, "We must also fight inflation by improvements and better enforcement of our antitrust laws and by reducing government obstacles to competition in the private sector." Between Taft and Carter's last mention in 1979, antitrust appeared in nineteen State of the Union addresses: Wilson (1913); Hoover (1930, 1931,1932); Roosevelt (1934, 1937, 1938, 1939, 1944, 1945); Truman (1947, 1948, 1949, 1950, 1953); Eisenhower (1956); Kennedy (1962); Ford (1976); Carter (1978). http://www.presidency.ucsb.edu/ws/index.php. Carter's predecessors sounded similar antitrust themes. *See, e.g.*, Gerald R. Ford, Address Before a Joint Session of the Congress Reporting on the State of the Union (Jan. 18, 1976), http://www.presidency.ucsb.edu/ws/index.php?pid=5677&st=&st1= ("[T]o foster competition and to bring prices down for the consumer. . . [t]his administration. . . will strictly enforce the Federal antitrust laws. . . ."); John F. Kennedy, Annual Message to the Congress on the State of the Union (Jan. 11, 1962), http://www.presidency.ucsb.edu/ws/index.php?pid=9082&st=&st1= ("This administration has helped keep our economy competitive by widening the access of small business to credit and Government contracts, and by stepping up the drive against monopoly, price-fixing, and racketeering."); Dwight D. Eisenhower, Annual Message to the Congress on the State of the Union (Jan. 12, 1961), http://www.presidency.ucsb.edu/ws/index.php?pid=12074&st=&st1= ("A major factor in strengthening our competitive enterprise system, and promoting economic growth, has been the vigorous enforcement of antitrust laws over the last eight years and a continuing effort to reduce artificial restraints on competition and trade and enhance our economic liberties."); Harry S. Truman, Annual Message to the Congress on the State of the Union (Jan. 6, 1947), http://www.presidency.ucsb.edu/ws/index.php?pid=12762&st=&st1= ("We now find that to a greater extent than ever before, whole industries are dominated by one or a few large organizations which can restrict production in the interest of higher profits and thus reduce employment and purchasing power. In an effort to assure full opportunity and free competition to business we will vigorously enforce the anti-trust laws.").

25. For example, President Clinton mentioned antitrust in speeches or remarks on forty-six occasions, but an illustrative instance is his 1996 remarks welcoming the World Series champion Atlanta Braves, where he remarks: "Well, the Braves proved that last year. You had great hitting, great fielding, and great pitching. Tom Glavine and Greg Maddux have won every Cy Young Award for the past 5 years. You may have an antitrust suit on your hands, even with baseball's exemption. [Laughter]." Remarks Welcoming the World Series Champion Atlanta Braves (Feb. 26, 1996), http://www.presidency.ucsb.edu/ws/index.php?pid=52463&st=atlanta+braves&st1. In his first six years in office, George W. Bush mentioned antitrust in passing only three or four times.

26. The findings discussed here are based on a search of the electronic archives of the parties' platforms using the search terms "antitrust," "anti-trust," "trusts," and "monop."

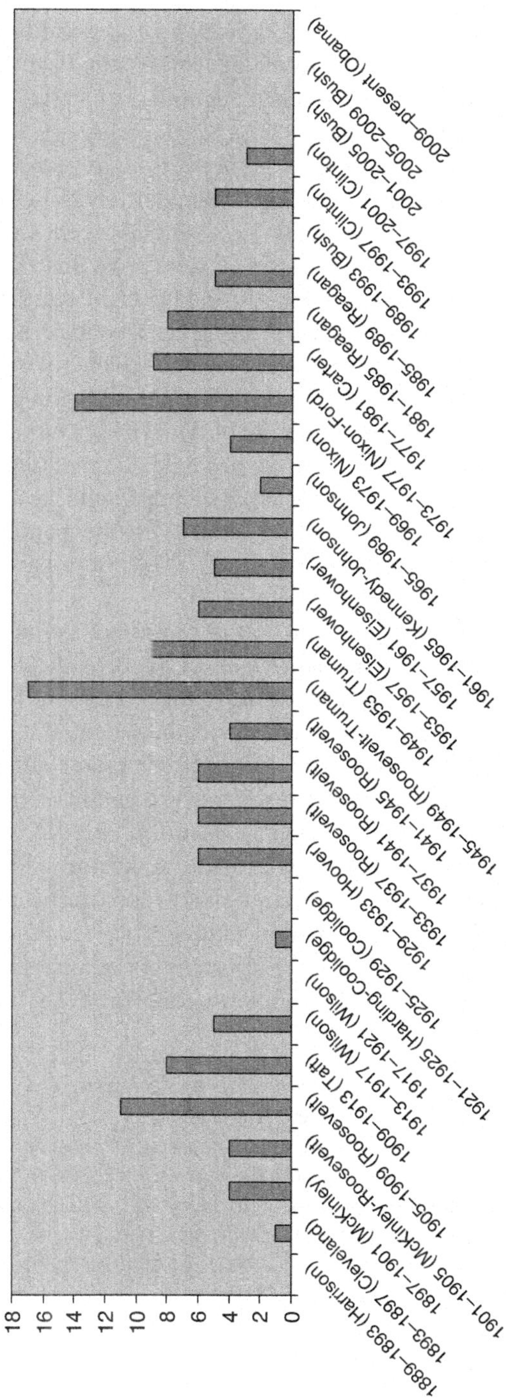

FIGURE 4.1 REFERENCES TO ANTITRUST IN MAJOR PRESIDENTIAL SPEECHES

Roosevelt and Taft terms and then in Woodrow Wilson's first term, followed by a drought during World War I and the early Depression, then a period a reinvigoration of references to antitrust in major speeches that continued with few lapses until George H. Bush's presidency beginning in 1989. George Herbert Walker Bush did not refer to antitrust in a single major speech. Bill Clinton made eight references in "major speeches" over his eight years, but all of them were in speeches on legislation, including some relatively minor acts, and none was made in a major televised forum like a convention acceptance speech, inaugural address, or State of the Union address.[27] George W. Bush did not mention antitrust in a major speech a single time during his eight years in office. There were brief signs that antitrust might reemerge as a political issue during the 2008 presidential campaign, when Barack Obama devoted portions of several speeches to antitrust enforcement, generally lamenting the neglect of enforcement during the Bush administration.[28] As of this writing, however, well over a year into his presidency, President Obama has made no mention of antitrust in a major speech. Since the Carter administration, presidents have stopped invoking antitrust in high-profile speeches intended for the population at large. Presidential antitrust references are statistically a story of peaks and valleys, but the latest valley is becoming a plain.

Antitrust has similarly dropped out of the two major political parties' quadrennial party platforms. From the passage of the Sherman Act in 1890 until the last quarter of the twentieth century, antitrust was a staple of the parties' platforms. The Democratic Party vowed vigorous enforcement of the antitrust laws and/or legislative reform—often with detailed policy prescriptions—in every platform from 1892 to 1988. Similarly, with the exception of the Hoover platforms in 1928 and 1932 and the Coolidge platform in 1924, the Republican Party platforms between 1892 and 1980 made mandatory (albeit sometimes unenthusiastic) reference to the importance of antitrust enforcement.

This has changed in the last quarter-century. The last time that antitrust was addressed in either of the parties' platforms was in a passing reference in the health-care plank of the 1996 Republican platform.[29] The last substantive

---

The archives searched were those maintained by the University of California at Santa Barbara. *See* http://www.presidency.ucsb.edu/ws/index.

27. Clinton's remarks concerned the National Cooperative Production Amendments of 1993, the International Antitrust Enforcement Assistance Act of 1994, the ICC Termination Act, the 1996 Telecommunications Act, the Curt Flood Act of 1998, and the Year 2000 Readiness Act. *See* http://www.presidency.ucsb.edu/ws/index.

28. Jeff Mason, *Obama Eyes Media with Promise of Antitrust Push*, Reuters (May 18, 2008) (reporting that presidential candidate Obama stated on the campaign trail: "We're going to have an antitrust division in the Justice Department that actually believes in antitrust law. We haven't had that for the last seven, eight years.").

29. Consistent with the recent Republican party's general antipathy to antitrust enforcement, the platform promised to "change anti-trust laws to let health care providers

discussion of antitrust in the Republican Party's platform was in 1976.[30] The last significant mention of antitrust in the Democratic Party's platform was in Walter Mondale's 1984 platform, which "complained that '[t]he FTC has run roughshod over the nation's antitrust laws, allowing 9 of the 10 largest mergers in history to occur,' called for 'vigorous enforcement of our antitrust laws,' and pledged that 'no Democratic Administration will forget the use of old fashioned antitrust policy to keep markets competitive—and prices down.'"[31] Despite this pledge, Michael Dukakis's 1988 platform made only two curt references to antitrust,[32] and it dropped out completely of the 1992, 1996, 2000, 2004, and 2008 Democratic platforms. Similarly, the 2000, 2004, and 2008 Republican platforms were silent on antitrust and, as noted, antitrust was effectively dropped as an issue after the 1976 platform.

One could ascribe the drastic cutback in antitrust references to various factors. Perhaps this dearth of antitrust references merely coincides with a quarter-century in which conservative, pro-business Republicans have held the White House for all but Bill Clinton's two terms and (thus far) the beginning of Barack Obama's presidency. But this does not explain the minimization of antitrust in the Dukakis platform and its complete absence from the Clinton, Gore, Kerry, and Obama platforms. Surely, if antitrust were politically salient, the Democrats would have made some mention of it.

Another possibility is that there simply was not much notable happening in the antitrust world during the last quarter-century. But this ignores the shadow of the *Microsoft* case, which dominated headlines during the late 1990s.[33] *Microsoft* is a good example of the political elite's withdrawal from antitrust discourse, precisely because it was a case involving much potential political intrigue. Politicians from the State of Washington (where Microsoft is headquartered) lobbied behind the scenes for Microsoft while politicians from Utah

---

cooperate in holding down charges." http://www.presidency.ucsb.edu/ws/index.php?pid=25848. A similar promise appeared in the 1992 platform ("modify outdated antitrust rules that prohibit hospitals from merging their resources to provide improved, cost-effective health care"). http://www.presidency.ucsb.edu/ws/index.php?pid=25847.

30. "The Republican Party believes in and endorses the concept that the American economy is traditionally dependent upon fair competition in the marketplace. To assure fair competition, antitrust laws must treat all segments of the economy equally." http://www.presidency.ucsb.edu/ws/index.php?pid=25843.

31. *See* http://www.presidency.ucsb.edu/ws/index.php?pid=29608.

32. The 1988 platform pledged to prevent "monopolistic mergers" and to "reinvigorate" the antitrust laws. http://www.presidency.ucsb.edu/ws/index.php?pid=29609.

33. *See* Edward Cavanagh, *Antitrust Remedies Revisited*, 84 Or. L. Rev. 147, 192 (2005) ("Media coverage of the [Microsoft] trial was unprecedented in scope, and as the Microsoft story migrated from the business pages to the front pages of daily newspapers and to lead story on the evening news, even antitrust junkies began to feel like overdose victims.").

(where Microsoft's rival Novell is located) lobbied against Microsoft.[34] In the meantime, Microsoft lavished its ample resources to make friends and influence people.[35] None of this is necessarily inconsistent with the technocratic shift story. Politicians naturally rise to defend their constituents' interests, and large corporate interests naturally try to exploit politics for their advantage. What is striking about *Microsoft* is that neither political party saw any gain from making the case *a political issue*. Indeed, as discussed below, President Clinton repeatedly disclaimed any participation in the case. The public had not necessarily lost interest in antitrust; it had simply ceased to view antitrust as a primarily political enterprise, and the political parties saw no gain from attempting to exploit it as one.[36]

B. Presidential Involvement in Antitrust Cases

A second way of studying antitrust's political salience is to examine the degree to which presidents publicly involve themselves in the administration of antitrust lawsuits brought by the Justice Department. A high degree of presidential superintendence of antitrust cases is inconsistent with the technocratic model of antitrust, which is premised on administration by detached, objective experts. Of course, presidents do not have the time to supervise the work of the Justice Department in the many antitrust matters with which the division is involved, so the relevant comparison should be of significant, nationally reported matters involving critical industries.

The *Standard Oil*, *AT&T*, and *Microsoft* cases provide useful reference points. All three were originally initiated by the Department of Justice and involved nationally important industries with defendants who produced products purchased by millions of end users. Thus, all three cases were potentially politically salient. In each case, the government sought major structural remedies—the breakup of the companies. The cases also coincide with three phases in antitrust's developmental history. The *Standard Oil* case was brought during the antitrust's formative era when antitrust was a highly salient and politically visible issue. The *AT&T* case was brought by a Republican administration during a period when a structuralist school of thought that generally supported increased

---

34. *See* Fred S. McChesney, *Economics Versus Politics in Antitrust*, 23 Harv. J.L. & Pub. Pol'y 133, 134 (1999) (describing political efforts made to influence Microsoft litigation).

35. *Id.*

36. To describe antitrust as an increasingly non-political enterprise is not to deny that even technocratic forms of antitrust administration are "political" in some sense of the word. *See* Richard O. Lempert, *Civil Juries and Complex Cases: Let's Not Rush to Judgment*, 80 Mich. L. Rev. 68, 84 (1981) ("[C]omplex cases—such as large-scale antitrust litigation—are some of the most 'political' cases that the system hears. Vast sums of money are involved, and the structure of the nation's largest companies may be at issue."). But antitrust is increasingly "nonpolitical" in the sense that it has ceased being subjects of partisan political discourse or control by the democratically elected branches.

antitrust intervention was dominant, but the Chicago School's more laissez faire perspective was ascendant.[37] The *Microsoft* case[38] was brought by the first Democratic administration after the Chicago School had become the dominant paradigm for antitrust analysis.

Theodore Roosevelt was significantly involved in the decision to bring the *Standard Oil* case and made several major public addresses on the issue, including a prelitigation May 4, 1906, Special Message to Congress that detailed findings of the Bureau of Corporations on Standard's anticompetitive practices.[39] After detailing Rockefeller's transgressions, Roosevelt concluded: "The Standard Oil Company has, largely by unfair or unlawful methods, crushed out home competition."[40] Roosevelt made several other references to the Standard Oil litigation in addresses to Congress.[41] The Democrats recognized Roosevelt's importance to the administration of the Standard Oil litigation, including in their 1912 platform a paragraph "condemn[ing] the action of the Republican administration in compromising with the Standard Oil Company and the tobacco trust

37. Posner, *The Chicago School*, *supra* n. 17 at 926–33.

38. The *Microsoft* case discussed here is the Justice Department action brought in 1998. The origins of the case date back to an earlier FTC investigation of Microsoft during the first Bush administration and a 1995 consent decree during Bill Clinton's first term. William E. Kovacic, *The Modern Evolution of U.S. Competition Policy Enforcement Norms*, 71 ANTITRUST L.J. 377, 453 n.275 (2003).

39. http://www.presidency.ucsb.edu/ws/index.php?pid=69667&st=standard+oil&st1=. Roosevelt made additional public speeches singling out Standard Oil as "the most dangerous members of the criminal class—the criminals of great wealth." EDMUND MORRIS, THEODORE REX 507 (2001). Although Roosevelt strongly approved of the government's action against Standard Oil, after he left office, he wrote privately that he disfavored the dissolution remedy sought by the government and eventually affirmed by the Supreme Court. Aug. 11, 1911 Letter From Theodore Roosevelt to Arthur B. Farquhar, reprinted in THEODORE ROOSEVELT: LETTERS AND SPEECHES 652 (Louis Auchincloss ed.,1951) ("I do not myself see what good can come from dissolving the Standard Oil Company into forty separate companies, all of which will still remain really under the same control. What we should have is a much stricter governmental supervision of these great companies, but accompanying this supervision should be a recognition of the fact that great combinations have come to stay and that we must do them scrupulous justice as we exact scrupulous justice from them.").

40. http://www.presidency.ucsb.edu/ws/index.php?pid=69667&st=standard+oil&st1=

41. Sixth Annual Message to Congress (Dec. 3, 1906), http://www.presidency.ucsb.edu/ws/index.php?pid=29547&st=standard+oil&st1= ("Rebates, for instance, are as often due to the pressure of big shippers (as was shown in the investigation of the Standard Oil Company). . . ."; Special Message to Congress (Jan. 31, 1908) ("The Standard Oil Corporation and the railway company have both been found guilty by the courts of criminal misconduct; both have been sentenced to pay heavy fines; and each has issued and published broadcast these statements, asserting their innocence and denouncing as improper the action of the courts and juries in convicting them of guilt. These statements are very elaborate, are very ingenious, and are untruthful in important particulars").

and its failure to invoke the criminal provisions of the antitrust law against the officers of those corporations after the court had declared that from the undisputed facts in the record they had violated the criminal provisions of the law."[42]

After antitrust's formative era, presidents continued to play some role in mobilizing public support for major antitrust matters. For example, in 1937, Franklin Roosevelt gave a press conference detailing the Attorney General's findings about collusion in the steel industry.[43] But antitrust was beginning its decline as a politically salient issue when the Justice Department initiated its antitrust suit against AT&T in 1974—an action that eventually led to AT&T's breakup into the "baby bells."[44] Unlike Roosevelt's fiery speeches about Standard Oil, President Ford did not take any initiative to discuss the matter publicly. But he did offer a tepid endorsement of the Justice Department's action, when pressed during a news conference:

> I was kept informed, but I don't think I should pass judgment on every antitrust suit that is contemplated by the Department of Justice. If they think they have a case, I think they ought to take the initiative within broad guidelines that I firmly believe in personally. Now in this case, as I understand it, it is not a suit aimed at AT&T simply because of its size. It is aimed at AT&T because of its alleged activities that result in noncompetition. Now the Antitrust Act says, in effect, that the elimination of competition is grounds for antitrust action by the Department of Justice. If that is the basis—and I understand it is—then in my opinion, the Department of Justice was acting properly.[45]

Fast-forward now to the *Microsoft* case, which originated in 1998. Unlike Roosevelt, who led the charge against Standard Oil as vigorously as he had led the Rough Riders up San Juan Hill, and unlike mild-mannered Jerry Ford who acknowledged being briefed on the *AT&T* case and offering his blessing, Bill Clinton refused to express *any opinion* on the actions of his Justice Department with respect to Microsoft. In a January 13, 2000, interview with CNBC's Ron Insana, Clinton expressed complete neutrality on whether Microsoft should be broken up: "Well, my response would be, first of all, that the decision would have to be made by a court and that, because it is a legal proceeding, I had nothing to do with what the Antitrust Division did, and I certainly can't have anything to do

42. http://www.presidency.ucsb.edu/ws/index.php?pid=29590&st=standard+oil&st1.

43. Franklin Delano Roosevelt Press Conference of April 27, 1937, http://www.presidency.ucsb.edu/ws/index.php?pid=15397&st=anti-trust&st1= (discussing details of attorney general investigation of collusion in steel industry).

44. *See* Marcellus S. Snow, *The AT&T Divestiture: A 10-Year Retrospective*, *in* BEYOND COMPETITION: THE FUTURE OF TELECOMMUNICATIONS 207 (Douglas M. Lamberton ed.,1995).

45. *See* http://www.presidency.ucsb.edu/ws/index.php?pid=4600&st=at%26t&st1.

with what the judge does."[46] In a February 14, 2000, interview with CNN's Wolf Blitzer, Clinton went even further, remarking that the *Microsoft* case was "handled in the Justice Department, strictly apart from the White House, so we had no role in that one way or the other."[47] Although Clinton may have decided not to touch the case because of Microsoft's popularity with the public,[48] neither of the two presidential candidates in the 2000 election tried to make a political case out of *Microsoft* either. Al Gore visited Microsoft's headquarters and warned obliquely against "the unfair use of market dominance in one sector to stifle innovation in another sector"[49] (which was not the principal issue in the *Microsoft* litigation), and George Bush refused to comment on the case altogether, saying that the matter was for the courts.[50]

These three cases illustrate antitrust's progression from populist to technocratic. In the democratic model, the president took responsibility for antitrust enforcement, especially in mobilizing public support for the Justice Department's actions. In the technocratic model, presidents purport to have nothing to do with antitrust enforcement, apart from ensuring that the right technocrats are selected to staff the enforcement agencies.

III. THE LEVEL OF FEDERAL ANTITRUST ACTIVITY

Antitrust has faded from national political dialogue, but that is not necessarily because it has become technocratic. It may simply be that antitrust is no longer discussed because it is no longer practiced. One frequently hears that the Reagan Administration dealt a near-fatal blow to federal enforcement of the antitrust laws.[51] Antitrust may be not so much technocratic as dying. Politicians may be

---

46. Interview with Ron Insana of CNBC's "Business Center" in New York City, *available at* http://www.presidency.ucsb.edu/ws/index.php?pid=58387.

47. Interview with Wolf Blitzer on CNN.com, February 14th, 2000, http://www.presidency.ucsb.edu/ws/index.php?pid=58086.

48. M. Broder, *Microsoft Tries Another Court: Public Opinion*, N.Y. TIMES, June 12, 2000, at A1 (reporting that a "Gallup poll taken in early May showed that 65% of the public had a favorable view of the company. The figure among computer users was even higher, 72%.").

49. *Id.*

50. *Id.*

51. *E.g.*, Yane Svetiev, *Antitrust Governance: The New Wave of Antitrust*, 38 LOY. U. CHI. L. REV. 593, 605 n.33 (2007) (describing Reagan Administration as period of nonenforcement of antitrust law); Albert A. Foer, *Half-Time at the Antitrust Modernization Commission*, 40 U.S.F. L. REV. 601, 617 (2006) (describing antitrust during Reagan administration as being in "severe retrenchment"); Daniel Goldberg, *Cornering the Market in a Post-9/11 World: The Future of Horizontal Restraints*, 36 J. MARSHALL L. REV 557, 577 (2003) (asserting that antitrust enforcement approached dormancy during the 1980s); David A. Balto,

content to let the antitrust agencies do their own thing because antitrust enforcement, as a share of the government's regulatory activity, has plummeted since the days of antitrust's highly visible public role.

One way to examine this possibility is to study the number of antitrust cases brought by the Department of Justice and see whether there is a significant decline in antitrust filings corresponding with the decline in political salience discussed in the previous section.[52] Measurement of the relevance of the antitrust division to the overall business of the public and private sectors must take into account not only the total number of case filings but also the amount of economic activity in the country. For example, the national economy of 2000 was about ten times larger in real terms than the national economy of 1940,[53] so one might expect that, all else being equal, a similarly aggressive antitrust agency would file ten times as many cases in 2000 as in 1940.

Figure 4.2 shows the level of Antitrust Division case filings adjusted for the amount of economic activity in the country.[54] The figure shows raw civil and criminal case filing numbers and antitrust filings as a percentage of real GDP,

---

Antitrust Enforcement in the Clinton Administration, 9 CORNELL J.L & PUB. POL'Y 61, 62–63 (1999) (discussing the Reagan Administration's view of antitrust enforcement as overly intrusive and the substantial reduction of antitrust enforcement during the Administration); Gregory J. Maier & Robert C. Mattson, *State Street Bank in the Context of the Software Patent Saga*, 8 GEO. MASON L. REV. 307, 321 (1999) (asserting that the Reagan Administration ended the era of antitrust ascendancy); Maurice E. Stucke, *Behavioral Economists at the Gate: Antitrust in the Twenty-first Century*, 38 LOY. U. CHI. L.J. 513, 540 (2007) (describing how the Chicago School's influence on the Reagan Administration resulted in the "wanement" of civil non-merger antitrust enforcement). Further sources calling the Reagan Administration a period of virtual nonenforcement are collected in Kovacic, *supra* n. 38.

52. There have been various empirical studies of the Antitrust Division's case filings over the years. *See* Richard A. Posner, *A Statistical Study of Antitrust Enforcement, reprinted in* THE CAUSES AND CONSEQUENCES OF ANTITRUST: THE PUBLIC CHOICE PERSPECTIVE, Fred S. McChesney & William F. Shughart II eds. (1995) (originally published in 13 J.L. & ECON. 365 (1970)). *See also* Joseph C. Gallo et al., *Department of Justice Antitrust Enforcement* 1955–1997*: An Empirical Study*, 17 REV. INDUS. ORG. 75, 90 (2000). Bill Kovacic's comprehensive survey of government antitrust enforcement from the 1960s through the early 2000s presents a more qualitative approach. *See* Kovacic, *supra* n. 38.

53. *See* Bureau of Economic Analysis *Current-Dollar and "Real" Gross Domestic Product* http://www.bea.gov/national/xls/gdplev.xls.

54. The underlying data are pooled from two sources. For 1938–2006, the data were provided to the author by the Department of Justice Antitrust Division. For earlier years, the data were drawn from Posner, *A Statistical Study, supra* n. 53, at 82, Table 5.5. Posner's data were compiled from the Commerce Clearing House (CCH). For the years in which there was overlap between Posner's CCH data and the data provided by the Department of Justice, there were slight but relatively insignificant differences. Real GDP numbers are chained 2000. Numbers from 1929 forward are collected from Bureau of Economic Analysis, http://www.bea.gov/national/xls/gdplev.xls. Pre-1929 numbers are collected from http://eh.net/hmit/gdp/.

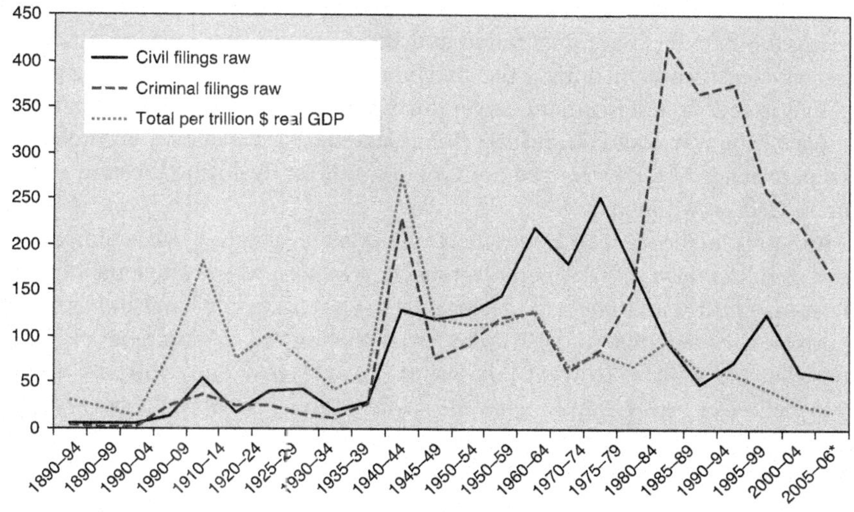

FIGURE 4.2 DOJ CASES FILED PER FIVE YEAR PERIOD

which allows a historical comparison of agency filings adjusted for overall economic activity.

The data support a story of federal antitrust enforcement in decline compared to the level of national economic activity, although the decline is perhaps not as significant as it appears at first blush. The two big spikes in enforcement correspond with abrupt shifts in antitrust policy and are relatively short lived. The first corresponds with the period immediately following the passage of the FTC and Clayton Acts and heightened enforcement during Woodrow Wilson's administration. During the Depression and the first half of the New Deal, antitrust went into remission. The second spike corresponds with the second half of the New Deal and the revitalization of the Antitrust Division under Robert Jackson and Thurman Arnold, beginning in 1937.[55] The revitalization's effect shows up dramatically in 1940 with a sharp increase in the number of filings, which increase was sustained for about three years until the beginning of U.S. involvement in World War II. For the remainder of the 1940s and'50s, federal antitrust enforcement levels remained fairly consistent. Thereafter, antitrust enforcement began to lose pace with economic growth, but the gap did not grow large until very recently. Contrary to common assumptions, enforcement during the Reagan Administration remained statistically consistent with the levels of enforcement

55. *See* Daniel A. Crane, *The Story of United States v. Socony-Vacuum: Antitrust and Hot Oil in the Two New Deals*, *in* ANTITRUST STORIES (Eleanor Fox & Daniel A. Crane eds., 2007).

during the 1970s, although the mix of cases changed considerably.[56] Enforcement during the first Bush administration and Bill Clinton's first term remained in line with enforcement during the previous two decades. The recent relative decline in federal enforcement began during Bill Clinton's second term, when the New Economy boomed, and case filings stayed fairly constant.[57] Enforcement as a percentage of GDP dropped even more significantly during the administration of George W. Bush.

Although Justice Department enforcement (as measured by case filings) has been trending down of late, perhaps reflecting a more conservative political climate, case filings and political ideology do not go uniformly hand in hand. For example, between 1900 and 1910 the "trust-busting" administrations of Teddy Roosevelt and William Howard Taft brought an average of one antitrust case per $100 billion of real GDP, roughly the same number as brought by Franklin Roosevelt's administration in 1938, Jimmy Carter's in 1979, Ronald Reagan's in 1985, and Bill Clinton's in 1995.[58]

Counting the number of cases filed is not a perfect way to measure the intensity of federal antitrust enforcement.[59] Another measure is the level of funding.[60]

---

56. What is interesting about the data from the Reagan years is that the total number of filed cases remained in line with the filings from the previous four or five administrations, but the ratio of criminal to civil cases swung dramatically in favor of criminal cases, in line that the Reagan administration prosecuted cartel cases far more vigorously than mergers and other civil matters. *See* Kovacic, *supra* n. 38 at 416–17. Although some commentators have disparaged the Reagan administration's "criminal antitrust program as commercially unimportant [and] a pedestrian exercise in bringing the same comparatively trivial case repeatedly," Kovacic shows that the Reagan administration's criminal enforcement against bid-rigging in the public contracting and major infrastructure sectors was important and effective. *Id.*

57. The gap between antitrust enforcement and economic growth does not necessarily signal a failure of antitrust, since it is possible that the growth areas of the new economy require less policing than traditional smokestack industries. Arguably, however, new economy industries—which are characterized by low marginal costs, tremendous scale economies, and network effects—require more, not less, policing. *See* Daniel L. Rubinfeld & John Hoven, *Innovation and Antitrust Enforcement, in* DYNAMIC COMPETITION AND PUBLIC POLICY: TECHNOLOGY, INNOVATION, AND ANTITRUST ISSUES 65 (Jerry Elig ed. 2001).

58. *See, e.g.,* Posner, *Statistical Study,* supra n. 53 at 82, Table 5.5.

59. *See* Kovacic, *supra* n. 38 at 407 (explaining some limitations with a "raw count[] of cases" approach to measuring federal antitrust enforcement).

60. Although comparing both the Antitrust Division and FTC's budgets and antitrust enforcement activities to GDP would provide a fuller analysis, the FTC did not began separately reporting its antitrust budget until the 1950s, and its data on antitrust case filings only go back to 1978. Accordingly, I have used Justice Department statistics as the most reliable historical proxy for the level of federal antitrust enforcement. A comparison of the Antitrust Division and total FTC budgets appears in Figure 2.1 in Chapter 2.

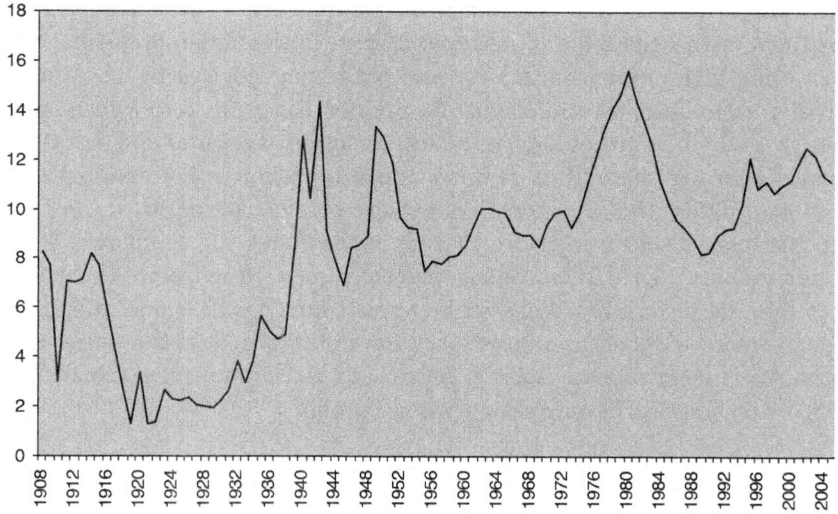

FIGURE 4.3 ANTITRUST DIVISION EXPENDITURES PER MILLION OF GDP

Figure 4.3 shows the division's budget as a fraction of GDP in real terms—again, in order to reflect the fact that a bigger economy requires more antitrust enforcement. Significantly, the data reveal that the Antitrust Division has been far better funded, even in proportion to total economic activity, during the second half of the twentieth century than during the first, and that there is no correlation between the decline in case filings since the 1940s and the level of funding. Despite the decline of antitrust's political salience, federal antitrust enforcement remains today as well funded as at almost any other time in American history.

This raises the question of what the Justice Department is doing, given that its real funding remains near historic highs while the number of civil and criminal cases it is brought has declined somewhat in the last few administrations. One factor, discussed further in Chapter 5 below, is that antitrust enforcement has shifted away from formal adjudication toward informal administration, which results in fewer case filings. In particular, the premerger notification system of the Hart-Scott-Rodino Antitrust Improvements Act of 1976[61] has had the effect of significantly decreasing the number of formal merger challenges because merger control is now usually handled administratively.[62] This account

61. *See* Hart-Scott-Rodino Antitrust Improvements Act of 1976, Pub.L. No. 94-435, 90 Stat. 1383 (codified in scattered sections of 15 U.S.C.).

62. *See* Robert H. Hahn & Anne Layne-Farrar, *Federalism in Antitrust*, 26 HARV. J.L. & PUB. POL'Y 877, 891 (2003) ("At the federal level, the Hart-Scott-Rodino Act pre-merger notification rules provide antitrust authorities with substantial information on the merging companies, which tends to weed out mergers unlikely to cause anticompetitive harm, resulting in fewer merger cases scrutinized by federal authorities reaching litigation").

is consistent with the view of an increasingly technocratic antitrust apparatus, working quietly behind the scenes to fix market concentration problems rather than filing high-profile court cases. Another factor, reflected in the Antitrust Division's workload statistics, is that the division has come to view its mandate more broadly than just enforcing the federal antitrust statutes and that it now spends a greater share of its resources on competition policy advocacy[63] and other nonadjudicatory activities. Finally, it also possible that antitrust cases have become more resource intensive because of the increasing complexity of economic analysis, such that individual cases consume a greater share of resources than they did historically. Whatever the explanation, congressional support for federal enforcement of the antitrust laws has not waned, despite antitrust's significant decline in political salience. Federal antitrust enforcement remains well supported and active despite its low political profile.

IV. THE POLITICAL ELITE AND THE TECHNOCRATIC BARGAIN

On balance, the declining political salience of antitrust is not correlated with a substantial decline in antitrust activity. With the exception of the relative decline in enforcement during Bill Clinton's second term and second Bush administration, both the levels of federal enforcement and federal funding have remained generally consistent with those of earlier periods, even as antitrust has been relegated to the fringes of national political discourse. And private enforcement levels, though sharply down from their spike in the 1960s and'70s (see Figure 3.1 in Chapter 3), are consistent with levels from eras characterized by political rhetoric calling for activist antitrust interventions.

This suggests that antitrust has become technocratic but in a particular kind of way. It has become technocratic in the mind of the political elite—presidents and their close circle of advisers that determine the content of presidential addresses and the president's level of involvement in antitrust administration; Republican and Democratic Party officials who draft party platforms; members of Congress who appropriate money to the antitrust enforcement agencies; and the political appointees who determine the course of the antitrust agencies' business. These political elites have accepted that antitrust is an important but largely technical matter that should be administered vigorously but without great public fanfare. They see relatively little party or personal gain to be had from trumpeting antitrust as a political issue and expect that antitrust developments will be followed only by their counterparts in the private sector and academia: business

63. This includes filing amicus curiae briefs in civil matters and other agencies' cases, negotiating with and giving advice to foreign governments and international organizations, and engaging in industry outreach. *See* Kovacic, *supra* n. 38 at 409 (explaining the value of agency "advocacy and research").

and legal elites and academics. The quid pro quo for antitrust's diminished political salience is that the enforcement agencies are largely left alone to do their work, free from strong external pressures.[64] This is the essence of the technocratic bargain.

To what can we attribute the technocratic bargain? Three factors suggest themselves. First, over time, a widespread consensus emerged among courts, the antitrust enforcement agencies, and antitrust practitioners and scholars about the goals of the antitrust enterprise.[65] During much of the history of U.S. antitrust law, there was vigorous debate over what antitrust law should seek to accomplish. Among the possible goals raised in legislative history, judicial opinions, and wider commentary were preserving a decentralized economy, protecting small businesses, preserving local ownership, guaranteeing vocational freedom, dispersing political power, protecting consumers from monopoly, and maintaining economic efficiency.[66] Since these goals were often in conflict, antitrust required political mediation. Over time, however, a broad consensus emerged that consumer welfare and economic efficiency are the overriding, if not exclusive, goals.[67] While there are occasions when economic efficiency (or total welfare) and consumer welfare suggest differing resolution of antitrust questions,[68] such occasions are relatively rare. In most instances, conduct that maximizes aggregate social welfare also benefits consumers, and conduct that harms aggregate social welfare also harms consumers; hence the antitrust

---

64. *See* Daniel A. Crane, *Antitrust Modesty*, 105 MICH. L. REV. 1193, 1210 (2007) (describing an implicit bargain in which antitrust enforcers trade political salience for independence).

65. HERBERT HOVENKAMP, THE ANTITRUST ENTERPRISE: PRINCIPLE AND EXECUTION 1 (2005) reporting that consensus has been reached on the goals of antitrust law); Cavanagh, *supra* n. 33 at 220 ("Over the last fifteen years, a bipartisan consensus has emerged regarding the goals of antitrust enforcement."); Robert Pitofsky, *Antitrust at the Turn of the Twenty-First Century: A View from the Middle*, 76 ST. JOHN'S L. REV. 583, 585 (2002).

66. *See* HOVENKAMP, THE ANTITRUST ENTERPRISE, *supra* n. 66 at 1–2; ROBERT H. BORK, THE ANTITRUST PARADOX: A POLICY AT WAR WITH ITSELF 15–45 (1978); Herbert Hovenkamp, *Distributive Justice and the Antitrust* Laws, 51 GEO. WASH. L. REV. 1, 1 (1995); Robert H. Lande, *Wealth Transfers as the Original and Primary Concern of Antitrust: The Efficiency Interpretation Challenged*, 50 HASTINGS L.J. 871, 911–35 (1999). On the legislative history of the Sherman Act, *see* WILLIAM LETWIN, LAW AND ECONOMIC POLICY IN AMERICA: THE EVOLUTION OF THE SHERMAN ANTITRUST ACT 53–99 (1965).

67. Report and Recommendation of the Antitrust Modernization Commission Chapter I.A (April 2007) http://www.amc.gov/report_recommendation; HOVENKAMP, THE ANTITRUST ENTERPRISE, *supra* n. 66 at 1; POSNER, ANTITRUST LAW 2 (2d ed. 2001); Thomas O. Barnett, *Substantial Lessening of Competition—The Section 7 Standard*, 2005 COLUM. BUS. L. REV. 293, 296 (2005); Thomas G. Krattenmaker et al., *Monopoly Power and Market Power in Antitrust Law*, 76 GEO. L.J. 241, 244 (1987).

68. Oliver E. Williamson, *Economies as an Antitrust Defense: The Welfare Tradeoffs*, 58 AM. ECON. REV. 18 (1968).

enforcement agencies do not spend much of their time deciding whether to apply a total welfare or consumer welfare standard.[69] Antitrust's goals are no longer in great controversy, and they are conjunctive, relatively well specified, and narrow. Most antitrust issues are thus about means, not ends.

Second, most contentious issues in antitrust are nonideological and no longer require appealing to endogenous preferences or foundational views about the legitimacy of the capitalist order, the meaning of human liberty (particularly freedom of contract and property), and the legitimacy of state intervention in private-market ordering. During earlier periods, contention over these and similar matters required a large degree of political involvement in the antitrust enterprise.[70] But today, there is relatively widespread consensus in the United States that the capitalist order is legitimate, that the freedoms of contract and property do not entail an unlimited right of corporations to engage in anticompetitive behavior, and that the state has a role to play in maintaining the efficiency and fairness of private markets. Given the commonality of view on these foundational issues, antitrust does not need the same degree of political superintendence that it once required.

Third, while modern antitrust analysis requires trade-offs,[71] it generally does not entail explicit decisions about how to value one person's interests against another's. While antitrust outcomes certainly have inter-class distributive consequences, these consequences are often unknowable and are not the focus of antitrust decision making. Antitrust specialists are far better at predicting whether a merger or other event will create market power and/or efficiencies than they are at predicting how the abuse of the market power or the benefits of the efficiencies will be distributed.[72] Since inter-class distributive issues do not play an explicit role in most antitrust cases, the political elite has found antitrust a less likely font of political intrigue and demagoguery.

It would be naïve to expect that the status quo represents antitrust's final idyllic resting place. The history of U.S. antitrust is one of sharp paradigmatic dislocations, of vast differences in antitrust views during different epochs.[73] Although

---

69. *See, e.g.*, Barnett, *supra* n. 67 at 297. Barnett, a former assistant attorney general in charge of the Antitrust Division, reported that "the consumer welfare and total welfare standards can diverge, although I think it is a rare case in practice." *Id.*

70. Hovenkamp, The Antitrust Enterprise, *supra* n. 66 at 11 (describing history of U.S. antitrust law as "overly ideological"); William H. Page, *Ideological Conflict and the Origins of Antitrust Policy*, 66 Tul. L. Rev. 1, 28–29 (1991) *see generally* Rudolph J.R. Peritz, Competition Policy in America: 1888–1992: History, Rhetoric, Law (1996).

71. *See, e.g.*, Peter J. Hammer, *Antitrust Beyond Competition: Market Failures, Total Welfare, and the Challenge of Intramarket Second-Best Tradeoffs*, 98 Mich. L. Rev. 849 (2000); Bork, *supra* n. 66 at 79–80 (describing "[v]alue trade-offs in antitrust litigation").

72. I develop this argument more fully in Daniel A. Crane, *Technocracy and Antitrust*, 86 Tex. L. Rev. 1159, 1213–16 (2008).

73. *See* Crane, *Antitrust Modesty*, *supra* n. 64 at 1201–11.

there is presently wide consensus on antitrust's goals, legitimacy, and limitations, the antitrust statutes are highly general and open textured and thus provide vehicles for implementing many vastly different political agendas.[74] As noted, President Obama made a modest attempt at reinvigorating antitrust as a political issue on the campaign trail. Further, the 2008–2009 financial crisis reinvigorated the public conversation about the relationship between the government and industry concentration. Yet, for now, there is little evidence that the political elite have any strong desire to reintroduce antitrust as an ideological issue or to disturb the technocratic bargain that has increasingly prevailed since at least the 1960s.

V. THE MISMATCH AND ITS IMPLICATIONS

For now, antitrust remains politically underground, controlled by a small cadre of economists and lawyers in government, the elite private bar (both plaintiff and defense), and elite economic consulting firms like Charles River Associates, NERA, LECG, and Lexecon. Elite policy makers are content to allow Hofstadter's "differentiated, specialized, and bureaucratized" institutions to run their own show, free from external interference, so long as they stay within their understood bounds.

This technocratic shift story has but one major glitch: Antitrust's populist institutional infrastructure remains largely unmodified. The technocratic bargain emerged quietly over time rather than explicitly as part of a legislative reexamination of antitrust's institutional structure. Even while implicitly accepting Hofstadter's assessment as an acceptable fact, Congress never amended antitrust's statutory infrastructure. Antitrust lost its populist ideology even while retaining its populist institutions. All of the populist institutions deputized at antitrust's founding: juries, generalist judges, generalist prosecutors, private litigants, etc., remain wholly intact. This historical slippage between values and institutions has created a mismatch between ends and means with important implications for the functioning of the entire system.

With this pregnant observation, we conclude the first part of our account of antitrust's institutional development in the United States. Thus far, we have viewed the institutional development primarily as the dialectic between corporate regulatory and crime-tort models. To recap briefly: The curious existence of two federal antitrust agencies owes in large part to the competition between these two models; private enforcement sprung out of the crime-tort model and eventually elicited a strong backlash from judges no longer sympathetic to its populist assumptions; the populist impulses that drove antitrust's institutional

74. *Id.*

formation faded over time in favor of a technocratic conceptualization more sympathetic to the corporate regulatory ideal, even though the institutions themselves remain intact.

In Part II of this book, we will examine specific ways in which antitrust's populist institutions interact poorly with antitrust's modern technocratic conceptualization. We will see, for example, that the civil jury cannot keep pace with antitrust's highly technical demands, that the FTC has struggled to find a norm-creative role in a system where antitrust norms are created by generalist judges in the shadow of private litigation, and that private litigation remains hampered by a focus on achieving compensation and deterrence. We will also examine some ways in which antitrust institutions have quietly adapted to the modern technocratic conceptualization and consider other ways in which they might do so in the future.

PART II

OPTIMIZING INSTITUTIONAL PERFORMANCE

5. REGULATION, ADJUDICATION, AND ADMINISTRATION

We begin our critical evaluation of U.S. antitrust institutions with a typology of approaches to the antitrust problem, which will inform the critiques and proposals in the following chapters. Part One of this book described a historical dialectic in U.S. competition policy between "crime-tort" and "corporate regulatory" approaches. These approaches correspond roughly in modern parlance with "antitrust" and "regulation."

It is common to describe antitrust and regulation as the two competing choices facing governments wishing to place controls on market economies.[1] For example, as a judge on the First Circuit, Stephen Breyer—a longtime fan of technocratic solutions[2]—described antitrust and regulation as substitutable legal controls:

> "[R]egulation" and "antitrust" typically aim at similar goals—i.e., low and economically efficient prices, innovation, and efficient production methods—but they seek to achieve these goals in very different ways. Economic regulators seek to achieve them *directly* by controlling prices through rules and regulations; antitrust seeks to achieve them *indirectly* by promoting and preserving a process that tends to bring them about.[3]

In this chapter, we will consider some of the stakes in the antitrust vs. regulation dichotomy. More fundamentally, we will consider the possibility that the typology is too limiting to capture the full range of conceptual and institutional approaches to market power problems. We will consider a third category—*administration*—lying somewhere between antitrust and regulation that already characterizes some of the most successful institutional approaches to solving the sorts of problems with which the antitrust enterprise is concerned and offers an appealing model for further institutional evolution.

---

1. *See*, e.g., W. Kip Viscusi, John M. Vernon & Joseph E. Harrington, Jr., Economics of Regulation and Antitrust xix (3d ed. 2000) (describing ordinary textbook approach as describing antitrust and regulation as separate policy mechanisms aimed at common goals).

2. *See* Ken I. Kersch, *Justice Breyer's Mandarin Liberty*, 73 U. Chi. L. Rev. 759, 760–61 (2006) (describing Justice Breyer's technocratic outlook).

3. *Town of Concord, Mass. v. Boston Edison Co.*, 915 F.2d 17, 22 (1st Cir. 1990).

I. REGULATION AND ITS DISCONTENTS

As we saw in Chapter 1, during antitrust's formative era and extending into the New Deal, there was a realistic possibility that the control of market power would turn in a regulatory rather than adjudicatory direction. Proposals for an expanded Bureau of Corporations would have granted a federal agency strong regulatory role over large interstate corporations. Indeed, the federal agency that most directly descends from the Progressive Era's regulatory agitations over corporate dominance is not the Federal Trade Commission, which at least on the antitrust side is not a true regulatory body (more on this in Chapter 7), but the Securities and Exchange Commission, which has extensive regulatory powers.[4] While it has no competition policy authority, the SEC's historical genesis dates from before the 1929 stock market crash and the Great Depression to the 1902 Industrial Commission Report, which dealt extensively with competition issues.[5]

During the Progressive Era, the regulatory model was associated with the Interstate Commerce Commission, which was created three years before the Sherman Act and had regulatory control over national railroads.[6] The ICC was the first independent regulatory body in the United States[7] and provided an early representation of the technocratic-regulatory model.[8] The commissioners were to be railroad experts insulated from political influence who would engage in the technical business of rate setting, ex ante rule making, and general administration of the nation's railroads.[9]

It is symbolic of the regulatory model's demise that, in 1996, after years of contracting its authority, Congress finally abolished the ICC.[10] By that time, an antiregulatory spirit had been sweeping through Washington for the better part of two decades, with high-profile relaxations of regulatory controls in many

---

4. *See generally* JOEL SELIGMAN, THE TRANSFORMATION OF WALL STREET; A HISTORY OF THE SECURITIES AND EXCHANGE COMMISSION AND MODERN CORPORATE FINANCE (3d ed. 2003).

5. *See* Chapter 1.

6. HERBERT HOVENKAMP, ENTERPRISE AND AMERICAN LAW 1836–1937 163–68 (1991).

7. Paul Stephen Dempsey, *The Interstate Commerce Commission: The Disintegration of an American Ideal*, 34 AM. U. L. REV. 1, 2 (1984).

8. *See, e.g.*, Randolph J. May, *Defining Deference Down: Independent Agencies and Chevron Deference*, 58 ADMIN. L. REV. 429, 445 (2006) (describing technocratic origins of ICC); Keith E. Whittington, *Dismantling the Modern State: The Changing Structural Foundations of Federalism*, 25 HASTINGS Const. L.Q. 483, 493 (1998) (describing "the ICC [as] illustrat[ing] the administrative ethic, with its focus on technocratic expertise").

9. Dempsey, *supra* n. 7 at 2.

10. ICC Termination Act of 1995, Pub. L. No. 104-88, 109 Stat. 803 (codified as amended in scattered sections of 49 U.S.C.). *See generally* Mark F. Kightlinger, *Nihilism with a Happy Ending; The Interstate Commerce Commission and the Emergence of the Post-Enlightenment Paradigm*, 113 PENN ST. L. REV. 113 (2008).

industries, including airlines, telecommunications, trucking, power generation, electricity, natural gas, and securities. At least prior to the "Great Recession" of 2008–2009, it was hard to find anyone in the antitrust community—whether on the Right or the Left—that embraced regulation as an appropriate model for policing problems of market power. Consider the words of Alfred Kahn, the father of airline deregulation:

> Regulated monopoly is a very imperfect instrument for doing the world's work. It suffers from the evils of monopoly itself—the danger of exploitation, aggressively or by inertia, the absence of pervasive external restraints and stimuli to aggressive, efficient and innovative performance. Regulation itself tends inherently to be protective of monopoly, passive, negative, and unimaginative. . . . Regulation is ill-equipped to treat the more important aspects of performance—efficiency, service innovation, risk taking, and probing the elasticity of demand. Herein lies the great attraction of competition: it supplies the direct spur and the market test of performance.[11]

Consistently with Kahn's admonition, within the last several decades, the discussion has been about whether greater or lesser antitrust interventions are desirable, not about whether private competition subject to antitrust rules should be replaced with top-down regulation.

In the aftermath of the Great Recession, it remains to be seen whether we will witness a revival of the regulatory spirit. As of this writing, regulatory solutions are back on the table in the consumer financial and banking sectors. A Consumer Financial Protection Agency has come into being with regulatory powers over consumer financial products. New banking legislation has established a Financial Services Oversight Council to monitor systemic threats in banking and financial services and, in conjunction with the Federal Reserve, break up large financial institutions that began to pose a risk to the wider economy. But despite these pressures, a wholesale reversion to a regulatory model of competition policy seems highly unlikely. For the reasons discussed next, adjudicatory control over market power remains the preferred modality.

II. THE VIRTUES AND LIMITATIONS OF ADJUDICATION

When the Sherman Act was framed three years after the Interstate Commerce Act and the FTC Act twenty-seven years later, following the ICC model of

11. 2 Alfred E. Kahn, The Economics of Regulation: Principles and Institutions 325–26 (Mass. Inst. of Tech. 1988) (1971). Justice Breyer articulated a similar point of view in Stephen Breyer, Regulation and Its Reform 15–35 (1982) (explaining the various justifications and subsequent critiques, for regulating the marketplace, including the "existence of a 'natural monopoly'").

regulation was a possibility.[12] But Congress chose not to create an antitrust regulatory body along the lines of the ICC. Instead of regulation as an antitrust mode, Congress chose adjudication. The Sherman Act and FTC Acts create highly generalized and open-textured antitrust norms—no restraints of trade, monopolization, or unfair trade practices[13]—which the courts then flesh out through a process of common law-like iteration in active disputes.[14]

The adjudicatory mode has many potential advantages over the regulatory mode. Judges tend to create law with actual facts in sight, which helps to make the liability norms concrete, specific, and functional.[15] Adjudicatory decision making tends to be more fact specific, incremental, adaptive, and flexible than regulation.[16] Whereas regulation tends to concentrate power in a few powerful hands, adjudication disperses decision-making power: horizontally, among the

---

12. *See* MARTIN J. SKLAR, THE CORPORATE RECONSTRUCTION OF AMERICAN CAPITALISM, 1890–1916: THE MARKET, THE LAW, AND POLITICS 324 (1988) (describing the two possible models for controlling the trusts as a statist regulatory model along the lines of the ICC and a nonstatist model of indirect regulation along the line of the Sherman and FTC Acts).

13. *See* William H. Page, *Interest Groups, Antitrust, and State Regulation: Parker v. Brown in the Economic Theory of Legislation*, 1987 DUKE LJ. 618, 659 (1987) (describing Sherman Act's open texture).

14. *See, e.g., Nat'l Soc'y of Prof. Eng'rs v. United States*, 435 U.S. 679, 688 (1978) ("Congress, however, did not intend the text of the Sherman Act to delineate the full meaning of the statute or its application in concrete situations. The legislative history makes it perfectly clear that it expected the courts to give shape to the statute's broad mandate by drawing on common-law tradition."); William F. Baxter, *Separation of Powers, Prosecutorial Discretion, and the "Common Law" Nature of Antitrust Law*, 60 TEX. L. REV. 661, 663 (1982) ("Congress adopted what is in essence enabling legislation that has permitted a common-law refinement of antitrust law through an evolution guided by only the most general statutory directions."); Frank H. Easterbrook, *Statutes' Domains*, 50 U. CHI. L. REV. 533, 544 (1983) ("The statute books are full of laws, of which the Sherman Act is a good example, that effectively authorize courts to create new lines of common law."); 1A PHILIP AREEDA & HERBERT HOVENKAMP, ANTITRUST LAW ¶ 103d2 (2d ed. 2000) (stating that the legislative history of other antitrust statutes demonstrates that the Sherman Act "invest[ed] the federal courts with a jurisdiction to create and develop an 'antitrust law' in the manner of the common law courts").

15. *See, e.g.,* Oliver Wendell Holmes, Jr., *Codes, and the Arrangement of the Law*, 5 AM L REV 1, 1 (1870), reprinted in Sheldon M. Novick ed., 1 THE COLLECTED WORKS OF JUSTICE HOLMES 212 (Chicago 1995) ("It is the merit of the common law that it decides the case first and determines the principle afterwards." For a recent exchange on the merits of common law rule making, *see* Emily Sherwin, *Judges as Rulemakers*, 73 U. CHI. L. REV. 919 (2006) (defending common law adjudication based on its focus on real-world disputes) and Frederick Schauer, *Do Cases Make Bad Law?*, 73 U CHI. L. REV. 883 (2006) (arguing that cognitive biases distort adjudicatory rule making).

16. *See* Peter H. Schuck, *Mass Torts: An Institutional Evolutionist Perspective*, 80 CORNELL L. REV. 941, 974–76 (1995) (discussing advantages of adjudication over regulation).

many different judges who may draw a case; and vertically, as decisions of a lower court can be appealed to a higher court.[17] Generalist judges may avoid the tunnel vision, power-aggrandizing tendencies, and agency-capture problems of administrative agencies.[18] The adjudicatory method lends itself to private enforcement and compensation of injured parties, whereas the regulatory method concentrates responsibility in government bureaucrats.[19]

On the other hand, adjudication has significant drawbacks. It requires a binary determination about the conformity of the defendant's comportment with abstract norms.[20] There are only two solutions in an antitrust trial—either the defendant did or did not violate the relevant norm.[21] Antitrust adjudication does not solve industrial organization problems so much as it announces winners and losers in legal contests.

Consider an example. In the most general sense, the antitrust problem is how to extract the efficiencies from large aggregations of capital without suffering the inefficiencies that result from market power.[22] Antitrust approaches its three paradigmatic evils—collusive collaborations, monopolistic exclusion of rivals, and mergers that enhance market power—by asking two common analytical questions: (1) Does the conduct enhance market power? and, (2) If so, do

---

17. *Id.*

18. Caleb Nelson, *Statutory Interpretation and Decision Theory*, 74 U. CHI. L. REV. 329, 351 (2007) (discussing tunnel vision and agency capture concerns that may lend generalist judges some advantages over specialized agencies).

19. *But see* Richard A. Nagareda, *Turning from Tort to Administration*, 94 MICH. L. REV. 899 (1994) (discussing models of public agency involvement in private mass tort litigation to help achieve appropriate compensation terms).

20. Carrie Menkel-Meadow, *Whose Dispute Is It Anyway?: A Philosophical and Democratic Defense of Settlement (in Some Cases)*, 83 GEO. L.J. 2663, 2674–75 (1995) (arguing that adjudication, by producing "binary win-lose results," fails to "recognize the ambiguities and contradictions in modern life,"); *see also* WOLF HEYDEBRAND & CARROLL SERON, RATIONALIZING JUSTICE: THE POLITICAL ECONOMY OF FEDERAL DISTRICT COURTS 45–57, 81–89 (1990) (analyzing shift from adjudication toward "technocratic administration" in the federal courts).

21. It is possible, of course, that the fact finder might find the defendant guilty or liable on some counts but not others, but as to each count, there are only two possibilities: guilty/liable or nonguilty/not liable.

22. *See*, e.g., Alan J. Meese, *Monopolization, Exclusion, and the Theory of the Firm*, 89 MINN. L. REV. 743, 781–82 (discussing economic perspectives on simultaneous increase in market power and economies of scale brought about by aggregations of capital); Andrew T. Guzman, *Is International Antitrust Possible?*, 73 N.Y.U. L. REV. 1501, 1509 (1998) (noting that a merger can simultaneously create productive efficiencies and economies of scale); Oliver Williamson, *Economies as an Antitrust Defense: The Welfare Trade-Offs*, 58 AM. ECON. REV. 18 (1968) (discussing how even a merger to monopoly can increase social welfare if it results in increased economies of scale).

efficiencies also result from the conduct?[23] If the answer to the first question is no, there is no need to ask the second question; the defendant wins. If it is yes, and the answer to the second is no, then an antitrust violation is easily found. But the questions are often answered yes and yes. A joint venture reduces the production costs but also involves market-power enhancing coordination of production levels;[24] a dominant firm redesigns its product in a way that creates improvements but also forecloses rivals from the market[25]; two firms create research and development synergies through a merger and also happen to be the two largest firms in an already concentrated market.[26] What then? Has the conduct violated the relevant antitrust norm?

Antitrust as an adjudicatory mode struggles to find ways to answer this question. One solution is merely to balance the efficiencies versus the inefficiencies and announce an antitrust violation only if the inefficiencies outweigh the efficiencies.[27] But there are two problems with this approach. First, a determination that a violation has occurred if the efficiencies slightly outweigh the inefficiencies, would expose the defendant to treble-damages liability for practices that had some redeeming virtues but a few more anticompetitive vices as determined ex post by an antitrust tribunal. Such an approach would chill procompetitive behavior, since potential defendants would not want to risk crossing

---

23. *See, e.g., United States v. Visa U.S.A., Inc.*, 344 F.3d 229, 238 (2d Cir. 2003) (applying a three-step rule of reason antitrust including (1) initial proof by the plaintiff of that relevant agreement created market power; (2) proof by the defendant that the restraint created efficiencies sufficient to negate any anticompetitive effects; and (3) opportunity for the plaintiff to show that the restraint was not reasonably necessary to achieve alleged efficiencies); Spencer Weber Waller, *Microsoft and Trinko: A Tale of Two Courts*, 2006 UTAH L. REV. 741, 750 (2006) (asserting that "antitrust principally fears durable market power unaccompanied by substantial efficiencies"); Andrew I. Gavil, *Exclusionary Distribution Strategies by Dominant Firms: Striking a Better Balance*, 72 ANTITRUST L. J. 2, 54 n.193 (2004) (asserting that "much of modern antitrust law today is driven by common, core concepts, such as market power, entry, and efficiency, which are relevant to the application of Sections 1 and 2 of the Sherman Act, and Section 7 of the Clayton Act").

24. *See* Thomas A. Piraino, Jr., *A Proposed Antitrust Approach to Collaborations Among Competitors*, 86 IOWA L. REV. 1137, 1187–88 (2001) (discussing situations where joint ventures create both efficiencies and market power).

25. *See, e.g., Berkey Photo, Inc. v. Eastman Kodak Co.*, 603 F.2d 263 (2d Cir. 1979) (holding that a court may not balance improvements in a dominant firm's products against anticompetitive effects on the dominant firms' rivals).

26. *See generally*, Alan A. Fisher, *Efficiency Considerations in Merger Enforcement*, 71 CAL. L. REV. 1580, 1599–1600 (1983) (discussing R&D synergies in merger enforcement).

27. *See, e.g.*, Christopher R. Leslie, *Trust, Distrust, and Antitrust*, 82 TEX. L. REV. 515, 671 (2004) ("Federal judges should balance any expected productive efficiencies against the possibility of allocative inefficiencies caused by cartel-like agreements spawned by the joint venture relationships.").

the line slightly.[28] Recognizing this, courts and the antitrust agencies tend to resist formulations of antitrust norms in ways that suggest that the question is one of open-ended balancing.[29]

Second, even if the good outweighs the bad, this does not necessarily mean that the good was achieved in the most desirable way possible. For example, suppose that a joint venture between three firms enhances efficiency in a way that outweighs any anticompetitive effects, but it is also the case that a merger between just two of the firms would achieve slightly fewer efficiencies and considerably less market power. One could condemn such a joint venture on the ground that there was a manner less restrictive of competition to achieve the efficiencies, as some courts have suggested.[30] But requiring the use of the least restrictive alternative upon pain of a treble-damages judgment raises the same problem as open-ended balancing—the absence of a margin of error for firm decision making and chilling desirable competitive behavior. So most authorities prefer a much more deferential articulation of the reasonableness test, which essentially awards market actors a business judgment privilege to achieve efficiencies in whatever way they choose, so long as there is not some markedly less restrictive way to achieve those efficiencies.[31]

The result is that antitrust law leaves considerable gaps between the good and the best. This has increasingly been the case as modern economic analysis has shown that many practices once considered anticompetitive—such as tying, exclusive dealing, bundling, aggressive price discounting, vertical contractual restraints, vertical and conglomerate mergers, and various forms of competitor

28. *See* Daniel A. Crane, *Rules Versus Standards in Antitrust Adjudication*, 64 WASH. & LEE L REV. 49, 99–100 (2007).

29. *See* HERBERT HOVENKAMP, THE ANTITRUST ENTERPRISE: PRINCIPLE AND EXECUTION 108 (2005) (outlining problems with an antitrust approach that turns on balancing social costs of monopoly versus increases in efficiency from the challenged practice).

30. *Sullivan v. National Football League*, 34 F.3d 1091, 1102 (1st Cir. 1994) ("One basic tenet of the rule of reason is that a given restriction is not reasonable, that is, its benefits cannot outweigh its harm to competition, if a reasonable, less restrictive alternative to the policy exists that would provide the same benefits as the current restraint."); *Mozart Co. v. Mercedes-Benz of North America, Inc.*, 833 F.2d 1342 (9th Cir. 1987) ("A tie-in does not violate the antitrust laws 'if implemented for a legitimate purpose and if no less restrictive alternative is available.'") (citation omitted).

31. *See, e.g., National Football League v. North American Soccer League*, 459 U.S. 1074, 1079–80(1982) (Rehnquist, J., dissenting from the denial of certiorari) (criticizing Second Circuit for adopting a least restrictive alternative test in antitrust case and arguing that such an approach is inconsistent with Supreme Court precedent); FTC & U.S. DEP'T OF JUSTICE, ANTITRUST GUIDELINES FOR COLLABORATIONS AMONG COMPETITORS ¶ 3.36b (2000), *available at* http://www.ftc.gov/os/2000/04/ftcdojguidelines.pdf (explaining that the agencies do not demand showing that restraint was essential to achieving the efficiencies but merely that the efficiency could not have been achieved by "practical, significantly less restrictive means").

collaboration—may have substantial efficiency justifications.[32] The recent tendency of the law has been to substantially scale back liability rules as to such practices, thus creating an underinclusive body of antitrust law, rather than engage in close-cutting balancing or less restrictive alternative analysis.[33] Since adjudication gives only two choices: condemn the practice; or bless it, the tendency has been increasingly toward blessing.

Part of the problem with the adjudicatory method as a regulatory tool is that it forces antitrust litigants into a "good versus evil" typology where the term "procompetitive" is a synonym for "good" and "anticompetitive" a synonym for "bad." It is a virtually theological proposition that antitrust law creates a national industrial policy, founded on competition. The Supreme Court has explained that "[t]he Sherman Act reflects a legislative judgment that ultimately competition will produce not only lower prices, but also better goods and services. 'The heart of our national economic policy long has been faith in the value of competition.'"[34] Within the antitrust community, it is heretical to question the value of competition in creating lower prices and spurring quality and innovation.

Yet many markets are uncompetitive, either temporarily or semipermanently. Sometimes, markets are not competitive because dominant firms undertake identifiable "bad acts" to exclude or suppress competition. More often, the cause is governmental intervention. For example, the grant of a patent right on a pioneer drug without ready substitutes often confers monopoly power on the drug maker for many years. Similarly, complex regulatory schemes may serve as entry barriers that keep out new competition for lengthy periods of time.[35] Sometimes, markets are not competitive in a conventional sense because they are natural monopolies. Natural monopolies include markets where high fixed costs,

---

32. *See* Herbert Hovenkamp, *Post-Chicago Antitrust: A Review and Critique*, 2001 Colum. Bus. L. Rev. 257 (2001) (discussing Chicago School's insights on efficiency of various competitive practices).

33. *See, e.g.*, William E. Kovacic, *The Intellectual DNA of Modern U.S. Competition Law for Dominant Firm Conduct: The Chicago/Harvard Double Helix*, 2007 Colum. Bus. L. Rev. 1, 72 (2007) (noting that both the Chicago and Harvard Schools of Antitrust have contributed to underinclusive liability norms for dominant firm behavior); Frank X. Schoen, *Exclusionary Conduct After Trinko*, 80 N.Y.U. L. Rev. 1625, 1647 (2005) (noting that the Supreme Court has created deliberately underinclusive liability norms for refusals to deal by dominant firms); Joseph F. Brodley, *Antitrust Standing in Private Merger Cases: Reconciling Private Incentives and Public Enforcement Goals*, 94 Mich. L. Rev. 1, 23 n.88 (1995) (noting that predatory pricing plaintiffs "must overcome deliberately underinclusive liability rules").

34. *Nat'l Soc'y. of Prof. Eng'rs v. United States*, 435 U.S. 679, 695 (1978) (quoting *Standard Oil Co. v. FTC*, 340 U.S. 231, 248 (1951).

35. *See* Robert H. Bork, The Antitrust Paradox: A Policy at War with Itself 347 (Free Press,1993) (1978) (observing that the "proliferation of regulatory and licensing authorities at every level of government" has allowed governmental officials to "control and qualify the would-be competitor's access to the marketplace").

network effects, or other features make it unlikely that more than one firm will be in the market at any given time.[36] In such cases, there may still be a form of competition in play—Schumpeterian competition or "competition for the market"—but a single dominant firm will still occupy the market for protracted periods of time.[37] The computer operating system market at issue in the *Microsoft* case may have such characteristics.[38]

Adjudication is oriented toward locating bad acts that impair the competitiveness of markets. Often, this means either forcing competition on industrial functions not suited to competition or else abandoning markets altogether, on the theory that the lack of competitiveness is not the result of a bad act. Adjudication thus falls into the "splitting" dilemma created by the crime-tort model. Under this model, an industrial practice is either a sinner or a saint. In other words, either the practice violates the relevant legal norm (usually decided on a post hoc basis during the course of litigation), in which case it is subjected to the harsh penalty of treble damages, or else it is found to be "competition on the merits," in which case it escapes any sanction whatsoever. This harsh dualism leaves no middle ground for practical legal solutions to market power problems.

For a real world example, consider the multibillion dollar antitrust litigation over payment systems that has been waged in many courtrooms over the last decade.[39] Payment systems like credit or debit cards are two-sided markets, meaning that payment card systems issue products demanded by two different

---

36. *See generally* Michael L. Katz & Carl Shapiro, *Network Externalities, Competition, and Compatibility*, 75 AM. ECON. REV. 424, 424 (1985) (cataloging instances where a product's utility depends on the number of "network" users of the same product and explaining that the "central feature of the market that determines the scope of the relevant network is whether the products of different firms may be used together"); Howard A. Shelanski & J. Gregory Sidak, *Antitrust Divestiture in Network Industries*, 68 U. CHI. L. REV. 1, 6–15 (2001) (detailing two methods of understanding such continued periods of market dominance—network effects and "Schumpeterian" Rivalry).

37. *See* Harold Demsetz, *Why Regulate Utilities?*, 11 J.L. & ECON. 55, 57 (1968) (critiquing the natural monopoly theory by noting that rival bidders may still compete in market negotiations, but implying that after contractual negotiations, only the winning bidder will remain—a distinction between "competition for the field" and "competition within the field").

38. *See United States v. Microsoft*, 253 F.3d 34, 49–50 (D.C. Cir. 2001) (noting Microsoft's argument that the operating system market is the type of dynamic, technological, innovation-based market-consuming academic debate over monopoly doctrine but declining to determine the validity of such a label).

39. *See* Steven Semeraro, *Credit Card Interchange Fees: Three Decades of Antitrust Uncertainty*, 14 GEO. MASON L. REV. 941, 941–42 (2007) (explaining that in 2005, numerous private antitrust cases "were consolidated before the Judicial Panel on Multi-District Litigation" where "potential damages [have been] said to exceed the annual pre-tax profit of the entire U.S. banking industry").

but interrelated sets of clients: buyers and merchants.[40] The payment systems are ultimately indifferent as to whether the buyers or merchants pay for the payment service, just as a newspaper is ultimately indifferent as to whether its revenues come from subscriptions or advertising. An antitrust intervention on one side of the market—for example, a prohibition on "honor all cards" policies[41]—may simply cause the payment systems to exact their tolls from the other side of the market by increasing fees to card carriers. Thus, the search for a "bad act" on either side of the market may have unintended and harmful effects on the other side of the market.

The situation is still more complicated because competition within payment systems occurs along multiple vectors. Until their recent IPOs, the Visa and MasterCard systems were joint ventures owned by banks that also issued individually branded credit and debit cards.[42] When a consumer swipes her credit card at a retailer, two different banks within a payment system are implicated.[43] The merchant's bank (the "acquiring bank") must pay an interchange fee to the consumer's bank (the "issuing bank"). Interchange fees are ultimately passed down to merchants, and merchants are unhappy because the fees are determined by bargaining between competitor banks who, given their dual status as acquirers and issuers, may not have very strong incentives to keep the rates low.[44] Another opportunity is presented for private antitrust litigants to weigh in and condemn the setting of interchange fees as an unreasonable horizontal restraint. Consider, again, what happens to the entire system if a particular practice is categorically condemned. Costs are likely to reemerge at some other juncture in the system, with potentially unfortunate results. For example, to the extent that the payment system was previously allocating fees to the less demand-elastic side of the market, a shift to the other side of the market could lead to a reduction in output.[45]

The analytical tools provided by the adjudicatory model do not lend themselves to regulation of such a vast and complex enterprise. The dualistic bottom line of private litigation, sinner or saint, does not allow for the sorts of incremental fixes and accommodations necessary to control the market power in the system without harming interests on another side of the market.

---

40. Benjamin Klein et al., *Competition in Two-Sided Markets: The Antitrust Economics of Payment Card Interchange Fees*, 73 ANTITRUST L. J. 571, 571 (2006).

41. Visa and MasterCard's "honor all cards" policy required merchants that accepted Visa and MasterCard credit cards to honor their debit cards as well. *Wal-Mart Stores, Inc. v. Visa U.S.A., Inc.*, 396 F.3d 96, 101 (2d Cir. 2005).

42. Klein, *supra* note 40 at 572.

43. *Id.*

44. *Id.* at 572–74.

45. Dennis W. Carlton & Alan S. Frankel, *Transaction Costs, Externalities, and "Two-Sided" Payment Markets*, 2005 COLUM. BUS. L. REV. 617, 629, 637 (2005).

III. THE ADMINISTRATIVE ALTERNATIVE

A third approach to problems of market power is what I call "administration." Like the regulatory model, the administrative model of antitrust is characterized by an emphasis on problem solving rather than assigning blame for norm violation.[46] Yet, like the adjudicatory model, it seeks to avoid top-down, command-and-control governmental commands. It is geared toward informal solutions and negotiated agreements rather than formal adjudication or rule making—although it is not merely a form of alternative dispute resolution. It is compatible with the common law's incrementality and does not necessarily entail centralization of decision making. It can be practiced by private parties as well as government enforcers, by both generalists and specialists. In short, the administrative model of antitrust has sufficient flexibility to accommodate technocratic values without entailing many of the criticisms of the regulatory model.

A leading example of the administrative model is merger review under the Hart-Scott-Rodino Antitrust Improvements Act of 1976.[47] Hart-Scott specifies that, as to certain classes of stock and asset acquisitions, the acquiring and/or acquired person must file a premerger notification with the Department of Justice and FTC.[48] Unless the agencies give early termination, the merger or acquisition cannot close for thirty days following the filing.[49] Prior to the termination of the thirty-day waiting period, the agencies can issue a "second request," a species of subpoena for categories of documents and information additional to those that must automatically accompany the initial filing.[50] The agencies can then extend the waiting period for thirty days following satisfaction of the second request[51] Formally, compliance with Hart-Scott does not mean that a merger is approved or that the merger is deemed legal.[52] But the effect of Hart-Scott has been to create a de facto administrative regime of merger approval by government economists and antitrust lawyers who consider, ex ante, the likely structural consequences of a merger and negotiate with the merging parties for

46. *See generally* A. Douglas Melamed, *Antitrust: The New Regulation*, 10 Fall Antitrust 13 (1995) (discussing differences between an approach to antitrust that focuses on whether past conduct violates legal norms and a regulatory approach that tends to focus prospectively on establishing conditions conducive to economic welfare).

47. Pub. L. No. 94-435, 90 Stat. 1383 (1976) (codified in relevant part at 15 U.S.C. § 18a).

48. 15 U.S.C. § 18a (a).

49. *Id.* at § 18a (b) (1).

50. *Id.* at § 18a (e).

51. *Id.* at § 18a (e) (2).

52. Nor does the agency's negotiation of a divestiture package preclude private parties from arguing that the agencies did not go far enough to ensure a competitive market. *See Six West Retail Acquisition, Inc. v. Sony Theatre Management Corp.*, No. 97 Civ. 5499(DNE), 2000 WL 264295, at *23 (S.D.N.Y. Mar. 9, 2000).

divestiture packages or conduct commitments sufficient to alleviate competitive concerns.[53] Merger practice has become a quasi-scientific and comparatively predictable administrative enterprise conducted by federal industrial policy experts with wide powers to specify the structure and competitive behavior of merging corporations.[54]

Modern merger control is not primarily either adjudicatory or regulatory in character. It usually does not involve litigation to determine whether a particular merger violates Section 7 of the Clayton Act. Instead of answering that formal question, the government and merging parties engage in informal dialogue to address the concerns that underlie the statute and find satisfactory solutions. Nor does merger review involve heavy-handed ex ante rule making or other features of a strong system of regulation. Although the enforcement agencies have promulgated merger review guidelines,[55] these are merely frameworks for analysis, not inflexible rules.[56]

Merger control is primarily a publicly administered function, but there are other examples of administrative antitrust that are either public-private or purely private. A leading example of public-private antitrust is the rate-setting mechanism under the BMI and ASCAP consent decrees, which is now codified in a federal statute.[57] BMI and ASCAP are music performance rights clearing houses that aggregate and license millions of individual artists' performance rights.[58] The transactions costs of individual licensing negotiations between each artist and each potential licensee make the clearinghouses very economically efficient.[59] At the same time, the aggregation of millions of licenses in the hands of large collective bargaining agents creates a substantial amount of market power and the potential for anticompetitive abuse. The solution has been a long-term

53. *See* E. Thomas Sullivan, *The Antitrust Division as a Regulatory Agency: An Enforcement Policy in Transition*, 64 Wash. U. L.Q. 997, 1025–42 (1986).

54. Daniel A. Crane, *Antitrust Antifederalism*, 96 Cal. L. Rev. 1, 52–57 (2008).

55. Dep't of Justice & Fed. Trade Comm'n, Horizontal Merger Guidelines (rev. ed. 1997). The Justice Department and Federal Trade Commission are currently considering revisions to the Guidelines.

56. The FTC and Antitrust Division quite candidly admit that their actual practice quite often deviates from the impressions given by the Guidelines. *See* FTC & U.S. Dep't of Justice, Merger Challenges Data, Fiscal Years 1999–2003 (2003), http://www.ftc.gov/os/2003/12/mdp.pdf.

57. *See* W. Jonathan Cardi, *Über-Middlemen: Reshaping the Broken Landscape of U.S. Copyright*, 92 Iowa L. Rev. 835, 846–47 (2007); Tim Wu, *Copyright's Communications Policy*, 103 Mich. L. Rev. 278, 304–11 (2004). The essential mechanisms of the BMI decree are discussed in *U.S. v. Broadcast Music, Inc.*, 426 F.3d 91, 95 (2d Cir. 2005). The rate-setting provision is codified in 17 U.S.C.A. § 513 (2007).

58. The economic justifications for the *BMI* and *ASCAP* system are discussed in *Broadcast Music, Inc. v. Columbia Broadcasting Sys., Inc.*, 441 U.S. 1 (1979).

59. *Id.*

consent decree resulting from an antitrust action brought by the Justice Department. Under the consent decrees, BMI and ASCAP must make through-to-the-listener licenses available for public performances of their music repertoires and provide applicants with proposed license fees upon request. If the clearinghouses and the applicant cannot agree on a fee, either party may apply to the rate court for the determination of a reasonable fee.[60]

The BMI and ASCAP matters started out as adjudicatory actions by the government, but the consent degree mechanism under which the companies have been operating for over forty years is largely administrative in character. A court called upon to address the clearinghouses' market power by setting a rate "adjudicates" in one sense of the word, but it is not the sort of binary adjudication—liable or not liable—that characterizes most adjudicatory antitrust litigation. The court is acting as a rate regulator, determining the reasonable price of the license, rather than deciding whether the parties' conduct conformed to some abstract norm. There is no jury involved and hence no jury avoidance and no need to worry about the complexities of antitrust law. The rate-setting proceeding is not an antitrust proceeding at all but a quasi-contractual solution designed to address an antitrust problem.[61]

There are also models of purely private antitrust administration. One fairly recent example is the voluntary use of "reasonable and nondiscriminatory" (RAND) licensing commitments by members of standard setting organizations (SSOs) and patent pools.[62] As in the BMI and ASCAP situations, the SSOs and patent pools may result in very substantial efficiencies and very substantial market power.[63] Unlike ASCAP and BMI, however, some SSOs and patent pools have not waited for a government suit before announcing quasi-contractual antitrust fixes designed to make disputes over licensing administrative rather than adjudicative. A typical antitrust fix is a commitment by the members of the SSO to license their patents on RAND terms to anyone wishing to practice the standard.[64] These commitments often include contractually created mechanisms

---

60. Broadcast Music, 426 F.3d at 95.

61. In a study highly critical of many antitrust consent decrees, Richard Epstein generally approves of the BMI and ASCAP decrees as conforming by and large "to the golden rule: Keep consent decrees simple, and tie them to the core violations to which they are directed." RICHARD A. EPSTEIN, ANTITRUST CONSENT DECREES IN THEORY AND PRACTICE: WHY LESS IS MORE 39 (2007).

62. *See* Daniel A. Crane, *Patent Pools, RAND Commitments and the Problematics of Price Discrimination*, *in* WORKING WITHIN THE BOUNDARIES OF INTELLECTUAL PROPERTY LAW 371-94 (Rochelle Dreyfuss, Diane L. Zimmerman & Harry First eds., Oxford University Press 2010) (describing voluntary acceptance of RAND commitments by members of standard-setting organizations).

63. Crane, *Patent Pools*, *supra* n. 62.

64. *Id.*

for expert determination of appropriate licensing terms.[65] In theory, these commitments might also be enforced contractually in the courts.[66]

Private administrative commitments have the potential to diffuse some of the suboptimal elements of antitrust adjudication, even while preserving a role for private enforcement. Conceptually, the RAND commitment is a voluntary undertaking that allows a technology joint venture to capture efficiencies while giving assurance that it will take the good without giving the bad. It replaces ideological struggle over antitrust norms with pragmatic problem solving, usually by technology experts.

A common objection to these sorts of administrative solutions to problems of market power in intellectual property is that it forces judges or private arbitrators into an uncomfortable rate-setting role.[67] To be sure, judges or arbitrators would occasionally have to intervene. But the goal of such a system would be to set the stage for private bargaining over royalty rates for intellectual property in a context where the licensees held a credible threat to counter the licensor's implicit hold-out threat. Since a judge or arbitrator would theoretically assign a royalty rate that stripped the excessive market power out of the IPRs, but neither party could predict exactly what the judge would view as excessive, so both parties would have an incentive to bargain toward a reasonable royalty rate. The mere threat of a rate-setting proceeding would curtail the IPR's ability to charge an excessive rate.[68]

This is not idle speculation. In a recent study, I examined fifty-two antitrust consent decrees that contained liability rule provisions for patents or copyrights.[69] In essence, these provisions required the defendants to license their patents or copyrights on reasonable and nondiscriminatory terms and reserved jurisdiction in the court to set the rate in the event that the parties could not agree.[70] In only

---

65. *Id.*

66. *Id.*

67. *See, e.g.*, Brief for the United States at 64–69, *United States v. Nat'l Lead Co.*, 1947 WL 44396 (U.S. 1947) (explaining that a liability rule treatment would impose on the courts "an onerous and absorbing administrative burden").

68. *See* Daniel A. Crane, *Bargaining in the Shadow of Rate-Setting Courts*, 76 ANTITRUST L.J. 207, 208 (2009) (describing "'jurisdiction retention' judgments," which do not necessarily involve a court in ever setting a rate but create a "threat of rate setting").

69. *Id.* at 311–12.

70. The following consent decree language—from a rare case in which the district court actually did set a rate—is typical: "Upon application for a license under the provisions of this Section, the defendant to whom application is made shall state the royalty which it deems reasonable for the patents to which the application pertains. If the parties are unable to agree upon a reasonable royalty, the defendant may apply to this Court for the determination of a reasonable royalty, giving notice thereof to the applicant and the Attorney General, and he shall make such application forthwith upon request of the applicant. In any such proceeding, the burden of proof shall be upon the defendant to whom

three out of fifty-two cases was the district court ever called on to set a rate.[71] In only one case, *ASCAP*, did a substantial amount of activity appear.[72] Between 1950 and 2009, the Southern District of New York has set rates for ASCAP about eight times, which is a significant amount of activity compared to other cases but still a relatively small number compared to the magnitude of ASCAP's licensing activities, the length of time at issue, and the pervasiveness of the consent decree in regulating ASCAP's activities.[73] In most cases, the bargaining over copyright or patent royalty rates happened quietly in the shadow of the rate-setting courts.[74]

Administrative systems focused on limiting future exercises of market power in intellectual property are much more effective than the adjudicatory systems focused on punishing IPR holders when they stray too far. This is particularly true given that many IP-intensive industries are subject to rapid change and innovation. The adjudicatory system is too slow and cumbersome to keep up.

It is not my purpose to argue that administrative solutions are always preferable to regulatory or adjudicatory ones. Administrative solutions are neither feasible nor desirable in all circumstances. Still, there is ample room within the current legal and regulatory environment to move more functions in an administrative direction. For example, in Chapter 7, we will consider further ways in which the FTC could pursue administrative solutions, and in Chapter 9, we will consider different administrative modalities that could replace private enforcement's misguided focus on compensation and deterrence. Policy makers should shed the overly narrow assumption that "regulation" and "antitrust" are the only two available modalities for policing market power in capitalist economies and consider the administrative option, which has quietly taken over important areas of competition policy and could extend its reach even further.

---

application is made to establish by a fair preponderance of evidence, a reasonable royalty, and the Attorney General shall have the right to be heard thereon." *United States v. Am. Optical Co.*, 95 F.Supp. 771, 772 (S.D N.Y. 1950).

71. Crane, *Rate-Setting Courts, supra* note 68, at 312.

72. *Id.* at 311.

73. *Id.* at 310.

74. A similar result occurs with respect to statutory copyright licenses. Copyright royalty judges, who have statutory jurisdiction to set copyright rates for compulsory licenses, have to exercise their powers relatively infrequently. More often, the parties bargain to a mutually agreeable solution in the shadow of the copyright judges. *See* Daniel A. Crane, *Intellectual Liability*, 88 TEX. L. REV. 253, 295 (2009).

6. THE MUCH-MALIGNED ANTITRUST JURY

No U.S. antitrust institution is more maligned than the jury. Antitrust experts frequently bemoan the incompetence of juries and criticize them as unsuited to determining complex antitrust matters. For adherents to Chicago School views, generally inclined to laissez faire perspectives, the undesirability of populist juries is a given.[1] But, as we saw in Chapter 3, many of the most aggressive denunciations of antitrust juries have come from Chicago's Left flank. Stephen Breyer has led the charge on the Supreme Court, usually lumping together non-expert judges and juries.[2] Harvard School academics, not bound like judges to be courteous to jurors, have dismissed the antitrust jury completely. Donald Turner, one of the past "deans" of the Harvard School advocated getting rid of the antitrust jury in civil cases altogether.[3] Herbert Hovenkamp, the current dean of the Harvard School, opines that "[j]ury trials in front of intelligent but nonspecialist judges is a truly miserable way to make economic policy," and that "juries remain a very weak link in a system where most of the relevant evidence is economic and technical."[4]

If the technocratic elite so distrusts antitrust juries, what accounts for their persistence? For one, the Seventh Amendment to the Constitution probably guarantees parties a right to jury trial in most civil antitrust cases, and the Sixth Amendment certainly guarantees it in criminal cases. The parties can waive these rights and, as we shall see, often do. But there is a second reason that there

---

1. *See, e.g.*, Frank H. Easterbrook, *Allocating Antitrust Decisionmaking Tasks*, 76 Geo. L. J. 305, 310 (1987) ("I am suspicious of booting to juries, and deferring to their conclusions on, questions that we—meaning judges, lawyers, economists, and other professions taken together—know very little about.").

2. *See, e.g., Credit Suisse Secs., (USA) LLC v. Billings*, 551 U.S. 264, 127 S. Ct. 2383, 2395 (2007) (observing the risks of inconsistency entailed in entrusting decisional authority to "different nonexpert judges and different nonexpert juries"); *Leegin Creative Leather Prods., Inc. v. PSKS, Inc.*, 551 U.S. 877, 127 S. Ct. 2705, 2730 (2007) (Breyer, J., dissenting) (arguing that "[o]ne cannot fairly expect judges and juries in [resale price maintenance] cases to apply complex economic criteria without making a considerable number of mistakes, which themselves may impose serious costs").

3. Donald F. Turner, *The Durability, Relevance, and Future of American Antitrust Policy*, 75 Cal. L. Rev. 797, 813 (1987) ("I see no overriding disadvantages to eliminating jury trials of private antitrust suits.").

4. *See, e.g.*, Herbert Hovenkamp, The Antitrust Enterprise: Principle and Execution 4, 63, 80–81 (2005) (opining that and that juries are usually unqualified to distinguish between competent and incompetent expert testimony). *See also* Douglas W. Ell, *The Right to an Incompetent Jury: Protracted Commercial Litigation and the Seventh Amendment*, 10 Conn. L. Rev. 775, 775–76 (1978).

is little movement for a major structural change to reign in antitrust juries. The legal system has already found ways to avoid antitrust jury trials and cabin juror power. A culture of jury avoidance permeates antitrust litigation, rendering actual jury trials rare and quaint events.

In this chapter, we shall consider the jury as a distinct institution. We shall consider the available evidence on how juries actually perform in antitrust cases (both criminal and civil), the systemic effects of the jury on antitrust adjudication, and possible reforms that could help to rationalize the jury within the increasingly technical and technocratic antitrust domain.

I. HOW DO CIVIL JURIES ACTUALLY PERFORM?

Despite a very broad consensus that civil juries must do a terrible job in antitrust cases, we do not actually know much about how antitrust juries actually perform. Part of the problem is that very few civil antitrust cases go to juries. Only about 1 percent of all civil antitrust cases go to a jury. These numbers are not very different from the jury trial rates in comparable fields. Figure 6.1 below shows the total number of jury trials in private antitrust, copyright, patent, and trademark cases for the 2003–2008 period. Antitrust is not unusual on a percentage basis, with copyright and trademark showing a smaller percentage and patent a larger one. But antitrust shows a small absolute number of jury trials. Over the five-year period, there were only forty-four antitrust jury trials, fewer than ten a year, which does not provide a very large pool of information for study.

	Number of Civil Jury Trials	Percentage of All Case Terminations
Antitrust	44	1.2
Copyright	101	0.5
Patent	331	2.4
Trademark	131	0.7

FIGURE 6.1 CIVIL JURY TRIALS IN FEDERAL COURT 2003–2008[5]

5. These data are pulled from the Annual Reports of the Administrative Offices of the U.S. Courts.

To my knowledge, there have been no systematic efforts to study the actual performance of civil antitrust juries. Most of the information available is anecdotal, and this information is not encouraging. The richest pool of information comes from an account by Arthur Austin, a law professor at Case Western University, of jury interviews he conducted after four antitrust cases in the mid-1990s, including the *Brooke Group v. Brown & Williamson:* predatory pricing that ended up in the Supreme Court.[6] Consistently with the intuitions described at the beginning of this chapter, Austin described jurors as utterly incapable of discharging their functions: "[T]he jurors were overwhelmed, frustrated, and confused by testimony well beyond their comprehension. I concluded that at no time did any juror grasp—even at the margins—the law, the economics or any other testimony relating to the allegations or defense."[7] Austin continued: "[A]t no time have I ever encountered a juror who had the foggiest notion of what oligopoly, market power, or average variable costs meant, much less how they applied to the case. Typical is the response I received when I asked a juror whether he remembered average variable cost. The juror replied, 'Yes, explain it to me. I still don't know what it means.'"[8]

To antitrust insiders, the average variable cost admission is particularly disturbing. For years, antitrust policy wonks and judges have been debating the "appropriate measure of cost" to use in predatory pricing cases, as though the technical definition of predatory pricing had great significance for the life of our economy.[9] The jurors were instructed that they could not find Brown & Williamson liable for predatory pricing unless it had priced below average variable cost.[10] For the juror to concede that he had no idea what the instruction even meant was to concede that he had willfully acted lawlessly in returning a plaintiff's verdict and, perhaps more offensively, ignored the considered

6. *See* Arthur Austin, *The Jury System at Risk from Complexity, the New Media, and Deviancy*, 73 DENV. U. L. REV. 51, 52–60 (1995). *See Brooke Group Ltd. v. Brown & Williamson Tobacco Corp.*, 509 U.S. 209 (1993).

7. Austin, *supra* n. 6 at 54.

8. *Id.*

9. *See, e.g.*, Phillip Areeda & Donald F. Turner, *Predatory Pricing and Related Practices Under Section 2 of the Sherman Act*, 88 HARV. L. REV. 697, 709–10 (1975); F.M. Scherer, *Predatory Pricing and the Sherman Act: A Comment*, 89 HARV. L. REV. 869, 883–85 (1976); Paul L. Joskow & Alvin K. Klevorick, *A Framework for Analyzing Predatory Pricing Policy*, 89 YALE L.J. 213, 223 (1979); William J. Baumol, *Quasi-Permanence of Price Reductions: A Policy for Prevention of Predatory Pricing*, 89 YALE L.J. 1, 21 (1979); Patrick Bolton, Joseph F. Brodley & Michael H. Riordan, *Predatory Pricing: Strategic Theory and Legal Policy*, 88 GEO. L.J. 2239, 2242–62 (2000); Aaron S. Edlin, *Stopping Above-Cost Predatory Pricing*, 111 YALE L.J. 941 (2002); Einer Elhauge, *Why Above-Cost Price Cuts To Drive Out Entrants Are Not Predatory—and the Implications for Defining Costs and Market Power*, 112 YALE L.J. 681, 711–14 (2003).

10. *Brooke Group*, 509 U.S. at 222.

judgment and policy design of the brightest and best economists, law professors, and judges.

So if the legal instructions were not influencing the juror's decision, what did? Austin listed a number of factors, from the lawyers' haberdashery to a Brown & Williamson's lawyer's cross-examination where he forced a tobacco wholesaler to admit his lack of education. The jurors perceived this as an "elitist attack."[11] Austin also describes the influence of "dominant jurors" motivated by ideology. A dominant juror named "Cleo," who Austin describes as "a classic Southern populist," explained that "B&W got too greedy. All of them (big businesses) are crooks."[12] Austin explains that "[d]ominant jurors intuitively know that the issue is ideology and gravitate toward evidence which supports their vision. Cleo's primary weapon was something antitrust lawyers dread, a 'smoking gun' document in which B&W executives made comments like 'bury them' and 'put a lid on Liggett.'"[13] Cleo was able to dissuade his fellow jurors from crediting the testimony Brown & Williamson's principal economic expert, the eminent University of Virginia economist Ken Elzinga, by deploying an argument made by Liggett's economist that "fact always trumps theory."[14] This argument appealed to jurors "with a high school education."[15]

The jury was not devoid of free-market advocates. A young man that Austin identifies as "Rocky" was a holdout for Brown & Williamson and a counterweight to Cleo on the jury. But, the jury hung together for so long during the trial and deliberations that it developed a family personality. As Rocky underwent a divorce, another juror became his counselor. Ultimately, Rocky decided to capitulate rather than to allow a hung jury, explaining: "A lot of people were tired. It was hell, I respect my elders, I loved them."[16]

Austin's findings are supported by other empirical or experimental studies that have shown that jury trials in antitrust cases may be tilted in a populist, anti-big-business direction. One study found that "[i]n some venues, as many as 75 percent of jurors think that large corporations regularly use unethical and unfair tactics to bully smaller competitors and squeeze them out of the marketplace."[17] Experimental work suggests that juries may routinely disregard judges' instructions on damages. For example, one study has shown that mock antitrust juries award significantly lower damages when they are told that the damages award

11. Austin, *supra* n. 6 at 54.
12. *Id.* at 55.
13. *Id.* at 56.
14. *Id.* at 56.
15. *Id.*
16. *Id.* at 57.
17. Barbara S. Swain & Dan R. Gallipeau, *Jurors Attitudes in Antitrust Cases*, 9 ANTITRUST 14, 15–17 (1994).

will be automatically trebled by law, unless the policy reasons for automatic trebling are explained to them.[18]

Given the limited anecdotal, empirical, and experimental evidence available and the widespread belief that it is representative of what actually happens in jury rooms, it is not surprising to find that most scholars and antitrust practitioners today (at least those on the defense side) believe, with Herbert Hovenkamp, that the jury is the "weak link" in the antitrust system. But even without further evidence of how juries actually perform, it is not hard to see that the populist ideal of the jury conflicts with the modern technocratic notion of antitrust.

Few institutions could be further from the technocratic model of expert administration than a randomly selected group of lay fact finders. As Tocqueville recognized, the jury is a quintessentially political institution that serves to balance and accommodate competing social forces.[19] The Supreme Court has upheld jury service as a form of democratic participation.[20] Constitutional historian Akil Amar notes that "[i]f we seek a paradigmatic image underlying the Bill of Rights, we cannot go far wrong in picking the jury. . . . The jury summed up—indeed embodied—the ideals of populism, federalism, and civic virtue that were the essence of the original Bill of Rights."[21] Those who continue to support some continued use of antitrust jury trials generally do so on populist political grounds.[22]

As described in Chapter 4, antitrust populism is long dead. Since at least the Chicago School revolution in the 1970s, antitrust law has been almost entirely divorced from norms of fairness or distributive justice that lie within the ken of the average layperson. The antitrust jury is not called upon to serve as the moral compass of the community, since antitrust is no longer thought to be a moral enterprise.[23] Nor is the jury usually asked to lend its competence on matters

---

18. Shari Seidman Diamond & Jonathan D. Casper, *Blindfolding the Jury to Verdict Consequences: Damages, Experts, and the Civil Jury*, 26 LAW & SOC'Y REV. 513, 557 (1992).

19. ALEXIS DE TOCQUEVILLE, 1 DEMOCRACY IN AMERICA 281 (Alfred A. Knopf ed., 15th ed. 1985) (1830).

20. *Powers v. Ohio*, 499 U.S. 400, 407 (1991) (noting that "with the exception of voting, for most citizens the honor and privilege of jury duty is their most significant opportunity to participate in the democratic process.").

21. Akil Amar, *The Bill of Rights as a Constitution*, 100 YALE L.J. 1131, 1190 (1991).

22. Gary Miranda, *Antitrust at Century's End*, 48 SMU L. REV. 1749, 1763 n.71 (1995) (arguing that "antitrust jury trials have served an important function in preserving the 'populist goals' of the antitrust movement.").

23. Indeed, leading antitrust scholars argue that antitrust law has no moral character at all. *See* HERBERT HOVENKAMP, ANTITRUST ENTERPRISE, *supra* n. 4 at 47 ("Antitrust is not good at transferring wealth, and cannot be defended on that basis in any event. Nor does it have any moral content of its own, and it is not well designed to provide rules of business ethics."); *id.* at 10 ("Antitrust is an economic, not a moral, enterprise."). *See also United States v. United Shoe Mach. Corp.*, 110 F. Supp. 295, 345 (D. Mass. 1953) ("The violation

involving basic human nature, such as the truthfulness of witnesses or the intent of the parties. The relevant questions are highly technical: What is the relevant market, as determined by cross-elasticity of demand between products;[24] does the defendant have market power in the relevant market, as determined by whether the defendant has the power to raise price without regard to competitive response;[25] did the defendant's actions harm the competitive process, as opposed to merely bringing harm to competitors[26]; were the defendants' actions justified by efficiency considerations[27]; does the anticompetitive effect of the conduct outweigh the pro-competitive benefit, and were there means less restrictive of competition to achieve the pro-competitive efficiencies[28]; and, in private cases, has the plaintiff suffered "antitrust injury," which is injury of the kind the antitrust laws were intended to prevent?[29] The Supreme Court has repeatedly stressed that antitrust does not impose rules of fair or ethical competition but merely specifies a technically defined norm of competition on the merits.[30]

---

with which United is now charged depends not on moral considerations, but on solely economic considerations."), *aff'd per curiam*, 347 U.S. 521 (1954).

24. *United States v. E.I. du Pont de Nemours & Co.*, 351 U.S. 377, 393–404 (1956) (holding that the relevant market is determined by whether there is "cross-elasticity of demand" between cellophane and other wrappings); *Brown Shoe Co. v. United States*, 370 U.S. 294, 325 (1962) (holding that the boundaries of a product market are determined by "interchangeability of use or the cross-elasticity of demand between the product itself and substitutes for it").

25. *National Collegiate Athletic Ass'n v. Board of Regents*, 468 U.S. 85, 109 n.38 (1984) ("Market power is the ability to raise prices above those that would be charged in a competitive market.").

26. *NYNEX Corp. v. Discon, Inc.*, 525 U.S. 128 (1998) (holding that plaintiff cannot succeed in antitrust case without showing harm to competitive process; even conduct that may be fraudulent, tortious, or otherwise unlawful does not implicate antitrust unless it causes harm to the competitive process).

27. *U.S. v. Microsoft Corp.*, 253 F.2d 34, 59 (2001) (holding that once plaintiff succeeds in showing that defendant's conduct was anticompetitive, burden shifts to defendant to offer efficiency justifications).

28. *Id.* (holding that once defendant shows that there are pro-competitive justifications for its conduct, burden shifts back to plaintiff to show that anticompetitive effects outweigh pro-competitive effects).; *U.S. v. Brown University*, 5 F.3d 658, 679 (3d Cir. 1993) ("Once a defendant demonstrates that its conduct promotes a legitimate goal, the plaintiff, in order to prevail, bears the burden of proving that there exists a viable less restrictive alternative.").

29. *Brunswick Corp. v. Pueblo Bowl-O-Mat, Inc.*, 429 U.S. 477 (1977) (holding that plaintiff in private antitrust cases for damages must show not only anticompetitive conduct but also that the harm suffered by the plaintiff was of the kind that the antitrust laws were intended to prevent).

30. *See, e.g., Brooke Group*. 509 U.S. at 225 ("Even an act of pure malice by one business competitor against another does not, without more, state a claim under the federal antitrust laws.").

Often, the critical evidence is documentary or interpretive, and there is not so much a dispute as to the occurrence of facts (i.e., whether someone attended a meeting or what a firm's revenues were) but instead as to their economic significance. Similarly, many courts have dismissed subjective intent as relatively unhelpful in determining antitrust cases.[31] Instead, antitrust has become focused almost entirely on a technical conception of economic efficiency. In this vision, antitrust is designed to encourage economic rivalry as a means of preventing output reduction attendant to collusive or exclusionary conduct.[32] Intent, truthfulness, and moral responsibility—three topics that juries might have some comparative advantage at divining—have been relegated to the margins of antitrust adjudication.

The antitrust jury sticks in the modern craw not merely because factual evidence suggests that antitrust juries systematically underperform, but also because the very democratic-populist justification for the jury conflicts with the modern account of antitrust law. Even without much empirical evidence on how juries actually perform in antitrust cases, the modern antitrust community has largely concluded that juries can't be expected to competently perform antitrust adjudication because juries necessarily lack the skill set demanded.

II. THE JURY'S LONG SHADOW

Given the small number of cases that actually land before antitrust juries, one may wonder whether all of the worry about jury underperformance is overblown. Perhaps antitrust juries are too trivial a player in modern antitrust adjudication to fret over. Yet, juries exert an influence well beyond the cases in which they sit as fact finders. Indeed, the entire system of civil antitrust adjudication is animated by a spirit of jury avoidance that affects the shape of both the substantive and procedural norms.

As we saw in Chapter 3, courts often frame antitrust liability rules to be deliberately underinclusive, at least partly to prevent many antitrust cases from reaching juries or resting on the jury's conclusions. *Brooke Group*, the case in which Cleo's populism prevailed in the jury room, is a case in point. The Supreme Court usually grants certiorari to decide abstract questions of general applicability, disdaining to consider the sufficiency of the evidence or other routine appellate reviews of the record. Yet, in *Brooke Group*, the Court took the extraordinary

---

31. Some judges and commentators see subjective intent as more helpful than others. *See* Ronald A. Cass & Keith N. Hylton, *Antitrust Intent*, 74 S. Cal. L. Rev. 657 (2001).

32. *See* Hovenkamp, Antitrust Enterprise, *supra* note 4 at 15–20 (explaining antitrust's model of consumer harm).

step of conducting sufficiency of the evidence review, parsing through the dense factual record, to reverse Liggett's verdict.[33]

Even stronger evidence of antitrust jury avoidance appears in the culture of motions to dismiss and, especially, summary judgment practice. The Supreme Court's *Matsushita*[34] decision directs trial courts to inquire into the economic plausibility of the plaintiff's claims before allowing them to go to a jury.[35] Lower courts even speak of a presumption in favor of summary judgment in antitrust cases.[36] Critics of the Supreme Court's summary judgment jurisprudence argue that *Matsushita* and similar cases have deprived the jury of many of its traditional functions.[37] This may be exactly what the Supreme Court intended. The litigation history of the *Matsushita* case suggests a direct linkage between a fear of incompetent juries and an aggressive summary judgment standard in antitrust cases.

Matsushita involved a claim by American television manufacturers that their Japanese competitors had engaged in a prolonged conspiracy to price predatorily in the United States. The case was factually dense and economically complex—the very kind of matter that a lay jury would be hard pressed to understand. During the course of the litigation, the United States Court of Appeals for the Third Circuit entertained an appeal from a pretrial order of the district court holding that parties to antitrust cases have an automatic right to a jury trial. While not deciding whether there was a jury trial right in the *Matsushita* case, the Third Circuit held that a party does not have a Seventh Amendment right to jury trial in an antitrust case if the trial would be so complex that the jury could not

---

33. In a predatory pricing case, the plaintiff claims that the defendant priced below its cost in order to drive a rival firm out of the market and thereafter recoup the costs of predation through supra-competitive pricing.

34. *Matsushita Elecs. Indus. Co. v. Zenith Radio Corp.*, 475 U.S. 574 (1986).

35. *Id.* at 587. Citing concerns about the cost and complexity of discovery, the Supreme Court recently appeared to extend this economic rationality inquiry back to the motion to dismiss stage. *See Bell Atl. Corp. v. Twombly*, 550 U.S. 544, 556 (2007) (holding that complaint alleging violation of Section 1 of the Sherman Act must allege facts sufficient to create "plausible grounds to infer an agreement").

36. *See, e.g., Thompson Everett, Inc. v. Nat'l Cable Adver., L.P.*, 57 F.3d 1317, 1322 (4th Cir. 1995) (stating that summary judgment may be a particularly appropriate and useful tool for sorting out the "unusual entanglement of legal and factual issues frequently presented in antitrust cases"); *Valley Liquors, Inc. v. Renfield Imp., Ltd.*, 822 F.2d 656, 660 n.4 (7th Cir. 1987) (stating that "summary judgment should be a favored practice in antitrust cases"); *Merck-Medco Managed Care, Inc. v. Rite Aid Corp.*, 22 F. Supp. 2d 447 (D. Md. 1998) (same); *Healthco Int'l, Inc. v. A-dec, Inc.*, 1989 2 Trade Cas. (CCH) ¶ 68,703, at 61,689 (D. Mass. 1989) (summary judgment in antitrust actions is "a desirable means of securing the just and speedy resolution of such actions").

37. *See, e.g.*, Arthur R. Miller, *The Pretrial Rush to Judgment: Are the "Litigation Explosion," "Liability Crisis," and Efficiency Clichés Eroding Our Day in Court and Jury Trial Commitments?* 78 N.Y.U. L. Rev. 982 (2003).

rationally perform its function.[38] That provocative decision never reached the Supreme Court because it was preempted by another way of avoiding jury trial in complex antitrust cases. After rejecting the defendants' motion to strike the plaintiffs' jury trial demand, the district court entered summary judgment for the defendants on the merits.[39] Aggressive use of summary judgment moots the need to take the politically sensitive step of dismissing the jury directly.

A recent example of jury avoidance appears in the Supreme Court's decision in *Bell Atlantic Corp. v. Twombly*, where the Court appeared to institute a heightened pleading standard in antitrust cases alleging conspiracy.[40] Justice Stevens's dissenting opinion accuses the majority of being overly concerned that jurors mistakenly find conspiracy when there is only evidence of parallel conduct—a matter which, per Justice Stevens, could be cured by "lucid instructions to juries."[41] What is interesting about this statement is that the majority opinion says nothing at all about juries or jury error, except to respond to Justice Stevens's argument by noting that "lucid instructions to juries" would not solve the problem of excessive discovery costs forcing the defendant into an early settlement.[42] Perhaps Justice Stevens's description of the majority's motivation is based on discussions in conference that the majority did not care to make part of its formal opinion.[43] In any event, the unstated fear of jury competence explains the underinclusive liability rules and aggressive motion to dismiss summary judgment standards that the courts have imposed as antitrust has become increasingly technical and complex.[44]

This unstated concern over jury competence may have spillover effects far beyond antitrust. As Arthur Miller noted about the Supreme Court's *Matsushita* decision, the antitrust summary judgment standard was seemingly based on antitrust-specific concerns but has been used much more broadly in civil

---

38. *See In re Japanese Elec. Prod. Antitrust Litig.*, 631 F.2d 1069 (3d Cir. 1980).

39. *See Zenith Radio Corp. v. Matsushita Elecs. Indus. Co.*, 494 F. Supp. 1190 (E.D. Pa. 1980).

40. *Twombly*, 550 U.S. 544.

41. *Id.* at 1975.

42. *Id.* at 1967.

43. The possibility of jury error was discussed tangentially in the parties' briefs. *See Bell Atlantic Corp. v. Twombly*, Respondents' Brief in Opposition to Petition for Certiorari, 2006 WL 1465524, *18 (May 24, 2006).

44. In another antitrust case contemporary with *Twombly*, the Court justified its holding that securities law preempted antitrust lawsuits against initial public offering syndicates by noting the risk that "the threat of antitrust mistakes" and "error" in the adjudication of antitrust lawsuits. *Credit Suisse Securities (USA) LLC v. Billings*, 127 S. Ct. 2383, 2396 (2007). *See generally* Daniel A. Crane, *Antitrust Antifederalism*, 96 Cal. L. Rev. 1, 33–38 (2008) (discussing earlier precedents evidencing concern over false positives in antitrust jury trials).

litigation.[45] Similarly, there is reason to believe that *Twombly's* motion to dismiss standard may spill over to other fields where democratic modalities may be more appropriate than they are in antitrust. The antitrust jury is a populist thorn in antitrust's side; and the remedies administered may affect adjacent bodies as well.

Adjudicatory statistics reveal that judicial jury avoidance has become a dominant characteristic of private antitrust litigation. Three-quarters of all federal antitrust cases are dismissed on a motion to dismiss or for summary judgment.[46] The effect on antitrust decision making is pernicious. Many important decisions that would best be made following the give-and-take of cross-examination and expert testimony in a courtroom or administrative proceeding are, instead, made under the artificial strictures of procedural rules that were not designed with the complexity of industrial policy making in mind. For instance, on motions to dismiss and for summary judgment motions, the district judge is supposed to ask whether the plaintiff's theory is economically plausible.[47] This requires a generalist judge (or, often, her clerk)—who is usually not trained in economics—to speculate about the economic plausibility of the plaintiff's assertions based initially on a set of supported allegations and later on a dense paper record collected, sifted, and spun by the lawyers. In making this determination, the judge cannot take live testimony; ask clarifying questions of witnesses; or rely on recommendations by neutral experts, who generally are only employed at trial.[48]

---

45. Arthur R. Miller, *The Pretrial Rush to Judgment: Are the "Litigation Explosion," "Liability Crisis," and Efficiency Clichés Eroding Our Day in Court and Jury Trial Commitments?*, 78 N.Y.U. L. Rev. 982, 1032 (2003) ("Thus, there are compelling arguments that the Supreme Court's holding in Matsushita, declaring the plaintiffs' requested inference implausible, was mandated by substantive antitrust law and the traditional conception of summary judgment, not by any heightened standard to be generally imposed on parties defending against the motion."); *id.* at 1055 (describing courts' willingness to take the Supreme Court's willingness to grant summary judgment in a complex antitrust action as a signal to be receptive to the motion in other contexts as well).

46. Between 2001 and 2005, 3766 private antitrust cases were terminated in the federal courts. Eight hundred sixty-one, or about 23 percent, were terminated through voluntary dismissal or private settlement. Seventy-five percent of the cases, or 2828, were dismissed by order of the court before trial, most often in response to a defendant's motion to dismiss or for summary judgment. Only 77 cases, about 2 percent of the cases, went to trial, and of these, only 45 cases were tried to juries. These data were collected from the administrative offices of the U.S. Courts..

47. *Twombly*, 550 U.S. at 556–57; *Matsushita*, 475 U.S. at 595–600.

48. *See* Hovenkamp, Antitrust Enterprise, *supra* note 4, at 89–90 (advocating greater use of neutral experts in antitrust trials); Posner, Antitrust Law 277–78 (2d ed. 2001) (suggesting the use of a neutral expert agreed upon by each party's expert); Learned Hand, *Historical and Practical Considerations Regarding Expert Testimony*, 15 Harv. L. Rev. 40, 56 (1901) (advocating for "a board of experts or a single expert, not called by either side, who shall advise the jury of the general propositions applicable to the case which lie within his

The dynamics of the courtroom and its truth-seeking structure are replaced by the mismatch of a mundane pretrial mechanism and an esoteric economic inquiry that most judges are ill equipped to make in a vacuum.

III. THE CRIMINAL JURY

Most of the anti-jury rhetoric has probably been motivated by a negative perception of civil juries. Do criminal juries share the infirmities of civil juries? Arthur Austin, who performed the civil jury interviews described earlier, argues that the civil jury's problems are modest compared to those of the criminal jury, but he has in mind celebrity trials like the media circus surrounding O.J. Simpson's murder prosecution.[49] With a few exceptions, antitrust prosecutions do not attract much media attention. Notable exceptions include the Archer Daniels Midlands lysine cartel—later made into a Hollywood movie called *The Informant*, due to the quirky personality of its central figure—and the Christie's/Sotheby's auction house commission price-fixing case, which involved flamboyant personalities in the world of high art.[50] Most cartel cases involve relatively obscure intermediate manufactured goods like cement, graphite, and glass rather than consumer goods that might show up in the newspaper headlines.[51] Despite the billions of dollars in costs to consumers, these cases seldom generate much public attention.

Today, criminal enforcement is reserved for hard-core cartel behavior, such as price-fixing, bid rigging, market division, and related practices. Criminal enforcement has become highly effective in recent years with significant enhancements in enforcement techniques including international cooperation and an amnesty program that has pressured cartel members to cooperate with the authorities.[52] Many jurisdictions outside the United States are moving toward U.S.-style

---

province"); John E. Lopatka & William H. Page, *Economic Authority and the Limits of Expertise in Antitrust Cases*, 90 CORNELL L. REV. 617, 628 (2005) (discussing use of neutral experts in antitrust cases).

49. Austin, *supra* n. 6, at 66.

50. *See* KURT EICHENWALD, THE INFORMANT: A TRUE STORY (2000); CHRISTOPHER MASON, THE ART OF THE STEAL: INSIDE THE SOTHEBY'S—CHRISTIE'S AUCTION HOUSE SCANDAL (2004).

51. *See* John M. Connor, *Cartels & Antitrust Portrayed: Private International Cartels from 1990–2008*, http://papers.ssrn.com/sol3/papers.cfm?abstract_id=1467310.

52. *See* Gary R. Spratling, *Making Companies an Offer They Shouldn't Refuse: The Antitrust Division's Corporate Leniency Policy-An Update*, Address Before the Bar Association of the District of Columbia's 35th Annual Symposium on Associations and Antitrust 1–2 (Feb. 16, 1999) (noting greater success in criminal enforcement against international cartels since the adoption of the amnesty policy), *available at* http://www.usdoj.gov/atr/public/speeches/2247.pdf.

criminal enforcement, essentially endorsing the U.S. criminal enforcement model as a success.[53]

Criminal enforcement is a small fraction of overall antitrust enforcement. The federal government files an average of fewer than fifty criminal cases a year, and the majority of these terminate in a pretrial plea bargain.[54] Beyond the similarly low absolute numbers, the statistics with respect to criminal antitrust enforcement evidence a very different juridical culture than that of the jury-avoidant civil antitrust system. Two figures stand out: First, whereas courts dismiss on pretrial motion about three-quarters of private civil antitrust cases that would otherwise be bound for a jury,[55] they dismiss charges against only about 2 percent of criminal antitrust defendants.[56] Second, whereas only about 2 percent of all civil antitrust cases are tried, half to a jury half to a judge,[57] criminal antitrust defendants go to trial before juries about 11 percent of the time.[58] In contrast to civil practice where the parties consent to a bench trial in about half of the cases that go to trial, there have been no reported bench trials in criminal cases in the last ten years.[59]

A partial explanation for these differences is that criminal and civil antitrust are conceptually and culturally very different enterprises. In the post-Chicago School era, civil antitrust law has become an increasingly complex and technical regulatory enterprise where economic experts play the starring role. On the other hand, criminal antitrust enforcement has retained an individualistic, constitutionalistic, and moralistic criminal law culture that partakes more of the culture of federal criminal law—suppression hearings, leniency agreements, sentencing guidelines, etc.—than it does of the culture of civil antitrust. Unlike civil antitrust and like other similar kinds of white collar offenses—such as RICO and securities fraud—criminal antitrust remains interested in the intent, truthfulness,

---

53. *See generally* International Competition Network, *Trends and Developments in Cartel Enforcement* (April 29, 2010), available at http://www.internationalcompetitionnetwork.org/uploads/library/doc613.pdf.

54. United States Antitrust Division, *Workload Statistics: FY* 1997–2006 (2007) [hereinafter Antitrust Division Workload Statistics], *available at* http://www.usdoj.gov/atr/public/workstats.pdf.

55. *See* Crane, *Antitrust Antifederalism, supra* n. 44 at 37.

56. The statistics reported here are based on the Annual Reports of the Director of the Administrative Offices of the U.S. Courts for the years 1997–2006. The data are collected from the Detailed Statistical Tables for U.S. District Courts, *available at* www.uscourts.gov, Table D-4 (Defendants Disposed of, by Type of Disposition and Major Offense).

57. *See* Crane, *Antitrust Antifederalism, supra* n. 44 at 37.

58. Detailed Statistical Tables for U.S. District Courts, *available at* www.uscourts.gov, Table D-4. The underlying data are the following: Between 1997 and 2006, there were 336 defendant dispositions, 7 by dismissal, 10 by jury trial acquittal, 288 by plea bargain, and 21 by jury trial conviction.

59. *Id.*

knowledge, and moral culpability of the individual.[60] These are the sorts of matters on which lay juries may have some comparative advantage over experts and for which the jury's democratic function may be well suited. It is thus not surprising that the jury avoidance that so strongly characterizes civil antitrust enforcement is manifested more weakly in criminal cases.

The political dynamics of criminal adjudication are also very different than in civil adjudication. Whereas many large corporate defendants are terrified to go before juries in cases involving smaller business plaintiffs or consumer class actions due to a fear of latent populist bias, it is not clear whether there is any particular directional bias in price-fixing cases. The government can play "greedy rich businessmen" themes, but the defendants—particularly the individual defendants—can equally well play antigovernment themes appealing to populist-libertarian sentiments. Unlike the received wisdom that big business should do anything to avoid juries in private cases, there is no comparable view that either the government or individual defendants should, all else being equal, seek to avoid a jury trial in a criminal price-fixing case. If there were, we would see defendants waiving their right to jury trials, which we seldom see.[61]

The upshot is that there is less reason to be suspicious of a continuing role for juries in criminal cases than there is in private civil cases.[62] Although criminal jury cases sometimes involve the same kinds of technical economic evidence that permeates private civil cases, criminal cartel cases are often not very different from other white collar prosecutions.

60. A good example of this is Justice Department's criminal prosecution of executives involved in the price-fixing conspiracy between Christies' and Sotheby's. After incriminating facts emerged it became apparent that a price-fixing conspiracy had been effectuated between the two firms, a matter which sealed the fate of the corporate defendants in the class action lawsuits brought by aggrieved buyers and sellers on the auction houses. Nonetheless, there remained ample questions for the jury's determination in the ensuing criminal case, which focused largely on *who* at the various firms was responsible for the illegal agreement, and to what degree. *See generally* Mason, *The Art of the Steal, supra* n. 50.

61. The government could theoretically demand a jury trial even if the defendant waived his Sixth Amendment right. *Singer v. U.S.*, 380 U.S. 24 (1965). However, it is unlikely that the government would often insist on a jury trial in antitrust cases if the defendant preferred a bench trial.

62. There are essentially no government civil jury cases, since such cases are almost always injunctive and hence require the trial judge, not a jury, to sit as the trier of fact.

IV. LIVING WITH ANTITRUST JURIES

Having now spent some time with antitrust juries and their systemic effects, we can ask what should be done about them. As we have just seen, part of the answer is to distinguish between civil and criminal juries. Whatever the infirmities of civil juries, these criticisms apply much less to criminal juries. Whatever reforms might be proposed should take into account the distinctiveness of the jury role in the civil and criminal contexts.

Another matter that deserves some consideration in any discussion about the competence of juries is the alternative—are generalist federal district court judges any better? As noted at the outset, many of the criticisms of juries have included criticisms of generalist judges as well. Alas, we know even less (on a systematic basis) about the actual workings of district court judges in antitrust cases than we do about juries, since juries have attracted some study as a discrete institution whereas trial judges have not. In Chapter 11, we shall look at models of specialized antitrust courts in other countries and ask about their advantages and disadvantages. But even without being part of specialized courts, federal district judges are unlikely to share all of the infirmities of juries in complex antitrust cases. Their background, education, socialization, promotion and reputational incentives, and other social and demographic qualities are very different from those of the average juror.

In any event, given the constitutional bar on eliminating civil antitrust juries by statute, we are largely stuck with antitrust juries as a feature of the adjudicatory system. The federal courts have already gone a long way—perhaps as far as they can go—to grant trial courts strong screening functions to prevent many cases from ever reaching juries. But a small number of cases, perhaps a quarter of all civil antitrust cases, will still pass the motion to dismiss, motion for summary judgment, and *Daubert*[63] stages and head toward juries. At that stage, most cases will settle on terms comparatively favorable to the plaintiff, since the defendant will often have more to fear (whether perceived or real) from the jury than the plaintiff. And then a few civil antitrust cases will still slip through and be tried by juries.

The question, then, is whether there are further controls on the management of actual jury trials that could improve the functioning of the private antitrust system. A range of options are possible. The strongest version—reflected in the Third Circuit's *Matsushita* decision discussed above—would be to take away entire cases from juries when they become overly complex. Whether or not such an option is broadly available is an open question. Several other

63. *Daubert v. Merrell Dow Pharm., Inc.*, 509 U.S. 579 (1993) (requiring trial judges to play role as gatekeepers to decide whether expert witnesses are adequately qualified as experts).

appellate courts have rejected such an exception,[64] and the Supreme Court has yet to decide the question.

An intermediate possibility is to selectively remove complex antitrust issues from juries while allowing them to decide less-complex questions (assuming there are any). In *Markman v. Westview Instruments*,[65] the Supreme Court endorsed a similar approach in patent cases, holding that judges, not juries, should construe patent claims (i.e., the specific features that the written patent claims to cover) even while allowing the jury to serve other functions in a patent infringement suit. Similarly, judges in civil antitrust cases might eliminate entire fact questions from juries, deciding, for example, the scope of the relevant market, the classification of costs as fixed or variable, and the percentage of the market foreclosed and leaving to juries more general questions such as whether the defendant had predatory intent or whether a competitor's product had a reasonable chance of market acceptance. Whether such an approach would survive constitutional scrutiny is also an open question.

An alternative less invasive of the jury's traditional role and more clearly within constitutional bounds would be to more carefully frame the questions that the jury is asked to answer. The practice in civil antitrust cases is often to give juries very broad instructions on the kinds of antitrust issues presented and then to give them a verdict form, calling for up or down decisions on the different counts of the complaint.[66] However, under Rule 49 of the Federal Rules of Civil Procedure, courts have the option of giving juries general verdicts with interrogatories or special verdict forms instead. While there are clear disadvantages to moving away from general verdicts, a more cabined form of judicial questionnaire to the jury has a greater likelihood of avoiding the sort of unbridled jury populism described in the preceding pages by revealing inconsistency in jury decisions, evidencing a fundamental misunderstanding of the relevant law and economic concepts.[67]

Scholars concerned about the continuing viability of civil juries in a world of increasing legal and regulatory complexity have offered various proposals along these lines. For instance, Cass Sunstein, Daniel Kahneman, and David Schkade have advocated a form of "technocratic populism" for punitive damages awards in tort cases in which the judge translates the jury's "punitive intent" into an appropriate damages figure.[68] The jury would be asked to rank or rate the severity

---

64. *See SRI Intern. v. Matsushita Elec. Corp.*, 775 F.2d 1107, 1130 (Fed. Cir. 1985); *In re United States Fin. Sec. Litig.*, 609 F.2d 411, 430 (9th Cir. 1979).

65. 517 U.S. 370 (1996).

66. *See* Model Jury Instructions in Civil Cases: 2005 Edition (ABA 2005).

67. *See generally Developments in the Law: The Civil Jury*, 110 Harv. L. Rev. 1408, 1493–1503 (1997).

68. Cass R. Sunstein et al., *Assessing Punitive Damages (With Notes on Cognition and Valuation in the Law)*, 107 Yale L.J. 2071, 2120–21 (1998).

of the defendant's wrongdoing, and the judge would then perform the technocratic task of determining the amount of money necessary to achieve the punitive goal identified by the jury.[69] In this model, the jury would retain its traditional democratic functions as to matters well suited to democratic reasoning, even while the judge would prevent more technically intensive matters from falling into the jurors' hands. Although in antitrust cases, the multiplier is set by statute at three and therefore no determination of a damages multiplier is required,[70] the use of special interrogatories or verdict forms on other matters could help to channel the jury's intuitions into a more consistent, reliable, and robust adjudicatory methodology.

There is no silver bullet that will instantly solve the problem of civil antitrust juries, given its constitutional foundations. Further, as observed at the outset, it is not even clear how deep the problem really is—to put it bluntly, how either incompetent or biased civil antitrust juries really are. For now, then, the best that can be done is to systematically study the behavior of performance of antitrust juries and continue to experiment with procedural mechanisms to bring their judgments more in line with the modern, technical, and economic concepts of antitrust.

---

69. *Id.*

70. 15 U.S.C.A. § 15 (2007).

7. ENHANCING FEDERAL ENFORCEMENT

Chapter 2 considered the reasons for the existence and persistence of two federal antitrust enforcement agencies. It concluded that dual enforcement's conceptual flaws and frequent malfunctions justified reconsideration of the division of responsibility between the agencies. Yet, it also acknowledged that the political will for such institutional redesign is presently lacking. This chapter considers some ways to enhance the enforcement powers of the two agencies without radically altering the institutional status quo. It turns out that there is more to say about the FTC than about the Antitrust Division, not because the FTC is a failure and the Antitrust Division a success. This is because there is more latitude for experimentation and institutional remodeling with a freestanding commission than with a comparatively small branch of the Justice Department.

There are doubtless many changes that could be made in the agencies' internal organization and resource allocation, for example, with respect to the departmental organization of economists and lawyers or the internal review processes for agency decisions with respect to subpoena compliance or other document requests.[1] Consistent with the broader themes of this book, however, this chapter is primarily concerned with improving the agencies' norm-creation capabilities and powers in relation to the roles of other institutional players such as generalist judges, private litigants, and juries.

I. IMPROVING THE ANTITRUST DIVISION

As discussed in Chapter 3, the Justice Department's Antitrust Division is sometimes a captive to norms created in private litigation since private suits vastly outnumber its own enforcement actions, and it enforces the same statute as the private litigants enforce. Unlike the FTC, to be discussed momentarily, the Antitrust Division does not have the option of declaring independence from the Sherman Act and enforcing some separate governmental enforcement statute. Perhaps unavoidably, the courts construed the Sherman Act as having the same substantive content in public and private cases.[2] This lack of an independent statutory norm-creation assignment is sometimes problematic and sometimes largely irrelevant.

1. *See generally* Antitrust Modernization Commission Report (2007).

2. *U.S. v. Microsoft Corp.*, 253 F.3d 34, 59 (D.C. Cir. 2001) (noting that "no less in a case brought by the Government" the plaintiff "must demonstrate that the monopolist's conduct harmed competition, not just a competitor").

In at least one context, private enforcement is almost entirely irrelevant to public enforcement. As we saw in Chapter 5, the lack of an independent statutory role is no longer a problem for the Antitrust Division in the merger control area. Since the 1976 Hart-Scott-Rodino Act, the Antitrust Division and FTC have largely created merger norms without interference from private litigants and with only occasional input from the courts. Modern merger control is the leading successful model of an administrative technocratic solution to problems of market power. Although the Justice Department has lost some high-profile merger cases in court,[3] those losses have not been due to private litigation overhang and have not been generally representative of the department's enforcement activities.[4] Merger control, which accounts for a large portion of the Antitrust Division's work, requires no fundamental institutional change.

The Antitrust Divisions' two other primary functions—criminal anti-cartel enforcement and civil monopolization and restraint of trade enforcement—are a different story. In both of these areas, the Antitrust Division enforces the same Sherman Act provisions as courts apply in private Sherman Act cases and thus must contend with the baggage of private litigation.

The problem is less acute on the criminal than on the civil enforcement side. In criminal cases, the Justice Department is usually the first to detect the cartel, bring an indictment, and either plea bargain or go to trial. The Justice Department has many investigatory tools, such as leniency offers, intergovernmental cooperation, search warrants, wiretaps, and grand jury subpoenas that enable it to crack concealed cartels long before the private plaintiffs' bar discover their existence.[5] Since the government gets to bring and try the case first, it is usually not beholden to any private litigation precedent already created with respect to the particular cartel in question.

The government is still beholden to general price-fixing norms, many of which will have been created in other private price-fixing cases—usually involving alleged cartels that the Justice Department decided not to prosecute. Thus, for example, many of the most significant decisions about the meaning of

---

3. *See, e.g., U.S. v. Oracle Corp.*, 331 F. Supp. 2d 1098 (N.D. Cal. 2004).

4. Merger cases that end up in litigation are not very representative of merger cases more generally. Because of the structure of the Hart-Scott-Rodino pre-merger notification and second request system, even parties who think that they might win a court battle have a strong incentive to settle on the terms demanded by the Justice Department (usually by divesting assets) or even to abandon the merger. The few cases that ultimately make it to court involve parties who have the unusual luxury of waiting out the lengthy Hart-Scott and litigation processes to see if their merger will be allowed. *See* Daniel A. Crane, *Antitrust Antifederalism*, 96 CAL. L. REV. 1, 52–57 (2008).

5. *See generally* Scott D. Hammond, Deputy Assistant Attorney General for Criminal Enforcement, Antitrust Division, U.S. Dept. of Justice, *The Evolution of Criminal Antitrust Enforcement Over the Last Two Decades* (Feb. 25, 2010), available at http://www.justice.gov/atr/public/speeches/255515.htm.

"agreement" for purposes of the requirement that a plaintiff prove the existence of a "contract, combination, or conspiracy" have come from private cases.[6] So there is still some private litigation overhang on criminal cartel cases, but it is probably not so significant as to require major institutional changes in anti-cartel enforcement.

The area where the Justice Department most clearly experiences the consequences of norms being created in private litigation is in rule-of-reason cases against joint ventures and monopolization lawsuits against dominant firms—the Department's two major areas of non-cartel, nonmerger antitrust enforcement. The effects are subtle, which is perhaps why private enforcement overhang has not been raised as a great concern. It does not appear from the Justice Department's recent track record in litigation that its enforcement powers in these areas have been significantly impaired. In the last several decades, it has won most of the important stages of cases it has chosen to litigate, including the high-profile *Microsoft* case (where it won the core of its case on liability),[7] its case against Visa and MasterCard's exclusivity rules,[8] its challenge to the National Association of Realtors' limitations on online real estate brokerage,[9] and an exclusive dealing case against a dental lab supplier.[10] Its only major loss in a joint venture or monopolization case was the American Airlines predatory pricing case (discussed in Chapter 3), where the overhang of private litigation almost certainly played an important role.[11]

But it would be misguided to judge the effect of private litigation on the Justice Department's litigation results solely by its track record in cases it decides to bring. The Antitrust Division only brings cases it thinks it can win, and its judgment about what cases it thinks it can win is affected by its analysis of prevailing legal norms, which are heavily affected by private litigation. There is little doubt, for example, that the Obama Justice Department would like to bring cases that prevailing legal norms would make it very difficult to win.[12]

---

6. *See, e.g.*, *Monsanto Co. v. Spray-Rite Service Corp.*, 465 U.S. 752 (1984); *Theater Enterp., Inc. v. Paramount Film Dist. Corp.*, 346 U.S. 537 (1954).

7. *Microsoft*, 253 F.3d 34.

8. *U.S. v. Visa USA, Inc.*, 344 F.3d 229 (2d Cir. 2003).

9. *U.S. v. Nat'l Ass'n of Realtors*, No. 05 C 5140, 2006 WL 3434263 (N.D. Il. Nov. 27, 2006).

10. *U.S. v. Dentsply Int'l, Inc.*, 399 F.3d 181 (3d Cir. 2005).

11. *U.S. v. AMR Corp.*, 335 F.3d 1109 (10th Cir. 2003).

12. For example, in her first major speech as the Assistant Attorney General for the Antitrust Division, Christine Varney discussed the Supreme Court's *Aspen Skiing* decision as an example of a "balanced" and "leading" case. Christine A. Varney, *Vigorous Antitrust Enforcement in this Challenging Era*, Remarks as Prepared for the Center for American Progress (May 11, 2009), available at http://www.justice.gov/atr/public/speeches/245711.htm (citing *Aspen Skiing Co. v. Aspen Highlands Skiing Corp.*, 472 U.S. 585 (1985)). However, *Aspen Skiing's* approach to unilateral refusals to deal by dominant firms is almost

This is not to say that the restrictive liability norms are necessarily wrong or that the Justice Department should enjoy carte blanche in bringing antitrust cases. Rather, the point is that a rational antitrust policy requires that norms be adapted to their institutional context. The current dogma, which treats the meaning of the Sherman Act as a platonic abstraction to be applied uniformly in all cases, misses the realist understanding that norms depend heavily on institutions and dulls the effectiveness of public litigation for reasons that have little to do with public enforcement.

There is no easy way to circumvent this problem without an improbable wholesale statutory revision of the antitrust laws. However, three smaller steps—two of which the Justice Department could pursue on its own initiative and one of which would require a modest intervention by Congress—are feasible.

A. Making Policy in Private Litigation Wastelands

The Justice Department can best reclaim a norm-creative role by marketing itself as the enforcer of antitrust policy in circumstances where private litigation is ineffective, inadequate, or impossible. Private antitrust litigation sometimes has difficulty reaching entire industries because of semiprocedural, semisubstantive doctrines like standing, causation of injury, and antitrust injury. The Justice Department does not face these obstacles. While it is nominally allowed to seek treble damages on behalf of the federal government,[13] it usually seeks only injunctive remedies. A plaintiff cannot prevail in an injunctive case without proving the existence of an antitrust violation,[14] but the Supreme Court has relaxed standing rules when plaintiffs seek injunctions rather than damages.[15] This means that the government never has to wade through the often case-dispositive threshold standing issues that often bog down private litigation. Similarly, unlike a private plaintiff, the government need not prove harm to itself—only to the competitive process. Thus, while a competitor plaintiff can only establish a right to damages if it shows that it was excluded from the market, the government can prevail even without proof that defendants excluded actual or potential competitors.[16] Similarly, while a private plaintiff must prove not only an injury causally related to an antitrust violation but also "antitrust injury"—that its injury was the

---

completely moribund in the Supreme Court. In *Verizon Communcs. Inc. v. Law Offices of Curtis V. Trinko, LLP*, 540 U.S. 398, 409 (2004), the Court referred to *Aspen Skiing* as residing "at or near the outer boundary of § 2 liability," a polite way of confining *Aspen Skiing* to its facts.

13. 15 U.S.C. § 15a (reversing holding of *United States v. Cooper Corp.*, 312 U.S. 600 (1941), which disallowed treble damages actions by the Government).

14. *See*, e.g., *Moore v. New York Cotton Exchange*, 270 U.S. 593 (1926).

15. *Cargill, Inc. v. Montford of Colorado, Inc.*, 479 U.S. 104, 111 n.6 (1986).

16. *American Tobacco Co. v. U.S.*, 328 U.S. 781, 810 (1946).

kind that antitrust law was meant to prevent[17]—the government bears no such burden since it does not have to prove an injury of any kind to itself.

The Justice Department can exploit these private enforcement gaps by bringing suit in industries or industry circumstances that private litigation has not yet reached. For example, imagine a dominant pharmaceutical company that has completely monopolized an industry by keeping rivals far from entering the market. The rivals could not bring suit, since they could not show the "intention and preparedness" to enter, and customers could not bring suit, either, since their injury would depend on a showing that some rival was prepared to enter.[18] Although in such cases the Justice Department would still be somewhat beholden to general antitrust norms created in private litigation, it would enjoy greater freedom to mold the development of public enforcement norms by claiming a unique need for its enforcement activities and the unlikelihood that its lawsuit would engender follow-on private litigation.

It is overreaching to ask courts explicitly to differentiate substantive liability determinants in private and government cases, but it is underreaching not to remind courts that norms and their applications depend heavily on institutions and remedies. As the Supreme Court once noted, the motivations of private and government enforcers are entirely different, and "[t]he scheme of the [antitrust] statute is sharply to distinguish between Government suits, either criminal or civil, and private suits for injunctive relief or damages. Different policy considerations govern each of these."[19] In order to reemerge as a norm entrepreneur, the Antitrust Division needs to lay claim to a unique role in circumstances where private litigation is ineffective and unique "policy considerations" apply.

B. Eliminating Private Enforcement Collateral Estoppel

A further step to limit the overhang of private litigation would be to limit the collateral estoppel effects of judicial determinations in injective cases on subsequent damages cases. Under present law, if the Justice Department prevails in an injunctive case, private plaintiffs suing the same defendant can claim as conclusively established any finding of fact or law in the prior case if the finding was critical and necessary to the prior judgment.[20] Thus, for example, when private plaintiff sued Microsoft after the Justice Department case, any of Judge Jackson's finding of fact or law that were essential to his holding were conclusively established against Microsoft.[21] In light of this reality, even if courts were otherwise sympathetic to adapting liability norms to the institutional context,

17. *Brunswick Corp. v. Pueblo Bowl-O-Mat, Inc.*, 429 U.S. 477 (1977).

18. *See*, e.g., *Meijer, Inc. v. Biovail Corp.*, 533 F.3d 857, 862 (D.C. Cir. 2008).

19. *U.S. v. Borden Co.*, 347 U.S. 514, 518–19 (1954).

20. *In re Microsoft Corp. Antitrust Litig.*, 355 F.3d 322, 328 (3d Cir. 2004). *See also Parklane Hosiery Co. v. Shore*, 439 U.S. 322 (1979).

21. *In re Microsoft*, 355 F.3d at 328.

they may be reluctant to do so because of the collateral consequences in a different institutional context.

Congress has already recognized that follow-on treble-damages actions can dull the effectiveness of the public agencies' enforcement powers. Under the Antitrust Criminal Penalty Enhancement and Reform Act of 2004,[22] when the Justice Department enters into leniency agreements with price-fixing defendants, private plaintiffs in subsequent cases can recover only single damages—not the ordinary treble damages. More fundamentally, the federal statute on antitrust judgments provides that final judgments or decrees in civil or criminal antitrust cases brought by the Justice Department can be the basis for collateral estoppel in subsequent private cases, but that collateral estoppel does not apply to consent decrees or FTC actions.[23] These provisions recognize that the defendants will be reluctant to settle or cooperate with the Antirust Division if that sets them up for greater exposure in subsequent private litigation. It also recognizes that the FTC will likely face greater scrutiny in reviewing appellate courts if there are extensive collateral consequences in private litigation.

A simple statutory amendment could allow the Justice Department to unshackle itself from subsequent private litigation spillovers by allowing the Justice Department to make a formal filing at the outset of the litigation declaring that the case would have no collateral estoppel or evidentiary consequences in subsequent private cases. Such a declaration—if made binding and effective by statute—could act as a signal to the judge to consider the liability and remedial issues solely within their immediate institutional context. Should the Justice Department prefer to allow private plaintiffs to free ride on its efforts in a particular case, it could simply decline to exercise the option.

C. Embracing the FTC's Unique Statutory Position

A final step would require the Justice Department to swallow some of its pride and invite cooperation from the FTC. The FTC was designed as a complement to, not as a substitute for, the Justice Department. The FTC Act's legislative history evidences a Congressional intent that "[f]ar from being regarded as a rival of the Justice Department . . . the [FTC] was envisioned as an aid to them."[24] The FTC Act contains several mechanisms for collaborative antitrust enforcement between the two agencies, in particular on questions of remedy. Section 6(c) of the act calls for the Commission to monitor compliance with antitrust decrees obtained by the Justice Department.[25] Section 6(e) allows the attorney general to request that the FTC "make recommendations for the readjustment of the business

---

22. § 213(a), Pub. L. 108-237, 118 Stat. 666 (2004) (codified in scattered sections of 15 U.S.C. and accompanying notes).

23. 15 U.S.C. § 16(a).

24. *FTC v. Cement Inst.*, 333 U.S. 683, 692–93 (1948).

25. 15 U.S.C. § 46(c).

of any corporation alleged to be violating the Antitrust Acts in order that the corporation may thereafter maintain its organization, management, and conduct of business in accordance with law."[26] Section 7 of the act allows district courts to refer Department of Justice antitrust cases to the FTC to sit as a "master of chancery" and determine the appropriate form of relief.[27]

Despite Congress's obvious intention that the two agencies collaborate in antitrust matters, these statutory provisions have been seldom used. In a 1962 letter to the chairman of the FTC, referring a decree matter to the FTC under Section 6(c), the attorney general stated the section had been "virtually unused since its enactment in 1914,"[28] and the neglect of 6(c) has continued since that time. Throughout the history of U.S. antitrust, the practice has largely been to treat the agencies as substitutes rather than complements. They have essentially divided industries and negotiated a clearance processes to decide which agency will handle a particular case.[29] Apart from the FTC's recent threat to bring monopolization cases in traditional Justice Department industries if the Antitrust Division became overly conservative,[30] the agencies have treated their respective fiefdoms as implicitly jurisdictional—fighting over turf only when the jurisdictional boundaries were murky.

The Justice Department could signal a clear institutional separation from private litigation by inviting the FTC's cooperation in high-profile antitrust cases. Although embracing the Commission model and interweaving its statutory advantages into its own cases would require some sharing of authority, such a move could eventually enhance the Justice Department's strength and litigation position. At least that would be the case if the FTC reemerged as an independent norm-creative power: the subject to which we now turn.

II. IMPROVING THE FEDERAL TRADE COMMISSION

A quick review of some key themes from the first part of this book will help set the stage for some thoughts on improving the performance of the FTC in its antitrust capacity. In Chapters 1 and 2, we saw that the FTC was a product of the Progressive Era, but that it was denied a fully technocratic norm-creation role associated with that era's values. In Chapter 3, we saw that one consequence of the rise and dominance of private enforcement in the post-war era was that the

26. 15 U.S.C. § 46(e).

27. 15 U.S.C. § 47.

28. *U.S. v. Int'l Nickel Co. of Can.*, 203 F.Supp. 739 (S.D.N.Y. 1962)

29. *See* the discussion of Justice Department/FTC clearance issues in Chapter 2.

30. FTC Commissioners React to Department of Justice Report, "*Competition and Monopoly: Single-Firm Conduct Under Section 2 of the Sherman Act*," (Sept. 8, 2008), http://www2.ftc.gov/opa/2008/09/section2.shtm.

creation of antitrust norms shifted from government cases to private cases. In large part due to this shift, the FTC lost the power to create antitrust norms on its own and became subservient to norms created by generalist courts, usually in private litigation. The Commission has become beholden to constricted norms embedded with institutional concerns that do not reflect its unique institutional position.

Whatever the optimal level of antitrust enforcement, there are no sound reasons of institutional design for treating the FTC as simply an ordinary antitrust litigant—a norm taker rather than a norm maker. If the Commission does not enjoy sufficient independence from private litigation to shape the formation of antitrust norms, there is not much of a reason to have one. Consider the following passage from Cass Sunstein's seminal work, *After the Rights Revolution*:

> Imagine. . . the multiple problems that would arise if private litigants were permitted to bring suit against "unfair and deceptive" advertising in the event that the Federal Trade Commission refused to act. Courts would be required to define in the first instance the statutory terms "unfair" and "deceptive." The process of regulatory implementation would be removed from the agency. Administrative expertise and accountability, so important in giving content to open-ended statutory terms, would be unavailable. All of the factors that gave rise to the agency would be undermined by independent judicial decisions.[31]

Sunstein's hypothetical ruminations about the loss of the FTC norm-creation authority in its consumer protection function uncannily describes what has actually occurred on the antitrust side. The Commission has lost an independent norm-creation power, and with it, "all of the factors that gave rise to the agency."

Of course, those who do not embrace the technocratic expert commission model may cheer the demise of an independent, norm-creative FTC and hope that its relegation to conventional law enforcement spells its continued marginalization and perhaps, in the footsteps of the Interstate Commerce Commission and the Public Utilities Holding Company Act, its eventual elimination. Without trying to mount a complete defense of technocratic agency expertise, let me offer two brief thoughts to those in this camp.

First, as discussed in Chapter 2, the FTC has survived repeated calls for its elimination and is unlikely to disappear any time soon. Hence, the pragmatic question is how to optimize the Commission's institutional performance in its present environment, not how to make it go away.

Second, it should be remembered that institutional modifications involve trade-offs. The political pressures that give rise to the antitrust impulse will not vanish if the FTC is marginalized; they will merely reappear at different junctures. The growth of private litigation meant an increase in the comparative influence of

---

31. Cass Sunstein, After the Rights Revolution: Reconceiving the Regulatory State 222–23 (1990).

juries, generalist trial judges, private plaintiffs, and treble damages. The backlash to private litigation led to a contraction of antitrust norms across the board. Now, the "post-Chicago" backlash to the backlash is bringing pressure for antitrust vigor to reemerge somewhere.[32] Who will be the institutional winners in any antitrust reemergence? Broadly speaking, the choice is between reinvigorating private litigation and its institutional baggage and reinvigorating the public enforcement agencies. Whatever the liabilities of the expert agency model, it is has substantial advantages over the institutional realities of private litigation.

As with the Antitrust Division, I propose three measures that could help to restore a norm-creative role for the FTC.

A. Preventing Appellate Forum Shopping

One relatively quick statutory fix that would considerably enhance the FTC's litigation position would be to amend the appellate review provision of the FTC Act to change the procedure for appeals from Commission decisions. Under the current statute, which dates back to the Commission's founding in 1914, a losing defendant may appeal the Commission's order "within any circuit where the method of competition or act or practice in question was used or where such person, partnership, or corporation resides or carries on business."[33] What this unique appellate review statute means, in effect, is that a large corporate defendant doing business throughout the United States can chose any of the twelve federal courts of appeal (not including the specialized Court of Appeals for the Federal Circuit) in which to lodge its appeal.[34] This means that large corporate defendants always have the advantage of litigating in the shadow of the most sympathetic appellate court in the nation and can shape their defenses accordingly.

---

32. On the backlash to the Chicago School, see How the Chicago School Overshot the Mark: The Effect of Conservative Antitrust Analysis on U.S. Antitrust (Robert Pitofsky, ed, 2008).

33. Under the FTC Act, a losing defendant may appeal to any of the federal appellate courts 15 U.S.C. § 45(c).

34. There are a few other appellate designation statutes that employ similarly broad language, but they are unlikely in practice to have the effect of creating a virtual free choice of circuit for most defendants. Under the Commodities Futures Trading Act, a losing defendant can in some cases appeal to the "United States court of appeals of the circuit in which the petitioner is doing business." 7 U.S.C. § 9. However, since much commodities trading work is localized around particular exchanges or particular traders, this is unlikely to create a broad choice of appellate courts. Similarly, the National Labor Relations Act allows an appeal to the circuit court "wherein the unfair labor practice in question was alleged to have been engaged in." 29 U.S.C. § 160(f). While some labor practices may be national, and hence give rise to an open choice of appellate jurisdiction, many challenged labor practices are local—at a particular plant or facility or involving a particular employee—and hence give rise to more limited appellate options.

The appellate forum shopping that this creates is particularly problematic in light of the fact that the Supreme Court has been relatively uninterested in antitrust cases, in general, and FTC cases, in particular, in the last four decades. During the 1960s, the FTC sought certiorari on substantive antitrust issues fifteen times, and the Supreme Court granted certiorari in eleven of those cases.[35] Since the 1960s, the FTC has filed eleven certiorari petitions in antitrust cases and has been granted Supreme Court review only four times. Given current odds, the FTC knows that it is likely that the appellate court selected by the defendant will have the final say in the case.

An example of such judicial hostility to an agency decision recently appeared in *Schering-Plough,* where the Eleventh Circuit testily rebuked the Commission for failing to follow its *Valley Drug* decision—a private treble-damages case—on patent settlements.[36] Of course, the case only ended up in front of the Eleventh Circuit because the defendants lodged their appeal there and not, say, in the Sixth Circuit that had held similar settlements per se illegal[37] or in any of the other circuits that had not yet decided the issue.

Forum shopping is, of course, not limited to appellate review of FTC cases. Private plaintiffs flock to file all sorts of cases in the fora they deem most advantageous. However, there are a variety of procedural tools at courts' disposal to limit such forum shopping, such as the personal jurisdiction and forum non conveniens doctrines. The FTC itself has the power to engage in some limited forum shopping by choosing to file in district court, as it did with various patent

---

35. The following court of FTC certiorari petitions since the 1960s only includes cases in which the Commission sought certiorari on the merits of an antitrust question decided by the court of appeals. It does not include cases involving purely administrative law questions. The Commission unsuccessfully sought certiorari in the following cases: *FTC v. Rambus,* 129 S. Ct. 1318 (2009); *FTC v. Schering-Plough Corp,* 548 U.S. 919 (2006); *FTC v. Detroit Auto Dealers' Ass'n,* 506 U.S. 973 (1992); *FTC v. Official Airlines Guides,* 450 U.S. 917 (1981); *FTC v. Adolph Coors Co.,* 419 U.S. 1105 (1975); *FTC v. Columbia Broadcasting System, Inc.,* 397 U.S. 907 (1970); *FTC v. American Motors Corp.,* 390 U.S. 1012 (1968); *FTC v. American Oil Co.,* 377 U.S. 954 (1964); *FTC v. Timken Roller-Bearing Co.,* 371 U.S. 861 (1962); *FTC v. Exquisite Form Brassiere, Inc.,* 369 U.S. 888 (1962); The Commission obtained a writ of certiorari in *FTC v. Ticor Title Ins. Co.,* 504 U.S. 621 (1992); *FTC v. Superior Court Trial Lawyers' Ass'n,* 493 U.S. 411 (1990); *FTC v. Superior Court Trial Lawyer's Ass'n,* 476 U.S. 447 (1986); *FTC v. Sperry & Hutchison Co.,* 405 U.S. 233 (1972); *FTC v. Texaco, Inc.,* 393 U.S. 223 (1968); *FTC v. Fred Meyer, Inc.,* 390 U.S. 341 (1968); *FTC v. Universal-Rundle Corp.,* 387 U.S. 244 (1967); *FTC v. Procter & Gamble Co.,* 386 U.S. 568 (1967); *FTC v. Dean Foods, Inc.,* 384 U.S. 597 (1966); *FTC v. Brown Shoe Co.,* 384 U.S. 316 (1966); *FTC v. Borden Co.,* 383 U.S. 637 (1966); *FTC v. Consolidated Food Corp.,* 380 U.S. 592 (1965); *FTC v. Sun Oil Co.,* 371 U.S. 505 (1963); *FTC v. Anheuser-Busch, Inc.,* 363 U.S. 536 (1960); *FTC v. Travelers Health Ass'n,* 362 U.S. 293 (1960).

36. *Schering-Plough Corp. v. FTC,* 402 F.3d 1056 (11th Cir. 2005).

37. *In re Cardizem CD Antitrust Litig.,* 332 F.3d 896 (6th Cir. 2003).

settlements cases after losing *Schering-Plough* in the Eleventh Circuit.[38] But it seems poor public policy to force the Commission to abdicate its administrative norm-creation function simply to prevent the defendant from having a trump card in the choice of appellate forum.

Several possible statutory fixes would improve matters. One possibility is to make all FTC antitrust decisions appealable to the U.S. Court of Appeals for the D.C. Circuit, which already has such a function with respect to many other administrative agencies.[39] This would not only defeat appellate forum shopping to the most restrictive court of appeals, it would also have the benefit of creating a comparatively specialized antitrust court. In Chapter 11, we will return to specialized antitrust courts and inquire about their benefits and liabilities.

A more modest change would make the administrative case appealable to a single federal circuit or limited number of federal circuits. For example, the case could be appealable to the federal circuit of the defendant's principal place of business or U.S. headquarters (in the case of a foreign corporation), as is the case for appeals from various decisions of the CFTC, SEC, FDA, EPA, and OSHA.[40] If there were multiple defendants with different principal places of business, this would result in a choice of appellate jurisdictions but still cut down on the number of forum-shopping possibilities.

B. Invoking an Independent Section 5

The FTC Act gives the Commission a seemingly simple mandate: Detect and prohibit "unfair methods of competition. . . and unfair or deceptive [trade] practices."[41] The Commission's powers under Section 5 are at least coextensive with the substantive reach of the Sherman Act—in other words, that anything that is illegal under the Sherman Act is also illegal under the FTC Act.[42] But the Supreme Court has also held that the FTC may go further than the Sherman Act and "stop in their incipiency acts and practices which, when full blown, would violate those Acts."[43] Thus, "the standard of unfairness under the FTC Act. . . encompass[es] not only practices that violate the Sherman Act and the other antitrust laws. . . but also practices that the Commission determines are against public policy for other reasons."[44]

---

38. *See FTC v. Watson Pharma., Inc.*, 611 F. Supp. 2d 1081 (C.D. Cal. 2009); *FTC v. Cephalon, Inc.*, 551 F. Supp. 2d 21 (D.D.C. 2008).

39. Often, defendants are given a choice of appealing to the Circuit Court for their principal place of business or to the D.C. Circuit. *See*, e.g., 15 U.S.C. § 77i(a) (SEC); 21 U.S.C. § 355(h) (FDA).

40. *See* 7 U.S.C. § 8 (CFTC); 15 U.S.C. § 77(i), U.S.C. § 80a-42(a) (SEC); 21 U.S.C. § 660; 21 U.S.C. § 360kk (OSHA); 42 U.S.C. § 7525 (EPA).

41. 15 U.S.C. § 45.

42. *FTC v. Cement Inst.*, 333 U.S. 683, 694 (1948).

43. *FTC v. Brown Shoe Co.*, 348 U.S. 316, 322 (1966).

44. *FTC v. Indiana Federation of Dentists*, 476 U.S. 447, 454 (1986).

All of this is promising given the need to move public norms away from private norms. But, alas, in recent years, the Commission has frequently tied itself to the Sherman Act, claiming that in enforcing Section 5 of the Sherman Act, it is merely enforcing Sherman Act norms.[45] And that, of course, means accepting all of the Sherman Act's private litigation baggage. Why would the Commission do that? Of late, the FTC has been shell-shocked by its treatment in the courts when it has invoked an independent Section 5. There is a wide gulf between the theoretical availability of an expansive Section 5 and actual judicial affirmation of FTC decisions to enjoin behavior that would not violate the Sherman Act. The courts have frequently quashed the FTC's efforts to develop an independent Section 5, even while paying lip service to the independence principle.[46] As former Chairman Bill Kovacic has remarked, it is difficult to find even ten successfully litigated Section 5 antitrust cases over the Commission's nearly hundred-year history.[47]

As usual, the reason is institutional. Courts tend to be jealous of their jurisdiction. To cite a venerable precedent, courts are loathe to abandon their prerogative "to say what the law is."[48] In an early decision—subsequently overruled but never quite forgotten—the Supreme Court applied a *Marbury v. Madison* thematic to the FTC: "The words 'unfair competition' are not defined by the statute and their exact meaning is in dispute. It is for the courts, not the commission, ultimately to determine as a matter of law what they include."[49] Courts are wary of agency assertions that the agency should be accorded independent space to develop *legal* norms. As FTC former Chair Robert Pitofsky has explained, a construction of Section 5 that would make the same behavior lawful at the Department of Justice and unlawful at the FTC is politically "untenable."[50]

Hence, while legal doctrine theoretically allows space for an independent Section 5, and there are good policy reasons for some movement away from the constraints of the Sherman Act, great care needs to be taken in the formulation of a "separation strategy." It simply will not due for the FTC to declare independence from the Sherman Act and then proceed to formulate its own antitrust

45. *See*, e.g., *Rambus, Inc. v. FTC*, 522 F.3d 456, 462 (D.C. Cir. 2008) (observing that the Commission had expressly limited its theory of liability to conduct that would violate Section 2 of the Sherman Act).

46. *See generally* FTC Workshop, Opening Remarks of Chairman William Kovacic, Official Transcript at 4-20, available at http://www.ftc.gov/bc/workshops/section5/transcript.pdf.

47. *Id.* at 10.

48. *Marbury v. Madison*, 5 U.S. (1 Cranch) 137, 177 (1803) ("It is emphatically the province and duty of the judicial department to say what the law is.").

49. *FTC v. Gratz*, 253 U.S. 421, 427 (1920)

50. *See* FTC Workshop, Remarks of Robert Pitofsky, Official Transcript, *supra* n. 46, at 64.

policy, as the Commission appears to have done in its recent case against Intel.[51] A "just trust us, we're the FTC," strategy has little chance of success in the courts. Rather, the FTC needs to pursue a cautious and incremental Section 5 independence strategy. Critical to this strategy is explaining in each case what it is about the particular context of that case that justifies an independent Section 5. I propose six contexts in which judicial deference to Commission norm creation may be particularly justified. Cases that involve a combination of these contexts are particularly likely to secure judicial deference to an independent Section 5.

First, courts are most likely to defer to administrative agency judgments in cases involving commercial practices about which the courts have not developed a deeply rooted body of precedent. In such cases, the courts may allow some administrative experimentation and testing, even though they might not have reached the same result as the agency if they had analogized to conduct already covered by established liability norms. Conversely, courts are least likely to defer when they have already spoken to the exact practice on many occasions and developed a time-tested body of liability rules to govern it. Refusal by the agency to honor the judicially created precedents may look—to judges at least—like intransigence.[52] It is human nature (and judges are human after all) to be more open to an idea on which one has not yet expressed an opinion than to approve of an idea that contradicts one's prior assertion. Hence, the FTC is most likely to be accorded a norm-creative role on issues that have not yet received a significant airing in the courts, rather than in seeking to reform well-worn areas of precedent like predatory pricing or exclusive-dealing law.

Second, one area where many commentators have urged the Commission to assert Section 5 independence is where there is a gap between Sections 1 and 2 of the Sherman Act.[53] Although Sections 1 and 2 plausibly could be read to cover all commercial conduct of an anticompetitive nature seamlessly, judicial construction of the statutory texts has created some coverage gaps. Section 1 requires a "contract, combination, or conspiracy"—and hence agreement between at least two unrelated actors—which precludes coverage of purely unilateral acts, such as the unilateral adoption of practices that facilitate tacit price coordination or unsuccessful attempts to induce others to join a cartel. Section 2 requires monopoly power, thus precluding application to anticompetitive acts involving a lesser degree of market power. Further, there is a serious juridical question about the

---

51. For a fuller discussion of the *Intel* case, see Daniel A. Crane, *Thoughts on Section 5 of the FTC Act and the FTC's Case Against Intel*, Antitrust Chronicle (February 2010). In the interests of full disclosure, I prepared the above paper while an academic consultant for Intel.

52. *See* FTC Workshop, Pitofsky Remarks, *supra* n. 46, at 65 ("The Federal Trade Commission really cannot overrule the Supreme Court. I don't care what Section 5 says.").

53. *See id.*

viability under Section 2 of "joint monopolization" offenses where the defendants did not agree on a concerted pattern of conduct but adopted parallel measures, such as exclusive dealing contracts, that effectively lock up the market to new entrants.

During the 1970s, the FTC brought cases that sought to fill these statutory gaps with the seamless and open-ended text of Section 5.[54] Though it was rebuffed by the courts, the Commission is surely on strong ground when asserting Section 5 as a catch-all, intended by Congress to avoid end-runs around the Sherman Act. The FTC Act's legislative history evidences such as congressional intent.[55] Further, it is not hard to explain to courts why the act should be read broadly to capture conduct that, for statutory construction as opposed to public policy reasons, falls outside the purview of the Sherman Act.

Third, the Commission is on strongest grounds when challenging market power created by fraud or deception. The FTC's original mission, incorporated in the 1914 act creating the Commission, was to prohibit "unfair competition." In the 1938 Wheeler-Lea Amendment, Congress added a prohibition on "unfair or deceptive" trade practices. Although these prohibitions are juridicially separate and not every "unfair method of competition" need involve "deception," there are obvious statutory synergies between the amended statute's competition and deception prongs. It follows that the Commission should enjoy the greatest independence from the constraints of Sherman Act law when advocating against market power acquired by deception or in antitrust cases that otherwise involve misrepresentation or fraud.[56]

Consider Justice Breyer's dissenting opinion in *FTC v. California Dental*, where he and three other justices assumed that the Commission should be afforded an extra measure of discretion when dealing with a dentist's organization's prohibition on price and quality advertising that was ostensibly justified by the prevention of fraud.[57] All four justices who signed onto Justice Breyer's opinion are still on the Court and Justice Souter, who wrote the majority opinion, has been replaced by Justice Sotomayor. The best test case in the Supreme Court for an independent Section 5 would be one where the Commission could argue for

---

54. *See, e.g., Boise Cascade Corp. v. FTC*, 637 F.2d 573 (9th Cir. 1980) (rejecting FTC's efforts to challenge unilaterally adopted basing point pricing systems).

55. See Marc Winerman, *The Origins of the FTC: Concentration, Cooperation, Control, and Competition*, 71 ANTITRUST L. J. 1, 74–75 (2003).

56. *See, e.g., FTC v. Texaco, Inc.*, 393 U.S. 223, 226 (1968) (observing that FTC determinations are entitled to "great weight" when the FTC has previously studied and examined a particular issue on multiple occasions).

57. *California Dental Ass'n v. FTC*, 526 U.S. 756, 787 (1999) (Breyer, J., concurring in part and dissenting in part) (observing that the FTC "an expert in the area of false and misleading advertising," found no basis for the association's claim that a prohibition on price and quality advertising was necessary to protect consumers against misleading claims).

a norm-creation role in areas involving deception or fraud, justified by its unique statutory mandate and expertise with such matters.

Fourth, the Commission is likely to find greater judicial receptivity to its norm creation in cases involving consumer decision making. The FTC brands itself as first and foremost a consumer protection agency.[58] The Commission enjoys its greatest prestige in that capacity, as manifested by the extreme popularity and positive reputational benefits for the Commission of the Do Not Call Registry. Indeed, the courts have afforded the Commission deference almost exclusively in its consumer protection capacity.[59] It follows that the Commission is most likely to secure deference from the courts for an independent Section 5 construction when the Commission is acting directly for the benefit of consumers.

To secure maximum deference, the Commission should not only invoke a general consumer welfare justification for its actions—all antitrust actions should be justified on consumer grounds, whether or not consumers are directly involved in the market segment at issue. Rather, the Commission should pursue an independent Section 5 program primarily in cases that directly involve choices and decisions by consumers and where the Commission can explain how its expertise with consumer psychology, values, and practices justifies a more liberal construction of Section 5 than might be justified under the Sherman Act.

For example, a good bit of the Justice Department's enforcement action against Microsoft involved claims about consumer behavior. Operating system users allegedly were confused by the existence of multiple browsers on a desktop, which meant that if Microsoft indelibly engraved Internet Explorer on the Windows desktop, OEMs would be reluctant to add Netscape Navigator for fear that their support lines would be overwhelmed by confused and irate consumers.[60] Thus, even in a case involving primarily commercial practices between businesses (operating systems, browsers, programmers, OEMs, etc.), consumer mentality, habits, and vulnerabilities played a major role. In a case like *Microsoft*, the Commission could stake a strong claim to Section 5 independence by invoking its expertise about, and protection of, consumers.

Fifth, agency expertise may be most useful—and hence call for the greatest judicial deference—where it concerns predictions about future consequences of

---

58. *See*, e.g., Prepared Statement of the Federal Trade Commission on "Proposed Consumer Financial Protection Agency: Implications for Consumers and the Federal Trade Commission;" Before the House Committee on Energy and Commerce Subcommittee on Commerce, Trade, and Consumer Protection, United States House of Representatives (July 8, 2009), available at http://www.ftc.gov/os/2009/07/090708Acfpatestimony.pdf (noting that the "Commission also appreciates the proposal's recognition of the FTC's role as the nation's consumer protection agency.").

59. *See* Daniel A. Crane, *Technocracy and Antitrust*, 86 TEX. L. REV. 1159, 1206–07 (2009).

60. *U.S. v. Microsoft Corp.*, 253 F.3d 34, 61 (2001).

incipient behavior. In such cases, courts may be comparatively ill equipped to divine the future and more likely to trust an agency's prediction based on its superior familiarity with the type of conduct at issue. Conversely, courts are less likely to defer when the relevant conduct has been in place for some time and its actual effects can be tested using judicial empirics—discovery and adversarial procedures. Judges are more confident in answering the question "have prices gone up" or "has innovation been stifled" than "are prices likely to go up" or "is innovation likely to be stifled." The more confident that judges are in their own abilities to work out the facts, the less likely they are to defer to administrative agencies.

In the classic formulation of an expansive Section 5 power, the Supreme Court held that the FTC Act "was designed to supplement and bolster the Sherman Act and the Clayton Act. . . to stop in their incipiency acts and practices which, when full blown, would violate those Acts. . . as well as to condemn as 'unfair methods of competition' existing violations of them."[61] As this quotation makes clear, the FTC's prophylactic Section 5 powers—the power to reach beyond the Sherman Act—exist as to categories of incipient behavior that could "when full blown" blossom into Sherman or Clayton Act violations. Conversely, as to practices that are not incipient but fully developed, *Brown Shoe* suggests that the FTC Act is merely coextensive with the Sherman Act.

Finally, as with the Justice Department, the Commission needs to pay careful attention to the relationship between theory of liability and theory of remedy. One of the chief justifications for giving the FTC prophylactic powers beyond the reach of the Sherman Act is that Section 5 remedies are prospective and preventative rather than compensatory, punitive, or structural.[62] The Commission should be accorded the greatest deference on liability norms when it simply orders the defendant to cease and desist from conduct that could impair the competitive functioning of a market in the future. When the Commission seeks extraordinary remedies—such as those that radically restructure an allegedly damaged market and seek to restore competition—the likelihood of judicial deference on liability norms is much smaller.

The Sherman Act's criminal penalties and treble damages require a strict construction of the act, whereas the semiregulatory nature of the FTC Act creates greater room for a broad enforcement mandate. As explained in the first treatise

---

61. *FTC v. Brown Shoe Co.*, 384 U.S. 316, 322 (1966) (*quoting FTC v. Motion Picture Adv. Serv.* Co., 344 U.S. 392, 394–95 (1953)).

62. *See*, e.g., *FTC v. Texaco, Inc.*, 393 U.S. 223, 226 (1968) (observing that the FTC Act was intended to delegate power to "'an administrative body of practical men' who will be able to apply the rule enacted by Congress to particular business situations, so as to eradicate evils with the least risk of interfering with legitimate business operations") (citation omitted).

on the FTC, written the year after the Commission's formation (by the son of the first Justice Harlan and the father of the second Justice Harlan):

> The word "unfair" is undeniably indefinite in sense and meaning. What one person may consider "unfair" in competitive trade, another may perhaps regard as legitimate. Conceivably, members of a court may disagree as to whether or not, under the circumstances of a particular case, a given method of competition is "unfair," just as in one case they were unable to agree and adjudge whether or not certain regulations there involved constituted an "unreasonable" restraint of trade within the purview of the Sherman Law. That, however, is of no consequence, so far as concerns the validity of the Trade Law [the FTC Act]. The Trade Law does not purpose to denounce any competitive act as a crime. It does not provide for the imposition of a fine upon, or for the imprisonment of, any person guilty of practicing "unfair methods of competition." Whatsoever the peril, under the Sherman Law, of practicing "unfair methods of competition," a person resorting to such practices incurs no other risk, under the Trade Law, than that the Trade Commission, by proceeding as pointed out in the statute, may obtain the order of a court requiring him to cease and desist from such practice.[63]

At least that is true where the FTC seeks truly prospective, corrective, and nonpunitive remedies akin to cease and desist orders. For example, in the *nData* case, the Commission invoked Section 5 to require an intellectual property licensor to comply with its preexisting commitment to license on particular terms.[64] There was nothing punitive or deterrence-oriented about that remedy. It was thus consistent with the FTC's broad prophylactic powers to declare conduct unlawful, combined with narrower remedial possibilities than the other antitrust laws. Even if the Sherman Act might not have allowed a finding of liability, the Commission may have had the power under Section 5 to correct a market failure based on industry participants' reasonable reliance on nData's prior representations. This is a positive model for successful assertion of an independent Section 5.

C. Engaging in Formal Rule Making

This book has primarily analyzed the FTC as a distinct antitrust institution, but many of the judicial deference issues presented are not unique to the FTC but are part of the broader fabric of administrative law. Part of the difficulty in articulating the case for an FTC norm-creation role is that there is a muddle in Supreme Court's administrative law jurisprudence over the criteria necessary

---

63. John Maynard Harlan & Lewis Wilson McCandless, The Federal Trade Commission, Its Nature and Powers: An Interpretation of the Trade Law and Related Statutes 31 (1916).

64. *In re Negotiated Data Solutions, LLC*, 2008 WL 258308 (F.T.C.).

for the application of judicial deference to agency interpretation of federal statutes—the question of "*Chevron* deference."[65] Elsewhere, I have explored some of the difficulties with a claim of *Chevron* deference for the FTC.[66] For now, I will simply note one possible route out of administrative quagmire—framing formal antitrust rules through notice and comment rule making. Although it has issued numerous rules on the consumer protection side, the Commission has issued almost no antitrust rules.[67] Changing that practice might change the strength of its claim to deference.

Arguably, the format of the Commission's rule making—whether adjudicatory or legislative—should not matter to the deference question so long as Congress has delegated the Commission "interpretative" powers, and it has the power to act with the force of law.[68] Still, going through a legislative rule-making process might help to refocus the deference question by highlighting the FTC's administrative (as opposed to law enforcement) character and underlying the agency's statutory rule-making powers. At the very least, this theory is worth testing.

Why has the FTC not framed explicit antitrust rules to date? The primary objection to legislative rule making at the FTC seems to be that antitrust issues

---

65. *See generally* Lisa Schultz Bressman, *Deference and Democracy*, 75 G.W. L. Rev. 761 (2007); Cass R. Sunstein, *Chevron Step Zero*, 92 Va. L. Rev. 187 (2006); Ronald M. Levin, *Prospective Exercises of Discretion*, 54 Admin. L. Rev. 771 (2002); Thomas W. Merrill, *Chevron's Domain*, 89 Geo. L. Rev. 833 (2001); Thomas W. Merrill, *The Meade Doctrine: Rules and Standards, Meta-Rules and Meta-Standards*, 54 Admin. L. Rev. 807 (2002).

66. *See* Crane, *Technocracy and Antitrust, supra n.* 59 at 1206–10.

67. In 1968, the FTC did issue one antitrust rule, pursuant to the Clayton Act, concerning discrimination in men's and boys' tailored clothing. Discriminatory Practices in Men's and Boys' Tailored Clothing, 16 C.F.R. pt. 412 (1968). The Commission repealed the rule in 1993, after never using it in law enforcement. Notice of Repeal, 59 Fed. Reg. 8527–28 (Feb. 23, 1994). *See* C. Scott Hemphill, *An Aggregate Approach to Antitrust: Using New Data and Rulemaking to Preserve Drug Competition*, 109 Colum. L. Rev. 629, 678, nns. 197, 198 (2009).

68. *See* Levin, *supra* n. 65 at 773 (arguing that when an agency has the power to implement a statute with the force of law, "the 'format' or procedural vehicle in which such an administrative interpretation appears should not matter"). Although *Chevron* deference may only apply to agency decisions that have "the force of law," *United States v. Mead Corp.*, 533 U.S. 218 (2001), this should not be an obstacle for the FTC. Cass Sunstein has asserted that "the FTC's rules do not have the force of law" because the Commission issues orders that cannot be enforced without a judicial proceeding, Sunstein, *Chevron Step Zero, supra* n. 65 at 223, but this is probably a mistaken view of legal effectiveness of the FTC's orders. Since 1973, violation of the FTC's orders, whether or not those orders have been confirmed by a court, give rise to strict liability for fines. *See* Thomas W. Merrill & Kristin E. Hickman, *Chevron's Domain*, 89 Geo. L. J. 833, 890–91 n.275 (2001) (describing legislative changes that made FTC's orders "self-enforcing" and hence binding "with the force of law" for Chevron purposes).

do not lend themselves to categorical resolution.[69] But, in fact, the FTC has sometimes made adjudicatory pronouncements that were thoroughly rule-like. The Commission decision on patent settlements in the *Schering-Plough* case is a good example.[70] Although framed in adjudication, the Commission's $2 million limit on patent settlement "reverse payments" announced a bright-line rule that was meant to apply generally to the pharmaceutical industry.[71] One wonders whether the patent settlement issue—which is currently steering toward a categorical resolution in Congress—might have followed a different path if the Commission had gone through notice-and-comment rule-making and framed a rule of the sort that it tried to achieve through adjudication, with embarrassing results.

There are obviously contexts when categorical rules would not work well. Still, the Commission should look for contexts where rules make sense and test the courts' willingness to accept some antitrust rules. In combination with the other two proposed steps, this could significantly advance the cause of public antitrust enforcement.

---

69. *See Report of the American Bar Association Section of Antitrust Law Special Committee To Study the Role of the Federal Trade Commission*, reprinted in 58 Antitrust L.J. 43, 91 n.103 (1989) ("[W]e are not optimistic about the chances that the FTC could codify antitrust-oriented prohibitions on specific types of business conduct."); *see also* Mark Lemley & Christopher R. Leslie, *Categorical Analysis in Antitrust Jurisprudence*, 93 Iowa L. Rev. 1207 (2008) (arguing against categorical antitrust decision making in certain contexts);

70. *Schering-Plough Corp.*, 402 F.3d at 1056.

71. *Id.* at 1062.

8. ANTITRUST FEDERALISM

In recent years, there has been a good bit of discussion in the United States about issues that can be broadly grouped under the heading "antitrust federalism." Federalism issues in antitrust, or elsewhere, are not unique to the U.S. system but arise in any system in which political power is shared by separate governments at national and regional levels, or, as in the case of the European Union, at transnational and national levels. Other present or former British Commonwealth countries, such as Australia and Canada, also must wrestle with the optimal allocation of antitrust authority and preemption in the relations between the federal and provincial governments.[1] This chapter deals with a series of long-standing, and sometimes-vexing federalism issues in the United States.

At a high level of generality, the important questions often come down to a decision about whether federal antitrust law or federal antitrust agencies should preempt inconsistent decisions by the states. In this context, "the states" could mean any of the branches of state government, whether the executive, legislature, judiciary, or administrative agencies. Significantly, federal preemption arguments involve both state efforts to be *more* and *less* aggressive in antitrust enforcement than the comparable federal norms. Sometimes, federal preemption would result in less aggressive enforcement and sometimes in more.

For convenience, this chapter groups federalism questions into three categories. First, it will briefly consider the ability of states to loosen federal competition norms by allowing or requiring economic actors to engage in activities that would otherwise be unlawful under federal law. Here, somewhat perversely, the prevailing legal norm allows the states to reverse-preempt federal law so long as the anticompetitive policy originates legitimately from the state as sovereign, and some state actor supervises the regulatory scheme that displaces competition.

We will then turn to the flip side—to the power of states to be more aggressive in antitrust enforcement than the federal government. We will first consider the power of state attorneys general to enforce the antitrust laws in the face of a federal agency decision to enforce those laws less aggressively. We will then consider the power of states, whether by legislative or judicial decision, to permit private party antitrust suits under state law that would not be allowed under the comparable federal statute. Finally, we will consider the three moving pieces of Federalism in combination and consider whether the consistent principle that emerges—essentially one of reverse preemption by the states—should be adjusted.

1. *See generally* ELEANOR M. FOX & DANIEL A. CRANE, ANTITRUST GLOBAL READER Ch. 7(D) (West Pub. 2010).

I. STATE REGULATORY SCHEMES THAT DISPLACE FEDERAL COMPETITION NORMS

State regulations often displace competition in favor of some other market-ordering mechanism or political expedient. Think of exclusive garbage collection franchises, limitations on billboard advertising, resale restrictions on liquor dealers, and agricultural proration statutes. It is neither possible nor desirable for federal antitrust law to preempt every state regulatory scheme that in some way displaces competition in the name of the state's police powers to promote health, safety, and general welfare. And, as Frank Easterbrook has pointed out, regulation almost always displaces competition.[2]

Under the prevailing legal norm, federal antitrust stands aside and allows the state regulatory scheme so long as the scheme satisfies a two-part test. Under the *Midcal* test, the anticompetitive policy must be "clearly articulated and affirmatively expressed as state policy" and actively supervised by agents of the state.[3] The instinct behind the *Midcal* test is grounded in sound political theory. If states want to displace competition, they may, but they must do so in a way that creates political accountability. Citizens affected by potentially higher prices and reduced quality attendant to the lessening of competition must be able easily to trace the policy back to state politicians and hold them accountable at election time. Should the citizenry fail to see net gains from the exchange, state politicians will feel it at the polls.

This account of antitrust federalism has strong resonances in more general theories of federalism. To paraphrase Oliver Wendell Holmes and Louis Brandeis, states should be given room to act as regulatory laboratories.[4] Nationwide, we will all learn and benefit from these state and regional experiments. Citizens who are dissatisfied with state or regional restrictions on competition can "vote with their feet" by moving to other states. If a California entrepreneur finds local laws too restrictive, she can pack up and move to Nevada. So far so good for the political rationalization of the states' power to reverse-preempt federal law.

Alas, the rhetoric of Holmesian social laboratories and citizens voting with their feet works well only as to a subset of state regulatory preemption cases. The account works reasonably well as to regulatory schemes that benefit local producers (or some subset of local producers) at the expense of local consumers.

---

2. Frank H. Easterbrook, *Antitrust and the Economics of Federalism*, *in* COMPETITION LAWS IN CONFLICT: ANTITRUST JURISDICTION IN THE GLOBAL ECONOMY 189, 189 (Richard A. Epstein & Michael S. Greve eds., 2004) (reprinted from the Journal of Law and Economics (1983)).

3. *California Retail Liquor Dealers Ass'n v. Midcal Aluminum, Inc.*, 445 U.S. 97, 105 (1980).

4. *See, e.g., Truax v. Corrigan*, 257 U.S. 312, 344 (1921) (Holmes, J., dissenting); *New State Ice Co. v. Liebmann*, 285 U.S. 262, 311 (1932) (Brandeis, J., dissenting).

Thus, for example, a zoning ordinance that restricts billboard advertising in Columbia, South Carolina, benefits the incumbent billboard company, harms its would-be rivals, and imposes costs on Columbia residents who presumably have to pay more for goods and services because the cost of advertising increases or because there is less available information if the amount of advertising goes down.[5] The ordinance may also reduce eyesore and crass commercialism. Local voters and community activists will have to balance the cost increases against the aesthetic benefits, all of which is the stuff of ordinary politics.

But this noble political accountability story does not work well as to anticompetitive regulations whose benefits are captured mostly by local producers and costs externalized to consumers who cannot vote in the jurisdiction that imposed the anticompetitive regulation. Consider the facts of *Olsen v. Smith*,[6] the first Supreme Court decision to consider the relationship between the Sherman Act and anticompetitive state regulations. The plaintiffs were pilots whom the State of Texas had granted an exclusive right "to pilot sail vessels or registered steamers, bound to or from foreign ports, in or out of the port of Galveston."[7] They sued a pilot, not lucky enough to be part of the monopoly, for unlawfully diverting business. One might sympathize with the state's regulatory ambition—after all, who wants want unskilled pilots driving boats through Galveston harbor? But it turns out that the state's "regulatory" scheme had nothing to do with protecting the health and safety of innocent longshoremen. The statute exempted vessels "owned in the state of Texas, and licensed in the district of Texas, when arriving from or departing to any port of the state of Texas."[8] The statute was simply designed to exact rents from foreign vessels and/or foreign commerce while immunizing local vessels in local commerce. The defendant raised the Sherman Act as a defense, to no avail. The Court held that the power to regulate included the power to create monopoly.[9]

An equally striking example of externalization of monopoly costs can be seen in *Parker v. Brown*, the case that created the modern doctrine of antitrust immunity for state regulations.[10] *Parker* involved a California agricultural proration statute Significantly, at the time of *Parker*, half of the world's raisins and 95 percent of raisins sold in the United States came from California.[11] Further, more than 90 percent of the raisins grown in California were shipped outside of the state.[12] Hence, California raisin producers had significant market power and

---

5. *See City of Columbia v. Omni Outdoor Advertising, Inc.*, 499 U.S. 365 (1991).
6. 195 U.S. 332 (1904).
7. *Id.* at 338.
8. *Id.* at 340–41.
9. *Id.* at 344–45.
10. 317 U.S. 341 (1943).
11. *Id.* at 344.
12. *Id.*

were able to export most of the costs of their cartel to consumers who had no say in California politics. Nonetheless, the Supreme Court held that the California scheme was categorically immunized from antitrust challenge.

As we will see in Chapter 11, the *Parker* conundrum is but a microcosm of the larger problem of the export cartel—a beggar-thy-neighbor strategy that plays out on a global scale. Not surprisingly, many anticompetitive schemes immunized from antitrust scrutiny under the *Parker* doctrine impose costs primarily on consumers who cannot vote in the relevant jurisdiction. For example, anticompetitive schemes by convention centers and hotels impose costs primarily on out-of-staters but receive antitrust immunity if organized by a duly authorized municipal authority.[13]

For another example of possible externalization of costs on nonvoters, consider the facts of *Town of Hallie v. City of Eau Claire*.[14] The towns of Hallie, Seymour, Union, and Washington were unincorporated areas adjacent to the city of Eau Claire, Wisconsin. The citizens of those towns could not vote in Eau Claire, although it was evidently Eau Claire's intentions to annex those territories. Eau Claire received federal funds to build a sewage treatment plant in the Eau Claire service area, which included the four towns.[15] The city then refused to supply sewage treatment services to the towns. It agreed, however, to provide treatment services to select homeowners within the towns if a majority of the voters in the area voted by referendum to have their homes annexed by the city and to use Eau Claire's sewage collection and transportation services.[16] According to the towns, the effect of this scheme was to prevent the towns from emerging as effective competitors to Eau Claire in sewage collection and transportation. It also may have allowed Eau Claire to increase costs to nonresidents, even while using the higher prices as leverage to bring them (and presumably their property taxes) into the city. Nonetheless, because the anticompetitive policy was approved by the state and sufficiently supervised by its agents, it was immune from federal antitrust scrutiny.

Perversely, *Midcal* and its progeny create an even worse problem than the ordinary export cartel. Recall that for a state regulatory scheme to qualify for *Parker* immunity, it must be affirmatively expressed as state policy and actively supervised by agents of the state. This means that it is usually not enough for a state to passively allow anticompetitive conduct to take place. It must require it—or at least come very close to requiring it[17]—and then actively monitor it.

---

13. *See, e.g., Helen Brett Enterprises v. New Orleans Metropolitan Convention and Visitors Bureau*, Inc., 1996 WL 346314 (E.D. La. June 25, 1996).

14. 471 U.S. 34 (1985).

15. *Id.* at 37.

16. *Id.*

17. A state regulatory policy can qualify for *Parker* immunity even if the state does not compel market actors to adhere to the regulatory scheme. *Southern Motor Carriers Rate*

The upshot is that states often play the role of cartel ringmaster, thus solving the cartel's perennial problem of preventing defection. Thus, unlike mere private market cartels, which may eventually collapse under their own weight, state-run cartels are backed by the coercive power of the state and hence are stable and perniciously effective. Think of Porter Brown, the producer and packer of raisins who wanted to sell more than his cartel allotment and would have done so if not for the threat of a misdemeanor conviction and the possibility of a fine or imprisonment.[18] Government coercion was effective at achieving what private agreement could not. Antitrust-immunized state-run cartels are highly effective methods of externalizing costs on people who have no say in the matter.

Anticompetitive state regulatory schemes do not impose costs solely on nonvoters. A body of public-choice theory suggests that anticompetitive schemes may be the product of regulatory capture by powerful industries and the diffusion of costs over a wide body of consumer who do not have a sufficient individual interest to mobilize politically and resist.[19] However, even if these accounts are not fully persuasive as to states' exploitation of their own citizens,[20] there is little doubt that states and their subdivisions at least sometimes use their antitrust immunity to benefit local producers and externalize monopoly costs on nonvoters. Robert Inman and Dan Rubinfeld have proposed an approach that would make *Parker* immunity turn on the absence of monopoly spillovers to nonvoters.[21] Such a move would go a long way toward improving a substantial defect in the structure of antitrust federalism.

Conf., Inc. v. U.S., 471 U.S. 48, 61 (1985). Nevertheless, state compulsion is often considered the "best evidence" that the policy of displacing competition is clearly articulated and affirmatively expressed as state policy. *Id.*

18. 317 U.S. at 347.

19. *See, e.g.*, Merrick B. Garland, *Antitrust and State Action: Economic Efficiency and the Political Process*, 96 YALE L.J. 486 (1987); John Shepherd Wiley, Jr., *A Capture Theory of Antitrust Federalism*, 99 HARV. L. REV. 713 (1986).

20. William H. Page, *Interest Groups, Antitrust, and State Regulation: Parker v. Brown in the Economic Theory of Legislation*, 1987 DUKE L.J. 618 (1987).

21. Robert P. Inman & Daniel L. Rubinfeld, *Making Sense of the State Action Doctrine: Balancing Political Participation and Economic Efficiency in Regulatory Federalism*, 75 TEX. L. REV. 1203, 1207 (1997). Inman and Rubinfeld would ask: "1) Does a state regulation generate significant monopoly spillovers onto nonresidents?; and 2) Was the state regulation decided without political participation of the affected nonresidents as evidenced by the lack of interstate regulatory agreement? If the answer to both questions is yes, then the state regulation fails the spillover test for economic efficiency, and a Sherman Act review of the regulation is appropriate." *Id.*

II. ENFORCEMENT BY STATE ATTORNEYS GENERAL

State attorneys general can, of course, enforce their states' antitrust laws, but they can also enforce the federal Sherman and Clayton Acts.[22] The 1976 Hart-Scott-Rodino Act granted the attorneys general the power to bring parens patriae suits on behalf of the consumers of their states.[23] In the same year, Congress sought to encourage expanded state antitrust activity by appropriating $25 million over three years to aid state antitrust enforcement. As a result, twenty-five states were able to establish new antitrust offices in their attorneys general offices.[24] Today, most states have at least a few dedicated personnel working on antitrust issues, and some of the bigger states have substantial antitrust bureaus.

Since the 1970s, the relationship between the state attorneys' general and the federal agencies has been alternately cordial and prickly, depending at least in part on the administration in office in Washington. During the Reagan administration, the relationship became adversarial. Many state antitrust enforcers believed that Reagan's antitrust enforcers had abdicated their antitrust enforcement responsibility. Lloyd Constantine, the head of New York's antitrust bureau and a particularly outspoken critic of the Reagan (and later George W. Bush) administrations, called the 1980s a "'dark age' for antitrust when favored economic theory was elevated above marketplace reality and the rule of law" and accused Reagan's antitrust enforcers of engaging in "civil disobedience" for their supposed neglect of enforcement.[25]

In 1983, out of their dissatisfaction with the Reagan Administration, the state attorneys formed a Multistate Antitrust Task Force within the National Association of Attorneys General—NAAG for short and also for poetic reasons. NAAG then promulgated its own guidelines for vertical restraints (1985) and horizontal mergers (1987),[26] articulating much more restrictive standards than those beginning then followed by the Antitrust Division and Federal Trade Commission. The stage was set for confrontation. But before anything too nasty could happen, there was a change in the White House. Under the leadership of

22. The states cannot enforce the Federal Trade Commission Act, but many states have "mini deceptive and unfair trade practices acts" modeled on the FTC Act. Private parties often have standing to sue under those acts. *See* Mark E. Swirbalus, *New Rubric of Risk: Unfair Trade Practices*, SN003 ALI-ABA 77 (2007).

23. 15 U.S.C. § 15c.

24. Alan D. Maness, *State Antitrust Enforcement: Its Evolution and Future Direction*, 27 ANTITRUST BULL. 831 (1982).

25. Lloyd Constantine, *The Mission and Agenda for State Antitrust Enforcement*, 36 ANTITRUST BULL. 835, 826 (1991). *See generally* Michael DeBow, *State Antitrust Enforcement: Empirical Evidence and a Modest Reform Proposal*, in COMPETITION LAWS IN CONFLICT: ANTITRUST JURISDICTION IN THE GLOBAL ECONOMY 267, 269–70 (Richard A. Epstein & Michael S. Greve eds., 2004).

26. DeBow, *supra* n. 25 at 270.

George H. W. Bush's antitrust division head, Jim Rill, an Executive Working Group on Antitrust was established, consisting of the five FTC commissioners, the Antitrust Division head, and five NAAG representatives.[27] The working group was supposed to coordinate state and federal law enforcement activities and, generally, to lower the temperature between Washington and the state capitals.

During most of the Clinton administration, relations between federal and state antitrust enforcers were smooth, since their ideologies generally converged. But late in the Clinton administration, there arose the mother of all state-federal antitrust disputes, a case that was to create a cottage industry of antitrust federalism papers and discussions—*Microsoft*.

The views on exactly what happened in *Microsoft* and what its implications should be for antitrust federalism policy are disputed. One popular account holds that the states obstructed the federal effort to secure an early settlement, thus evidencing a defect with the status quo in antitrust federalism. The evidence for this view comes primarily from Judge Richard Posner, and it is perhaps because Posner—a hugely influential figure in antitrust and American law, more generally—is behind it that the "federalism is broken" theme has sounded so loudly in recent years. Let us briefly review the facts.

The Justice Department brought the *Microsoft* case—actually, the third federal *Microsoft* case but the one most people think of as "*Microsoft*"—in 1999.[28] Nineteen states brought suit also, and the cases were consolidated before Judge Thomas Penfield Jackson in the D.C. District Court. Among the more unusual twists and turns in the case, Professor Larry Lessig was appointed special master, and Judge Posner was appointed mediator. In early 2000, after Judge Jackson issued his findings of fact but before he issued his conclusions of law, Judge Posner mediated the case. The parties were unable to reach a settlement. Judge Jackson issued his conclusion of law and subsequently ordered Microsoft broken into two separate companies: an operating systems company and a browser company. The U.S. Court of Appeals for the D.C. Circuit affirmed the decision in part but reversed some key findings, including the remedy, and ordered the case remanded to a different district judge. Then, in November of 2002, the Bush administration reached a settlement with Microsoft. Of the nineteen state plaintiffs, one (South Carolina) dropped its suit, sixteen agreed to the federal settlement, and two states—Massachusetts and West Virginia—objected to the settlement.[29] Judge Kollar-Kottelly eventually issued a final decree close to the one proposed by the Bush administration.[30]

---

27. *Id.*

28. *U.S. v. Microsoft*, 253 F.3d 34 (2001).

29. De Bow, *supra* n. 25, at 267.

30. William H. Page & John E. Lopatka, The Microsoft Case: Antitrust, High Technology, and Consumer Welfare 72 (2007).

The antitrust federalism questions mostly center on differing accounts of what occurred during the failed 2000 mediation. In press accounts, Judge Posner blamed the state attorneys general for obstructing a mediated resolution.[31] Subsequently, Judge Posner has argued that states should be "stripped of their authority to bring antitrust suits, federal or state, except under circumstances in which a private firm would be able to sue."[32] Alternatively, he has proposed giving federal authorities a "right of first refusal" to bring antitrust cases and strip states and private parties from suing over the same matter.[33] Without mentioning *Microsoft* specifically, he has developed a theory that state attorneys general follow a "strategy consist[ing] of bringing high-profile lawsuits that attract publicity to the attorney general and promote the interests of politically influential state residents. . . at the expense of nonresidents."[34] Judge Posner's arguments are widely understood as a rebuke of the state attorneys general who participated in *Microsoft*.

Other participants in the failed 2000 mediation efforts have disputed Posner's accounts. Harry First, a prominent antitrust scholar at NYU who was then working for the New Attorney General's Bureau, has suggested that Posner may be at fault for failing to consult the states in the early phases of the mediation and then rejecting the state proposals as "unreasonable" and coming too late.[35] First believes that Posner gave up prematurely on the possibility of a settlement because of a "blinkered" on the competence of the states and that "Posner's impatience with the states may have kept the parties from a result that, in the end, all of the parties would have preferred."[36] First notes that the states contributed significantly to the litigation effort, including evidentiary support for the remedy that Judge Jackson ultimately ordered.[37]

It has hard to know what to make of the states' participation in *Microsoft*. One possibility is that the states' insistence on remedies more stringent than those that the Clinton Justice Department was willing to accept may have resulted in a weaker eventual decree than would otherwise have been possible. The failure of

---

31. *See* Ken Auletta, *What Kept Microsoft from Settling Its Case?*, New Yorker (Jan. 15, 2001), at 40.

32. Richard A. Posner, *Antitrust in the New Economy*, 68 Antitrust L.J. 940, 940 (2001).

33. *Id.* at 941.

34. Richard A. Posner, *Federalism and the Enforcement of Antitrust Laws by State Attorneys General*, in Competition Laws in Conflict: Antitrust Jurisdiction in the Global Economy 252, 257 (Richard A. Epstein & Michael S. Greve eds., 2004).

35. Harry First, *Delivering Remedies: The Role of the States in Antitrust Enforcement*, 69 Geo. Wash. L. Rev. 1004, 1033 (2001).

36. *Id.*

37. *Id. See also* Jay L. Himes, *Exploring the Antitrust Operating System: State Enforcement of Federal Antitrust Law in the Remedies Phase of the Microsoft Case*, 11 Geo. Mason L. Rev. 37 (2002) (arguing that states played a beneficial role in the Microsoft remedies phase).

the mediation in 2000 meant that the case was litigated to the D.C. Circuit, which issued an opinion that affirmed some aspects of Judge Jackson's liability findings but reversed others and, particularly, cast doubt on the viability of a break-up remedy.[38] The failure of the mediation meant that the Bush Administration rather than the Clinton Administration had the opportunity to settle the case post-appeal and did so on terms more sympathetic to Microsoft. If, as many believe, the eventual Microsoft consent decree was a failure,[39] then one could claim that the states' refusal to follow the federal lead in 2000 resulted in the ultimate failure of the government's enforcement action.

But that story, even if partly true, may simply show "but for" causation rather than "proximate" causation. To say that "but for" the states' refusal to follow the federal lead the ultimate decree might have been stronger is hardly a sufficient reason to impugn the states or otherwise consider state antitrust enforcement a failure. It is equally true that "but for" the Supreme Court's decision in *Bush v. Gore*,[40] the Gore Justice Department might have insisted on more aggressive remedies after the D.C. Circuit opinion, but it would make little sense to pin the failure of the *Microsoft* case on the Supreme Court's resolution of the disputed 2000 election. Precisely because *Microsoft* is a once-in-a-generation, larger-than-life matter with enormously complicated facts, it would be mistaken to extrapolate a general theory of the relationship between state and federal antitrust enforcers from that particular case.

Indeed, *Microsoft* is probably an outlier case insofar as it involved state attorney general participation in national antitrust litigation and alleged "interference" with the federal agenda. Michael DeBow's study of state attorney general enforcement between 1993 and 2002 suggests that state enforcement is relatively infrequent and focused, quite properly, on local matters.[41] DeBow found that the states filed 120 antitrust actions over the ten-year period he studied. A large percentage of the cases involved bid rigging or price-fixing in local industries—just the sorts of cases that seem most unobjectionable for state attorneys general to bring.[42] DeBow found little evidence of parochialism or localist bias.[43]

A more recent empirical study by Michael Greve finds evidence of parochialism in state attorney general antitrust enforcement but not because of

38. *See generally* A. Douglas Melamed & Daniel L. Rubinfeld, *U.S. v. Microsoft: Lessons Learned and Issues Raised, in* ANTITRUST STORIES 287–310, 293–94 (Eleanor M. Fox & Daniel A. Crane eds., 2007).

39. *See* HERBERT HOVENKAMP, THE ANTITRUST ENTERPRISE: PRINCIPLE AND EXECUTION 298–304 (2005).

40. 531 U.S. 98 (2000).

41. DeBow, *supra* n. 25.

42. *Id.* at 272–74.

43. *Id.* at 275 ("While parochialism and externality concerns are theoretically well grounded, they do not find much empirical support in the states' actions to date.").

overenforcement against out-of-state interests.[44] Greve found that states almost never challenge their sister state's anticompetitive conduct and have "consistently advocated a partial surrender of state regulatory authority."[45] As interesting as Greve's findings are, however, they suggest that state attorneys general are not so much obstacles to effective federal antitrust authority as irrelevancies. Apart from *Microsoft*—where the facts are, as noted, in dispute—it is difficult to find cases where state attorneys general affirmatively obstructed federal antitrust enforcement.

Even if most state attorney general enforcement is proper, yoeman work defending the state's citizens from local cartels or anticompetitive mergers, big national antitrust cases do create opportunities for political grandstanding. One needs no better evidence of this than New York Attorney General Andrew Cuomo's announcement of a solo effort to sue Intel in the fall of 2009, just weeks before the FTC filed its own enforcement action. It is difficult to imagine what New York's citizens had to gain from a Quixiotic—and surely enormously expensive—lawsuit about the global trade practices of one of the world's largest corporations that had already been investigated by European and Asian antitrust authorities and was about to be sued by the FTC.[46] Not coincidentally, at the time he brought the case, Cuomo was considered the front-runner for the Democratic nomination for New York governor.

Political grandstanding by state (and federal) politicians is hardly unique to antitrust enforcement, and it is hard to imagine that there is any strong federal interest in tweaking the structure of antitrust federalism to avoid it. Nor is there any general need to reign in state antitrust enforcers. If there is a need for a modification of existing antitrust federalism principles in the public enforcement domain, it is to give federal agencies the ability to resolve national antitrust cases preemptively. Whether or not *Microsoft* is a real example of state interference with federal management of a complex national case, there could be some small number of cases in which federal law enforcers need a free hand to resolve a matter in their perception of the public interest. The relevant statutory amendment could be something like the following: If at any point during a federal antitrust enforcement proceeding, the assistant attorney general or Federal Trade Commission (by a majority vote of its commissioners) certifies that continued state involvement in the matter would be detrimental to the federal interest, the court would dismiss the state action with prejudice, and the dismissal would serve as res judicata to bar assertion by any state—whether or not a party to the proceeding—of any claim that was or could have been asserted in the federal lawsuit.

---

44. Michael S. Greve, *Cartel Federalism? Antitrust Enforcement by State Attorneys* General, 72 U. Chi. L. Rev. 99 (2005).

45. *Id.* at 101.

46. I should disclose that I have received funding from Intel for academic papers relating to the FTC's enforcement action.

To be sure, such an approach would strip away the power of the states to act as a check on abdication of responsibility during periods of excessively conservative federal antitrust enforcement—if such a thing exists. Whether a federal preemptive power is warranted depends in large part on whether the greater risk is that federal antitrust enforcers will be overly lax or that state antitrust enforcers will be overly aggressive. And that, of course, depends on one's priors about the optimal level of antitrust enforcement: an issue that I will not attempt to address here.

III. PRIVATE ENFORCEMENT UNDER STATE LAW

If antitrust enforcement by state attorneys general is of relatively modest significance in the overall scheme of antitrust enforcement, private enforcement of state antitrust laws is much more significant. As noted in Chapter 3, private antitrust enforcement outnumbers public enforcement by a 10-1 ratio. Further, unlike *Microsoft* in the public context, which is perhaps more trope than fact, the deviation between federal and state private enforcement is large and important.

In Chapter 3, we sketched a brief historical narrative about purchaser standing in private antitrust cases. To recap, the federal story is a play in three acts. In *Hanover Shoe* in 1968, the Supreme Court held that a private plaintiff who is a direct purchaser from a defendant who is able to raise the price of goods because of unlawfully obtained market power has a right of action to recover the full extent of the overcharge, even if the plaintiff passes on the entire overcharge downstream and therefore suffers no economic damage.[47] Thus, for example, if a wholesaler purchases goods from a manufacturer who is involved in a price-fixing cartel but then simply raises the price of the goods when he sells to retailers and sees no decline in volume (because downstream demand is inelastic), the wholesaler can still recover the full extent of the overcharge. Then, in *Illinois Brick* in 1977, the Court held that an indirect purchaser bearing the real economic brunt may recover nothing.[48] Thus, in the previous example, the retailer who buys from the wholesaler or the customer who buys from the retailer and ultimately pays the passed-on overcharge does not have standing to sue under federal antitrust law.

The Supreme Court's vision in the *Hanover Shoe/Illinois Brick* tandem of creating a uniform, administrable national rule was quickly shattered as state policy makers began to react. Particularly unpalatable to many state officials was the possibility that large corporate middlemen—whether wholesalers or retailers—would received huge windfall damages awards while consumers who paid the ultimate price could recover nothing. The states began to rebel against *Illinois*

---

47. *Hanover Shoe Inc. v. United Shoe Machinery Corp.*, 392 U.S. 481 (1968).
48. *Illinois Brick Co. v. Illinois*, 431 U.S. 720 (1977).

Brick's prohibition on direct purchaser suits, which led to the third act in the play—*Arc America*.[49]

ARC America was an antitrust suit brought by four states—Alabama, Arizona, California, and Minnesota—against cement producers who the states accused of price-fixing. The states were purchasers of cement but often did so through middlemen and hence counted as indirect purchasers (at least in part). Nonetheless, the states asserted claims under state antitrust statutes as well as under the Sherman Act. The Alabama, California, and Minnesota statutes explicitly allowed indirect purchaser claims.[50] The Arizona statute was modeled on the Clayton Act, but Arizona argued that the statute should be interpreted to allow indirect purchaser suits.[51]

The Supreme Court had to decide whether the state laws were preempted by federal law. Nothing in Section 4 of the Clayton Act—the statute creating the private right of action—suggested an intention to displace state indirect purchaser suits since, indeed, nothing in the text of the Clayton Act predetermined the results in *Hanover Shoe* or *Illinois Brick*. Further, the Court noted that the purpose of the Sherman Act was to supplement state antitrust laws rather than to displace them.[52] Thus, the only question was whether "state laws permitting indirect purchaser recoveries pose[d] an obstacle to the accomplishment of the purposes and objectives of Congress."[53] The Court concluded that neither *Hanover Shoe* nor *Illinois Brick* found any general congressional policy about private antitrust claims, only about private *federal* antitrust claims. Those cases, the Court reasoned, had only been about the management of the federal system. How the states wanted to run their private litigation systems was their own business. If the federal courts did not want to hear the state law indirect purchaser claims because they were too complicated or burdensome, they could simply decline to exercise supplemental jurisdiction over those claims.[54] Indirect purchaser claims under state law simply were not a federal problem.

Since *ARC America*, the trend toward state allowance of indirect purchaser litigation has continued. Twenty-five states and the District of Columbia have adopted "*Illinois Brick* repealer statutes," permitting either their own states' consumers or their attorneys general as parens patriae to bring indirect purchaser claims.[55] Additionally, courts in Massachusetts, Nebraska, Vermont, Florida, and

---

49. *California v. ARC America Corp.*, 490 U.S. 93 (1989).

50. *Id.* at 98, n.3.

51. *Id.*

52. *Id.* at 101–02.

53. *Id.* at 102.

54. *Id.* at 103–04.

55. Daniel R. Karon, "*Your Honor, Tear Down That Illinois Brick Wall,*" *The National Movement Toward Indirect Purchaser Antitrust Standing and Consumer Justice*, 30 Wm. Mitchell L. Rev. 1351, 1361 (2004).

New Jersey have ruled that indirect purchasers can sue under their consumer protection statutes, and Arizona, Iowa, North Carolina, and Tennessee courts have ruled that their citizens can sue under their state antitrust statutes.[56] Thus, a majority of states have rejected *Illinois Brick* and allowed some form of indirect purchaser suits.

This would not necessarily be of concern if (1) state and federal law governed separate spheres of commercial behavior, and (2) state courts limited themselves to applying their indirect purchaser rules to local cases involving their own citizens. Alas, these two conditions have not held.

First, there is virtually no federal antitrust case that cannot also be brought under state law. Given modern jurisdictional understandings, federal law can reach even principally local matters, and state law can reach even national and international matters. For example, after Judge Jackson entered his findings against Microsoft, plaintiffs' lawyers filed more than 150 antitrust class actions against Microsoft under both state and federal law on behalf of indirect purchasers of Microsoft software.[57] The damages potentially facing Microsoft were tremendous, not simply because of the scale of Microsoft's business but also because of the likelihood of multiple duplicative recoveries, each trebled. If an intermediary such as an original equipment manufacturer or retailer purchased Microsoft Windows and then bundled it into a hardware product or resold the software at retail, the intermediary would typically be entitled to recover the full overcharge, times three given the automatic trebling rule. But, under state *Illinois Brick* repealer statutes and rulings, that would not stop consumers from also recovering the full overcharge they paid, possibly times three—even though the total recovery from Microsoft totaled many times more than any actual overcharge.[58] State indirect purchaser standing has dramatic effects on the liability incurred by companies operating on a national or global level.

The second condition, that state courts only apply indirect purchaser standing to local cases involving their own citizens, also has not held or has held only very unevenly. Some state trial judges have actually certified class action lawsuits that would have applied the antitrust laws of the judge's home state to citizens of other states.[59] For example, in one case, a California trial court certified a class of indirect copper purchasers in nineteen states and announced that it would apply

---

56. *Id.*

57. *Bettendorf v. Microsoft Corp.*, 2009 WL 4984079, at n.2 (Wis. Ct. App. 2009).

58. Some states allow the defendant to assert a "pass-on defense" to limit the defendants' recoveries. *See* Kathleen Foote, *State Antitrust Enforcement*, 1542 PLI/Corp 585 (2006). The exercise of such a defense is complicated by the fact that the direct and indirect purchaser cases may be asserted in different courts and determining the amount of the overcharge pass-on may be difficult.

59. *See* Indirect Purchaser Litigation Handbook, 84–90 (ABA 2005).

California antitrust law to the entire class.[60] Such efforts, however, have generally been denied. In the copper case, the California appellate court quashed the trial court's class certification decision,[61] and other trial judges have usually rejected the plaintiff's request for a single multistate class applying the favorable antitrust laws of the home jurisdiction.[62] But although judges have generally resisted the call to formally export their antitrust norms to citizens of other states, many judges (both state and federal) have found no difficulty in certifying indirect purchaser classes on behalf of citizens of other states that, in principle, recognize indirect purchaser standing.[63] Hence, a single judge would preside over a conglomeration of twenty-five or thirty class actions, each class coinciding with an *Illinois Brick* repealer jurisdiction.

In one sense, there is nothing problematic about a single judge simultaneously applying the indirect purchaser laws of various different states. Since each state made the decision to allow indirect purchaser claims, the mere adjudication of the claims in a conglomerated class action in another state does not necessarily offend federalism principles. In practice, however, plaintiffs' lawyers tend to file suit in the jurisdictions they perceive as friendliest to antitrust complaints. The practical effect is that the most pro-plaintiff trial judges get to decide antitrust norms for not only the citizens of their own states but those of other states as well.

Not only did the acceptance of this practice encourage forum shopping, but it created enormous complexities of judicial administration. For, in the grand tradition of federalist idiosyncrasy, the states did not part with *Illinois Brick* in a tidy and uniform manner. Rather, they occupied the space created by *ARC America* with a huge variety of indirect purchaser allowances and limitations. Thus, for example, Idaho allows individual indirect purchaser actions but prohibits class actions by anyone other than the attorney general, Michigan allows indirect purchaser actions only if the violation is "flagrant;" Mississippi allows for single damages for indirect purchasers plus a $500 civil penalty; and New York, Rhode Island, and South Dakota admonish courts to take steps to avoid "duplicate recovery."[64]

In 2005, Congress passed the Federal Class Action Fairness Act,[65] which allows the federal courts to assert diversity jurisdiction over class actions where the amount in controversy exceeds $5 million and in which any member of the plaintiff class is a citizen of a different state than the defendant. The act allows removal to federal court of some indirect purchaser class actions and hence lessens some

60. *J.P. Morgan & Co. v. Superior Court*, 6 Cal. Rptr. 3d 214, 217 (Cal. App. Ct. 2003).

61. *Id.*

62. *See* Indirect Purchaser Litigation Handbook, *supra* 59.

63. *Id.* at 86.

64. Foote, *supra* n. 58 at 599.

65. Pub. L. No. 109-2, 119 Stat. 4 (codified in scattered sections of 28 U.S.C.).

(but not all) of the forum-shopping problems.[66] But now all of the administrative complexities that the *ARC America* Court was confident the federal courts could avoid are dumped, once again, into the federal lap. Indeed, the complexities are now greater, since federal courts now have to sort through a crazy quilt of varying legal standards and defenses recognized by state laws before turning to the convoluted economic proof of overcharge, pass-on, and duplication.[67]

The bipartisan Antitrust Modernization Commission has sensibly called for a reform that would accommodate the political impulses for indirect purchaser recoveries even while improving the administration of these cases.[68] The AMC proposes legislation that would overrule both *Illinois Brick* and *Hanover Shoe* and hence allow both indirect and direct purchasers to bring antitrust claims. The statute would then provide that damages in such actions could not exceed the overcharges (trebled) incurred by the direct purchasers. Defendants would pay a trebled-damages award for the direct purchaser overcharge into the court's coffers, and the direct and indirect purchasers could then seek an apportioned share of the damages pot, up to their actual damages.

The AMC declined to recommend legislative overruling of *ARC America* and preemption of state indirect purchaser laws. Citing considerations of "federalism and political pragmatism," the Commission instead endorsed legislation that would allow removal of state indirect purchaser actions to federal court to the full extent permitted by Article III of the Constitution.[69] Under a multidistrict litigation process, all of the federal and state direct and indirect claims would be consolidated in a single district court for all purposes, including both discovery and trial.[70] Although state law would nominally remain preemptive of federal antitrust standards, it is likely that over time federal judges would homogenize state and federal practices in these consolidated proceedings.

IV. RECONSIDERING STATE SUPREMACY

We have now seen three ways in which antitrust runs counterclockwise on federalism's grandfather clock. Under the ordinary constitutional principle, federal

66. Various end runs around the statute are possible. *See, e.g.*, *Tanoh v. Dow Chem. Co.*, 561 F.3d 945 (9th Cir. 2009) (finding that seven separate toxic tort actions filed in state court, each with fewer than one hundred plaintiffs, were not a removable class action).

67. *See, e.g.*, *In re Flonase Antitrust Litig.*, 2010 WL 234858 (E.D. Pa. Jan. 21, 2010).

68. Report and Recommendation of the Antitrust Modernization Commission Chapter Two (April 2007) http://www.amc.gov/report_recommendation/.chapter3.pdf.

69. *Id.*

70. This would require legislatively overruling (as to antitrust cases) the Supreme Court's decision in *Lexecon v. Milberg Weiss Bershad Hynes & Lerach*, 523 U.S. 26 (1998), which allows multidistrict litigation consolidation for discovery, class certification, summary judgment, and other pretrial motions, but requires remand to the originating court for trial.

law reigns supreme over inconsistent state law.[71] But in antitrust, it is exactly the opposite. State law trumps federal law. If the states decide to be more permissive than federal law, they get their way, and if they decide to be more restrictive, they also get their way.

It is hard to see the justification for this supremacy reversal in sound principles of political design. Let us examine three conventional arguments for distribution of power between the state and federal governments and see whether they fit the reverse-preemption norm in antitrust.

First, one of the chief impulses of the American system of government is to distribute power among the different branches of government and between different governments so that the different branches and different governments act as a check on each other.[72] But this Madisonian impulse does not provide a strong normative explanation for the current structure of antitrust federalism. Under current principles, the states do not so much provide a check on federal power as to displace it.

Second, one common argument that we have already encountered is that the states should be allowed to act as social laboratories, providing data that other states and the national government can evaluate in deciding their own policies. As we have seen, that argument does not work well as to activities that externalize costs on citizens of other states. It also does not work well when the decisions of one state are permitted to trump the decisions of another state. Thus, for example, if a few dissenting states held up an early settlement in *Microsoft* or aggressive state judges certified nearly nationwide indirect purchaser class actions, it is hard to justify that as part of the natural laboratory of federalism. We expect scientists to confine their experiments to their own laboratories and not to go meddling in the laboratories of others.

Finally, and relatedly, one might want to see the antitrust decision making occurring at the state level in order to allow optimal matching of people with different tastes for antitrust intervention and different levels of antitrust enforcement.[73] Such a description may work well for regulatory areas like environmental law, where regulatory externalities (whether positive or negative) may be largely contained within the regulatory jurisdiction, but does not work well for modern large-scale antitrust, where state borders are usually irrelevant to the flow of commerce and the litigation response. What one tends to get instead is either a

---

71. The Supremacy Clause of Article IV of the U.S. Constitution provides that the Constitution and federal law made pursuant to it "shall be the supreme Law of the Land; and the Judges in every State shall be bound thereby, any Thing in the Constitution or Laws of any State to the Contrary notwithstanding." U.S. Const. art. VI, cl. 2.

72. *See* The Federalist No. 51 (James Madison).

73. *See, e.g.*, Richard L. Revesz, *Rehabilitating Interstate Competition: Rethinking the "Race-to-the-Bottom" Rationale for Federal Environmental Regulation*, 67 N.Y.U. L. Rev. 1210 (1992).

race to the bottom or a race to the top. In Chapter 1, we saw that in the late nineteenth and early twentieth centuries, a "race to the bottom" in corporate law eliminated the states' ability to use corporate law to restrict the market power of large aggregations of capital. Modern federalism principles allow both races to the top and races to the bottom. By permitting the externalization of costs on nonvoters, federalism principles encourage a race to the bottom in the regulated economy—the beggar-thy-neighbor realities of international trade. Conversely, in the unregulated economy, federalism principles encourage a race to the top. The state attorneys general with the most aggressive antitrust policy may exercise disproportionate influence on what commercial practices that businesses engage in nationwide. The states that go the furthest in allowing indirect purchaser suits largely moot the choices of states that would prefer a more conservative standing rule, at least as to businesses that operate nationally and cannot adjust their practices on a state-by-state basis. Neither the "top" nor the "bottom" is likely to be the optimal locus of antitrust policy.

Unlike some other institutional issues that implicate constitutional questions (such as jury trials discussed in Chapter 6), fixing the status quo of implicit state supremacy in antitrust merely requires congressional legislation. There is no doubt that federal law has the constitutional right to supremacy. It is up to Congress to reclaim this supremacy.

9. RETHINKING PRIVATE ENFORCEMENT

The United States is unique in the world insofar as private enforcement of the antitrust laws vastly outstrips public enforcement. As discussed in Chapter 3, there are roughly ten private federal cases for every case brought by the Department of Justice or Federal Trade Commission. Almost all of these private cases are oriented exclusively toward damages. While the plaintiff usually asks for an injunction against further misconduct, everyone understands that the case is all about the treble damages or, more likely, the settlement that the defendants inevitably pay if the case survives summary judgment.[1]

Efforts to correct the perceived infirmities of the U.S. private enforcement system by tweaking the mechanics of enforcement—standing rules, discovery principles, claim aggregation mechanisms, damages rules, and the like—are futile. The shortcomings of private enforcement are existential, not technical. They go to foundational assumptions about the goals and purposes of antitrust law and competition policy. Private antitrust in the United States has rarely advanced the two assumed goals of private enforcement: namely, deterrence and compensation. As other jurisdictions around the world consider adopting a private enforcement model, they should begin by reevaluating the goals of private enforcement. Only once the goals are properly specified does it make any sense to discuss the more technical implementation details.

To critique the U.S. system of private litigation is not to call for a governmental monopoly of antitrust enforcement, which is the de facto rule in most countries. Those who distrust private economic monopolies should also distrust public governmental monopolies. A system of private enforcement allows for decentralized decision making and individualized bargaining. It supplies a set of "on-the-street" enforcers closer to the relevant problems, along with enhanced enforcement resources and continued enforcement during downturns in public enforcement. Private antitrust enforcement should be retained but reconceived.

1. In the current system, the possibilities for injunctive relief are slim. Only about eighteen private antitrust cases go to trial every year in the federal system, out of about 800 cases that reach a final disposition. *See* Daniel A. Crane, *Antitrust Antifederalism*, 96 CAL. L. REV. 1, 35 n.188 (2008). Even assuming that half of these cases succeed at trial, that is, only about nine cases a year which would even be candidates for permanent injunctive relief. Of course, it is possible that the parties would enter into a settlement agreement calling for the entry of a stipulated injunction, but such settlements are exceedingly rare in private cases.

I. THE FAILURE OF THE COMPENSATION AND DETERRENCE GOALS

The Supreme Court has repeatedly stated that the private right of action for treble damages under the antitrust laws serves two purposes: compensating injured victims of unlawful conduct and attracting enforcement resources to supplement the government's deterrence-oriented efforts.[2] Unfortunately, modern private antitrust enforcement does not serve either one of these objectives very well.

A. Compensation

From a political perspective, it is doubtlessly important to pay lip service to the notion that private antitrust remedies exist to compensate people injured by wrongdoers.[3] If one is trying to sell a new private enforcement system to a skeptical public, this is certainly the right tack. Alas, private antitrust litigation does a very poor job at compensating injured victims. Antitrust injuries are conventionally classified into two categories: static and dynamic.[4] Static injuries concern the effects on consumers from an increase in price, attendant to the exercise of monopoly power.[5] Dynamic injuries arise when a dominant firm stifles innovation or new product development.[6] Private antitrust litigation could, in theory, attempt to compensate injured victims for both types of losses, but it fails at both tasks.

---

2. *See, e.g., Pfizer, Inc. v. Gov't of India*, 434 U.S. 308, 314 (1978) (stating that "§ 4 [of the Clayton Act] has two purposes: to deter violators and deprive them of 'the fruits of their illegality,'" and "to compensate victims of antitrust violations for their injuries.") (citations omitted); *Am. Soc'y of Mech. Eng'rs, Inc. v. Hydrolevel Corp.*, 456 U.S. 556, 572 n.10 (1982) ("Congress created the treble-damages remedy. . . precisely for the purpose of encouraging *private* challenges to antitrust violations. These private suits provide a significant supplement to the limited resources available to the Department of Justice for enforcing the antitrust laws and deterring violations.") (*citing Reiter v. Sonotone Corp.*, 442 U.S. 330, 344 (1979)); *Tex. Indus., Inc. v. Radcliff Materials, Inc.*, 451 U.S. 630, 636 (1981) (referring to deterrence as "one of the important purposes of the treble-damages action under § 4 of the Clayton Act"); *Ill. Brick Co. v. Illinois*, 431 U.S. 720, 746 (1977) (asserting that compensation and deterrence are the twin goals of § 4 of the Clayton Act); *see also* Phillip Areeda, *Antitrust Violations Without Damage Recoveries*, 89 Harv. L. Rev. 1127, 1127 (1976) (stating that two purposes of private antitrust enforcement are compensation and deterrence).

3. The framers of the Sherman Act justified the treble-damages remedy as necessary to achieve compensation for injured victims of the trusts. Robert H. Lande, *Wealth Transfers as the Original and Primary Concern of Antitrust: The Efficiency Interpretation Challenged*, 50 Hastings L.J. 871, 911–35 (1999).

4. To be more precise, antitrust scholars generally speak about "static efficiency and dynamic efficiency." The loss of one or other of those forms of efficiency due to anticompetitive injury is what I call static or dynamic injury.

5. *See generally* Herbert Hovenkamp, Federal Antitrust Policy: The Law of Competition and Its Practice 19–20 (3d ed. 2005).

6. *See generally* Herbert Hovenkamp, *Restraints on Innovation*, 29 Cardozo L. Rev. 247 (2007).

1. **Static Injuries** In a static model of competitive injury, the clearest social cost of an antitrust violation falls upon a class of people who will often not be able to sue—those who stopped purchasing from the defendant because the price increased too much. When a firm acquires market power through collusion or exclusion of rivals, it typically will raise its price to a monopoly level. Two classes of consumers suffer harm. First, some consumers who would otherwise have purchased the product are no longer willing to purchase it at the higher price. Hence, they substitute to a second-best preference. These consumers' loss is a "deadweight" loss—a class of foregone transactions that should, in a competitive market, have taken place.[7] Economists identify deadweight loss as the primary *social* cost of anticompetitive behavior.[8] It is a social cost because it results in a misallocation of scarce social resources. Customers must buy their second-best, rather than their first-best, preferences.

The second class of harm accrues to consumers who continue to purchase the product at the higher price. Their injury is a wealth transfer from consumers to producers.[9] This is not necessarily economically inefficient, since it merely transfers money from one person to another and does not directly affect the deployment of scarce resources.[10] There is nothing that says a priori that the money is better off in the hands of consumers than the producers. For example, if the price-fixed product is a luxury good, then price-fixing may act as a progressive tax on rich consumers for the benefit of poor artisans.

Private parties who sue antitrust defendants typically do not sue to vindicate the interests of the consumers who stopped buying the goods because they were too expensive. Instead, private parties sue only for the purchasers who did buy and actually incurred an overcharge.[11] For example, imagine the difficulty of representing a class of purchasers who *stopped* buying vitamins because of a vitamins cartel or, even worse, who never *started* buying vitamins because of excessive prices. How could one prove who the consumers were or quantify their injury? It is much easier to recover damages on behalf of purchasers who made the purchase but paid too much. In this case, the formula is simply to posit a but-for price and use the difference between the actual price and the but-for price as damages.[12]

---

7. Herbert Hovenkamp, *Antitrust's Protected Classes*, 88 MICH. L. REV. 1, 30 (1989).

8. KENNETH G. ELZINGA & WILLIAM BREIT, THE ANTITRUST PENALTIES: A STUDY IN LAW AND ECONOMICS 6–7 (1976); William M. Landes, *Optimal Sanctions for Antitrust Violations*, 50 U. CHI. L. REV. 652, 653 (1983).

9. Hovenkamp, *Antitrust's Protected Classes*, *supra* note 7, at 9–11.

10. To the extent that would-be monopolists expend resources trying to effectuate wealth transfers, such expenditures may be inefficient. RICHARD A. POSNER, ANTITRUST LAW 13 (2d ed. 2001). However, private enforcers do not sue to recover such wasted expenditures.

11. *See* Hovenkamp, *Antitrust's Protected Classes*, *supra* note 7, at 36.

12. *Chattanooga Foundry & Pipe Works v. City of Atlanta*, 203 U.S. 390, 396, 399 (1906) (holding that damages in overcharge cases are the "difference between the price paid and the market or fair price").

The fact that private damages recoveries are automatically trebled under the Clayton Act[13] (save for a few exceptional cases) is no reason to believe that deadweight losses are being recovered after all. One could rationalize the treble-damages allowance as necessary to capture a set of damages that are difficult to identify or recover in private litigation, including the deadweight loss.[14] Although this may be an argument for the deterrent purpose of treble damages, it is not a particularly good argument for their compensatory function. A consumer who recovers treble damages may be entirely different from a consumer who forgoes the relevant purchase after the monopoly price increase. Private antitrust enforcement tends to focus on a set of purchasers and injuries that are secondary in the hierarchy of antitrust concerns. Private enforcement does not seek compensation for, nor does it meaningfully analyze, the key concern of deadweight loss.[15]

Assume, however, that compensating for wealth transfer is every bit as important a goal of antitrust as preventing deadweight losses.[16] How well does private antitrust enforcement do on this score? As to consumers, the answer is "not very well." The widely distributed nature of the overcharge and the difficulty in locating the real economic victims work against this goal.

To see why private enforcement fails at compensating for wealth transfer, consider the effects of a typical antitrust claim. A dominant durable medical equipment manufacturer enters into exclusive dealing contracts with hospitals and the group purchasing organizations (GPOs) that bargain on the hospitals' behalf.[17] The exclusive contracts unlawfully lock out potential competitors and allow the manufacturer to charge a monopoly price. In the first instance, the monopoly overcharge is paid by distributors that stock goods for the hospitals. The hospitals have complex billing arrangements with the distributors in which some, but not all, of the overcharge is passed on to the hospital. The hospitals then pass along some, but not necessarily all, of this overcharge to their patients. The patients are often not directly affected by the overcharge. This is because the patients' co-pay for using hospital services remains initially unaffected; their insurance companies

13. 15 U.S.C. §15(a) (2006).

14. *See generally* Robert H. Lande, *Are Antitrust "Treble" Damages Really Single Damages?* 54 Ohio St. L.J. 115 (1993).

15. On the other hand, public enforcers typically seek penalties, not damages, and do not have to establish standing to sue or make their case on behalf of any particular class of purchasers. Rather, they can focus on the overall social harm of the conduct and pursue remedies designed to deter and prevent such conduct in the future.

16. *See* Lande, *supra* n. 3, at 911–35 (arguing based on legislative history that Congress intended the Sherman Act to prevent wealth transfers from consumers to producers).

17. *See, e.g., Del. Valley Surgical Supply, Inc. v. Johnson & Johnson*, 523 F.3d 1116 (9th Cir. 2008); *Southeast Missouri Hosp. v. C.R. Bard, Inc.*, 2009–1 Trade Cas. (CCH) 76, 461 (E.D. Mo. 2008); *Natchitoches Parish Hosp. Serv. Dist. v. Tyco Int'l*, 247 F.R.D. 253 (D. Mass. 2008).

pay the bulk of the passed-on overcharge. The insurance companies may eventually increase their premiums or co-pays, but these future increases may fall on a different set of insureds than those who received monopoly-priced services. For large classes of patients, such as the indigent and the elderly, any overcharge borne by the hospitals may be passed onto taxpayers in the form of Medicare, Medicaid, or direct hospital subsidization. This complex scenario has countless analogs in the world of manufacturing, sales, and distribution. Thus, a monopoly overcharge often produces endless ripples in the economy.[18]

The law has a practical answer to the above scenario: just as a person can be damaged without legal injury,[19] so also can a person be legally injured without actual damage. Under the current U.S. system of standing, a private plaintiff who is a direct purchaser from an overcharging monopolist has a right of action to recover the full extent of the overcharge, even if the plaintiff passes on the entire overcharge downstream and therefore suffers no economic damage.[20] Conversely, an indirect purchaser bearing the real economic brunt may recover nothing.[21] Proposals for reform would grant some standing to indirect purchasers,[22] but even that would not necessarily result in the real economic victims being compensated. The question remains: Who are the proper indirect purchasers? Are they the hospitals, patients, insurance companies, or taxpayers? Figuring out which, if any, of these groups suffered the real economic harm is often difficult or impossible given the complexity and variability of the relevant economic relationships.

---

18. *See* Robert G. Harris & Lawrence A. Sullivan, *Passing on the Monopoly Overcharge: A Comprehensive Policy Analysis*, 128 U. Pa. L. Rev. 269, 276 (1979) (noting that "in a multiple-level chain of distribution, passing on monopoly overcharges is not the exception: it is the rule").

19. See *Steel Co. v. Citizens for a Better Env't*, 523 U.S. 83, 103 n.5 (1998) (recognizing the principle of *damnum absque injuria*—harm without legal injury).

20. *Hanover Shoe, Inc. v. United Shoe Mach. Corp.*, 392 U.S. 481 (1968).

21. *Ill. Brick Co. v. Illinois*, 431 U.S. 720 (1977). It bears noting that the *Illinois Brick* and *Hanover Shoe* rules only apply in federal lawsuits. In *California v. ARC America Corp.*, 490 U.S. 93 (1989), the Supreme Court held that federal antitrust law does not preempt state antitrust laws that allow indirect purchaser suits. A number of states have allowed such indirect purchaser suits.

22. The congressionally appointed Antitrust Modernization Commission recently made a recommendation for legislative reforms that would overrule both *Hannover Shoe and Illinois Brick* and allow for removal of state cases to federal court and consolidation of all damages claims as to a particular violation. Antitrust Modernization Comm'n, Report and Recommendations ch. 2 (2007), *available at* http://govinfo.library.unt.edu/amc/report_recommendation/chapter2.pdf. The court would then make a determination of what the total monopoly overcharge was, treble the overcharge, and allocate the damages pot to the different plaintiffs based on the proportion of their individual injuries to the total.

This brings us to the second problem with pursuing a compensation goal. Even if the real economic victims of an overcharge as a class could be identified, identifying the actual people who suffered injury and issuing them a check is often so expensive that administrative costs swallow the whole recovery.[23] The U.S. experience on this is instructive. Realizing that the costs of issuing checks to the members of the injured class were often prohibitive, creative lawyers invented other ways in which the injured consumers could be compensated. For example, the settling lawyers would have the defendants agree to issue coupons to class members. These coupons could be used for future purchases from the defendants. The coupons often go unclaimed and unused, however.[24] Further, the issuance of coupons may simply encourage the defendants to raise the price of their products, thus wiping away any compensatory benefit, or it may cause inefficient overconsumption by the compensated class.[25] In 2005, Congress passed the Class Action Fairness Act,[26] which was designed, in part, to rein in perceived abuses in coupon settlements. Still, after lawyers' fees and administrative fees are accounted for, each consumer's share of the recovery is negligible, even though the harm to the class is great.[27]

Nevertheless, private antitrust litigation continues to have a strong defenders. For example, in a recent study, Professors Robert Lande and Joshua Davis provided an empirical analysis of forty recent private antitrust cases that resulted in substantial damages awards.[28] They concluded that private antitrust litigation "very significantly compensates victims of illegal corporate behavior and is almost always the only way these victims can receive redress."[29] One may question how much compensation of injured victims actually occurred. The forty cases resulted in the recovery of $18.006 to $19.639 billion in cash,

---

23. *See* Richard A. Posner, *Oligopoly and the Antitrust Laws: A Suggested Approach*, 21 Stan. L. Rev. 1562, 1590 (1969) (arguing that "[t]he class action, save for large institutional purchasers, is a delusion. There is no feasible method of locating and reimbursing the consumer who several years ago may have paid too much for a toothbrush. . . .").

24. *See* Christopher R. Leslie, *The Need to Study Coupon Settlements in Class Action Litigation*, 18 Geo. J. Legal Ethics 1395, 1396–97 (2005) (reporting redemption rate of 26.3 percent).

25. *See* A. Mitchell Polinsky & Daniel L. Rubinfeld, *A Damage-Revelation Model of Coupon Remedies*, 23 J.L. Econ. & Org. 653, 653 (2007). Polinsky and Rubenfield summarize the literature critical of coupon settlements, but argue that coupons may be socially efficient if they are designed as an alternative to cash and make the defendant bear costs that better reflect the harms they have caused. This may be a strong deterrence argument, but it does little for the compensation goal.

26. Class Action Fairness Act, Pub. L. 109–2, 119 Stat. 4 (2005).

27. *See* Edward Cavanagh, *Antitrust Remedies Revisited*, 84 Or. L. Rev. 147, 214 (2005).

28. Robert H. Lande & Joshua P. Davis, *Benefits from Private Antitrust Enforcement: An Analysis of Forty Cases*, 42 U.S.F. L. Rev. 879 (2008).

29. *Id.* at 880.

depending on how the calculations are performed.[30] Of the total recovery, "$12.088 to $13.438 billion, in thirty-two cases, was recovered by direct purchasers; $1.815 billion, in six cases, was recovered by indirect purchasers; and $4.028 to $4.311 billion, in six cases, was recovered by competitors."[31] Since direct purchasers often pass along a substantial portion of any overcharge downstream, over two-thirds of the recoveries studied likely failed to compensate the parties who ultimately absorbed most of the economic injury.

The above is primarily a feature of U.S. standing rules, so one should also consider the $1.815 billion recovered in the six indirect purchaser cases. While this mathematically results in an average recovery of about $300 million per case, the numbers are skewed by the *El Paso* litigation, which resulted in a $1.4 billion recovery for the indirect purchasers. Eliminating this outlier results in an average indirect purchaser recovery of $77.6 million. In each case, the settlement pot was further reduced by an attorney's fee award, generally in the 20–33 percent range.[32] It is doubtful how much the disbursement of the remaining settlement amount benefited the downstream consumers.

For example, take the *Augmentin* case, which is one of the six indirect purchaser recoveries in the study.[33] In the *Augmentin* case, the indirect purchaser settlement value was $29 million, of which 25 percent was awarded to class counsel as attorney's fees, leaving $21.75 million to be distributed to the indirect purchasers.[34] However, the indirect purchaser class consisted of both insurers and state governments in addition to consumers.[35] The insurers, perhaps not having standing as direct purchasers and hence counting as indirect purchasers, likely passed along most of the overcharge to their insureds. What was the outcome for the injured consumers themselves, that is, those who took the antidepressant drug Remeron? They were awarded only 32.8 percent of the settlement fund, or $7.134 million after attorney's fees.[36] The settlement opinion does not reveal their precise number, but it does state that over 800,000 notices were sent to potential class members.[37] Given these numbers, it is unlikely that the settlement yielded more than a few dollars per injured class member.

There is another way of looking at the compensation in such cases. The *Augmentin* settlement opinion reveals that out of the 800,000 consumers to whom

30. *Id.* at 891.

31. *Id.* at 899.

32. *Id.* at 911–12, tables 7a–c.

33. *Id.* at 879.

34. *Id.* (providing further detail on the *Augmentin* case).

35. *In re Remeron End-Payor Antitrust Litigation*, Nos. Civ. 02-2007 FSH, Civ. 04-5126 FSH, 2005 WL 2230314, at *1, 6 (D.N.J. Sept. 13, 2005).

36. *Remeron*, 2005 WL 2230314, at *25.

37. *Id.* at *19.

notice was given, only 65,000 filed proofs of claim.[38] Assuming that all 65,000 claims were allowed, each member received an average of about $109 from the settlement, which may not be an insignificant sum to many families. Should this modest compensation to about 8 percent of the injured parties count as a success? Perhaps those who filed proofs of claim were the members who felt most aggrieved by the violation and hence were most in need of compensation. Still, it is more likely that they were the members with the time and education to file proofs of claim. By contrast, the remaining 92 percent simply absorbed their losses.

The outlier *El Paso* case, which resulted in a recovery of $1.4 billion for indirect purchasers, involved claims that natural gas suppliers artificially inflated the price of natural gas in California.[39] The indirect purchasers consisted of 13 million California consumers and 3000 businesses.[40] Naturally, the possibility of a check payout in *El Paso* was unsatisfactory because of the substantial administrative costs in maintaining mailing addresses and printing checks.[41] Instead, the settlement provided for a complex scheme of remittances to the California Public Utilities Commission and for natural gas rate reductions over fifteen to twenty years.[42] Because natural gas is rate regulated in California,[43] the settlement amounted to an agreement about rate-regulation principles for the next two decades.

One may describe the *El Paso* scheme as compensating consumers as a class, but such a description would be largely inaccurate. This is because consumer injuries occurring in the past correspond only roughly to future consumer gains. Injured consumers who died, moved away from California, or discontinued natural gas service over the rate-reduction period received no compensation or received compensation that bore little relation to the amount of their injury. On the other hand, consumers who moved to California or otherwise began natural gas consumption after the violation received a windfall. In sum, consumers whose consumption patterns or volume changed significantly from the violation to the rate-reduction period were either overcompensated or undercompensated. The *El Paso* settlement did not amount to a serious effort to identify persons who suffered economic harm and compensate them in proportion to their loss. As the above examples illustrate, identifying, locating, and compensating the real economic victims of an antitrust overcharge is often impossible. Compensation, therefore, is a noble but ultimately unrealistic goal.

---

38. *Id.* at 19.

39. *Id.* at 77.

40. *Id.*

41. *Id.* at 84.

42. *Id.* at 84–86.

43. California Public Utilities Commission, Natural Gas and California, http://www.cpuc.ca.gov/puc/Energy/gas/natgasandca.htm (last visited Feb. 11, 2010).

There exists one class of interests to which the foregoing observations do not apply with equal force. When competitors are injured by an exclusionary practice, they are not overcharged. Instead, they lose profits. In a small sense, the ripple-effects principle of economic injury still applies to competing firms. For example, a manufacturer plaintiff that loses sales because of an antitrust violation may mitigate its losses by laying off employees, borrowing less money from banks, or demanding fewer raw materials from suppliers. However, the adversely affected employees, banks, and suppliers do not have standing to sue because their injury is too remote from the violation.[44] Still, the competitor plaintiff usually will have experienced the majority of the economic injury; and, in this sense, the competitor is situated like an ordinary tort victim. Further, it is not hard, in most cases, to identify competitors that have lost profits. Because their injury is concentrated, it is generally cost-effective to award them damages.

There are several problems with justifying a compensation-oriented private remedy on the grounds that competitors are good candidates for compensation. First, there is a widespread and probably legitimate concern that competitor plaintiffs frequently use antitrust law for anticompetitive purposes.[45] If anything, private competitor lawsuits make it harder for consumers to receive full compensation, since courts often react to competitor lawsuits by contracting liability norms in a way that stymies consumer suits as well.

Second, competitor harm—or at least the kind of harm recognized by antitrust law—does not occur in many antitrust cases. If a cartel raises prices, a firm that does not join the cartel nonetheless benefits from it.[46] If an anticompetitive merger harms a rival firm because in the but-for world it would have faced less competition, the rival firm has not suffered "antitrust injury" and may not recover damages.[47] On the other hand, it is also possible that antitrust violations harm competitors without harming consumers, as is true in cases of attempted monopolization, where a dominant firm harms its rival but fails to obtain monopoly power.[48] But in those cases, the ordinary justification for allowing the competitor suit is a prophylactic one: namely, that it is better to prevent antitrust violations before they occur.[49] This is not a compensation justification; rather,

---

44. *See generally Associated General Contractors. v. Carpenters,* 459 U.S. 519 (1983).

45. *See* William J. Baumol & Janusz A. Ordover, *Use of Antitrust to Subvert Competition,* 28 J.L. & Econ. 247 (1985); Frank H. Easterbook, The *Limits of Antitrust,* 63 Tex. L. Rev. 1 (1984); Daniel A. Crane, *The Paradox of Predatory Pricing,* 91 Cornell L. Rev. 1, 5–32 (2005); R. Preston McAfee & Nicholas V. Vakkur, *The Strategic Abuse of the Antitrust Laws,* 2 J. Strategic Mgmt. Educ. 37, 37–38 (2005); Edward A. Snyder & Thomas E. Kauper, *Misuse of the Antitrust Laws: The Competitor Plaintiff,* 90 Mich. L. Rev. 551 (1991).

46. *See Matsushita Elec. Indus. Co. v. Zenith Radio Corp.,* 475 U.S. 574, 586 (1986).

47. *See generally Brunswick Corp. v. Pueblo Bowl-O-Mat, Inc.,* 429 U.S. 477 (1977).

48. *See generally Spectrum Sports, Inc. v. McQuillan,* 506 U.S. 447 (1993).

49. *Swift & Co. v. United States,* 196 U.S. 375 (1905).

it is a deterrence argument in which the rival's lawsuit is merely a means to achieve the end of consumer welfare.

Relatedly, any harm suffered by an excluded competitor is incidental to the economic purposes of antitrust law. The Supreme Court has often declared that "[t]he purpose of the antitrust laws. . . is 'the protection of competition, not *competitors*.'"[50] Therefore, individual competitors serve as means to the end of consumer welfare. While antitrust may do a comparatively better job of compensating them than other classes of victims, this is not the major purpose of antitrust law.

2. **Dynamic Injuries** Economists and antitrust scholars increasingly view static consumer injuries as far less significant than dynamic injuries.[51] The major dispute concerning competition policy and innovation is not whether innovation creates more consumer welfare than static efficiency but whether antitrust enforcement can meaningfully advance dynamic efficiency. For those who follow the tradition of Joseph Schumpeter, all significant competition is dynamic, and static efficiency is of dubious importance.[52] Because the path of innovation is unpredictable, some economists in the Schumpeterian tradition doubt whether antitrust law does much to advance consumer welfare.[53] On the other side, those who follow the tradition of Kenneth Arrow contend that antitrust law is critical to

---

50. *Leegin Creative Leather Products, Inc. v. PSKS, Inc.*, 551 U.S. 877, 906 (2007) (*citing* Atlantic Richfield Co. v. USA Petroleum Co., 495 U.S. 328, 338, (1990). Whether the "competition, not competitors" maxim applies with equal force in the European Union has been the subject of much discussion. *See* Damien Gerardin, *The Perils of Antitrust Proliferation: The Globalization of Antitrust and the Risks of Overregulation of Competitive Behavior*, 10 CHI. J. INT'L L. 189, 207 (2009). Nonetheless, the European Commission seems to have come around to a consumer welfare orientation. DG Competition Discussion Paper on the Application of Article 82 to Exclusionary Abuses, 4. Dec. 2005, *available at* http://ec.europa.eu/comm/competition/antitrust/art82/discpaper2005.pdf. It would thus be anomalous even in the European Union to justify the expense, burden, and systemic effects of private antitrust litigation if all it did was compensate aggrieved competitors.

51. *See* Hovenkamp, *Restraints on Innovation*, supra note 6 at 253 (stating that "today no one doubts [Robert M. Solow's] basic conclusion that innovation and technological progress very likely contribute much more to economic growth than policy pressures that drive investment and output toward the competitive level."); Michael E. Porter, *Competition and Antitrust: A Productivity-Based Approach*, in UNIQUE VALUE: COMPETITION BASED ON INNOVATION: CREATING UNIQUE VALUE FOR ANTITRUST, THE ECONOMY, EDUCATION AND BEYOND 154, 156–57 (Charles D. Weller ed., Innovation Press 2004).

52. JOSEPH SCHUMPETER, CAPITALISM, SOCIALISM, AND DEMOCRACY 84–85 (Harper and Brothers 1942).

53. *See* Harold Demsetz, *How Many Cheers for Antitrust's 100 Years?* 30 ECON INQ. 207 (1992); Michael L. Katz & Howard A. Shelanski, *Mergers and Innovation*, 74 ANTITRUST L.J. 1, 3 (2007) ("In the light of the potential tension between competition and innovation, and in the light of the uncertainty that innovation creates for predictions about competitive

fostering consumer welfare, since oligopolistic markets tend to foster lower rates of innovation than more competitive ones.[54] Still, whether one follows Schumpeter or Arrow, there is general agreement that innovation and technological progress are vital to the advancement of consumer welfare, and that they are probably far more significant than short-term pricing and output effects.[55]

Private antitrust litigation is no better at compensating consumers for dynamic injuries than for static injuries. Indeed, it is probably worse. With respect to static injuries, it is possible for economists to estimate the amount of the overcharge, though the estimate may sometimes be speculative. In contrast, measuring the amount of dynamic efficiency loss and quantifying this loss in dollars often amounts to little more than guesswork.[56] Dynamic efficiency losses suffer from an incommensurability problem, and commensurability is usually considered the very heart of legal compensation models.[57]

For example, suppose that Microsoft undertakes a campaign to quash the development of a multiplatform Java programming system in order to prevent Java from developing a program that could compete with Microsoft's Windows operating system.[58] As a result, Microsoft retains its operating system dominance and overcharges consumers for Windows. The overcharge portion of the static harm, although not the deadweight loss, can be quantified and reduced to a damages award in litigation. But the much larger harm may be the loss of an unknown amount and variety of technological innovation that would have followed had Microsoft not stymied Java programmers in creating a competitive alternative.[59] Since operating systems function as a platform to other applications, technological innovations in the operating systems field could have led to untold innovations in applications.

---

effects of mergers and future conditions in relevant markets, a growing body of commentary has questioned the relationship of antitrust law to innovation.").

54. Kenneth J. Arrow, *Economic Welfare and the Allocation of Resources for Invention, in* THE RATE AND DIRECTION OF INVENTIVE ACTIVITY: ECONOMIC AND SOCIAL FACTORS 619–22 (Richard Nelson ed., 1962). *See generally* Jonathan B. Baker, *Beyond Schumpeter vs. Arrow: How Antitrust Fosters Innovation*, 74 ANTITRUST L.J. 575 (2007).

55. *See, e.g.*, Thomas O. Barnett, *Maximizing Welfare Through Technological Innovation*, 15 GEO. MASON L. REV. 1191, 1194 (2007–2008) (arguing that "dynamic efficiency—particularly leapfrog dynamic efficiency—accounts for the lion's share of efficiency/welfare gains.").

56. Hovenkamp, *Restraints on Innovation*, supra note 6 at 257.

57. *But see* Margaret Jane Radin, *Compensation and Commensurability*, 43 DUKE L.J. 56, 57 (1993) (arguing for an alternative view of compensation form of redress based on "affirming public respect for the existence of rights and public recognition of the transgressor's fault with regard to disrespecting rights").

58. *See* Hovenkamp, *supra* note 13 at 257–59.

59. *Id.* at 257.

Unsurprisingly, very few antitrust plaintiffs seek compensation for dynamic injuries. Even when they do seek such compensation, courts are inhospitable to their claims. Proving the but-for world of competitive innovation is far too speculative an endeavor to meet the evidentiary burden required by civil litigation. Thus, courts have rejected claims against Microsoft for stifled innovation.[60] For example, the Fourth Circuit held that "[i]t would be entirely speculative and beyond the competence of a judicial proceeding to create in hindsight a technological universe that never came into existence. . . . It would be even more speculative to determine the relevant benefits and detriments that non-Microsoft products would have brought to the market and the relative monetary value. . . to a diffuse population of end users."[61] As the Fourth Circuit observed, the problems of proof were not limited to the specific facts of the *Microsoft* case: "At bottom, the harms that the plaintiffs have alleged with respect to the loss of competitive technologies are so diffuse that they could not possibly be adequately measured. The problem is not one of discovery and specific evidence, but of the nature of the injury claimed."[62]

Damages for these sorts of harms are almost never recovered in private litigation. Again, one might posit that the treble-damages remedy is a rough proxy for some unquantifiable dynamic injury, but such an argument is weak. The installed base of consumers who continued to purchase the defendant's products after the monopolistic price increase are often the very consumers who would have continued to purchase from the defendant even if an innovative competitive product had entered the market. The consumers most likely to have purchased the hypothetical innovative product are the ones who stopped purchasing from the defendant and substituted to less-desirable second choices after a price increase or who never began purchasing from the defendant in the first place.[63] Awarding treble damages to the consumers who paid the overcharges does not compensate the consumers who likely suffered most of the dynamic injuries.

Just because private antitrust litigation does not compensate consumers for the harms of stifled innovation does not mean that private litigation is not useful in deterring conduct that stifles innovation. In the same way that private litigation may prevent static deadweight losses by deterring antitrust violations, so too may it prevent conduct that stymies innovation. What private antitrust litigation cannot do, in most cases, is recover damages for foregone technological development or purchases. Since most scholars would agree that these injuries are by far

---

60. *Id.* at 258–59

61. *Kloth v. Microsoft*, 444 F.3d 312, 324 (4th Cir. 2006) (*quoting In re Microsoft*, 127 F. Supp. 2d 702, 711 (2001)).

62. *Id.*

63. For example, in the case of Microsoft, the most likely victims of the suppression of innovation are users of Linux or other operating systems who would have seen the development of a more innovative operating system market in the but-for world.

the most troubling ones, antitrust damages thus seem incapable of achieving compensation for the most significant antitrust injuries.

B. Deterrence

Those who believe that antitrust law exists primarily to promote economic efficiency argue that deterrence, and not compensation, should be the primary purpose of private antitrust enforcement.[64] In their view, antitrust damages supplement criminal fines by removing any expected profitability from antitrust violations.[65] Decision makers in dominant firms will perceive that they are better off by not violating antitrust law, given the likelihood of detection multiplied by the penalty. Unlike other fields of law in which the deterrent value of private enforcement has been questioned,[66] the deterrent success of private antitrust enforcement is largely taken for granted.[67]

In order to evaluate this deterrence claim, one must ascertain who is being deterred. The primary class of relevant decision makers is corporate managers, although one must also consider the possibility that vigilant shareholders will rein in managers who fail to respond to antitrust incentives. With respect to these managers, the argument that private antitrust litigation provides effective deterrence is increasingly doubtful. Two converging trends—the increasing length of antitrust proceedings and the increasing shortness of managerial tenure—make it likely that corporate managers severely discount the threat of future damages litigation.

First, the time gap between the planning of antitrust violation (which is presumably the moment at which deterrence should take root) and antitrust judgment day is increasingly long. While current statistics on the duration of antitrust litigation are not readily available, it is possible to make reasonable assumptions

---

64. *See, e.g.*, William H. Page, *The Scope of Liability for Antitrust Violations*, 37 Stan. L. Rev. 145, 1451 (1985) (arguing that "the deterrent function must predominate"); Posner, Antitrust Law, *supra* note 10 at 266 (arguing that compensation should be a "subsidiary" goal to deterrence).

65. *See generally* Gary S. Becker, *Crime and Punishment: An Economic Approach*, 76 J. Pol. Econ. 169 (1968). As Bill Landes has explained, "[t]he optimal penalty should equal the net harm to persons other than the offender, adjusted upward if the probability of apprehension and conviction is less than one." William M. Landes, *supra* n. 8 at 678.

66. *See, e.g.*, John C. Coffee, Jr., *Reforming the Securities Class Action: An Essay on Deterrence and Its Implementation*, 106 Colum. L. Rev. 1534, 1535–36 (2006) ("As presently constituted, securities class actions produce wealth transfers among shareholders that neither compensate nor deter.").

67. Some commentators have questioned whether treble damages are adequate to achieve optimal deterrence. *See, e.g.*, Robert H. Lande, *Five Myths About Antitrust Damages*, 40 U.S.F. L. Rev. 651 (2005–2006). However, the general view is that the prospect of antitrust damages is a successfully conveyed message to the firm, even if the exact size of the multiplier should be higher.

based on the available data. For the last decade, the average disposition time for all civil cases in the federal system has been steady at between eight and nine months. The average time from filing of the case to trial has steadily increased from around 18.5 months in 1996[68] to 24.6 months in 2007.[69] This suggests that early disposition of cases, whether due to motions to dismiss or early settlement practice, has been relatively constant, but that cases going all the way to trial take much longer than before because of the increasing complexity of modern litigation and the increasing burden of discovery.[70] The Georgetown study, discussed in Chapter 3, found that antitrust cases take, on average, about three times longer than other federal cases from initiation of the lawsuit to disposition.[71] While this ratio has likely not remained constant, the average antitrust suit almost certainly lasts for three or four years. In 2007, there were 378 federal antitrust cases that had been pending for over three years, an immense number considering that there were only a thousand new antitrust filings, and that many cases are quickly disposed of on motions to dismiss.[72]

The time from filing to trial tells only part of the story. The average interval from the filing of a notice of appeal to final disposition is now over a year for all cases.[73] The average interval for antitrust cases is likely even longer due to their monetary significance and complexity. Certiorari petitions to the Supreme Court typically add another year to the delay, during which the appellate court's mandate and the corresponding obligation to pay the judgment are stayed.[74] Moreover, the misconduct at issue usually begins at least a year or two, and often many years, before the complaint is even filed. Hence, in the average private antitrust

---

68. *See* U.S. District Court Judicial Caseload Profile, http://www.uscourts.gov/cgi-bin/cmsd2001.pl.

69. *See id.* at http://www.uscourts.gov/cgi-bin/cmsd2007.pl

70. *See* Fed. R. Civ. P. 26 (b) (2) 2006 advisory committee notes (describing increased burdens from electronic discovery).

71. The Georgetown study found that the average time for the termination of all cases was 24.9 months, with a median of 16.6 months. *See* Steven C. Salop & Lawrence J. White, *Economic Analysis of Private Antitrust Litigation*, 74 Geo. L. J. 1001, 1009 (1986). For comparative purposes, the median length of federal civil cases at the time of the Georgetown study was about nine months. *Id.*

72. Administrative Office of the U.S. Courts, Judicial Business of the U.S. Courts, tbls. S-11 & C-2 (2007), *available at* http://www.uscourts.gov/judbus2007/contents.html. To put the antitrust numbers in perspective, it may be useful to consider the ratio between three-year-old cases and new filings for other classes of private lawsuits. The following are some other categories of cases by (1) new filings, (2) three-year-old cases, and (3) ratio between (1) and (2): breach of contract: 33,939; 1,358, 25:1; civil rights: 31,756, 2,077, 15:1; environmental: 767, 214, 4:1; labor: 18,674, 532, 35:1; RICO: 653, 122, 5:1. Antitrust, with fewer than three new filings per three-year-old case shows a significantly greater disposition toward lengthy cases than other common categories of business litigation.

73. *Id.* at tbl. B-4.

74. Fed. R. App. P. 41(d)(2).

case, the time from the beginning of an anticompetitive scheme until judgment day is at least five years and may be closer to ten years or more.

The relevant time intervals in two recent private antitrust cases, in which the plaintiffs won substantial damages awards at trial and had them affirmed on appeal, are instructive. In *LePage's Inc. v. 3M*,[75] the allegedly anticompetitive bundled rebates were put in place in 1992, and LePage's filed suit in 1997 but did not prevail until 2004, when the Supreme Court denied certiorari. In *Conwood Co. v. U.S. Tobacco Co.*,[76] the plan to eliminate Conwood was hatched in 1990, Conwood sued in 1998, and the Supreme Court denied certiorari in 2003. In both cases, the time between the decision to engage in the challenged conduct and the end of the legal process was well over a decade.

This time lag should be paired with the fact that the managers who put into place anticompetitive schemes are increasingly unlikely to be around to internalize their effects at judgment day. During the 1980s, the turnover rate among senior managers in large corporations was just above 10 percent.[77] By all accounts, the turnover rate has increased significantly, and perhaps even doubled, in the 1990s and 2000s, as various capital market factors accentuated shareholder demand for short-term performance.[78] Today, the average CEO holds her job for about six years.[79] Mid-level executives, such as divisional managers, typically hold their jobs for an even shorter period, perhaps less than four years.[80] Thus, most of the executives responsible for an antitrust violation will no longer be with the firm by the time a damages award is entered against the company.

---

75. *LePage's Inc. v. 3M*, 324 F.3d 141, 144 (3d Cir. 2003).

76. *Conwood Co.v. U.S. Tobacco Co.*, 290 F.3d 768, 772, 775 (6th Cir. 2002).

77. *See* Anne T. Coughlan & Ronald M. Schmidt, *Executive Compensation, Management Turnover, and Firm Performance: An Empirical Investigation*, 7 J. Acct. & Econ. 43, 52 tbl.1 (1985) (documenting an average CEO turnover of 12.7 percent for all firms listed in *Forbes* compensation survey from 1978–1980); Jerold B. Warner, Ross L. Watts & Karen H. Wruck, *Stock Prices and Top Management Changes*, 20 J. Fin. Econ. 461, 461 tbl. 1 (1988) (calculating average annualized rate of 11.5 percent for arrivals or departures by top management including CEO, chairman, or president positions based on *Wall Street Journal* reports from 1963–1978).

78. Kathleen A. Farrell & David A. Whidbee, *Impact of Firm Performance Expectations on CEO Turnover and Replacement Decisions*, 36 J. Acct. & Econ. 165, 173 tbl.1 (2003) (recording a 9 percent turnover rate from 1986–1997); Steven N. Kaplan & Bernadette A. Minton, *How Has CEO Turnover Changed? Increasingly Performance Sensitive Boards and Increasingly Uneasy CEOs* 2 (Nat'l Bureau of Econ. Research, Working Paper No. 12465, 2006) (reporting that in the period 1998–2005, CEO turnover increased to 16.5 percent, implying an average CEO tenure of just over six years).

79. Kaplan & Minton, *supra* note 84, at 2.

80. R.M. Bushman, R.J. Indjejikian, & A. Smith, *Compensation Contracts in Hierarchical Organizations: Determinants of Incentive Pay for Business Unit Managers*, (Univ. of Chi. Working Paper 1994) (reporting 3.7 year average tenure for division managers).

High managerial turnover rates might not thwart the deterrence objective if managers were to internalize some of the detrimental effects of antitrust judgments rendered after they leave the defendant firm. In particular, managers might incur a reputational cost in lost future employment opportunities or take a prestige hit in the business community by virtue of their past roles in a later-adjudicated antitrust violation.[81] But there is scant evidence suggesting that individual managers' reputations are much affected by antitrust judgments against their former employers. Individual managers are not often named as codefendants in private antitrust cases and usually do not appear in any public pronouncement of liability. Liability in complex antitrust cases seldom turns on the culpability of a single manager but rather on a cluster of managerial decisions over time, making it difficult to pinpoint blame.[82] Relatedly, judicial opinions in private antitrust cases often omit the names of individual managers, referring instead to the acts of an impersonal corporation or "the defendant." For example, in the much-publicized *LePage's Inc. v. 3M* case,[83] neither the district court nor the Third Circuit opinion referred to a single 3M executive by name. In most cases, an outsider to the litigation would find it difficult to impose a reputational sanction against any present or former firm manager.

In light of these facts, it is difficult to see how the threat of a future damages judgment disciplines managerial decision making. When managers plan conduct that brings immediate large profits but only potential liability at some future date, the extent to which the future liability deters them from choosing immediate profits is a function of their implicit discount rate for the potential damages award. The longer the perceived time until judgment day, the more likely it is that managers will discount the threat of damages. If managers believe that they are unlikely to be employed by the firm at the distant judgment day, they will tend to disregard the threat of future liability altogether.

Yet, the story is not so simple. One must consider the possibility that private antitrust litigation forces managers and shareholders to internalize the costs of an antitrust violation long before any legal judgment day. Efficient capital markets may punish the firm and, by extension, its managers, as soon as a lawsuit is threatened or filed. According to one study, the filing of a securities class action lawsuit by investors more than doubled the likelihood of CEO turnover.[84] It is unlikely,

81. *See* Christopher R. Leslie, *Antitrust Amnesty, Game Theory, and Cartel Stability*, 31 J. Corp. L. 453, 459–60 (2006).

82. Things may be different in price-fixing cases, where a single rogue manager may collude with someone outside the firm. For other reasons discussed below, private damages actions have a more plausible deterrent effect when they are follow-ons to criminal prosecutions. *See infra* text accompanying note 106.

83. *LePage's Inc. v. 3M*, 324 F.3d 141 (3d Cir. 2003).

84. *See* Philip E. Strahan, *Securities Class Actions, Corporate Governance and Managerial Agency Problems* 22 (June 1998), *available at* http://papers.ssrn.com/abstract=104356

however, that the mere filing of a private antitrust suit brings about severe consequences for a defendant firm's managers. Unlike securities lawsuits, which may impair shareholder confidence in the integrity of insiders, antitrust lawsuits may instead communicate that company managers are acting aggressively to expand market share and increase profitability. This is especially true in the case of private antitrust lawsuits, which many shareholders may rightly regard as signaling that rivals firms are merely disaffected by aggressive, but ultimately lawful, competition. While empirical work suggests that the filing of an antitrust action by the Department of Justice or Federal Trade Commission has an immediate and significant negative effect on a defendant firm's share price, the filing of a private antitrust lawsuit has only about a tenth of the effect of a public suit. Empirical studies have found that defendants lost, on average, 6 percent of their share value upon the filing of a government antitrust lawsuit[85] but only about 0.6 percent of their share value—with an average loss of $4 million—upon the filing of a private lawsuit.[86] A half-percent drop in market capitalization is unlikely to engender ruinous consequences to most managers, particularly if the gains from the challenged behavior were large.

There are two other ways that private antitrust lawsuits might mete out negative sanctions on corporate managers prior to judgment day. First, antitrust litigation is extremely expensive, and the costs are often borne disproportionately by defendants.[87] CEOs, CFOs, and particularly, general counsels, care a great deal about legal fees, but the divisional managers who often make the decisions that ensnare a firm in an antitrust suit may not care. A divisional manager typically seeks to maximize the reported profitability of her own business unit, not necessarily the value of her firm as a whole.[88] For accounting purposes, legal fees are often treated as operating expenses of the firm as a whole. Therefore, legal fees may not come directly out of a divisional manager's budget or count against her revenues for the purposes of divisional financial

(reporting that filing of a securities class action lawsuit by investors increased probability of CEO turnover from 9.8 percent to 23.4 percent).

85. *Kenneth D. Garbade* et al., *Market Reaction to the Filing of Antitrust Suits: An Aggregate and Cross-Sectional Analysis*, 64 Rev. Econ. & Stat. 686, 686–71 (1982).

86. John M. Bizjak & Jeffrey L. Coles, *The Effect of Private Antitrust Litigation on the Stock-Market Valuation of the Firm*, 85 J. Am. Econ. Rev. 436, 437 (1995).

87. *See* Frank H. Easterbook, *The Limits of Antitrust*, 63 Tex. L. Rev. 1, 34 (1984).

88. *See* Philip G. Berger & Eli Ofek, *Diversification's Effect on Firm Value*, 37 J. Fin. Econ. 39, 40 (1995) (discussing "misalignment between central and divisional managers"); Flora Guidry et al., *Earnings-Based Bonus Plans and Earnings Management by Business Unit Managers*, 26 J. Acct. & Econ. 113, 139–40 (1999) (divisional managers seek to maximize short-term profitability of business units rather than that of international conglomerate); Hyun-Han Shin & René Stulz, *Are Internal Capital Markets Efficient*, 113 Q.J. Econ. 531, 533 (1998)) (divisional managers can create deadweight costs through rent-seeking and internal politics).

reporting and incentive compensation. The threat of having to pay legal fees during a protracted and expensive lawsuit may have relatively little deterrent effect on the key decision makers who consider whether to engage in anticompetitive tactics.

A second way that private antitrust lawsuits could provide a deterrent shock before legal judgment day is through large settlement payouts, which are a sort of privately negotiated and accelerated judgment day. But with the exception of government case tag-along suits, which are discussed below, large settlement payouts in private cases usually do not occur until the eve of trial. Corporate managers and boards are usually unwilling to open up their corporate coffers for more than nuisance-value settlements until the threat of an adverse judgment is imminent. Thus, private settlements may accelerate judgment day by short-circuiting appeals, but the average time from the planning of anticompetitive conduct to the payment of any substantial settlement amount still probably exceeds five years.

If managers cannot be expected to respond reliably to the threat of distant and unpredictable liability judgments against their firms, what about shareholders? Two related factors suggest that shareholders do not have strong incentives or capabilities, either. First, the kind of industrial behavior that gives rise to antitrust claims creates the prospect of substantial long-run costs if an antitrust challenge is successful but offers significant short-run profits in the meantime. From an outsider's perspective, it is very hard to evaluate the risk that firm behavior will produce eventual antitrust liability. Whether conduct of the kind adjudged under antitrust's rule of reason and monopolization law's amorphous standards is likely to result in antitrust liability is difficult for antitrust experts to predict, let alone the average institutional investor. It is unlikely that many shareholders will try to curb behavior that increases a firm's market share and profits but that might eventually lead to antitrust liability. Even assuming that a large institutional investor with access to corporate insiders was aware that conduct was risky from an antitrust perspective, given the expected length of time until judgment day, it will often be a rational strategy to approve tacitly the risky conduct, hold the stock for a few years while its value increases, and then sell before an antitrust suit commences. The initial filing of the private lawsuit does relatively little damage to the issuer's share price, so savvy shareholders will have plenty of time to reap their profits and then exit.

Given all of the above factors, it is implausible that the threat of future private litigation does much to deter anticompetitive behavior. My own experience in a private antitrust case is illustrative. By the time the case settled during an appeal, it had been nine years since the lawsuit was filed and fifteen years since the alleged misconduct began. Only a handful of personnel who were with the company during the relevant events were still employed by the firm at settlement. Since the time that the underlying conduct had occurred, the company had witnessed multiple generations of senior management come and go. The company's capital structure had changed multiple times, too. First, it was part of a corporate conglomerate; then it was spun off as an independent publicly traded company; then it was acquired by another conglomerate; and shortly afterward, it was taken private. The managers and shareholders who had reaped the gains from any unlawful conduct, assuming that there was any, had long since moved on.

Of course, deterrence is not just about deterring the individual managers who undertook the wrongful acts from doing so again. Deterrence also seeks to set an example that others will heed.[89] But others will learn the lesson that is *actually* taught to the wrongdoers—and not the abstract lesson that antitrust law is *trying* to teach. If a manager at MegaFirm observes a successful private antitrust lawsuit against another dominant company and asks what it means for him, then the answer to his question may well be: "It is perfectly rational for me to beat up on my competitor, if that increases the success of my division, my incentive compensation, and the value of my stock options. By the time judgment day arrives, I will probably be in a job two times removed from this one and have diversified my stock portfolio so that MegaFirm's stock will account for a relatively small proportion of my wealth."

In theory, there is some cause to be optimistic about the deterrence potential of private lawsuits in cases brought as follow-ons to government criminal prosecutions against cartels.[90] The Justice Department's leniency program, which provides substantial incentives for early defection from cartels, leads many firms to enter guilty pleas as soon as a price-fixing conspiracy is detected.[91] Once a firm has entered a guilty plea, it will often pay out large private settlements quickly because its defenses are very limited.[92] Therefore, follow-on private damages actions in cartel cases provide a much swifter predicted judgment day than do other classes of private antitrust litigation. Although private follow-on suits have the potential to provide substantial deterrence "kickers," in order to make firms more willing to participate in the leniency program, a federal statute limits follow-on suits to single damages against defendants granted leniency.[93] The statute

89. *See* Michael K. Block & Jonathan S. Feinstein, *The Spillover Effect of Antitrust Enforcement*, 68 Rev. Econ. & Stat. 122, 122 (1986) (observing that antitrust deterrence is most effective when targeted at other firms in the same industry as the violator).

90. The government does not criminally prosecute any antitrust offenses except for hard-core cartel behavior. Kathryn K. Dyer & Garrett M. Liskey, *Antitrust Violations*, 45 Am. Crim. L. Rev. 195, 223–24 (2008) (discussing aggressive prosecution of international cartels).

91. *See* Donald C. Klawiter, *Corporate Leniency in the Age of International Cartels: The American Experience*, 14 Antitrust 13 (Summer 2000).

92. The firm is collaterally estopped to deny that it engaged in price-fixing. 15 U.S.C. § 16(a) (2006). It can still contest the standing of the class of purchasers and the amount of their damages.

93. Antitrust Criminal Penalty Enhancement and Reform Act of 2004, § 213(a), Pub. L. 108–237, 118 Stat. 666 (2004) (codified in scattered sections of 15 U.S.C. and accompanying notes).

cuts by two-thirds the deterrence effectiveness of many follow-on private suits and, essentially, orients such suits toward a compensation goal. In sum, effective private litigation deterrence is rare.

II. TOWARD PRIVATE ADMINISTRATION

Compensation and deterrence largely fail as goals of private antitrust litigation, but that does not mean that the whole enterprise should be abandoned. Instead, private enforcement should be reoriented toward achieving an attainable objective—that is, using the power of private litigation to frame private bargaining over problems of market power. Rather than looking backward toward remediating or punishing past bad acts, private antitrust enforcement should be oriented toward the future by preventing exercises of market power that harm consumers.

For example, many antitrust cases concern claims that certain contractual terms foreclose competition. There are many different species of potentially foreclosing contractual terms. A partial litany includes tie-ins,[94] exclusive dealing,[95] market share rebates,[96] bundled discounts,[97] loyalty clauses,[98] and volume discounts.[99] These kinds of contractual provisions have the potential to harm the competitiveness of a market by requiring entry on a large scale or preventing smaller rivals from reaching economies of scale that would permit them to act as a meaningful constraint on the dominant incumbent.[100] At the same time, there are many pro-competitive or competitively neutral reasons for these

---

94. Tying involves the seller of a monopoly product requiring the buyer to purchase a second product as well.

95. Exclusive dealing involves contractual commitment to exclusivity in either buying or selling.

96. Market share rebates are earned when a buyer makes specified percentages of its purchases from the seller.

97. Bundled discounts are given in return for the buyer's agreement to make minimum amounts of purchases in separate product categories.

98. There are various forms of loyalty clauses, all of which provide for one contractual party to do business with the other to the exclusion of other potential parties. For example, the buyer may commit to give its business to the seller so long as the seller matches the best price offered by other sellers.

99. Volume discounts are given when a buyer reaches a certain level of purchases, either units or dollars.

100. *See* Benjamin Klein, *Exclusive Dealing as Competition for Distribution "On the Merits,"* 12 GEO. MASON L. REV. 119, 122 (2003) (explaining how exclusive dealing "will force existing [non-exclusive] competitors and potential new entrants to operate at a cost disadvantage" and may prevent their entry "until sufficient distribution becomes available").

kinds of contractual terms.[101] The upshot of foreclosure is lengthy, fact intensive, and cumbersome litigation.

The usual course in such cases is something like the following: The plaintiff, usually a new entrant, sues, claiming that it is in dire risk of having to exit the market because of the defendant's contractual practices. The defendant counters that the contractual provisions in question bring benefits to customers; indeed, they may have been requested by customers. The defendant also contends that the reason the plaintiff failed is not because of the defendant's contracts but, instead, because of the poor quality of the plaintiff's product. A threshold motion to dismiss may be granted, in which case the entire case goes away. Otherwise, the parties hunker down into years of discovery and expert disclosures, at the end of which the defendant gets a last chance to avoid trial by moving for summary judgment. If the motion is denied, the defendant pays out a large monetary settlement but does not agree to modify its contractual practices. Often, the contractual practices at issue have been mooted by the expiration of the original contracts and subsequent market developments.[102]

If the plaintiff's case is successful, or if it appears to have a chance of succeeding, entrepreneurial class action lawyers will quickly cobble together a class of purchasers in order to make a claim for overcharges. If the class is not certified, the case vanishes. If the class is certified, the defendant settles again without changing its practices. Money changes hands, and the market moves on.[103]

As noted earlier, there is little reason to believe that any of this either results in meaningful compensation to antitrust law's intended beneficiaries or deters other firm managers from engaging in similar practices. Instead of looking backward to see if any such contract violated antitrust law, it would be preferable for judges or administrative agencies to entertain private claims with a view toward prospectively restructuring contracts, so as to allow the market to behave competitively.[104]

---

101. *See* generally *id.* at 137–60 (detailing the efficiencies of exclusive dealing, such as counteracting distributor "free-riding" and assisting manufacturers in contracting for distributor promotion).

102. *See*, e.g., *Masimo Corp. v. Tyco Health Care Group, L.P.*, No. CV 02-4770 MRP, 2006 WL 1236666, at *15 (C.D. Cal. 2006) (upholding jury verdict against defendant based on foreclosure effects of various contractual practices but declining to grant a permanent injunction because the market had changed considerably in the interim).

103. These observations are not new. In 1966, Everette MacIntyre, an FTC commissioner, wrote an article bemoaning the duration, expense, and damages orientation of private antitrust litigation and calling for a much greater focus on the possibility of injunctive remedies. Everette MacIntyre, *Antitrust Injunctions: A Flexible Private Remedy*, 1966 Duke L. J. 22 (1966). As noted earlier, the duration of private damages litigation has substantially increased over the intervening years.

104. Assuming that there is an antitrust problem at all.

For example, suppose that a defendant had contracts requiring major customers to make 80 percent of their purchases from the defendant in order to receive a particular level of discount.[105] Suppose also that a hearing were held limited to the questions of (1) the pro-competitive justifications for such market share discounts, (2) the foreclosure effect on the plaintiff, and (3) the feasibility of contractual modifications that would permit the plaintiff some breathing room in the market without impairing the defendant's legitimate interests. A judge might decide that some level of market-share commitment was justified, but that lowering the commitment to 70 percent would achieve most of the same efficiencies without denying the plaintiff the opportunity to reach the minimum viable scale. In this event, the judge might enjoin the defendant from denying any customer its contractual discounts so long as it reached at least a 70 percent share, thus effectively lowering the market share commitment by 10 percent.

Such a prospective-looking system would require some statutory innovation. Under the present antitrust statutes, a judge would not be justified in injunctively restructuring a contract unless she found a violation of some section of the antitrust law. This all-or-nothing nature of the search for a violation adds nothing but confusion, burden, and time to antitrust proceedings. If the proposed system has any chance of succeeding, it must be nimble and quick. It must strip away the need for lengthy discovery and trials on questions of intent, damages, history, and perhaps even the sinkhole of technical market definition. The trial itself must focus on objective economic facts: specifically, the need for and feasibility of adjusting contractual terms in order to remove entry barriers.

To be sure, more abbreviated proceedings than a full trial after extensive discovery would entail some risk of error. However, the incremental value of the information produced in traditional antitrust discovery rarely exceeds the cost of the delay that damages actions necessarily entail. Discovery often suffers from a severe case of diminishing marginal returns. Most of the information produced in discovery beyond the relevant contracts, cost and revenue data, and some basic business documents is not very useful in determining the ultimate *economic* questions necessary to correct market failures. Thus, the comparative advantages of more speedy determinations are apparent.

An overriding objection to such a system might be that coercively rewriting contracts is a regulatory, and not a judicial, function. Nevertheless, judges do routinely rewrite contracts in order to promote competition. One area where this occurs is in litigation over the enforceability of covenants not to compete. Under common law principles, covenants not to compete are only enforceable to the extent reasonably necessary to promote the employer's legitimate interests.[106] While some courts follow an all-or-nothing approach, under which a covenant

---

105. These are essentially the facts of *Concord Boat Corp. v. Brunswick Corp.*, 207 F.3d 1039 (8th Cir. 2000).

106. Restatement (Second) of Contracts § 188 (1981).

not to compete is either entirely enforceable or entirely unenforceable, a majority of courts follow some version of the "blue pencil" doctrine, which allows a judge to rewrite an overbroad covenant so as to be reasonable.[107] Judges, as lawyers by training, are familiar with the structure and meaning of contracts and may be better able to modify contracts than other business relationships.

Suppose, however, that judges should not be in the business of rewriting contracts in order to achieve competition objectives, because the necessary technical understanding to do so escapes the average judge. This is actually a broader argument against generalist judges assuming jurisdiction over complex antitrust cases and would mean that judges should not award damages for antitrust violations either. Assuming this argument is correct, it merely suggests shifting the contract-policing function to the Federal Trade Commission or another expert body. Since the remedy would be an injunction rather than monetary damages, there is nothing to prevent the FTC from acting as an administrative body to scrutinize contractual terms.[108] During the political wrangling leading up to the creation of the FTC, there were proposals to give the FTC power to approve or disapprove large corporate contracts.[109] A less-ambitious role for the FTC could include some sort of exhaustion of administrative remedies system, whereby any competitor unhappy with an exclusionary contract would have to go through an administrative process before bringing an action in court. This administrative proceeding could result in an administrative law judge recommending contractual modifications that, if adopted by the defendant, would bar the plaintiff from bringing a damages action in court.

Further, even assuming that both judges and administrative agencies are far inferior to contractual parties in drafting contracts, the adoption of a forward-looking private remedy system need not entail extensive contract rewriting by judges or administrative agencies in most cases. Just as most private damages actions are either dismissed by the courts or settle,[110] most private injunctive actions would be dismissed on the grounds that the plaintiff was not really foreclosed or else resolved through a negotiated settlement between the parties. The difference from damages litigation would be the speed with which the matter

---

107. Griffin Toronjo Pivateau, *Putting the Blue Pencil Down: An Argument for Specificity in Noncompete Agreements*, 86 Neb. L. Rev. 672, 682–89 (2008).

108. Proposals to give the FTC power to award damages have been unsuccessful. *See* Stephen Calkins, *Civil Monetary Remedies Available to Federal Antitrust Enforcers*, 40 U.S.F. L. Rev. 567, 580 n.59 (2006) (describing a failed bill "expressly authoriz[ing] the Commission to seek consumer redress after entry of a Commission cease and desist order"). Given the general view that civil antitrust claims entail a Seventh Amendment right to a civil jury, allowing the FTC to award compensatory damages for antitrust violations might be unconstitutional.

109. Crane, *Antifederalism*, *supra* note 1, at 16–18.

110. About three-quarters of private antitrust cases are involuntarily dismissed, almost a quarter settle, and just 2 percent are resolved through a trial. *Id.* at 35 n.188.

could be brought to resolution—months rather than years—and the nature of the agreed-upon remedy—contractual modification enhancing the competitiveness of the market, rather than monetary payments shifting money between pockets.

The solutions to contractual foreclosure are often relatively simple. Consider one recent example. Beginning in the 1990s, Johnson & Johnson (J&J) entered into contracts with group purchasing organizations (GPOs) that offered hospitals substantial discounts on endo products and sutures if the hospitals bought minimum amounts of their requirements in different product categories from J&J.[111] A medical products company that did not offer a full line of comparable products sued, claiming that the bundled discounts foreclosed its ability to compete, since it could not match the discount on J&J's full product line.[112] As soon as the competitor sued, J&J modified its contractual formula to make the market-share formula inapplicable to competitors that did not offer a full product line.[113] After this simple contractual modification, J&J's bundled discount system remained functional as a competitive device against J&J's full-line competitor Tyco but had no further exclusionary effect on small rivals, since purchases from smaller rivals would no longer count in determining whether hospitals had met their market-share requirements.[114] The court granted summary judgment in favor of J&J on the claims relating to these contracts, noting that the contractual modification had solved the foreclosure problem.[115]

It is tempting to view the J&J story as evidence that the threat of treble damages has a salutary deterrent effect on exclusionary conduct, but that would be the wrong conclusion. J&J did not modify its contracts until its competitor sued and did so then, only to score litigation points. J&J's "switch in time" did not stop the litigation from continuing for at least three more years; the court denied summary judgment on a number of other allegedly exclusionary contractual practices. The lesson to draw is that the fixes for contractual exclusion are often simple and could be administered prospectively without excessive complexity or delay.

It is perhaps overly optimistic to hope that private antitrust enforcement will ever look much beyond deterrence and compensation. The current system of private antitrust litigation is big business for lawyers on both sides and many other constituencies. Most importantly, the current system is not so obviously broken that there is great demand for reform. Billions of dollars flow from defendants to "victims," so compensation seems to be working, and this appears to sends

111. *See Applied Med. Res. Corp. v. Ethicon, Inc.*, 2006 WL 1381697, at *1 (C.D. Cal. Apr. 27, 2006) (explaining Johnson & Johnson's purchase agreements with the group purchasing organizations).

112. *Id.*

113. *Id.* at * 3–4.

114. *Id.*

115. *Id.* at *4.

message to potential offenders.[116] Still, hope remains for modest incremental reforms.

The best hope for reform lies in testing and proving forward-looking remedies on a small scale. The challenge for those interested in reforming private antitrust litigation is to create simple, workable models of future-oriented remedies that provide incentives to the relevant stakeholders to bargain toward mutually beneficial solutions to market-power problems. As such, when models are tried and proved on a small scale, they will provide hope for broader reforms.

116. *See* Lande & Davis, *supra* note 28, at 893–98 (finding that "private enforcement is significantly more effective at deterring illegal behavior than DOJ criminal antitrust suits").

PART III

COMPARATIVE AND INTERNATIONAL PERSPECTIVES

10. THE EUROPEAN MODEL

It is impossible to do thorough justice to "the European model" of antitrust enforcement in a single chapter. Europe's institutional arrangements are at least as complex as the American ones that have consumed nine earlier chapters. Further, speaking of a "European" model is somewhat misleading. There are twenty-seven Member States in the European Union, each with its own distinctive institutional structure.[1] Unlike the American states, which have largely homogenous institutional arrangements, there is a great degree of variety in the Member State's institutional arrangements.[2] Overlaying these country-specific institutions are the European Commission and the European courts. The interplay between the European-level and Member State institutions creates an even more complex set of federalism questions than are presented in the United States.

This chapter analyzes the "European model" primarily from the vantage point of the European Commission and European courts and their relationship to Member State institutions. Consistently with the broader themes of this book, it pays particular attention to four areas of contrast between the U.S. and European models: (1) the roles of expertise and independence, (2) the balance between inquisitorial and adversarial processes, (3) federalism—the distribution of power and responsibility between European-wide and member-state-specific institutions, and (4) private antitrust enforcement. Idiosyncratic arrangements in various Member States are not considered here, although some exemplars appear in the following chapter.

I. INTRODUCTION TO EUROPEAN INSTITUTIONS

A. Historical and Normative Foundations

The Treaty of Rome (now renamed the "Treaty on the Functioning of the European Union" or TFEU) became operative in 1958 against a backdrop of two disastrous world wars that wreaked havoc on the European continent. Initially, the treaty's

1. Further, significant economies like Switzerland and Norway have not joined the European Union and hence present distinctive institutional questions not addressed in this chapter.

2. *See generally* THE MODERNISATION OF EU COMPETITION LAW ENFORCEMENT IN THE EU (Dermot Cahill ed., 2004), which provides a country-by-country report on the Member State's institutional arrangements.

primary goals were political—to prevent another world war[3]—as well as economic. The treaty's predecessor, the European Coal and Steel Community Treaty of 1951, was primarily orchestrated between France and Germany and ensured that the two main commodities of war—coal and steel—would be freely and openly shared among the perennial military rivals. The Treaty of Rome also used economics as an instrument to achieve the political end of binding the European nations together economically so that their fates and fortunes were intertwined. The European economies had traditionally been heavily government owned or monopolized and segregated from each other at national borders. The animating spirit of the treaty was to break down national economic boundaries and create a single integrated European market.

Historically, the United States also needed to use economics instrumentally to bind together its obstreperous states, but it did not choose an antitrust policy to do so. For example, nothing bound the Union together so much as the creation of Alexander Hamilton's national bank (discussed in Chapter 1), which issued debt to so many constituencies that the failure of the bank would have meant the impoverishment of a wide swath of American society. The framing of the Sherman Act did share one similarity with the Treaty of Rome, however: it occurred within a generation of a disastrous war (the U.S. Civil War that ended twenty-five years before the framing of the Sherman Act). But even prior to the Civil War, the United States already possessed the legal tools necessary to achieve a common market—particularly the power of Congress over interstate commerce and the dormant commerce clause, which prohibited states from discriminating against interstate commerce. Unlike the Treaty of Rome, the Sherman Act was not primarily concerned with creating a common American market.

Over time, the functions of the European Union evolved away from a concern about political stability to greater concerns about economic growth and prosperity and shared moral and social values. The value of creating a common market remains an important part of the woof and warp of European competition law, but over time, other economic values less tied to the treaty's original political purposes have crept in as well. Increasingly, EU competition law seems oriented toward a consumer welfare standard, although one that is sometimes conceptually and ideologically different from the dominant strains in the United States. The key building blocks of modern EU competition law—prohibitions on anticompetitive agreements (TFEU Article 101) and mergers (the 1989 Merger Regulation) and abuses of dominance (TFEU Article 102)—are conceptually

3. Treaty Establishing the European Economic Community (Mar 25, 1957), Part One, art II, 298 UNTS 11, 15 ("It shall be the aim of the Community, by establishing a Common Market and progressively approximating the economic policies of Member States, to promote throughout the Community a harmonious development of economic activities, a continuous and balanced expansion, an increased stability, an accelerated raising of the standard of living and closer relations between its Member States.").

similar to the three main strains of U.S. antitrust law (Sections 1 and 2 of the Sherman Act and Section 7 of the Clayton Act).

B. Overview of European Institutions

At a European Union level (as opposed to the institutional arrangements within each Member State), the institutions most critical to competition law and policy are the Commission, the Council, and the Court of First Instance (CFI or General Court as it was renamed in November 2009) and the European Court of Justice (ECJ). The Commission theoretically acts as a collegial body for the good of the whole community. The members are expected not to pursue national interests. The Commission is often referred to as the executive body of the European Union. It initiates legislative process by drafting legislation in the form of Council Regulation, such as merger control; Commission Regulation, such as for group exemptions for certain common forms of agreement; and Commission Notices, such as safe harbors for de minimis restraints. Also, and very importantly for competition law, the Commission has adjudicative powers. It decides competition law cases that originate with the Commission and national competition authorities.

The Council, or Council of Ministers, is comprised of the head of state of each Member State. The constituency changes according to the subject matter at hand, so, for example, the economic ministers sit on economic matters. The Council exercises primary legislative power in the community. Increasingly in fields other than competition law, it shares power with the European Parliament.

Competition cases may be initiated in the Competition Directorate of the Commission (Directorate General for Competition or DG for short). Like the FTC, the Commission has both investigatory and prosecutorial powers. When the Commission wishes to proceed against a particular respondent, it files a Statement of Objections, which describes the conduct involved and contains a preliminary assessment. Settlements with the Commission are referred to as "undertakings" and do not have the binding character of U.S.-style consent decrees. Following an investigation, the case handlers within the Competition Directorate draft a preliminary decision. The draft is vetted by the Legal Service (lawyers' lawyers to the various directorates of the Commission and to the other institutions) and by an advisory committee of the Member State representatives. The resulting revised draft decision is submitted to and ordinarily adopted by the College of Commissioners. The firms involved or other persons with a special interest can seek annulment or modification of the decision in the CFI, which is comprised of a judge from each Member State. Either party can appeal the court judgment to the highest court of the European Union, the ECJ, which is comprised of a judge from each Member State. When an appeal is taken to the ECJ, an advocate general (AG) is assigned to the case. The advocate general—who has the standing of a judge of the court—hears the case along with the panel of judges and writes a usually learned opinion, analyzing the facts and law and expressing his or her opinion as to the appropriate outcome. The judgments of both courts must be by consensus; there are no published dissents.

The Commission cannot enforce the treaty's competition law provisions criminally nor can private litigants file cases before the Commission. The process is strictly civil and administrative. The Commission's essential coercive power is to order fines, which may be quite large (up to 10 percent of the defendant corporations' annual worldwide "turnover" or revenue).

Competition law cases may also be initiated by national competition authorities or by private litigants, in national courts. However, for reasons that will be discussed at the end of this chapter, private antitrust litigation is far less common in Europe than in the United States. If an issue of EC competition law arises in a national court, and the interpretation of EC law is not clear, the national court may refer the issue to the Court of Justice. This is called a preliminary reference.

II. EXPERTISE AND INDEPENDENCE

Unlike the United States, where much antitrust law is made by generalist judges or juries (or their shadow), European competition law is primarily the product of expert or semi-expert deliberation. Except in the case of private enforcement, which to this point has been very modest in vindicating European competition policy, European antitrust is created in the first instance by DG Comp or in antitrust agencies in Member States. On appellate review, it is created by the CFI or ECJ.

A. DG Comp and the European Commission

Like the FTC, DG Comp has two related but separate areas of authority—state aids (European law prohibits Member States from subsidizing industry in a way that distorts competition within the European market) and antitrust (including merger control). DG Comp's antitrust caseload appears similar to the FTC's. In 2008, for example, it adopted eight decisions and issued four statements of objections in cartel cases, adopted six decisions and issued four statements of objection in non-cartel antitrust proceedings, and reviewed three hundred forty-seven merger notifications, twenty-five of which were identified as problematic and were subject to remedies.[4] Similarly, the FTC typically conducts serious review

4. Directorate General for Competition Annual Activity Report 2008, *available at* http://ec.europa.eu/atwork/synthesis/aar/doc/comp_aar.pdf.

on twenty to thirty mergers and initiates ten to twenty nonmerger cases, although it does not handle cartel cases.[5]

Since September of 2003, the economic function at the Commission has been broken out into a separate office—the office of the chief competition economist (CCE).[6] The impetus for the movement was at least in several embarrassing defeats for the Commission where the European Court of Justice found that the Commission's decisions lacked sufficient economic foundation.[7] The office of the CCE consists of ten economists (less than a fifth the number employed at the FTC's Bureau of Economics), all of whom have a PhD in industrial organization.[8] Half are career Commission bureaucrats, and half are temporary appointees,[9] which means that the CCE has the opportunity for continuous contact with the worlds of academia and industry. Like the economists in the FTC's Bureau of Competition, CCE economists are assigned to work directly with the DG Comp case teams investigating particular matters. Separately, the CCE provides an independent opinion to the competition commissioner before she proposes her final decision to the College of Commissioners.[10]

DG Comp shares an important similarity to the Antitrust Division in one key respect: DG Comp is not an independent agency but rather a division of a larger unit of government. It has no authority to issue binding decisions of its own but must obtain ratification from the College of Commissioners. Just as the solicitor general's office tempers the independence of the Antitrust Division and conforms its legal positions to wider administrative policy positions, so too, the European Commission's Legal Service Division tempers the positions advocated by DG Comp and conforms them to the Commission's wider legal, political, and economic objectives. Whatever the merits of a strong external legal review function, legal service's interventions sometimes serve as a veto on DG Comp's increasing economic orientation. An example to be discussed momentarily involves a switch from a deterrence objective to a compensation objective for proposed private enforcement reforms.

In sum, from an economic and industry expertise perspective, DG Comp does not lag far behind the FTC or the Antitrust Division. It is less independent than the FTC, although as we noted in Chapter 2 the FTC has largely exchanged independence from the president for dependence on Congress.

---

5. *See, e.g.*, *The FTC in 2008: A Force for Consumers and Competition, FTC March* 2008, *available at* http://www.ftc.gov/os/2008/03/ChairmansReport2008.pdf.

6. Lars-Hendrik Röller and Pierre A. Buigues, *The Office of the Chief Competition Economist and the European Commission*, http://ec.europa.eu/dgs/competition/officechiefecon_ec.pdf

7. *Id*. at 4, citing *Airtours v. Commission* (case T-342/99 ECJ 2002) as an example.

8. *Id*. at 6.

9. *Id*.

10. *Id*.

B. The European Courts

The other major institutional players in the creation of EU antitrust law are the CFI (in November 2009, renamed the General Court) and the ECJ. The ECJ originated with the European Coal and Steel Community Treaty in 1951 and received expanded powers under the Treaty of Rome in 1958.[11] It is the highest appellate court on the meaning of the TFEU's antitrust provisions. It has jurisdiction over European Commission infringement decisions, can render decisions that Member States have failed to live up to their treaty obligations, and may provide preliminary rulings on treaty obligations to Member State courts upon those courts' referral of questions to the ECJ.[12]

The ECJ's wide-ranging jurisdiction makes it essentially a generalist court, not greatly different in the range of topics from the U.S. Supreme Court.[13] In comparison to the U.S. Supreme Court, however, the ECJ hears a substantial number of antitrust cases: about 5 percent of its docket. Between 2005 and 2009, the ECJ decided 115 competition cases out of a total of 2328.[14] By way of comparison, during the same period, the U.S. Supreme Court decided about eight antitrust cases out of a total of somewhat fewer than five hundred with written opinions. The ECJ is not only a significantly larger decider of antitrust cases on a percentage basis, but it also sees enough competition cases every year to see a representative distribution of competition law issues.

Since each Member State gets to appoint a judge to the ECJ, the Court is large and variable in quality. However, it may be misleading to focus on the quality of the judges rather than the quality of the advocate general, since the generally accepted (although empirically unprovable) view is that the Court often defers to the views of the advocate general.[15] There is no formal specialization among the advocates general, but there may be some informal allocation of economically minded AGs to complex antitrust matters. The senior-most member allocates the workload among the group of AGs and may take into account interests and expertise in making allocation decisions.

The CFI came into being in 1988 in reaction to a perception that the ECJ's docket was becoming overloaded.[16] Although partially an appellate court (in the sense that federal courts of appeal review decisions from the FTC), the CFI was meant to be a "specialised fact-finding tribunal with particular expertise in cases

---

11. Anthony Arnull, The European Union and its Court of Justice 5–7 (2d ed. 2006).

12. *Id.* at 33.

13. *See generally* Alicia Hinarejos, Judicial Control in the European Union: Reforming Jurisdiction in the Intergovernmental Pillars (2009).

14. European Court of Justice Annual Report 2009, at 9, *available at* http://curia.europa.eu/jcms/jcms/Jo2_7000/.

15. Arnull, *supra* n. 11 at 15.

16. *Id.* at 25.

concerning economic effects of complex factual situations."[17] From 1988 until 1993, competition cases represented a substantial portion of the CFI's docket, but Council decisions in 1993 and 1994 extended the CFI's jurisdiction more broadly, thus somewhat diminishing its competition law specialization. Following the Treaty of Nice in 2004, the CFI acquired even further jurisdiction, including nearly all acts or omissions of the European Commission.[18]

Even with these changes, competition and competition-related issues remain a substantial portion of the CFI's docket. Over the life of the CFI, approximately 12 percent of its docket has consisted of competition cases.[19] By comparison, between 2004 and 2009, the court decided 254 competition cases out of a docket of 2588, a 10 percent antitrust caseload.[20] Unlike the ECJ, however, a very substantial portion of the CFI's remaining caseload is in the closely related fields of state aid and intellectual property. In combination, competition, state aid, and intellectual property amount to about 45 percent of the CFI's cases.[21] This is a far higher percentage of cases in competition and competition-related fields than any comparable U.S. court, except for the Federal Court of Appeals for the Federal Circuit, which hears patent appeals.

One potentially important difference between judicial review of FTC decisions and CFI review of EC decisions concerns the standard of review. Exactly what the standard of review is in the European courts "has been the subject of intense debate and scrutiny among academics, practitioners, the Judiciary, and the Commission."[22] Nonetheless, it is clear that the intensity of judicial review on questions of fact and law varies considerably between CFI review of Commission decisions and appellate court review of FTC decisions. U.S. courts distinguish solely between questions of fact and questions of law (admitting the possibility that there are also mixed questions of fact and law). On factual questions, the courts defer to the FTC's judgments under a substantial evidence standard.[23] On questions of law, review is de novo, although the courts are supposed to accord the FTC "some deference as to its informed judgment that a particular practice violates the FTC Act."[24] The CFI similarly reviews issues of law de novo. It does not, however, defer to the EC's decisions on questions of fact but conducts its

17. *Id.* at 25.

18. *Id.* at 26.

19. Bo Vesterdorf, *Judicial Review in EC Competition Law: Reflections on the Role of Community Courts in the EC System of Competition Law Enforcement*, Competition Policy International (Autumn 2005), at 18.

20. CFI Statistics of Judicial Activity, http://curia.europa.eu/jcms/upload/docs/application/pdf/2009–03/ra08_en_tpi_stat.pdf.

21. *Id.*

22. Tony Reeves & Ninette Dodoo, *Standards of Proof and Standards of Judicial Review in European Commission Merger Law*, 29 Fordham Int'l L.J. 1034, 1034 (2006).

23. *Schering-Plough Corp. v. FTC*, 402 F.3d 1056, 106—63 (11th Cir. 2005).

24. *Id.* at 1063.

own independent review of the facts in the record.[25] Further, on "complex economic matters," the CFI applies a "manifest error" standard to Commission decisions.[26] The tripartite European review system recognizes, more explicitly than the U.S. system, that somewhere between the domain of law and fact lies a space for regulatory policy making on complex economic matters. To secure the advantages of agency expertise, the European courts defer to administrative decisions in that space.

In sum, the European courts (where the judges are political appointees with relatively short tenure) are probably less independent than the U.S. courts (where judges at political appointees but enjoy life tenure during good behavior) but more expert on antitrust matters since such matters occupy a considerably higher percentage of their caseload. It is difficult to say whether this translates into a higher average quality of decision or opinion, since such an assessment requires some view of the relative bents of U.S. and EU competition law—a matter outside the scope of this book.

Since the Treaty of Nice in 2003, there has been talk about the possibility of creating a specialized "EU Competition Court" under Article 225a of the EC Treaty.[27] The British House of Lords' European Union Committee considered, and rejected, such a proposal in 2007, concluding that specialization would not diminish complexity of lead to time savings.[28] Still, talk of a possible movement toward more expert competition law courts in Europe continues. In Chapter 11, we will return to the subject of specialized antitrust courts.

III. INQUISITORIAL AND ADVERSARIAL PROCESSES

A key difference between the U.S. and European antitrust models reflects the traditional difference between the U.S. and continental legal models more generally—at almost every stage of decision, the United States. employs an adversarial adjudicative or administrative model, whereas the European Commission generally employs an inquisitorial-administrative model.[29] This is not to say that every antitrust decision in the United States is made following the give-and-take of cross-examination and party contest. As noted in earlier chapters, much antitrust

25. Vesterdorf, *supra* n. 19 at 12–15

26. *Id.* at 15.

27. *See* Christopher Bellamy, *An EU Competition Court: The Continuing Debate, in* THE REFORM OF EC COMPETITION LAW: NEW CHALLENGES 31–52 (Ioannis Lianos & Ioannis Kokkoris eds., 2010).

28. *Id.* at 40.

29. *See generally* Wouter P.J. Wils, *The Combination of the Investigative and Prosecutorial Function and Adjudicative Function in EC Antitrust Enforcement: A Legal and Economic Analysis*, 27 WORLD COMP. 201 (2004).

policy making and implementation (particularly, most merger policy) occurs in behind-the-scenes negotiation in the shadow of formal proceedings. The formal proceedings, however, are predominantly adversarial. The Justice Department has no power to make binding decisions; it can only sue in court to enforce the law. The FTC follows an internal separation of powers model where the Complaint Counsel at the Bureau of Competition initiates an action (with the approval of the Commissioners), an impartial administrative law judge renders a decision, and the Commissioners then sit effectively as a court of appeals to hear the competing arguments about the ALJ decision from complaint counsel and the defendant's lawyers. By contrast, decision making within the Commission involves no formal taking of evidence or cross-examination of opposing witnesses or any of the other trappings of direct adversarial contest. Once the Commission or FTC takes a decision, and the defendant appeals to the courts, the processes largely converge.

As already noted, the administrative process within the Commission begins with the issuance of a "Statement of Objections," essentially an administrative complaint.[30] The competition commissioner can issue the Statement of Objections on her own initiative, after consultation with Legal Service.[31] The parties are entitled to submit evidence and contentions, both in writing and at an oral hearing. A hearing officer—a Commission official outside DG Comp—conducts the hearing, which is essentially the party's opportunity to submit its position and evidence. Thereafter, DG Comp prepares a draft decision, which is vetted by a peer review panel within DG Comp, Legal Service, other Commission services (if relevant), and an advisory committee comprised of competition authorities of Member States.[32] The DG's recommendation is ordinarily ratified by the Commission. Although the College of Commissioners may consult on the decision, they do not sit as a reviewing court like the FTC's commissioners.[33] Once the Commission adopts DG Comp's recommendation, the decision becomes binding unless annulled by the courts.

This tight combination of investigative, prosecutorial, and adjudicative functions with DG Comp has led to charges of prosecutorial bias, although it is difficult to substantiate or falsify such claims.[34] Even the FTC, which has significantly more robust internal checks and balances, has not been immune from similar criticisms.[35] The Commission's current streamlined approach has been defended

---

30. Wouter P.J. Wils, *The Increased Level of EU Antitrust Fines, Judicial Review and the ECHR*, World Comp. 8 (2010).

31. *Id.*

32. *Id.*

33. Wils, *Combination*, supra n. 29 at 7.

34. *Id.* at 14.

35. *See* Malcolm B. Coate & A.N. Kleit, *Does it Matter that the Prosecutor is Also the Judge? The Administrative Complaint Process at the Federal Trade Commission*, 19 Managerial & Decision Econ. 1 (1998).

primarily on the grounds of cost savings—with the American adversarial model described as overly time consuming and wasteful.[36]

At present, there appears to be some momentum for reforms that would inject further elements of adversarial contention into the Commission's administrative processes. An article in *The Economist* reported that lawyers who frequently appeared in competition matters felt that by the time of the hearing, the case teams were "wedded to their version of events, even if they hear a convincing defense."[37] Practitioners complained that the hearing lacked any serious purpose, without cross-examination or often the attendance of the competition commissioner.[38] One practitioner described the typical hearing as "just a bunch of lawyers showing PowerPoint slides."[39] Recently, the Commission was embarrassed when the EU's ombudsman found that during its investigation of the Intel case that ultimately resulted in a record $1.5 billion fine against Intel, DG Comp failed to make a written record of a meeting with a Dell executive that could have provided exculpatory evidence.[40] A more directly adversarial process might have drawn out the exculpatory facts.

Possible reforms of the Commission's processes range from the radical to the incremental. At the radical end, one could envision a system in which the Commission would be required to initiate antitrust proceedings in Member State courts, much as the FTC does when it sues in federal court. Such a change seems undesirable, since it would diminish many of the benefits of expertise discussed in the previous section. At the more modest end of the spectrum, the Commission might further liberalize its administrative processes, for example, by allowing cross-examination and formal fact finding at the hearing stage and an opportunity to be heard by the competition commissioner.

Finding the optimal balance between technocratic expertise, administrative flexibility, and the truth-sharpening mettle of adversarial processes is a tall order. Neither the United States nor the European Union can claim to have found the perfect balance. If the United States could benefit from some further institutional shifts in the directions of expertise and flexibility, the European Union could benefit from shifts in the direction of greater transparency and adversarial process.

---

36. Wils, *Combination, supra* n. 29 at 22–24.

37. *Unchained Watchdog: Businesses Think Europe's Trustbusters Should be Kept on a Tighter Leash*, ECONOMIST (Feb. 18, 2010).

38. *Id.*

39. *Id.*

40. Decision of the European Ombudsman Closing his Inquiry into Complaint 1935/2008/FOR against the European Commission, *available at* http://www.ombudsman.europa.eu/cases/decisions.faces/en/4164/html.bookmark.

IV. FEDERALISM

Like the United States, the EU system includes a trans-state (indeed, transnational) authority, the European Commission, trans-state (indeed, transnational) courts, the Court of First Instance and the European Court of Justice, and national competition authorities and courts in each state. Further, the TFEU overlays twenty-seven sovereign national governments that continue to engage in a broad array of regulatory functions that often have significant effects on competition. The relationships between these different institutions on a European and national level naturally create complex legal, political, and regulatory policy issues. Two fundamental issues are considered here: (1) the enforcement of the treaty's competition law provisions by Member States, and (2) the power of Member States to displace European competition norms in favor of other regulatory policies.

A. Shared EC and Member State Authority

One of the major moves in the EU in recent years has been an effort to decentralize competition law decision making and grant increased authority and responsibility to national competition authorities and courts. This has particularly been manifested with respect to the treatment of anticompetitive agreements—which in the United States would be analyzed under Section 1 of the Sherman Act and what in the EU is analyzed under Article 101 of the TFEU. Article 101 sets forth a two-stage process for assessing possible anticompetitive effects of such agreements. Article 101(1) catches agreements that prevent, restrict, or distort competition. Article 101(2) declares such agreements void. Article 101(3) states that Article 101(1) may be declared inapplicable if four conditions are met. In essence, the conditions are that the agreement must be on balance pro-competitive, that it was be efficient or technologically progressive, that competition must be restrained no more than necessary to fulfill these objectives, and consumers must get a fair share of these benefits.

Article 101 was implemented in 1962 by Regulation 17, which declared that the Commission alone could give Article 101(3) exemptions. Regulation 17 set out a structure for clearing and exempting agreements. Under this structure, if parties notified an agreement, the provision declaring the agreement void was stayed until the Commission ruled on the entitlement to the exemption. The centralized notification/exemption system required a huge amount of paperwork and analysis. By the 1990s, it had become clear that the paperwork and time and effort it took to analyze the thousands of filed agreements were extraordinary, and the workload increased geometrically with the admission of new accession states. Delays were long. The bureaucratic and reactive work drained resources, to the marginalization of other work. Moreover, the structure of the system had resulted in rigid and regulatory rules that were out of step with increasingly well-accepted modes of economic analysis.

In 2002, the Commission undertook a program of modernization and adopted Council Regulation (EC) No 1/2003.[41] The introduction of Regulation 1, which was prompted in substantial part by the growing number of Member States, reflected significant procedural reform whereby powers would devolve to Member States, but Member States would be obliged to carry out EC law and policy, and a new network of national authorities, combined with the continuing sharing of information about all relevant national court judgments, would assure consistency and coherence.

The core of Regulation 1 is the abolition of the requirement that agreements that fall within Article 101(1) must be notified. It makes Article 101(3) directly effective, so that national competition authorities and national courts, as well as the Commission, may decide whether agreements fulfill the requirements of Article 101(3). This sharing of power lightens the Commission's workload, giving it more time to consider more serious restraints of community-wide interest. It also makes national competition authorities full partners in the enforcement of European competition norms.[42]

Article 3 of Regulation 1 imposes two fundamental obligations on the courts and competition authorities of the Member States, to preserve the realm of EC law. First, where national competition law is applied to agreements and abusive practices that may affect trade between Member States, Article 3(1) imposes the obligation on national authorities and courts to apply Articles 101 and/or 102 concurrently with the national law. Second, Article 3(2) obliges the competition authorities and courts of the Member States not to invoke national law to prohibit agreements or concerted practices that may affect trade between Member States but that are not prohibited by community competition law. Member States may, however, be more aggressive than Article 102 in applying national laws against abuse of dominance.

The Commission retains the ability to deal with any case affecting trade between Member States, thereby relieving national authorities of their competence to apply EC law in a particular case. In addition, Article 10 equips the Commission with the sole power to adopt, on its own initiative and when the community public interest so requires, ex ante decisions finding that a particular agreement or practice does not infringe Articles 101 or 102. An exercise of Article 10 power precludes national courts and competition authorities from adopting decisions in the same case that would run counter to the Commission's decision. Hence, in contrast to U.S. federalism (discussed in Chapter 8), where states can press for an application of federal antitrust law in conflict with the views of the federal government, the "convergence rule" gives the European Commission has the power to advance a uniform

---

41. Council Regulation 1/2003 on the implementation of the rules on competition laid down in Articles 81 and 82 of the Treaty OJ [2003] L1/1.

42. D.G. Goyder & Joanna Goyder, Goyder's EC Competition Law 519 (5th ed. 2009).

administrative view of EC law without interference from the Member States (subject, of course, to the ultimate decision of the courts).[43]

In order to ensure the consistent application of EC competition law throughout the community, Regulation 1 creates mechanisms for information sharing and consultation among national competition authorities and the center through the creation of the European Competition Network (ECN), which has encouraged cooperation in handling cases, facilitated case allocation, and produced convergence of national laws and procedures. Also, national courts are entitled to ask the Commission for its support in the application of Articles 101 and 102, and both national competition authorities and the Commission are empowered to make amicus curiae submissions before the national courts.

The upshot of the Regulation 1 reforms has been to decentralize authority and responsibility to enforce the TFEU's competition provisions, even while ensuring a primary and preemptive role for the European Commission. In contrast to the relative unruliness of American antitrust federalism, this system achieves decentralization and power sharing even while ensuring that that a single supranational authority can speak in a unified voice for the executive function of EU antitrust enforcement.

B. Member State Authority to Displace Treaty Competition Norms

A second area of comparison to the United States on federalism issues involves the authority of Member States to authorize or require anticompetitive conduct that would otherwise violate treaty norms. Recall that under the *Parker v. Brown* doctrine discussed in Chapter 8, U.S. states can displace the federal competition norm so long as the displacement is clearly articulated as state policy and actively supervised by state actors. Not so in Europe. As the Court of Justice explained in the *Italian matches* case,[44] the treaty requires "the Member States not to introduce or maintain in force measures, even of a legislative or regulatory nature, which may render ineffective the competition rules applicable to undertakings."

Italian matches involved a circumstance with many similarities to the facts of *Parker*. The Italian government created a regulatory scheme for matches where the Ministry of Finance set the price for matches, and then a state-sanctioned consortium of match producers allocated production quotas. The ECJ found that the Italian authorities were compelled by the treaty to disapply national law

---

43. *See* Richard Whish, Competition Law 76–77 (Oxford University Press, 6th ed. 2009).

44. *Consorzio Industrie Fiammiferi (CIF) (Italian matches)*, Case C-198/01, judgment of September 9, 2003. *See generally* Eleanor M. Fox, *State Action in Comparative Context: What if Parker v. Brown Were Italian? in* International Antitrust Law & Policy 463–74 (Barry E. Hawk ed., 2004).

if it legitimized or reinforced private conduct that would otherwise violate Article 101.[45]

In Europe, then, the preemption norm runs in the opposite direction than in the United States. While treaty law does not preclude all regulation that displaces competition, it does prevent Member States from enlisting market actors in anti-competitive schemes. As Eleanor Fox has noted, if *Parker* had been a European case, "[t]he Italian Antitrust Authority would have disapplied the Italian law to the extent necessary to avoid undermining Article [101]; the national court would have set aside the law as void."[46]

This aspect of European federalism seems unambiguously superior to the American reverse-preemption norm. It is an odd treaty system that allows signatory states to frustrate treaty rules so long as they do so conspicuously and actively. One may object that EU competition law is directly a product of the treaty through its antitrust articles whereas the Sherman Act is a discretionary legislative undertaking within the ambit of the federal constitution—that Articles 101 and 102 are embedded in the treaty whereas the Sherman Act has no constitutional status. But that difference is merely formal, perhaps explaining the legal doctrines but not making normative sense of the institutional arrangements. Congress clearly could make the Sherman Act preemptive if it so chose; and it should so choose. On the federalism front, the United States. has much to learn from the EU.

V. PRIVATE ENFORCEMENT

Perhaps the starkest contrast between the U.S. and EU antitrust systems concerns the role of private enforcement. As discussed in earlier chapters, private enforcement now dominates the U.S. system. By contrast, there is no private enforcement at all at the EU level and only modest enforcement in most Member States. Traditionally, European jurisdictions have not been nearly as generous to private litigants on such matters as discovery, class actions, and proof of damages as the United States has been. Even the United Kingdom, whose common law provided the foundations of U.S. antitrust law, has had only a handful of successful private damages cases.[47] Germany seems to be the jurisdiction with the most active private enforcement. A recent study found up to 500 private cases raising competition law issues in the German courts between 2005 and 2007,

---

45. Due to the procedural posture of the case, the ECJ did not directly reach a second question—whether the Italian scheme precluded matchmakers from engaging in autonomous conduct, although it strongly hinted that if it reached that question it would find that the scheme did preclude autonomous competitive decisions.

46. Fox, *supra* n. 44 at 473.

47. *See* Michael D. Hausfeld, *Global Enforcement of Anticompetitive Conduct*, 10 SEDONA CONF. J. 9, 17 (2009).

although it is unclear whether all of these cases would be considered traditional antitrust matters.[48]

In 2008, the European Commission released a White Paper—essentially a blueprint for further action by the Commission—calling for expanded private antitrust enforcement within the European Union.[49] Two dominant themes emerge from the White Paper: (1) Europe needs more private enforcement but (2) *not* in the U.S. style. On virtually every major aspect of private litigation—including standing, discovery, claim aggregation, damages—the White Paper argues for an approach that essentially rejects the U.S. position.

A glimpse back three years before the issuance of the White Paper will illustrate the origin and nature of the White Paper's orientation. In a 2005 Green Paper—a kind of publicly disseminated draft of the White Paper—the Commission had taken the view that deterrence should be a primary goal of an expanded private enforcement regime.[50] But between 2005 and 2008, the Commission's Legal Service—populated, as we have already noted, by lawyers rather than economists—insisted that this U.S.-style economic perspective on private enforcement did not fit with European values, where deterrence was to be a largely governmental function and compensation the primary function of private litigation. Hence, the White Paper reports that "full compensation is. . . the first and foremost guiding principle" of private antitrust litigation and that "[m]ore effective compensation mechanisms mean that the costs of antitrust infringements would be borne by the infringers, and not by the victims and law-abiding businesses."[51]

This shift from deterrence to compensation has profound consequences for the remainder of the White Paper and, if ultimately accepted in European legislation, for the future of private enforcement in the EU. For all of the reasons identified in Chapter 9, compensation is a poor choice. The case for deterrence is weak but perhaps more attainable given a speedier adjudicatory system or

48. Sebastian Peyer, *Private Enforcement of Competition Law: An Empirical Study from Gemany* (draft, on file with author).

49. *Commission of the European Communities White Paper on Damages Actions for Breach of the EC Antitrust Rules*, COM (2008) 165 final (Apr. 2, 2008) [hereinafter *E.U. White Paper*].

50. Commission of the European Communities Green Paper, *Damages actions for breach of the EC antitrust rules* (Dec. 19, 2005), *available at* http://eurlex.europa.eu/LexUriServ/LexUriServ.do?uri=COM:2005:0672:FIN:EN:PDF (asserting that private enforcement should "contribut[e] significantly to the maintenance of effective competition in the Community (deterrence)."

51. *Id.* at 3. Interestingly, the white paper listed deterrence as a merely secondary goal for private enforcement. *Id.* In the United States, the situation is arguably the opposite. *See* William H. Page, *The Scope of Liability for Antitrust Violations*, 37 STAN. L. REV. 1445, 1452 (1985) (arguing that the Supreme Court has elevated deterrence over compensation as a value for private antitrust enforcement).

systemic refinements forcing managers to internalize the costs usually borne only by shareholders. On the other hand, whatever the theoretical desirability of compensating injured victims of antitrust violations, the case that private litigation accomplishes effective compensation is very weak. It is unlikely that procedural adjustments would fix the problem, since it is difficult to imagine any effective way of securing compensation for the downstream purchasers.[52] Indeed, compensation is even more likely to fail as a goal in the European Union, its Member States, and jurisdictions with similar legal regimes than it is in the United States. The choice of compensation as an objective often interacts with procedural and administrative rules that render private antitrust litigation ineffective at achieving *any* rational goal.

The mischievous effects of pursuing a compensation goal quickly become apparent in the remainder of the White Paper. First, the paper announces that because compensation is the goal, the real economic victim of the violation should always have standing to sue. Accordingly, indirect purchasers all the way down the distribution chain should have standing.[53] Indeed, the White Paper proposes a rebuttable presumption that end purchasers absorb the entire overcharge.[54] Conversely, since other parties in the distribution chain who pass the overcharge downstream do not suffer real economic injury, the antitrust violator should be allowed to assert a pass-on defense to the distributors' claims.[55]

The Commission's proposed standard is already the rule in a number of jurisdictions with emerging private antitrust enforcement. According to a 2007 study of a number of jurisdictions by the International Competition Network (ICN), while the vast majority of the jurisdictions surveyed had not explicitly considered either the direct purchaser rule or the "pass-on" defense, most would probably invoke unjust enrichment principles to deny recovery to a wholesaler or retailer who simply passes on the overcharge.[56] Conversely, the ICN study concluded that the vast majority of surveyed jurisdictions would probably allow suits by indirect purchasers.[57] To the extent that jurisdictions favor a compensation goal, they will presumably opt for indirect purchaser standing and the availability of a pass-on defense.

The effects of a compensation objective do not end with standing principles. The White Paper calls for "full compensation of the real value of the loss

52. *See* Richard A. Posner, *Oligopoly and the Antitrust Laws: A Suggested Approach*, 21 Stan. L. Rev. 1562, 1590 (1969).

53. *Id.* at 4.

54. *Id.* at 8.

55. *Id.*

56. International Competition Network Annual Conference, Moscow, May 2007, Report of the Cartels Working Group, *Interaction of Public and Private Enforcement in Cartel Case*, at 12.

57. *Id.*

suffered."[58] The White Paper goes on to make clear that this includes not only "actual loss" but also lost profits and interest.[59] While this all sounds generous to plaintiffs, there is a highly significant subtext: treble damages or other damages multipliers are inconsistent with a compensatory regime, since they award plaintiffs a windfall far in excess of their actual damages.

Two more procedural aspects of compensation-oriented regimes are significant. First, class action procedures are rare in continental systems.[60] The White Paper recognizes that the parties bearing the economic burden of antitrust violations have often "suffered scattered and relatively low-value damages," and that some form of claim aggregation is therefore necessary for private enforcement.[61] Still, the White Paper shies away from U.S.-style class actions, calling instead for "representative actions" by "qualified entities" such as state bodies or trade associations or "opt-in collective actions."[62] The ICN reports that class actions are available in only five of the jurisdictions it surveyed.[63]

Another procedural issue raised by the White Paper and commonly discussed in jurisdictions considering private antitrust enforcement is discovery. Here, again, the White Paper rejects the U.S. model. Although the White Paper recognizes the need for some information disclosure in litigation, it seems far more concerned about "the negative effects of overly broad and burdensome disclosure obligations, including the risk of abuses."[64] It proposes that any discovery should be court-ordered (rather than party-initiated as in the United States) and only available when the plaintiff has pleaded facts plausibly showing the existence of an antitrust violation[65]; satisfied the court that he cannot reasonably obtain the facts except through discovery; specified the precise categories of information to be disclosed; and demonstrated that the discovery requests are relevant, necessary, and proportionate.[66]

In sum, the proposed EU system, which is also characteristic of other emerging antitrust jurisdictions, has a compensation objective and, consequently, indirect

---

58. *E.U. White Paper, supra* note 49, at 7.

59. *Id.*

60. *See* Richard A. Nagareda, *Aggregate Litigation Across the Atlantic and the Future of American Exceptionalism*, 62 VAND. L. REV. 1, 2–3 (2009) (discussing European alternatives to U.S.-style class actions and concluding that "U.S.-style class actions are likely to remain exceptional from a trans-Atlantic perspective").

61. *E.U. White Paper, supra* note 49, at 4.

62. *Id.*

63. International Competition Network Annual Conference, Moscow, May 2007, Report of the Cartels Working Group, *supra* note 115, at 4.

64. *White Paper, supra* note 49, at 5.

65. On this score, the EU position does not differ from the U.S. position. *See Bell Atl. Corp. v Twombly*, 550 U.S. 544 (2007) (holding that, to survive the pleading stage, a complaint must possess allegations "plausibly suggesting" an antitrust violation).

66. *White Paper, supra* note 49, at 5.

purchaser standing, single damages, and restrictive rules on claim aggregation and discovery. By contrast, the U.S. Supreme Court has nominally recognized deterrence and compensation as co-equal objectives but has seemed to favor deterrence over compensation when the two interests diverged.[67] As previously noted, the United States generally follows a "direct purchaser" rule, in which the direct purchasers of the overpriced goods have standing to sue, even though they may pass on the overcharge by reselling the good at a marked-up price and thereby avoid economic injury[68] and denies standing to indirect purchasers.[69] The United States also allows automatic treble damages by statute[70] and liberal party-initiated discovery by rule.[71]

Consider now how effective the European model is likely to be at achieving compensation or in encouraging private antitrust litigation at all. If European courts chase the harm downstream to the ultimately injured party, they will find themselves with thousands or even millions of parties to compensate in the ordinary antitrust case. Not only will those parties be widely dispersed with many small injuries, they will also be denied the two features of the U.S. system, generous claim aggregation and treble damages, that provide hope that a suit will be brought and monies recovered. Further, if the purchasers sue, they will face sharp limitations on discovery. Discovery stinginess is particularly problematic in a system that gives standing to downstream purchasers who are remote from the defendant. Unlike the direct purchasers, who are often sophisticated contractual parties of the defendant, the indirect purchasers may know very little about the defendant's business and need generous amounts of discovery to make their case.

Ironically, a primarily deterrence-oriented system, like that of the United States, has less need of the very features of the U.S. civil litigation system that

67. *See* Barak D. Richman & Christopher R. Murray, *Rebuilding Illinois Brick: A Functionalist Approach to the Indirect Purchaser Rule*, 81 S. Cal. L. Rev. 69, 90 (2007).

68. *Illinois Brick Co. v. Illinois*, 431 U.S. 720, 744–47 (1977).

69. *Hanover Shoe, Inc. v. United Shoe Machinery Corp.*, 392 U.S. 481, 492–94 (1968). *But see supra* note 28 and accompanying text (noting that state antitrust law is not preempted from allowing indirect purchaser suits and that some states have allowed such suits). Further, the congressionally appointed Antitrust Modernization Commission recently made a recommendation for legislative reforms that would overrule both *Hannover Shoe* and *Illinois Brick* and allow for removal of state cases to federal court and consolidation of all damages claims as to a particular violation. Antitrust Modernization Comm'n, Report and Recommendations 265–78 (2007), *available at* http://govinfo.library.unt.edu/amc/report_recommendation/amc_final_report.pdf. The court would then make a determination of what the total monopoly overcharge was, treble the overcharge, and allocate the damages pot to the different plaintiffs based on the proportion of their individual injuries to the total. *Id.* at 270–78.

70. 15 U.S.C. § 15 (2006).

71. *See* Fed. R. Civ. P. 26.

continental systems often reject. It has less need for claim aggregation, since the direct purchasers are relatively fewer in number and have more concentrated injury. It has less need for treble damages, since the direct purchasers often have a sufficient incentive to sue for even single damages. Finally, it has less need for discovery, since the direct purchasers often know much more about the defendant's business practices and conduct than do the downstream purchasers.

None of this is to say that the EU would be wrong to reject direct purchaser rules, class actions, treble damages, liberal discovery, or other features of the U.S. system.[72] Even where these features are present, private antitrust litigation is not very successful at achieving compensation or deterrence. Rather, the point is that if compensation and deterrence have failed as objectives in the United States, they are even more likely to fail in the European Union and in other jurisdictions with similar legal regimes and cultures. Emerging private enforcement jurisdictions have an expanded set of reasons to resist implementation of a private enforcement system centered on either compensation or deterrence. Before locking in a private litigation system that inertia will later make difficult to change, these jurisdictions would be well advised to consider the failures of the U.S. system at a foundational level and then proceed from a different premise.

For now, it remains unclear whether the White Paper approach will be implemented. There has been considerable political dissent from the White Paper in the European Parliament, with legislators from some Member States arguing that a European mandate on private enforcement would interfere with the prerogatives and practices of the national courts. In March of 2010, the Commission's consumer commissioner announced that the White Paper's proposals would be considered in conjunction with broader consumer protection reforms and after intensive consultation with various stakeholders—a prescription for several years of delay. It seems that any serious reforms in the next few years are most likely to come from the initiative of individual Member States rather than from Brussels.

---

72. The disdain that many foreign governments hold for private U.S. antitrust litigation was barely concealed in a series of amicus curiae briefs filed in the U.S. Supreme Court on behalf of a number of foreign governments arguing that foreign purchasers from international cartels should not be permitted to sue in U.S. courts, an issue decided as the foreign governments desired in *F. Hoffmann-La Roche Ltd v Empagran SA,* 542 US 155 (2004). See, e.g., Brief for the United Kingdom of Great Britain and Northern Ireland, Ireland, and the Kingdom of The Netherlands as Amici Curiae Supporting Petitioners at 13, 542 U.S. 155 (No. 03-724) (quoting *Smith Kline & French Labs Ltd. v. Bloch,* [1983] 1 W.L.R. 730 (C.A. 1982) ('As a moth is drawn to the light, so is a litigant drawn to the United States. If he can only get his case into their courts, he stands to win a fortune."); Brief of the Federal Republic of Germany and Belgium as Amici Curiae Supporting Petitioners at 11, 542 U.S. 155 (2004) (No. 03-724) (asserting that "controversial features of the U.S. legal system include extensive discovery, jury trials, class actions, contingent fees, and punitive damages.").

11. EMERGING ANTITRUST INSTITUTIONS AROUND THE WORLD

Antitrust law is booming around the world. Over one hundred countries now have antitrust regimes in place, although not all are equally effective or aggressive. Many of the underlying laws and institutions are creations (or re-creations) of very recent vintage. For example, China, India, and Brazil, three of the largest developing economies, have overhauled or implemented entirely new antitrust enforcement structures since 2007. A number of other economically important countries are emerging as significant antitrust players. These include industrialized economies like Japan, South Korea, Canada, and Australia—and nations like South Africa that have emerged from seismic changes in their political, cultural, or economic identities.

This chapter provides an introduction to some of the enforcement structures in emerging antitrust regimes outside of Europe and the United States. Rather than attempting to provide a survey of every enforcement agency around the world, it focuses on a few jurisdictions—especially China, India, Brazil, South Africa, Canada, Australia, Japan, and Korea—that are particularly significant economic players or have representative or distinctively interesting institutional models.

The chapter begins with a brief, and necessarily incomplete, glimpse of historical and cultural elements that shape antitrust law in emerging regimes. It then introduces some agency models used in emerging antitrust regimes, with particular reference to the division of regulatory, investigatory, and adjudicatory powers. It then turns to the relationship between administrative agencies and the judiciary, as well as the development of specialized antitrust courts. Finally, it briefly considers the development of private litigation in the emerging antitrust world.

I. ANTITRUST INSTITUTIONS IN HISTORICAL, SOCIAL, AND POLITICAL CONTEXT

Understanding and comparing the enforcement structures of emerging antitrust regimes requires keeping in mind the cultural, political, and historical differences that animated the creation of these regimes. Many of these countries are only years or decades removed from dramatic political or economic upheaval and retain ambivalent or complex relationships with market economies, which are foundational to antitrust. The political forces that frame new antitrust institutions are sometimes as concerned with limiting the spread of rampant Western-style market competition as they are with stimulating it. In the United States, it is long settled that the economy will be organized around competition principles, and the great question for antitrust institutions is how much governmental intervention is required to make competition flourish. In much of the rest of the world, including in many emerging antitrust regimes, there remain profound doubts as to the wisdom of market competition in the first place.

When serious antitrust reforms occur, they often ride a wave of broader political-end economic reforms. Often, antitrust culture waxes during a period of economic and political liberalization and wanes during periods of democratic retrenchment. Many of the significant new, or newly remodeled, Asian regimes developed antitrust enforcement systems during periods of political liberalization following periods of political and economic statism. The U.S.-controlled Japanese regime introduced antitrust into Japan following World War II as a part of an effort to decentralize the concentration of economic power and increase market access.[1] Conversely, Korea's 1961 military coup resulted in the creation of an Economic Planning Board that exercised tight controls over the economy. It was only after a second coup in 1980 that the new Korean government implemented an antitrust regime that signaled a move from government-led economic development to free-market principles (even though the market reforms were not initially accompanied by greater political pluralism).[2]

This is not to say that political liberalization and the introduction of antitrust principles necessarily go hand in hand. For instance, modern antitrust principles came to Chile in conjunction with Augusto Pinochet's economic reforms.[3] Even though the Pinochet regime embraced Chicago School ideas about free-market competition, the regime understood the right to compete as a key political value, enshrining it in the 1980 Chilean Constitution.[4] As a consequence, Chilean competition authorities during the Pinochet regime viewed vertical restraints as anticompetitive.[5]

Some formerly or transitionally Communist states have adopted forms of antitrust law despite continuing with largely state-directed organization of enterprise. In the wake of the Soviet Union's collapse, Russia has moved forward cautiously with competition policy, "liberalizing" its economy through a mixture

---

1. Harry First, *Antitrust in Japan: The Original Intent*, 9 PAC. RIM L. & POL'Y J. 1 (2000).

2. *See* Youngjin Jung & Seung Wha Chang, *Korea's Competition Law and Policies in Perspective*, 26 NW. J. INT'L L. & BUS. 687 (2006); Sang-Seung Yi & Youngjin Young, *A New Kid on the Block: Korean Competition Law, Policy, and Economics*, COMPETITION POL'Y INT'L (Autumn 2007).

3. Elina Cruz & Sebastian Zarate, *Building the Trust in Antitrust: The Chilean Case* in COMPETITION LAW AND POLICY IN LATIN AMERICA 157–188 (Eleanor M. Fox & D. Daniel Sokol eds., 2009).

4. *Id.* at 157.

5. *Id.* at 158.

of underenforced competition laws and a price-regulatory "natural monopolies" law.[6] Critics contend that the Russian government uses its economic levers—including antitrust policy—primarily to advance nationalistic objectives rather than to stimulate the Russian economy.[7] But even if that is true for now, it is possible that competition law principles and institutions—once planted in an economy—will adapt and grow in an unforeseen direction over time. The U.S. story, told earlier in these pages, provides a ready illustration.

In many cases, the ultimate direction of new antitrust policies and institutions cannot be determined for a generation or more after their founding in a regime. China's newly minted Anti-Monopoly Law states that its primary purpose is "promoting the healthy development of the socialist market economy."[8] To the Western ear, the idea of a "socialist market economy" sounds like an oxymoron, and critics have complained that China's antimonopoly law may serve primarily to stymie foreign direct investment in China.[9] Less pessimistic observers note that China relies on economic growth to maintain its holy grail of political stability and sees antitrust law as a driver of economic growth.[10] Even this economic account of China's intentions implies a different version of Chinese antitrust than that favored in the West. In the Chinese calculus, producer surplus may count far more than consumer surplus, putting Chinese antitrust at odds with European and U.S. antitrust values.

In the same vein, India's new competition act lists "the economic development of the country" as a primary goal of the new regime.[11] India may be much more interested in long-term infrastructure development rather than short-run consumer welfare, which may result in the allowance of anticompetitive activities that

---

6. OECD Country Studies, *Russia: Peer Review of Competition Law and Policy* 11, 14 (2004), *available online at* <http://www.oecd.org/dataoecd/10/60/32005515.pdf> (visited Jan 11, 2009).

7. *See generally* OECD Economic Survey of Russia 2009: Improving Regulation in Russia's Goods and Services Markets, *available at* http://www.oecd.org/document/5/0,3343, en_2649_34833_43302341_1_1_1_37463,00.html (reporting that an "unusually important role of current or former politicians and senior bureaucrats in business, [] gives rise to multiple, distorting and costly conflicts of interest").

8. Anti-Monopoly Law of the People's Republic of China, Article 1, *available at* http://english.peopledaily.com.cn/90001/90776/90785/6466798.html.

9. *See, e.g.*, Mark Williams, *Foreign Investment in China: Will the Anti-Monopoly Law be a Barrier or Facilitator?*, 45 Tex. Int'l L.J. 127, 127–28 (2009).

10. *See* Zhenguo Wu, *Perspectives on the Chinese Anti-Monopoly Law*, 75 Antitrust L.J. 73, 79 (2008) ("The anti-monopoly legislation should promote the further integration of Chinese practice with the international market rules, make Chinese economic growth more attuned to the requirements of economic globalization, and better integrate China into the development patterns of the global economy.").

11. The Competition (Amendment) Act 2007, Preamble, *available at* http://www.cci.gov.in/index.php?option=com_content&task=view&id=18.

ostensibly contribute to "development" goals.[12] Similarly, many South American countries may be much more interested in the macroeconomic implications of antitrust as part of a broader suite of development, social mobility, and anti-inflation tools than in any immediate effect in stimulating consumer welfare.

And then there are countries where antitrust law is intended to play a unique role in displacing historical power structures. South Africa's Competition Act acknowledges "[t]hat apartheid and other discriminatory laws and practices of the past resulted in excessive concentrations of ownership and control within the national economy"[13] and states that a goal of the Competition Act is to "regulate the transfer of economic ownership in keeping with the public interest."[14] The Competition Commission of South Africa states as one of its purposes the promotion of "a greater spread of ownership, in particular to increase the ownership stakes of historically disadvantaged persons."[15] South Africa sees antitrust law as a means of dismantling white industrial hegemony left over from the apartheid era.

Given the diversity of political, historical, economic, and social contexts in which antitrust institutions take root, it is impossible to develop an idealized agency model or predict the path of any particular institutional structure. The optimal form of an agency depends not merely on the political, legal, and constitutional constraints under which antitrust institutions operate, but also on the purposes for which the regime adopts antitrust principles. In surveying antitrust institutions in emerging markets, we shall compare and contrast key features without suggesting an idealized form.

II. AGENCY MODELS

A. How Many Agencies?

How many antitrust agencies should a new antitrust regime create? Senior political officials from developing antitrust regimes often wonder whether they should be following the bifurcated U.S. example. For the reasons explored in Chapter 2, there is no good reason to design a multi-agency system from scratch. Nonetheless, for partly historical and partly political reasons, emerging antitrust regimes sometimes spread antitrust authority over several different agencies.

1. **Multi-Agency Models** Apart from the U.S., China provides the most dramatic example of a regime that disperses antitrust enforcement authority across

12. Aditya Bhattacharjea, *India's New Competition Law: A Comparative Assessment*, 4 J. Competition L. & Econ 609, 627 (2008).

13. Competition Act of the Republic of South Africa (1998), Preamble, *available at* http://www.compcom.co.za/assets/Files/pocket-book-2005-R.pdf.

14. *Id.*

15. CCSA website, "About Us," http://www.compcom.co.za/about-us/.

multiple agencies. Prior to the adoption of the Anti-Monopoly Law in 2007, three agencies shared the duties of enforcing anticompetitive conduct provisions in Chinese law. Despite a statement in Article 10 of the Anti-Monopoly Act that a new agency, the Anti-Monopoly Enforcement Authority, "shall be responsible for the anti-monopoly enforcement work," antitrust enforcement authority remains dispersed.

Three separate Chinese agencies enforce laws aimed at specific forms of anticompetitive conduct. The Ministry of Commerce has exclusive control over mergers and acquisitions and has created the Anti-monopoly Bureau to serve that function.[16] The State Administration for Industry and Commerce's (SAIC) enforcement authority covers unilateral abuse of dominance and cartels that do not involve price-fixing. The third enforcement agency, the National Development and Reform Commission (NDRC), which originally was responsible for price regulation under the State Planning Commission, is now responsible for regulating price-setting conduct that is not directly supervised by the Chinese government. In addition to the three enforcement agencies, the Anti-Monopoly Law also created a policy research body, the Anti-Monopoly Commission, which oversees the development of competition policy and suggests broad antitrust strategies.

This broad fragmentation of enforcement duties is unprecedented in the developing world of antitrust enforcement and raises important questions of bureaucratic efficiency. While other countries have spread enforcement authority among different agencies, China is perhaps the only country to separate enforcement duties based on the nature of the offense—as opposed to other criteria such as whether the enforcement is civil or criminal or which industry is implicated. It remains to be seen whether such a system can remain stable over time. It is often difficult to determine before an investigation is launched precisely what kind of anticompetitive conduct is at issue—for example, whether the issue will turn out to be price-fixing or market division.

For now, Brazil also follows a dispersed model of antitrust authority.[17] Beginning with the enactment of a comprehensive antitrust regime in 1994, Brazil has divided enforcement authority between three agencies. Brazil's comprehensive antitrust law, *Law* 8,884, designates a single administrative adjudicatory body, the Administrative Council of Economic Defense (CADE), an investigative and quasi-legislative agency, the Secretariat of Economic Law (SDE), and an agency which issues opinions on the economic consequences of mergers

16. On the institutional structure of the Chinese Anti-Monopoly Law, *see generally* Xiaoye Wang, *Highlights of China's New Anti-Monopoly Law*, 75 ANTITRUST L.J. 133 (2008); Bruce W. Owen, Su Sun & Wentong Zhang, *China's Competition Policy Reforms: The Anti-Monopoly Law and Beyond*, 75 ANTITRUST L.J. 231 (2008).

17. On competition law in Brazil, *see generally* Gustavo Mathias Alves Pinto, *Competition Law in Brazil*, 4 BUS. L. BRIEF 22 (2007); Gesner Oliveira, *Competition Policy in Developing Countries: The Case of Brazil*, 26 NW. J. INT'L L. & BUS. 619 (2006).

and acquisitions and other anticompetitive conduct—the Secretariat for Economic Monitoring (SEAE). The SEAE also serves a more general role of investigating infractions against the economy of Brazil.

The SDE, an agency within the Ministry of Justice, has quasi-legislative and investigative powers. It formulates and implements policies related to the protection of the economy from anticompetitive conduct. It also serves a more traditional investigative purpose, initiating and conducting investigations and administrative proceedings to determine whether an alleged act is anticompetitive. Following an administrative proceeding, the SDE then provides a recommendation to the CADE, an adjudicative body, on whether the conduct in question was anticompetitive. The CADE is an independent administrative agency in the Ministry of Justice that makes final administrative rulings that are only appealable to Brazilian courts.

It now appears likely that Brazil will fold its three agencies into a single agency superstructure. Under a bill introduced in 2008 that is expected to see fruition by the end of 2010, SDE will become an investigative unit within CADE. This unit will have the power to investigate cartel allegations and first-phase mergers before sending these cases to CADE, which will function as a tribunal. SEAE will be folded into a chief economist group within CADE.

China and Brazil provide models of clear separation of enforcement authority across different agencies. In other jurisdictions, there are multiple, separate antitrust institutions, although it is not always clear whether to think of some of the bodies as agencies or as courts. Canada, South Africa, and Australia—whose institutions we will survey at some length—follow a similar model involving delegation of initial investigatory work. But despite the commonality in apparent structure and agency titles, the powers granted to the investigative agencies and the tribunals vary significantly. The tribunals' powers range from a broadly administrative and nonjudicial function—which makes the tribunal largely a second agency—to a grant of first-instance quasi-judicial power—which makes the tribunal not so much a second agency as a specialized antitrust court.

In the case of the Australian Competition Tribunal, the name tribunal is deceiving. The adjudicative function of the Australian Tribunal does not include judicial power—the power to reverse over questions of law—but only the powers to reverse findings of fact, unreasonable exercises of discretion, or circumstances where discretion should not have been exercised at all.[18] The tribunal serves as a reviewing body of decisions of the Australian Competition and Consumer Commission ("ACCC") on grants of anticompetitive conduct exemptions and certain kinds of mergers, but not on questions of law. The Australian model thus represents a partial effort to separate the investigatory and prosecutorial functions

18. *Australian Competition and Consumer Commission v. Australian Competition Tribunal*, 232 ALR 153 (Fed. Ct. Australia 2006).

from the administrative-adjudicatory ones, while maintaining a distinct line between the administrative and judicial processes.

By contrast, the Canadian Competition Tribunal is the first-instance adjudicatory body for many civil matters. The tribunal is a quasi-judicial body with four judicial members who are sitting judges and eight nonjudicial members who have expertise in the area of business or economics. It sits in panels from three to five, and each panel must have a judicial member and a lay member. A judicial member must resolve all questions of law. The tribunal is a hybrid between an agency and a court, ostensibly bringing the virtues of economic and business expertise to the judicial function.

Unlike the more restrictive jurisdictions of the Australian and Canadian Competition Tribunals, the South African Competition Tribunal and Competition Appeal Court serve as a substitute to generalist court adjudication of antitrust cases. The South African Tribunal has original jurisdiction over large mergers and complaints about anticompetitive conduct but is not formally considered a court. In addition to its grant of original jurisdiction, the South African Tribunal also has the power to review decisions made by the South African Competition Commission regarding smaller mergers and grants of anticompetitive conduct exemptions. Like the Canadian Competition Tribunal, members of the tribunal must be qualified experts in the matters heard by them, and there must be at least one lawyer on each tribunal panel.

A unique feature of the South African model is the Competition Appeal Court, a judicial body that has the status of a High Court. The Appeal Court satisfies the South African Constitution's requirement that parties be able to appeal to an independent court and is vested with the power to review tribunal decisions for legal and jurisdiction errors. As a body holding the status of a High Court, its members must be exclusively drawn from High Court judges.

We shall return momentarily to the Australian, Canadian, and South African models. For now, observe that even the question of classifying jurisdictions based on whether they have a single agency or multiple agencies requires an analytic exercise on the distinction between administrative agencies and courts. Although having multiple law enforcement or administrative agencies in the U.S. style may be declining in popularity, a variety of hybrid organizational models have been used with success.

2. **Unified Agency Models** Despite the persistence of multi-agency models in some large and particularly salient economies, the decided trend in recent years has been in the opposite direction. Several European countries, including France and Portugal, have moved from multiple agencies to a single agency over the past few years. As previously noted, Brazil seems likely to do the same by the end of 2010. Most jurisdictions that have a specialized antitrust court treat the court as a true judicial body and not as an extension of the enforcement agency.

South Korea and Japan provide representative examples. Each relies on a single agency, the Fair Trade Commission, to investigate and adjudicate complaints of anticompetitive conduct. Decisions by the Fair Trade Commissions are only appealable to the country's High Court or Supreme Court, which are completely separate from the administrative system.

Following the implementation of the India Competition Act in 2002, in May 2009, the Indian enforcement structure also resembles a unified agency model. The Competition Commission of India is charged with the duty to enforce the Competition Act and is granted broad investigatory powers. It also has administrative adjudicatory powers, and after an inquiry into the alleged anticompetitive conduct may declare the conduct anticompetitive and illegal under the Competition Act. The Competition Commission has the power to order a party in violation of the Competition Act to discontinue the practice in question and to impose a monetary penalty on the party.

Appeals from a Competition Commission decision in India are made to a specialized appellate body, the Competition Appellate Tribunal. In addition to the Appellate Tribunal's power to hear appeals from Competition Commission decisions, it is also the judicial body that hears claims for damages caused by anticompetitive conduct. Claims for damages may only be filed following a finding of anticompetitive conduct by the Competition Commission. Decisions by the Appellate Tribunal are appealable to the Supreme Court of India. The Indian system differs from the Canadian, Australian, and South African examples discussed in the previous section insofar as its "Tribunal," the first reviewing court, is a true judicial body with no administrative functions.

B. Executive and Administrative Models

In Chapter 10, we noted that the European Commission has recently come under criticism for its administrative processes that may deny parties a sufficient opportunity to influence the Commission's internal deliberations before a decision is made. Separation-of-powers concerns are mostly cleanly addressed by delegating enforcement authority to executive-styled agencies that enforce antitrust law as litigants before separate judicial or quasi-judicial bodies. However, few countries draw their institutional structures with such clear Montesquiean lines. Still, for heuristic purposes at least, it may be useful to classify agencies as largely executive or largely administrative.

1. **Executive Models** The three former or present British Commonwealth countries previously introduced—Canada, Australia, and South Africa—provide examples of separation of powers achieved by creating a primarily executive antitrust enforcement body. But even these countries' agencies are not purely executive. One could imagine the antitrust authority as a law enforcement agency that investigates and prosecutes but has no power of compulsion, adjudication, or rule making; however virtually no antitrust authority in the world follows such a model. Even the U.S. Department of Justice Antitrust Division, in theory a purely executive body, has the authority to issue civil investigative demands (a form of

extrajudicial subpoena) without aid of a court.[19] Not surprisingly, even agencies that are oriented to be primarily executive usually may investigate and compel production of documents and other materials on their own initiative. Thus, for example, the Canadian and South African authorities—which are about as executive as agencies come—have the authority to open investigations upon their own initiative and to compel testimony and production of documents.

Unlike true administrative agencies, however, the Canadian and South African authorities must rely principally on the courts to enforce antitrust law. In Canada, the Competition Bureau must seek adjudication of anticompetitive conduct complaints through criminal courts, civil courts, or before the Competition Tribunal. Lawyers from the Department of Justice represent the CCB in cases before civil courts and the Competition Tribunal. Prior to a 2002 amendment to the Competition Act, a consent order had to be approved by the Competition Tribunal. The CCB is now permitted to enter into consent order agreements without aid of the courts, although third parties who may be directly affected by a consent order agreement may appeal to the Competition Tribunal to revise or rescind a term in the consent order.

The South African Competition Authority (SACC) is even more limited in its powers. The SACC must refer or close an investigation or bring suit in the courts within one year of commencing the investigation. Unlike the enforcement agencies in Australia and Canada (and like the Department of Justice, which must seek judicial approval for antitrust consent decrees under the Tunney Act),[20] the SACC does not have the power to enter into consent order agreements with parties without the imprimatur of the Competition Tribunal.

In Australia, if the ACCC believes that corrective action is necessary, it must decide between three primary actions. In cases where the ACCC assesses the anticompetitive risk from conduct to be low, it is permitted to enter into an administrative agreement with a party that requires the party to cease the conduct in question and compensate those who have suffered harm from the conduct. For more serious threats to competition, Section 87(b) of the Trade Practice Act grants the ACCC the power to enter into a court-enforced undertaking agreement that often includes the defendant admitting responsibility and remedying the conduct in question. For the most egregious conduct, the ACCC may authorize initiation of litigation to remedy the alleged anticompetitive conduct. The ACCC does not have the power to impose penalties and must rely on the courts to enforce any agreed upon remedial measures.

---

19. *See* 15 U.S.C. § 1312.

20. *See generally* Lawrence M. Frankel, *Rethinking the Tunney Act: A Model for Judicial Review of Antitrust Consent Decrees*, 75 ANTITRUST L.J. 549 (2008).

Despite their general classification as executive enforcement bodies, the three agencies discussed above exercise some quasi-judicial powers. In both Australia and South Africa, the ACCC and SACC have the power to grant exemptions for conduct that would otherwise contravene antitrust law. Additionally, the enforcement agencies of all three countries have merger authorization powers. In South Africa, the SACC may authorize mergers that are believed to have a low risk of anticompetitive effects, while mergers believed to have more pernicious effects must be reviewed by the South African Competition Tribunal. In addition to the quasi-judicial powers vested in these enforcement agencies, the CCB also initiates policy proposals and competition legislation for Industry Canada (the Canadian ministry of industry).

The design of the South African, Australian, and Canadian competition authorities reflects a sensibly differentiated view of executive authority on the separate questions of *permitting* and *prohibiting*. Agencies need independent power to clear the way for business practices that might otherwise draw antitrust scrutiny. Involving the courts in all such decisions would bog down the process and diminish the benefits of speed and certainty that are key drivers of dynamic economies. However, by requiring that the agencies act as prosecutors rather than judges when it comes to determining liability or assessing penalties, these jurisdictions have avoided some of the difficulties with structuring internal separations of power that have troubled the European Commission and, sometimes, the FTC.

Separating powers by creating distinctively executive enforcement agencies is one mechanism for creating checks and balances in antitrust adjudication. Another mechanism is to fragment power internally within the executive agency. For example, the enforcement powers of the ACCC are vested in a governing executive body composed of seven commissioners and three associate commissioners.[21] Enforcement decisions are made in formal meetings of the Commission and require a minimum of three commissioners (including the chair or deputy chair of the Commission) to be present. The Commission's professional staff presents reports on recommendations to initiate court proceedings, merger recommendations, and recommendations on applications for anticompetitive conduct exemptions. The Commission then votes to accept the recommendation or to pursue an alternative course of action.

On the other hand, most executive institutions are hierarchical with a single executive sitting at the peak of the organization. Whereas legislative and judicial bodies perform well with power dispersed among equal peers, multiheaded executive bodies tend toward instability. (Think of the Roman triumvirates). Consistently with the ordinary executive model, a single commissioner heads the

21. The Trade Practice Act does not specify a minimum or maximum number of commissioners. The only statutory constraint on the number of commissioners is the requirement that a quorum of three be present to constitute a formal meeting.

Canadian Competition Bureau (CCB) and the South African Competition Commission (which drew heavily from the Canadian model). Enforcement powers are principally vested in the commissioners of both the SCCC and the CCB, and actions taken by the SCCC or CCB must receive the express authorization of their respective commissioners.

2. **Administrative Models** At the other end of the spectrum from the executive agencies are the administrative agencies. Japan and Korea offer leading examples of an administrative model. The enforcement structures in both Japan and Korea concentrate adjudicatory, investigative, and regulatory powers in a single agency.

In Japan, the Fair Trade Commission (JFTC) may initiate an investigation on its own volition if it believes that an action has violated the Antimonopoly Act. Investigative powers vested in the JFTC are broad and include ordering witnesses to undergo interrogation by the Commission, ordering expert witnesses to give their expert opinions, ordering the surrender of documents related to the investigation, and entering business offices to investigate the conditions of the business and to examine documents and other materials. Following the investigation stage and a determination that a firm has violated the Anti-Monopoly Act, the JFTC may issue a cease and desist order. Upon issuance of the cease and desist order, the entity subject to the order may accept it, thus prompting the JFTC to issue a "Recommendation Decision" that places legal force behind the order or may contest it. Currently, the entity subject to the order must state its dissatisfaction within sixty days of its issuance. The JFTC will then initiate a hearing to consider the cease and desist order. During this hearing, the complainant presents its argument that the cease and desist order was wrongly issued. The investigating attorneys from the JFTC are the respondents in the case and defend the JFTC's issuance of the order.

Following the hearing, the "hearing examiners" draft a decision for submission to the Commission, which consists of five commissioners (including the chairman). The Commission renders its decision. Unlike the executive agencies discussed in the previous section, the JFTC has direct fining power. Upon the finding of an unreasonable restraint of trade, the JFTC must impose a surcharge of 6 percent of the sales amount of the product affected. A decision by the Commission following the hearing is appealable to the Tokyo High Court, which currently has exclusive jurisdiction to examine the validity of JFTC orders. Appeals from High Court rulings may then be appealed to the Supreme Court.

In a recent development, the JFTC has proposed that an expert panel at the Tokyo's District Court hear appeals pertaining to cease and desist orders, rather than the JFTC itself. If this proposed amendment to cease and desist order procedure was to be adopted, it would be a significant step toward a more executive model. The impetus for this proposed reform echoes some of the ongoing themes in the European discussion about separation of power, transparency, and due process. A process that relies on a single agency to initiate an investigation, issue an administrative order, and review that order raises concern about the independence of the JFTC actors involved in each phase of the adjudication process. Despite these concerns, some academics have advocated for the maintenance of the JFTC cease and desist order hearing process, noting that the JFTC has developed an expertise in competition matters and is the most competent body to adjudicate such matters.[22]

Like the JFTC, the Korean Fair Trade Commission (KFTC) is a unified enforcement agency with the power to initiate investigations and adjudicate alleged violations of the Monopoly Regulation and Fair Trade Act (MRFTA). The KFTC also has the authority to establish regulations for the implementation of the MRFTA. It may initiate an investigation if it suspects a violation of the MRFTA or if it is made aware of conduct that may violate the act. Following the investigation stage, the KFTC may "establish the standards for correction and recommend that the enterpriser or enterprisers' organization concerned comply with those standards." Upon receipt of the KFTC's correction recommendation, the defendant has ten days to state whether it will comply with the recommendation. If the defendant complies, the KFTC considers the matter closed. If the defendant does not agree to comply, the Commission hears the case, and each party has the opportunity to present oral arguments through the adversarial process. Following oral arguments, the Commission issues its opinion. If it finds a violation of the MRFTA, it may issue a cease and desist order or may impose a surcharge. Like the current Japanese structure, the initial appeal of the KFTC corrective measure is heard by the Commission. Following an appeal to the Commission, the defendant may then appeal to the High Court.

In both the Korean and Japanese enforcement models, the separation between investigation and adjudication is blurred, thus creating concerns regarding the legitimacy of the entire adjudicatory process. For example, in the KFTC, the secretary general's office is the investigative department of the agency. Investigators in the department prepare examination reports that are then referred by the secretary general to the Commission for adjudication. The Commission is composed of five standing commissioners (including the chairman) and four nonstanding commissioners. The Office of General Counsel serves as a resource to the commissioners during adjudication.

Despite the nominal separation between the secretary general's office and the Office of General Counsel, there are concerns that the two departments occasionally maintain ex parte contact throughout adjudication. Adding to these concerns are the personnel policies of the KFTC. Employees of the secretary general's office and the officer of the General Counsel are constantly rotated between the offices. Employee rotation between investigative and adjudicatory departments can

---

22. *See* Mitsuo Matshushita, *Reforming the Enforcement of Japanese Antimonopoly Law* (draft, on file with author).

increase adjudicatory efficiency but also aggravate existing doubts about the impartiality of adjudication.

Another criticism that has been leveled against the unified agency model is that it has the potential to result in the underdevelopment of legal precedent. The closer an enforcement model moves toward a regulatory bureaucratic model, the less likely there will be significant formulation of precedent addressing specific trade practices, and hence less concrete information available to businesses about what they can and cannot do. Bureaucratic agencies sometimes deal in broad abstract pronouncements on antitrust policy but fail to disclose concrete grounds for decisions.

The newly created Competition Commission of India provides a third example of a hybrid executive-administrative model. The new India enforcement regime was implemented in 2009, following seven years of development after the Competition Act was passed in 2002. Extensive amendments were made to the Competition Act in 2007 following constitutional challenges to the personnel structure of the Commission.

The Commission is the central authority entrusted with the enforcement of the Competition Act. Like the JFTC and KFTC, the Commission is built around a quasi-adjudicatory body. The chairperson and the six members of the Commission must be either qualified to serve as a judge on the High Court or have "special knowledge of, and professional experience of not less than fifteen years in international trade, economics, business, commerce, law finance, accountancy, management, public affairs" or other any other area that is deemed useful to the Commission. The central government may appoint a director general "for the purposes of assisting the Commission in conducting inquiry into contravention of any of the provisions of [the] Act."[23]

The Commission investigates potential anticompetitive agreements and abuses of dominance through a process of "inquiry." If the Commission believes that there is a prima facie case supporting a violation of the Competition Act, it may request the director general to investigate the matter.[24] Following the investigation, the director general must submit a report of his findings to the Commission. If the director general recommends a finding of contravention, the Commission may proceed with the inquiry into the alleged conduct. If, on the other hand, the director general's report states that there has been no contravention, the Commission may request further investigation of the matter or hear objections from the complaining party.[25]

Following a finding by the Commission of a violation of the Competition Act, the Commission has broad remedial powers. It may issue a cease and desist

23. Competition Act § 15.

24. T. Ramappa, Competition Law in India: Policy, Issues, and Developments 257 (2006).

25. Competition Act § 19.

order, impose a monetary penalty on the violator, modify the agreement in question, or pass "such other order or issue such directions as it may deem fit."[26] Unlike the unified agency models in Japan and Korea, the appeals process from Commission rulings begins outside of the Commission. The 2007 amendments to the Competition Act created a specialized appellate court to hear appeals from Commission decisions. The Competition Appellate Tribunal may hear an appeal by "the Central Government or the State Government or a local authority or enterprise or any person, aggrieved by any direction, decision or order" of the Commission.[27]

The Appellate Tribunal is designed to be both fully judicial and expert. Its chairperson must be or have been a member of the Supreme Court or a Chief Justice of the High Court. The remaining two members must have at least twenty-five years of experience in one of the same categories of matters that qualifies a person to be a member of the Commission. In carrying out its review powers, the Appellate Tribunal is not bound by the Indian Code of Civil Procedure and instead "shall be guided by the principles of natural justice."[28] Unlike the appellate courts of the United States, the Appellate Tribunal has broad powers to call witnesses and require testimony under oath and to require the discovery and production of documents. In addition to serving as an appellate court for appeals from Commission rulings, parties seeking compensation for conduct deemed by the Commission to violate the Competition Act may bring a claim before the Appellate Tribunal for adjudication. Appeals from Appellate Tribunal rulings may be made to the Supreme Court of India.

The Indian enforcement model is still in its infancy, and implications of its structure remain to be developed.[29] By creating an independent court to hear Commission appeals, India's structure may address, in part, the transparency and separation of powers concerns raised by the unified administrative model while still capturing the efficiencies created by a unified enforcement agency.

III. SPECIALIZED ANTITRUST COURTS

As already noted, a number of regimes employ specialized antitrust courts, and the list appears to be growing. At present, the list includes at least Austria, Canada, Chile, China, Denmark, India, Israel, South Africa, and the United Kingdom. There has been discussion over the years about a similar move in the United States, but it has not garnered much support. Perhaps the greatest obstacle to the implementation of such a model in the United States is uncertainty whether the nearly

---

26. Competition Act § 27.
27. Competition Act § 53B(1).
28. Competition Act § 53O.
29. The Appellate Tribunal's inauguration occurred in the fall of 2009.

three-decade experiment with a specialized patent court—the U.S. Court of Appeals for the Federal Circuit—has been a success.[30] Despite the apparently growing popularity of specialized antitrust courts in other jurisdictions, it remains to be seen whether such courts enjoy strong performative advantages over generalist courts.

As the complexity of antitrust increases, perhaps we should expect that more jurisdictions will migrate toward specialized antitrust courts. One of the major issues that many developing countries face in implementing an effective antitrust system is a lack of training and economic sophistication in the judiciary. Creating an antitrust court can alleviate some of these concerns, although there may be constitutional or administrative law reasons why this may be difficult or impossible in some jurisdictions.

On the other hand, there are reasons to be skeptical that specialized antitrust courts are better than generalist courts. Generalist courts may be better at seeing the big picture of economic and social consequences of particular decisions, more deferential to agency decision makers, and less likely to develop "tunnel vision." With the development of more specialized antitrust courts around the world, it will be interesting to compare the performance of generalist and specialized judges and see what lessons can be drawn about their comparative performance.

Part of the success or failure of specialized antitrust courts may turn on what they are called upon to do. In jurisdictions that follow a largely administrative model of first-instance antitrust decision making, the function of a specialized antitrust court is usually appellate. However, it may be that the greatest advantages of a specialized antirust court lie in its ability to bring expertise into fact finding, trial management, and first-instance decision making. A few specialized antitrust courts play such a role. The Canadian Competition Tribunal is one of two first-instance fora available for adjudication of civil antitrust matters in Canada. The Canadian Competition Bureau may bring actions in the civil courts of Canada or before the Tribunal, depending on the nature of the case. Similarly, in India, the Competition Appellate Tribunal hears appeals from orders by the Competition Commission of India, but is also the first-instance adjudicator for parties seeking compensation for conduct that the CCI has found to be in violation of the

30. The Federal Circuit was established in 1982. It has jurisdiction over all patent appeals arising from district court decisions. A wide variety of studies have tested different hypotheses about the effects of specialized courts, such as whether they increase uniformity or the influence of ideology on decision making. *See, e.g.*, Scott E. Atkinson, et al., *The Economics of a Centralized Judiciary: Uniformity, Forum Shopping, and the Federal Circuit*, 52 J.L. & Econ. 411 (2009) (finding weak evidence that the existence of the federal circuit has lead to an increase in uniformity rates on patent validity issues); Banks Miller & Brett Curry, *Expertise, Experience, and Ideology on Specialized Courts: The Case of the Court of Appeals for the Federal Circuit*, 43 Law & Soc. Rev. 839 (2009) (concluding that prior expertise enhances the effect of ideology but that accummulated experience does not).

Competition Act. This unique structure makes the Tribunal the trial court in private damages cases.

Specialized antitrust courts sometimes face constitutional obstacles that marginalize their influence in the scheme of judicial review and force them to cede decisional authority to other nonexpert courts. In South Africa, for example, framers of the post-apartheid competition regime intended for the CAC to have the status of a High Court and final adjudicator of competition matters. It was granted broad review powers that included review of legal errors, the substantive merits of any final decision by the SACT, and jurisdictional errors. However, the Supreme Court of Appeal held that under the Constitution, the Competition Appeal Court could not be a final court of appeal, and that, even in nonconstitutional matters, appeals could still be made to the Supreme Court of Appeal.[31] Accordingly, the South African Supreme Court has final say on matters of antitrust policy.

Because of such constitutional or administrative obstacles, some regimes choose to structure their nominal antitrust "tribunals" more as administrative agencies than as true courts. Australia's Competition Tribunal and Argentina's National Tribunal for the Defence of Competition do not have the status of courts but serve essentially administrative roles. By contrast, Chile's Competition Tribunal (TDLC), created in 2003, is an independent trial court that manages to capture the virtues of expertise without losing its judicial powers. It is headed by a chief judge who must be a lawyer with a minimum of ten years' experience in competition law, economics, or commercial law. The TDLC has four other expert members, two of whom must be lawyers and two of whom must be economists. All of the members of the court serve for six-year terms. 2009 amendments cemented the TDLC's judicial status, adding further protections on independence; conflicts of interest; impartiality; and regulating procedural and evidentiary matters such as the means of calling witnesses, statutes of limitation, and the introduction of evidence. TDLC decisions are ultimately subject to review by the Chilean Supreme Court, but the TDLC may exert significant influence over antitrust policy by virtue of its control over the creation of a factual record.

IV. PRIVATE ENFORCEMENT

Public enforcement remains the norm in most of the world. Where private enforcement nominally exists as a statutory right, practical obstacles such as limited discovery rights, the absence of claim aggregation mechanisms, limitations on damages, and a judicial culture of inhospitality to private litigation often render it ineffective. In India and Japan, for example, private lawsuits are only allowable

31. *American Natural Soda Corp. v. Competition Comm'n of South Africa*, Case No. 577/2002 (South Africa Supreme Ct. App. 2003).

as follow-ons to government suits, which prevent private enforcement from playing any role as a stimulus to, or substitute for, public enforcement. Other jurisdictions have eliminated the prior government action requirement. Korea did so by statute in 2005, and China has stated that an administrative finding of liability is not a prerequisite to private enforcement. Still, relatively few private cases—whether follow-ons or original claims—are brought in these jurisdictions.

As in Europe, however, there are signs of growing interest in expanded private enforcement throughout the developing antitrust world. Private enforcement has already taken off in South Africa and appears poised for expansion in many parts of South America and Asia. In the last few years, it has become common to hear of private enforcement "firsts" in regimes not otherwise known for vigorous antitrust enforcement. For example, in 2009, an Argentine court awarded damages in a private antitrust action for the first time, ostensibly paving the way for future damages cases.[32] Claimant Autogas alleged that gas producer and distributor YPF abused a dominant position in the market for liquid petroleum gas (LPG) by charging lower prices to foreign buyers than domestic buyers and then preventing foreign customers from reselling into Argentina. In 1999, Argentina's National Commission for the Defense of Competition found a violation and imposed a fine. The Buenos Aires court awarded $3.5 million in damages to Autogas and exempted it from paying legal expenses. However, it reduced Autogas's damages, finding that Autogas had passed on some of the overcharge to its customers.

Despite the view that class actions are a uniquely American pastime, other jurisdictions are cautiously experimenting with the class action mechanism. In 2009, the Ontario Superior Court of Justice issued the first decision by a Canadian court in a contested case certifying a price-fixing class action on behalf of a class including indirect purchasers.[33] U.S.-style class action cases have been available in Australia's Federal Court since 1992, although, to date, only one case—involving the international vitamins cartel—has been successful.[34]

Other jurisdictions are trying to expand the availability of claim aggregation mechanisms without fully embracing U.S.-style class actions. One interesting example is Brazil's Consumer Defense Code (Law 8078), which creates a series of state and local consumer protection agencies called "Procons" that are located in all 26 Brazilian states, in the Federal District (Brasilia), and in 670 municipalities. The Procons, either upon a consumer complaint or their own initiative,

32. Peter Scott, *Argentinian Court Awards Private Antitrust Damages*, Global Competition Review (Nov. 19, 2009).

33. In Irving Paper Limited et al. v. Atofina Chemicals Inc., [2009] O.J. No. 4021. Courts in British Columbia and other Canadian provinces have refused similar requests. See, e.g., Pro-Sys Consultants Ltd. v. Infineon Technologies AG, 2008 BCSC 575.

34. Brooke Dellavedova, Vince Morabito & Brendan Sweeney, *Private Antitrust Enforcement in Australia* (draft, on file with author).

can initiate class action lawsuits for damages on behalf of injured consumers.[35] Similarly, Brazilian law allows nongovernmental consumer organizations to file antitrust class actions seeking damages.[36] Very few such cases have been filed, but at least there is an indigenous model of claim aggregation that could be brought to bear on the collective action problems that cartels create.

For the reasons discussed earlier in this book, it would be a mistake for emerging antitrust jurisdictions to embrace private enforcement without regard to its systemic effects on public litigation and its questionable ability to deliver on compensation and deterrence objectives. Still, particularly in jurisdictions where public enforcement is chronically underfunded or otherwise sluggish, it is encouraging to see some cautious experimentation with private enforcement, if for no better reason than to stimulate the development of competition law norms and provide a supplement to public enforcement.

35. *OECD Peer Review Report*, above n 24, at 97.
36. *Id.* at 125.

12. TOWARD INTERNATIONAL ANTITRUST INSTITUTIONS?

We close this book with a largely Utopian topic—the possibility of international antitrust institutions with meaningful cross-border jurisdiction. Many people who pay attention to the rapid development of antitrust regimes across the globe hold two tenets in common. First, most of the relevant stakeholders would benefit if competition policy could be harmonized interjurisdictionally.[1] Second, and alas, this beneficial harmonization is unlikely to happen on a significant scale in the foreseeable future.[2] To many, antitrust harmonization is thus a noble but Utopian aspiration.

A certain degree of international harmonization can occur without the creation of new antitrust institutions. Countries can share best practices, as they do through the International Competition Network (ICN) and numerous other outlets for antitrust cross-fertilization. Organizations like the International Monetary Fund (IMF) and World Bank can continue to encourage developing countries to add Western-style antitrust norms to their packages of market-oriented reforms. But despite the possibilities for low-level harmonization, it is unlikely that significant degrees of harmonization can occur and remain stable without the creation of new antitrust institutions—or the assignment of an antitrust role to existing institutions like the World Trade Organization (WTO). Hence, in the first instance, discussing international antitrust harmonization means discussing the creation of global antitrust institutions and determining where they may or may not be necessary.

Since we do not have any real global antitrust institutions or prospects that any will be created in the immediate future, it is premature to spend much time on details of institutional structure. Rather, the important questions ask what sorts of international competition problems most urgently call for the creation of global institutions, what are the preconditions to the creation of such institutions, and what sorts of steps might set the stage for their eventual emergence.

1. *See, e.g.*, Andrew T. Guzman, *The Case for International Antitrust, in* COMPETITION LAWS IN CONFLICT: ANTITRUST JURISDICTION IN THE GLOBAL ECONOMY 99, 109–10 (Richard A. Epstein & Michael S. Greve eds., AEI, 2004).

2. *See, e.g.,*, Eleanor M. Fox, *International Antitrust and the Doha Dome*, 43 VA. J. INT'L L. 911, 931–32 (2003).

I. HARMONIZATION PRIORITIES

What does the world gain from international antitrust harmonization? In part, the answer depends on the exact problem that harmonization would supposedly remedy. Harmonizationists cite many different potential benefits from increased international homogenization of antitrust norms. Some are more compelling than others, and sorting through them is necessary in order to prioritize the difficult tasks ahead.

A. Less Compelling Justifications for Harmonization

One fundamental concern that has received a good deal of attention is discrimination against foreign firms' access to domestic markets. This is a real concern with many egregious illustrations, but it is not primarily an antitrust concern. Antitrust law tends to be concerned with the acquisition and exercise of market power, and trade barriers do not necessarily have anything to do with the acquisition of market power. For example, agricultural trade barriers often take place against a backdrop of intensely competitive local markets. Further, there are existing mechanisms under GATT and the WTO to deal with trade barriers that do not rely on antitrust principles.

The problem of trade barriers does not end with tariffs; there are other ways to discriminate against foreign firms. A more subtle version of parochial discrimination occurs when a jurisdiction allows anticompetitive activity in a way that blocks foreign competitors from accessing the domestic market. A case in point is the Kodak-Fujitsu dispute over consumer photographic film and paper distribution in Japan.[3] Japan effectively tolerated (and, indeed, encouraged) vertical exclusive dealing arrangements between manufacturers, wholesalers, and retailers that made it difficult for U.S. firms like Kodak to access the Japanese market.

But, again, international antitrust enforcement would not necessarily fit this set of problems. Tolerance of anticompetitive agreements in cases like the Kodak photographic film and paper matter exacts a toll on domestic consumers and potential domestic entrants to the market as well. The burden on foreign firms is incidental to the fact that the domestic regime may have adopted a poor antitrust policy that also threatens its own producers and consumers. This is perhaps an example of "bad" antitrust law, but the arguable dearth of antitrust law in some jurisdictions is not a sufficient reason to agitate for harmonization.

A more serious international problem is beggar-thy-neighbor extraction of monopoly rents through the allowance of export cartels. The problem is familiar from U.S. federalism cases. As noted in Chapter 8, the Supreme Court has

3. *See* World Trade Organization, Report of the Panel, *Japan—Measures Affecting Consumer Photographic Film and Paper* 10.378–10.382 WT/DS44/R (Mar. 31, 1998).

allowed states to mandate cartel behavior by their domestic producers who were primarily exporting out of state.[4] From the short-run perspective of domestic political regimes, this is a perfectly rational strategy to increase the well being of local producers without internalizing the costs of monopoly pricing. Though it is equally true that the world economy would gain if export cartels were prohibited, individual jurisdictions are not likely to follow this long-run strategy.[5] Unlike in the previous Kodak example, the costs of the anticompetitive restraint are almost entirely exported from the enacting jurisdiction, which means that there is virtually no domestic political constraint against the adoption and perpetuation of the restraint.

What is not at all clear is that the creation of global antitrust institutions is necessary to curb the harms of export cartels. Under the dominant "effects test" for antitrust jurisdiction, domestic authorities are competent to prosecute importers that have agreed to fix prices in the domestic market, even though the agreement was transacted in a foreign jurisdiction.[6] Further, since trading partners often carry a roughly equal balance of trade, there is no reason why bilateral trade agreements cannot prohibit export cartels between the signatories.[7] Curbing export cartels may seem like a good idea, but the current level of pressure for economic efficiency does not translate into a strong imperative for multilateral antitrust harmonization.

---

4. *See, e.g., Parker v. Brown*, 317 US 341, 360–61 (1943) (holding that California raisin prorating regulations that effectively prevented interstate commerce of certain crop was still within a state's power to regulate to preserve local well being, since the regulation was imposed before interstate shipment). *See also* Frank H. Easterbrook, *Antitrust and the Economics of Federalism*, 26 J.L & ECON. 23, 24 (1983).

5. Maggie Levenstein and Valerie Suslow note that most countries that allow export cartels do so implicitly by only prohibiting cartels that harm the domestic economy rather than explicitly by requiring registration of export cartels. Margaret C. Levenstein & Valerie Y. Suslow, *The Changing International Status of Export Cartel Exemptions*, http://papers.ssrn.com/sol3/papers.cfm?abstract_id=618201. Indeed, Levenstein and Suslow report that, in the last decade, at least ten countries have switched from explicit to implicit exemption models, which makes it difficult to track the amount and sort of export cartel behavior that is actually occurring.

6. *See, e.g.*, Paul B. Stephan, *Against International Cooperation, in* COMPETITION LAWS IN CONFLICT: ANTITRUST JURISDICTION IN THE GLOBAL ECONOMY 66, 82 (Richard A. Epstein & Michael S. Greve eds., AEI, 2004).

7. Disappointingly, the North American Free Trade Agreement (NAFTA) contains an explicit exemption for export cartels. The North American Free Trade Agreement Implementation Act, NAFTA Administrative Action Statement, ch. 15(B), 103rd Congress, 1st Sess (Sept. 3, 1993) in HR Doc No 103-159, vol. 1, 450, 623. *See also* Brendan Sweeney, *Export Cartels: Is There a Need for Global Rules?*, 10(1) J. INT'L ECON. L. 87, 104–05 (2007) (reporting that most bilateral trade agreements with competition provisions do not address export cartels).

One benefit of harmonization would come from the adoption of better substantive norms. Opponents of harmonization often point out that there is no reason to believe that harmonization will lead to improved antitrust norms.[8] However, even supposing that antitrust harmonization increases the average quality of antitrust laws around the globe through the leveraging of best practices, experience, and learning, there is no distinctive reason why harmonization-as-quality improvement should be more of a goal of antitrust than any other mandatory regulatory subject.[9] Interjurisdictional sharing of norms may increase the average quality of domestic law, but this is not a sufficiently powerful reason to advocate the abandonment of national sovereignty or distinctiveness on antitrust matters.

B. More Compelling Justifications for Harmonization

A more compelling reason for antitrust harmonization is to alleviate the burden on international business operations caused by heterogeneous domestic antitrust norms. In order to determine what forms of antitrust harmonization yield the greatest benefits, one must view antitrust heterogeneity from the perspective of the multinational business corporation. In general, the costs of antitrust heterogeneity fall into two categories: (1) increased transactions costs arising from the need to comply with multiple jurisdictions' procedural requirements and (2) conflicting domestic rules that do not easily mesh with corporations' business structures or technological design.

1. Complying With Inconsistent Procedural Requirements The transactions costs of complying with multiple jurisdictions' procedural requirements arise mostly in the merger context. The costs can be further subdivided into two types. First, compliance with merger notification requirements is expensive. For example, one estimate (prepared in 1997 and therefore somewhat dated) suggests that the preparation of Hart-Scott-Rodino premerger notification in the United States costs about $25,000 for mergers that are not investigated and $500,000 for mergers that are, not including the filing fee or indirect costs.[10] Over sixty jurisdictions have merger notification requirements,[11] and the idiosyncrasies of these various regimes require merging firms to retain local counsel and report different

---

8. *See, e.g.,*, Stephan, *supra* n . 6 *at* 66.

9. To be sure, the case for harmonization of mandatory regulatory regimes is stronger than for the harmonization of optional regulatory regimes—such as contract—where firms can choose from a menu of governing laws. In the latter case, there is essentially a market for good law, and weak regimes will tend to fail for want of business.

10. *See* Joe Sims & Deborah P. Herman, *The Effect of Twenty Years of Hart-Scott-Rodino on Merger Practice: A Case Study in the Law of Unintended Consequences Applied to Antitrust Legislation*, 65 ANTITRUST L.J. 865, 891–92 (1997).

11. International Competition Policy Advisory Committee Antitrust Division, *Final Report* 89 (2000), *available online at* <http://www.usdoj.gov/atr/icpac/chapter3.pdf> (visited Jan. 10, 2009).

information for each jurisdiction covered by the merger. A good deal of waste could be eliminated through multilateral adoption of a centralized filing system, which would require the creation of some form of global institution.

A deeper problem is that the variance in merger notification requirements can delay or even kill beneficial mergers. Country-by-country variances in notification requirements are so great that putting together an international merger is becoming very dicey work.

Take, for example, the timing of notification. Some countries have premerger notification requirements; others have postmerger notification requirements. This means that sometimes the same stock acquisition must be notified and reviewed before it closes in the United States and Europe and only after it closes in Japan and Korea.[12] From the perspective of international business development, this is the worst of all worlds. A business might reasonably prefer a premerger notification requirement on the ground that this gives ex ante certainty or it might prefer a postmerger notification system on the grounds that this prevents delay in the closure of mergers, but no one would prefer a mixed system where the premerger regimes delay the transaction *and* where, even after closing, parties will have no assurance that their transactions will stand because the postmerger regimes are just getting started with their own review. A uniform interjurisdictional rule (premerger, in my opinion) would be far preferable. However, such harmonization does not require the creation of a international merger body; it would be enough that the most important jurisdictions harmonize their procedures by agreeing on a model merger notification and review protocol and implement it through domestic legislation.

2. Inconsistent Treatment of Corporate and Technological Structure The second major cost of antitrust heterogeneity arises from the conflict between corporate business or technological structures and local norms. Consider the wide variety of business practices chosen by an international firm. Among other things, the firm must choose its corporate structure, develop its product, hire employees, select distribution methods, and enter into contracts with upstream suppliers and downstream customers. For the firm operating in many different jurisdictions, some of these practices can be fairly easily conformed to local requirements, and some cannot. For example, complying with local labor requirements (such as minimum wage and employee benefit laws) may be somewhat expensive, but one country's idiosyncratic requirements do not affect the firm's ability to operate in other jurisdictions.

Antitrust law does not typically address labor relations, but it does often address vertical contracting with suppliers or customers. Antitrust regimes around the world have a variety of different—and often conflicting—norms with

12. Country-by-country merger requirements are collected by the International Competition Network (ICN), *available online at* <http://www.internationalcompetitionnetwork.org/media/archive0611/merger_templates/> (visited Jan. 10, 2009).

respect to such issues as exclusive dealing, franchisee rights, loyalty rebates, predatory pricing, and intellectual property licensing terms. While an international firm's general counsel may find it annoying to have to learn each country's idiosyncratic antitrust requirements and conform local contracting accordingly, there is relatively little spillover from one country to another. With some exceptions, a country can seal off the contagion of bad antitrust norms outside its borders because contracting is adaptable on a country-by-country basis.

The case is very different when it comes to corporate structure and technological design. When the EU blocked General Electric's acquisition of Honeywell, this meant that the merger could not be consummated in the United States either (even though the U.S. Department of Justice had cleared the deal).[13] The EU thus made industrial policy not only for Europe but also for the United States.

There are two serious downsides to this sort of "everyone for himself" approach to merger policy. For one, it means that the significant economy with the most restrictive merger policy dictates industrial policy to the rest of the world.[14] Since there is no reason to believe that the lowest common denominator is usually the optimal outcome, a system that tends toward the lowest common denominator is likely to produce an unfortunate number of false positives—in other words, to disallow mergers that should be allowed.

But the problem is worse than that. Merger control is not just a "thumbs up, thumbs down" process. It frequently involves negotiation between competition authorities and the merging parties over divestiture packages and conduct remedies. Each competition authority has disproportionate leverage to extract concessions favorable to its own jurisdiction—for example, a promise not to close a domestic plant, a commitment to treat a local competitor with special favor—because each authority has the power to hold up the entire merger.[15] In this sense, the international merger landscape raises the same kind of holdout problems that justify granting eminent domain powers to the government. An international merger regime that allowed a central authority to eliminate these collective-action obstacles to efficient mergers would improve the welfare of all countries and their consumers.

---

13. *See* Eleanor M. Fox, *GE/Honeywell: The U.S. Merger that Europe Stopped—A Story of the Politics of Convergence, in* 9 Antitrust Stories 331, 355 (Eleanor M. Fox & Daniel A. Crane eds., Thomson/West 2007).

14. I say significant economy because the merging parties might decide to cease doing business in any insignificant jurisdiction that tried to hold up the deal.

15. *See, e.g.*, Richard M. Brunnell, *The Social Costs of Mergers: Restoring "Local Control" As a Factor in Merger Policy*, 85 N.C. L. Rev. 149, 192 n. 158 (2006) (reporting that Justice Department has taken local interests into account in deciding where to allocate bank divestitures from merger remedies). *See also* Bruce M. Owen, *Imported Antitrust*, 21 Yale J. Reg. 441, 451 n 37 (2004).

A semi-international example of a government's use of merger control to exact concessions occurred in 2001 when the Arkansas-based retailer Wal-Mart tried to acquire the Puerto Rican supermarket chain Supermercados Amigo.[16] The FTC resolved antitrust concerns by requiring a spin-off of four stores to an up-front buyer.[17] Nonetheless, the Puerto Rican secretary of justice, fearing that Wal-Mart would shift its purchases away from local suppliers and that the merger would eliminate Puerto Rican jobs, sued in the Puerto Rican courts under the Puerto Rican Anti-Monopoly Act to enjoin the merger.[18] She then sought to settle by exacting promises that Wal-Mart would retain Supermercados Amigo's employees and continue purchasing from local suppliers.[19]

The Supermercados Amigo debacle is only semi-international, because Puerto Rico is a partially autonomous U.S. Commonwealth subject to the constraints of the U.S. Constitution. Wal-Mart was able to secure a federal district court injunction against the justice secretary's attempted exactions on the ground that they violated the "negative" or "dormant" commerce clause of the U.S. Constitution, which generally prohibits a state (or commonwealth) from discriminating against interstate commerce.[20] As antitrust jurisdictions proliferate globally, however, it is not difficult to imagine many more such instances arising with no dormant commerce clause backstop. Further, the parochialism in Supermercados Amigo was easy to identify. In the future, well-schooled antitrust agencies may find more subtle ways to exact localist favors without triggering World Trade Organization (WTO) scrutiny on discrimination grounds.

Only slightly less problematic than heterogeneous treatment of corporate structure is heterogeneous treatment of technological structure. When antitrust jurisdictions impose differing requirements on a firm's technological design, this can greatly increase the costs of selling a single product around the world, create artificial incompatibility, and chill technological innovation.

A ready example is the EU's insistence that Microsoft "unbundle" its PC operating system, Windows, and its media player.[21] The EU decision effectively

---

16. *See Wal-Mart Stores, Inc v Rodriguez*, 238 F. Supp. 2d 395, 403 (D Puerto Rico 2002). The story of the Supermercados Amigo acquisition is told in Eleanor M. Fox, *An Anti-Monopoly Law for China—Scaling the Walls of Government Restraints*, 75 ANTITRUST L.J. 173, 183–84 (2008).

17. Federal Trade Commission, *In re Wal-Mart Stores, Inc and Supermercados Amigo, Inc*, Decision and Order, FTC Docket No C-4066, II.A (Feb 27, 2003), *available online at* <http://www.ftc.gov/os/2003/02/walmartdo.htm> (visited Jan. 11, 2009).

18. Fox, *Scaling the Walls*, *supra* n. 16 at 183.

19. *Id.* at 183–84.

20. *Wal-Mart Stores*, 238 F. Supp. 2d at 414.

21. Commission of the European Communities, Commission Decision of 24.03.2004 relating to a proceeding under Article 82 of the EC Treaty (Case COMP/C-3/37.782 Microsoft), art. 6(a), 2004 OJ (C900), *available online at* <http://ec.europa.eu/comm/competition/antitrust/cases/decisions/37792/en.pdf> (visited Jan .11, 2009).

required Microsoft to redesign its operating system for the European market, since Microsoft was permitted to continue to carry the "bundled" version of Windows in the rest of the world. In 2005, Microsoft complied with the EU's decision and began to make available "Windows XP Home Edition N," with the "N" conspicuously and clumsily—as if to make the point—standing for "not with Media Player." Although the European Court of First Instance eventually affirmed the Commission's decision,[22] "Edition N" proved highly unpopular with original equipment manufacturers serving the European market, and very few installed it on their computers. Microsoft thus redesigned its operating system for the European market only to find no takers.

Another example is France's quixotic battle with Apple's iPod MP3 player. Ostensibly to prevent music piracy, Apple's iTunes online music store embeds music download files with code that only allows iTunes songs to be played on iPods.[23] In 2004, Virgin Media accused Apple of abusing its dominance by linking its downloaded music with its MP3 player.[24] The French Competition Commission rejected the claim,[25] but France passed legislation in 2006 that would have required Apple to allow songs sold on iTunes to be played on other MP3 players.[26] In response, Apple threatened to pull its iTunes service out of France altogether rather than create a different digital rights system for the French market.[27] France subsequently softened the legislation, thus seemingly mooting the controversy, but this kind of confrontation seems increasingly likely to be played out in a technologically interconnected world.

Technological heterogeneity is vexing enough when created by differences in extralegal factors including custom, culture, history, independent development, turf protection, and accident. International standardization bodies like the International Standardization Organization work hard to reverse these effects. The creation of a global institution with the authority to prevent idiosyncratic domestic antitrust policies from thwarting technological progress would be desirable. However, though preventing artificial technological heterogeneity is a valuable goal, some preconditions need to be in place in order to achieve this objective.

---

22. *Microsoft Corp v. Commission*, Case T-201/04, [2007] 5 CMLR 11, ¶¶ 1345–66 (Sept. 17, 2007) (European Court of First Instance).

23. Deana Sobel, *A Bite out of Apple? iTunes, Interoperability, and France's Dadvsi Law*, 22 Berkeley Tech. L.J. 267, 267–68 (2007).

24. Daryl Lim, *Beyond Microsoft: Intellectual Property, Peer Production and the Law's Concern with Market Dominance*, 18 Fordham Intell. Prop., Media & Enter. L.J. 291, 317–18 (2008).

25. *Id.*

26. *Id.* at 317 n. 132.

27. Nika Aldrich, *A System of Logo-Based Disclosure of DRM on Download Products*, 8 J. High Tech. L. 57, 62 n. 30 (2008).

II. PRECONDITIONS FOR MEANINGFUL HARMONIZATION

The kind of international antitrust harmonization necessary to facilitate international business transactions faces a number of serious obstacles. Effective harmonization requires not only convergence on substance and procedure but also the creation of international antitrust institutions. Any such institution will necessarily be technocratic—expert and not directly politically responsive. Although there are examples of nontechnocratic international institutions—for example, the United Nations General Assembly or the Security Council—there would be no sense in trying to create a politically responsive international antitrust institution. Modern antitrust analysis is dense, technical, difficult, and not the sort of discipline that lends itself to negotiation and deal cutting in fifteen-member councils manned by career politicians. Effective international antitrust harmonization means agreeing on governing norms and committing them to the administration of politically independent economists and economically informed lawyers.

Before such harmonization can unfold, at least some formidable preconditions must be satisfied. In Chapter 4, we saw that a technocratic ideal became possible in the United States because of the satisfaction of three preconditions: broad ideological consensus on the legitimacy of regulated capitalism, consensus on the purposes of antitrust enforcement, and the absence of explicit interclass distributional considerations in antitrust decision making.

A primary precondition is a global consensus on the legitimacy both of market economies and of governmental controls on market economies. International technocratic administration of any aspect of antitrust is impossible so long as any participating country continues to face deep political ambivalence about whether private ownership and management of the means of production is legitimate and whether the government may legitimately intervene to correct failures of the private enterprise system. So long as these questions remain deeply in controversy, it will be impossible to entrust antitrust decision making to experts on an international level. The existence and stability of an antitrust regime assumes the legitimacy of a regulated market economy, an assumption still very much in doubt in many corners of the globe.

Second, harmonizing jurisdictions must agree on a common answer to antitrust's great existential questions: why do we have antitrust laws, and for whose benefit do we enforce them? It will do no good to agree on modes of antitrust analysis (that is, rule of reason, premerger notification, Herfindahl-Hirschman Index) without agreeing on why and for whose benefit the relevant technocrats are undertaking the endeavor.

Answering these existential questions is difficult enough within a mature antitrust jurisdiction like the United States. It is far more difficult to achieve a consensus on these questions across multiple jurisdictions that have very different understandings about why antitrust law exists. Consider, for example, the contrast between the ostensible goals of antitrust law in the United States and the EU. The essential purpose of the antitrust provisions in the TFEU is the creation of a European common market, whereas the essential purpose of the Sherman Act (at least in its modern iteration) is to enhance economic efficiency and consumer welfare. Whereas common markets often do enhance efficiency, the EU's distributive concerns sometimes lead to results that would be anathema in the United States.[28] To be sure, transatlantic differences sometimes reflect disagreement over means rather than ends,[29] but sometimes results look different simply because the two antitrust regimes are pursuing different goals.

Harmonizing goals is no easy task because goals are highly historically contingent. In Chapters 10 and 11, we saw that U.S., European, and other nations' antitrust regimes grew out of radically different historical contexts. On the other hand, differing historical foundations do not mean that shared normative goals cannot be achieved over time. Antitrust's existential purpose need not become frozen in time as of the regime's creation. The ostensible goals of U.S. antitrust, for example, have changed and adapted considerably over time. Such convergence on an international scale is possible as well. Indeed, some convergence on the existential question may be occurring already.[30]

A final precondition for the success of global harmonization is the adoption of a mode of antitrust analysis that does not require decision makers to entertain explicit distributive considerations as among identifiable interest groups—particularly interest groups with a nationally defined character. The technocratic competence of an international antitrust tribunal or agency would be shattered the moment it was directed to decide, for example, whether a merger that would entail reduced competition and price increases in the Russian market should be allowed because it would also entail enhanced competition and price reductions for consumers in the Canadian market. Technocrats simply have no politically legitimate way of deciding how much weight to give the interests of Russian or Canadian consumers and producers. These are inherently political questions.[31]

---

28. *See* Aditi Bagchi, *The Political Economy of Merger Regulation*, 53 AM. J COMP. L. 1, 11–12 (2005).

29. For example, in the GE/Honeywell matter, Mario Monti, the European competition commissioner, defended the European view as being in line with the U.S. consumer welfare approach insofar as *goals* were concerned. Fox, *GE/Honeywell, supra* n. 9 at 343–45. .

30. Anu Piilola, *Assessing Theories of Global Governance: A Case Study of International Antitrust Regulation*, 39 STAN. J. INT'L L. 207, 223 (2003) ("[T]he diverse goals that countries pursue through antitrust laws have in some ways converged in recent years").

31. In theory, the international regulators might try to balance the harm to one group against the gains to another group and only permit the merger if the gains exceed the harms. It is very unlikely, however, that such a mode of analysis in the hands of politically unresponsive technocrats would enjoy political legitimacy—particularly given that the measurements of the costs and benefits would be predictive and less than exact.

Fortunately, there are modes of antitrust law that do not rely on such inter-interest group balancing. In its *Philadelphia National Bank* decision,[32] the U.S. Supreme Court rejected the merging banks' arguments that any anticompetitive effects to retail banking customers in the Philadelphia markets would be more than offset by the fact that the increased lending limits of the merged bank would allow it to better compete with New York City banks that served large Philadelphia businesses. The Court rejected the suggestion that "anticompetitive effects in one market could be justified by procompetitive consequences in another."[33] The U.S. antitrust enforcement agencies generally continue to follow this principle, evaluating competitive effects market by market and insisting on relief that makes whole each affected market.[34]

Antitrust law is not devoid of distributive consequences. Indeed, antitrust enforcement *should* have distributive consequences—particularly preventing avoidable wealth transfers from consumers to producers. But there is a difference between a regulatory regime having distributive consequences and the assignment of a regulatory analytical mode that requires inter-interest group balancing. Such balancing is not inherent in modern antitrust law. If international antitrust harmonization is to succeed, such balancing must be excluded in favor of a single-minded antitrust mode that narrowly focuses on identifying and remedying concentrations of economic power with anticompetitive effects in defined relevant markets. Creating international antitrust institutions with a political mandate would be a recipe for disaster.

III. FEEDBACK LOOPS BETWEEN SUBSTANCE, PROCEDURE, AND INSTITUTIONS

If effective antitrust harmonization cannot succeed so long as the international community falls short of the criteria articulated in the previous section—political acceptance of regulated capitalism, agreement on antitrust ends, and

---

32. *United States v Philadelphia Natl Bank*, 374 U.S. 321 (1963).

33. *Id.* at 370.

34. Dep't of Justice & Fed. Trade Commission, *Horizontal Merger Guidelines* § 4 n 36 (rev. ed. 1997) (Noting that [T]he Agency normally assesses competition in each relevant market affected by a merger independently and normally will challenge the merger if it is likely to be anticompetitive in any relevant market. In some cases, however, the Agency in its prosecutorial discretion will consider efficiencies not strictly in the relevant market, but so inextricably linked with it that a partial divestiture or other remedy could not feasibly eliminate the anticompetitive effect in the relevant market without sacrificing the efficiencies in the other market(s). Inextricably linked efficiencies rarely are a significant factor in the Agency's determination not to challenge a merger. They are most likely to make a difference when they are great. and the likely anticompetitive effect in the relevant market(s) is small.).

an analytical mode free from explicit balancing of constituent interests—it is no wonder that there is so much pessimism about harmonization's prospects. Achievement of the first two criteria, in particular, seems remote. Further, general ideological acceptance of regulated capitalism so far exceeds the set of questions with which antitrust is concerned that the antitrust community is at the mercy of broader global currents. The long-run ideological and political consequences of the "Great Recession" of 2008–2009 remain to be seen.

Nonetheless, the antitrust community is not entirely impotent to press toward international harmonization. There are a number of small incremental steps that could be taken at present. Although these steps could not by themselves or jointly usher in an era of antitrust homogeneity, they could begin to set the stage for future harmonization if or when the preconditions begin to materialize.

The key to such incremental stage setting is to understand the relationship between harmonization's moving parts and to approach them strategically. International antitrust harmonization has three prongs: substance, procedure, and institutions. Ultimately, an optimal international antitrust regime requires some uniformity in all three prongs, although sequential development may be possible.

Procedure and substance are interrelated categories, and any effort to harmonize one without the other will result in frustration. Suppose, for example, that there was a uniform antitrust code of substantive norms applicable to all major economies, and yet each country was free to specify its own procedural norms. The practical meaning of the substantive norms would continue to be widely divergent based on each country's choice of procedure. For example, stringent pleading rules in cartel cases prior to discovery could severely limit the number of cartel cases brought or restrict such cases to causes of action based on governmental enforcement, despite the theoretical availability of a private right of action.[35] A rule that allocated the burden of proof to the defendant to prove efficiencies in a merger case would result in a very different merger regime than one that required the government to disprove the existence of efficiencies.[36]

The same is true of institutions. Even with uniform substantive and procedural rules, results would be heterogeneous without the commitment of decision making to international institutions. This is not to say that it is impossible for fairly uniform law to develop across adjacent sovereign institutions with a common cultural reference point. The development of U.S. common law in fifty sovereign state court systems provides proof that the law can develop fairly

---

35. Consider *Bell Atl. Corp. v Twombly*, 550 U.S. 544 (2007) (articulating pleading requirements in cartel cases that prevent plaintiffs from getting access to discovery until they have plausible evidence of the existence of a conspiracy).

36. Burdens of proof straddle substance and procedure. *See* Earl C. Dudley, Jr. & George Rutherglen, *Deforming the Federal Rules: An Essay on What's Wrong with the Recent Erie Decisions*, 92 VA. L. REV. 707, 729 (2006).

uniformly given virtually identical procedural codes and continual cross-reference on substantive norms. But the uniformity of U.S. common law, despite the dispersion of sovereign decision making is attributable to the shared legal culture of U.S. judges across the states. Elite U.S. judges are often products of national law schools with a national curriculum that pays relatively little attention to interstate idiosyncrasies. Judges from different countries interpreting and implementing an international treaty would not be able to draw on this sort of shared legal culture and could not be expected to develop a uniform body of competition law across national borders. National judges from different countries are known to give very different interpretations to the same treaty.[37] Of course, lower federal court judges often differ on the meaning of federal treaties, statutes, or the constitution as well, but at least in a unified federal system, there is an institution—the Supreme Court—with corrective powers. Without such an institution, the specification of uniform procedural and substantive norms is unlikely to bring about the kind of antitrust homogeneity necessary to advance international business.

Ultimately, a well-functioning system of international antitrust law requires harmonization in the strong sense—some international institution must interpret and implement the procedural and substantive competition policy norms. Harmonization ultimately needs to occur on all three fronts, but it need not occur simultaneously across them. Thus, for example, while substantive harmonization without procedural harmonization will prove fruitless in the long run and vice versa, tackling substantive harmonization before tackling procedural harmonization (or vice versa) is not out of the question. Indeed, harmonizing one first may make harmonizing the other easier. Shared understanding of a procedural norm's meaning makes it easier for decision makers to converge on an adjacent substantive norm's meaning.

Of the three prongs, it seems prudent to begin with the harmonization of procedure. Agreements on procedures seem less threatening to national sovereignty, less irrevocable, and less of a compromise on ideological principles than agreement on substantive norms or the delegation of power to international institutions. At the same time, harmonization of procedures would not only provide some immediate benefits (such as simplified merger notification) but also provide a framework for nations to share formal antitrust norms. Later agreements on substantive norms and international institutions would be much easier to accomplish against a history of procedural homogeneity.

---

37. See, for example, Melissa A. Waters, *Creeping Monism: The Judicial Trend Toward Interpretive Incorporation of Human Rights Treaties*, 107 COLUM. L .REV. 628, 654 (2007) (noting that while the U.S. Supreme Court confines its use of international human rights treaties to constitutional interpretation, courts in other common law countries use the same treaties to interpret statutes and update their common law).

Proposals for the internationalization of merger procedures, in particular, are not new.[38] Yet resistance to even procedural harmonization remains deep seated. For instance, in 2000, the Justice Department issued an International Competition Policy Advisory Committee report that contained a lengthy and detailed chapter on improving international merger procedures.[39] Its recommendations, however, stopped short of suggesting that jurisdictions formally attempt to harmonize their procedures. To the contrary, the Advisory Committee expressed the view that "many of the transaction costs imposed by merger regimes are rationally related to the efficient review of transactions that have the potential to create appreciable anticompetitive effects within the reviewing jurisdiction and therefore should be taken in stride as a cost of doing business."[40] Instead of recommending steps toward formal harmonization, the report recommended that each jurisdiction attempt to follow certain principles in framing its merger control provisions. Each jurisdiction should attempt to screen out mergers unlikely to generate appreciable anticompetitive effects within the reviewing jurisdiction, establish objectively based notification thresholds, act transparently, retain the authority to challenge mergers that do not trigger premerger notification requirements, and eschew reliance on merger notification fees to subsidize the enforcement agencies' budgets.[41]

Vague hortatory suggestions such as these are harmless but unlikely to enhance the efficiency of international business in a significant way. What is needed, for starters, is a formal multilateral commitment to a merger clearance process, which, even if not centrally managed on substance, would entail procedural convergence on merger clearance. If a critical mass of major economies could agree on even a common merger notification form, this would be a good start. There is no technological reason why multiple enforcement agencies could not share in a common notification system. For example, the United States has two merger clearance agencies with very different institutional structures and cultures, but they employ a single notification form. Their electronic filing system allows parties to submit their premerger notification form electronically via the Internet. Once the notification form has been processed, it is accessible by both the FTC and Justice Department via a shared database.[42] Although there

---

38. Merit E. Janow, *Transatlantic Cooperation in Competition Policy*, *in* ANTITRUST GOES GLOBAL: WHAT FUTURE FOR TRANSATLANTIC COOPERATION? 29, 48 (Simon J. Evenett, Alexander Lehmann & and Benn Steil eds., Brookings 2000); Jürgen Basedow, *Conflict of Laws, Comparative Law and Civil Law: International Antitrust: From Extraterritorial Application to Harmonization*, 60 LA. L. REV. 1037, 1051 (2000).

39. International Competition Policy Advisory Committee, *Final Report* at 33–39, *available at* <http://www.usdoj.gov/atr/icpac/chapter1.pdf> (cited in note10).

40. *Id.* at 94–95.

41. *Id.* at 155–56.

42. *See* Federal Trade Commission and Department of Justice, Hart-Scott-Rodino Electronic Filing System (May 13, 2008), *available online at* <https://www.hsr.gov/> (visited Jan. 11, 2009).

would have to be some hard detail work and compromise over such issues as confidentiality, initial disclosures, timing, and the like, there is no good reason that the United States, the European Union, and some jurisdictions with similar merger control regimes could not kick off a similar international system.

The point, of course, is not merely to create an international merger database. The point is to prove the feasibility of international harmonization through one procedural step, to extend from there to another procedural step, to allow success on procedural harmonization to set the stage for some modest substantive harmonization, and progressively to cede authority to an international institution on specified questions.[43] This assuredly will not happen quickly. But it will not happen at all if the small first steps on procedure are not taken.

International antitrust harmonization is not an undifferentiated good and is not likely to happen on a large scale anytime soon. But antitrust homogeneity is valuable enough to the efficient conduct of international business that it is worth investing current energy to lay the groundwork for future harmonization. Beginning with small steps such as a unified international premerger notification protocol could move us incrementally toward the long-term goal of antitrust homogeneity for international business.

43. For example, success with procedural coordination of premerger notification might pave the way for a treaty agreement on substantive merger norms for multinational corporations, which could in turn pave the way for an international body with jurisdiction to regulate mergers involving international corporations. In time, a positive experience with international regulation of multinational mergers could set the stage for expansion of the regulatory body's jurisdiction to adjacent issues, such as international joint ventures.

INDEX

CPSIA information can be obtained at www.ICGtesting.com
Printed in the USA
BVOW06*1915180816

459468BV00007B/23/P

9 780195 372656